CW01217877

Aid in Danger

PENNSYLVANIA STUDIES IN HUMAN RIGHTS

Bert B. Lockwood, Jr., Series Editor

A complete list of books in the series
is available from the publisher.

AID IN DANGER

The Perils and Promise of Humanitarianism

LARISSA FAST

PENN

UNIVERSITY OF PENNSYLVANIA PRESS

PHILADELPHIA

Copyright © 2014 University of Pennsylvania Press

All rights reserved. Except for brief quotations used
for purposes of review or scholarly citation, none of this
book may be reproduced in any form by any means without written
permission from the publisher.

Published by
University of Pennsylvania Press
Philadelphia, Pennsylvania 19104-4112
www.upenn.edu/pennpress

Printed in the United States of America on acid-free paper
10 9 8 7 6 5 4 3 2 1

A catalogue record for this book is available from the Library of Congress
ISBN 978-0-8122-4603-2

*To my parents, Darrell and Loretta, and especially
my Dad, who through their words and actions
taught me the meaning of humanity*

CONTENTS

Introduction	1
Chapter 1. Three Stories of Aid in Danger: From Baghdad and Muttur to Solferino	15
Chapter 2. The Twin Challenges for Contemporary Humanitarianism	46
Chapter 3. The Dangers They Face: Understanding Violence Against Aid Workers and Agencies	66
Chapter 4. The Dominant Explanations: Competing Discourses of Aid	89
Chapter 5. Explanations in the Shadows: Competing Images of Aid	127
Chapter 6. Coping with Danger: Paradigms of Humanitarian Security Management	173
Conclusion. Reclaiming Humanity	226
Notes	247
Bibliography	275
Index	305
Acknowledgments	323

Introduction

Humanitarianism is in crisis. More than a decade after 9/11 and the advent of the "war on terror," the dangers to aid workers have increased, as has the complexity of their operating environment. The humanitarian impulse to provide lifesaving assistance is under fire, literally and figuratively: literally, as aid workers from Afghanistan to Zimbabwe are attacked, injured, kidnapped, and killed, and aid agencies are prevented from accessing vulnerable populations; and figuratively, as the essence of humanitarian action—to provide life-sustaining assistance to those suffering as a result of war or natural disaster—is compromised by those who link such assistance to foreign policy or security goals. While many have analyzed the figurative challenges of conflating humanitarian action with other agendas, few have devoted attention to the literal challenge of violence against aid workers and its implications for providing aid. This issue and its attendant consequences provide a neglected yet essential lens through which to examine the state of the humanitarian system. Doing so exposes the practical and analytical challenges of providing assistance, crystallizes its ethos, and offers a pathway for reforming the system.

In 2011, 86 aid workers died, 127 were severely injured, and 95 were kidnapped in 151 incidents worldwide, representing the highest number recorded since researchers began systematically tracking such incidents in the mid-1990s (Stoddard, Harmer, and Hughes 2012). Humanitarian aid operations have evolved in complexity throughout their history, but following the "war on terror" after 2001 they changed more visibly, with an increasing sophistication and fortification in the provision of security for aid workers. These changes are both symptom and cause of the crisis in the humanitarian system. By delving into these changes, I seek not to explain why incidents are increasing but instead to explore the rhetorical constructions of explanations for violence against aid workers and the responses they engender. This project therefore entails examining from a multidisciplinary perspective the assumptions that underlie these constructions. At heart, aid work is a moral and practical good, that is, a compassionate and *relational* response to the suffering of others. Unfortunately, certain conceptualizations of the causes of the violence and the strategies to protect aid workers inhibit the effectiveness of those strategies, contribute to the normalization of danger in aid work, and undermine precisely those values they are supposed to uphold.

Those who manage security for aid operations must take into account a range of possible causes of and responses to violence against aid delivery. In some cases, local, national, or global political and social conditions sow the seeds of security incidents. From Libya to Sri Lanka, providing assistance in the midst of war and deadly conflict is inherently dangerous work. In Pakistan and Somalia, the politics of terror shapes the operating environment and augments the risks for individual aid workers and aid agencies. In Chechnya and the Democratic Republic of Congo, aid agencies have evacuated staff or suspended programs for security reasons. For some organizations and in some contexts, the concern for security trumps other considerations about where and how to operate. Others pay less attention to managing risk, calculating threat, and mitigating the effects of threats and actual safety or security incidents.

In all contexts, however, the risks to aid workers are also ordinary, even mundane. They are embedded in everyday decisions about whom to hire or where aid workers eat and live. Hiring practices can play into long-standing grievances and cause resentment between parties to a conflict or even among those with or without gainful employment. Lifestyle choices—for example, when aid workers frequent restaurants or entertainment establishments offering fare that exceeds the means of the local population—can magnify perceptions of the aid world as the domain of the "haves" in a sea of "have-nots." These actions can feed into stereotypes and perceived injustices that create the conditions that may result in security incidents. Obviously not every decision and program, whether individual or organizational, affects local perceptions of aid workers and organizations. Those who ignore these factors, however, do so at their own peril.

In analyzing threat and risk, it is tempting to rely on myopic explanations that emphasize the politicization of aid, the rise in global terror, or the increasingly blurred boundaries between civilian and military actors. Indeed, these oft-cited and compelling explanations have become axioms, accepted at face value and virtually unquestioned as the primary causal mechanisms of violence against aid workers. These factors undoubtedly complicate access to vulnerable populations and compromise the safety and security of aid workers and agencies. An exclusionary analysis of this kind, however, promotes an image of humanitarians as exceptions, operating outside of the conflict dynamics that surround them, and as exceptional, part of a special category of civilians deserving attention and protection.

Therefore, these explanations serve to perpetuate the lauded role of aid actors in the public imagination and to maintain an analytical lens that preserves the *exceptionalism* of humanitarian actors. Moreover, it privileges *external* factors, which are largely beyond the control of humanitarian actors, as responsible for an increase in violence against them and serves to silence those *internal*, micro-level factors over which humanitarians do exercise influence, such as personal behavior and choices, security protocols, or the hiring and firing policies of individual agencies. When providing aid in contexts of danger, this is not and cannot be enough. Instead, an analytical framing of these issues that challenges the axiomatic discourses and that seeks to more accurately capture the complexity of the interrelated dimensions characterizing aid in danger is necessary.

While focusing exclusively on internal vulnerabilities negates the contextual dimension of attacks, organizations that calculate risk and vulnerability by focusing exclusively—or even primarily—on external threats place themselves in a reactive mode to the violence around them. Addressing external threats privileges high walls, alarms, guards, and even counterthreats, such as armed escorts for aid delivery. Of course, humanitarians must anticipate external threats and prepare to mitigate the likelihood and impact of an attack. Equipping vehicles with blast plates on the undercarriage and covering windows with protective film that minimizes flying glass shards, for example, limit the impact of an explosion, should one occur. Such measures offer a degree of protection and address the symptoms, if not the causes, of attack. Unfortunately, a priori decisions to react and harden against attack create humanitarian fortresses that further separate aid workers from the populations they assist and help to create a situation in which fear threatens to eclipse the humanitarian imagination. These mechanisms may save lives, but at what cost? By contrast, providing assistance in ways that privilege the relational element of humanitarianism offers an antidote to exceptionalism and a way to reassert the humanitarian ethos in the midst of war and violence.

Exceptionalizing Aid

Humanitarian assistance has long been contested. Depending on the eye of the beholder, it is seen as an individual, compassionate response to the suffering of others, as altruistic (if paternalistic) charity from rich to poor, or as a symbol of a manipulative desire and intention to remake the recipient of aid in the image of the provider. These interpretations generate competing visions of who provides aid, how they provide aid, and what is their ultimate purpose.

By "aid," I refer to the emergency/relief and development assistance that nongovernmental organizations (NGOs) such as CARE, Oxfam, and Médecins Sans Frontières (Doctors Without Borders) and international organizations such as the United Nations (UN) and the International Committee of the Red Cross (ICRC) provide, and not to the bilateral and multilateral aid that governments provide and receive. At the risk of furthering the existing terminological confusion, however, I use the terms "humanitarian" and "aid worker" interchangeably throughout the book, employing them in a specific and limited way to refer to aid workers living and working in violent contexts. My focus, therefore, is on violence against aid workers and aid agencies that *provide aid in the context of violence or insecurity*. This approach necessitates an analysis of those actors that operate from a narrow and principled humanitarian approach, such as the ICRC, as well as those operating from a stance that expands or modifies these principles. The latter include relief and development NGOs that espouse a solidarist or faith-based stance and those that provide both emergency, short-term relief and long-term development assistance. In doing so, I join those seeking to move beyond the traditional debates that have defined the analysis of humanitarianism (Barnett 2011; Donini 2012), such as whether humanitarian action is political or apolitical in nature or how the transition between providing relief, on the one hand, and reconstruction or development assistance, on the other, should be managed. By contrast, I do not intend to conflate emergency relief with development or reconstruction activities or to equate these types of assistance, since their purposes and circumstances differ.

I use the terms "humanitarian" and "aid worker" synonymously for three interconnected reasons. First, most "humanitarians" are in fact aid workers.

They are employed by agencies that do not espouse, either in language or in practice, all four of the core principles of humanitarian action. The first of these, *humanity*, is central to my argument. Throughout the book, I use humanity to refer to the universal and inherent dignity and equality of the person, refined by an acknowledgment that humans are social, and therefore relational and interdependent, beings. The remaining three core principles are those of *neutrality* (not taking sides in a conflict), *impartiality* (providing assistance according to need and without discrimination based on characteristics such as religion or ethnicity), and *independence* (possessing autonomy of action). Aside from those who care deeply about terminological precision and its theoretical and practical implications, most people observing or benefitting from such assistance (and arguably the perpetrators of violence against them) do not distinguish one category from the other. Nevertheless, the principles remain analytically and operationally relevant. Humanitarians (in the principled, narrow sense) pursue their activities differently than do many development or multimandate agencies, with both reflecting their respective guiding principles and organizational missions. Irrespective of their principled stance, I propose that all aid actors operating in conflict zones need to reassert humanity as their central guiding principle.

Second, my area of inquiry in this book is the context of violence and the provision of assistance in situations of danger.[1] Thus, recognizing that aid workers in contexts of violence work both in a purely humanitarian capacity and on traditional development programs, I endeavor to move beyond the dichotomy of political and apolitical humanitarian actors to focus on the contexts in which they operate. Violent contexts are, more often than not, places where emergency humanitarian assistance prevails in scope and amount over other types of assistance. Moreover, violent contexts are high-stress environments in which international organizations tend to employ hardened security strategies and more expatriate staff, ratcheting up the importance of internal vulnerabilities, which are rooted in individual and organizational actions and inactions. This potent combination complicates the provision of aid in violent situations.

Third, all aid agencies, whether operating from a principled or politically engaged platform, experience security incidents as part of their operations in natural and human-caused, complex, emergency as well as nonemergency, "safe" contexts. To focus solely on the narrowly defined humanitarians misses a significant population for whom the issues I discuss in this book are or should be of central concern.

In what follows, I argue that a "humanitarian exceptionalism" characterizes conceptions of aid actors as a special category of actor in the international system, with particular implications for both the analysis of the causes of and the responses to the violence they experience. By exceptionalism I mean that aid actors are seen as outside of (as opposed to within) the conflict systems in which they operate, and that they are categorized as a special category of civilians deserving attention and protection. The implications of exceptionalism are threefold: as exceptions, aid actors are or should be immune from the violence within which they operate, while their exceptional nature creates hierarchies of ascribed internal (foreigner over national) and external (aid worker over other civilians) values that simultaneously privilege external threat as the primary cause of violence against them. I recognize that in writing this book, I am equally (and perhaps more so) guilty of exceptionalizing aid workers. Yet it is precisely this issue that I wish to interrogate further, even if to do so emphasizes the exceptionalism I hope to dismantle.

This humanitarian exceptionalism derives from images of aid workers as helpers and rescuers, and from the principles of neutrality and impartiality as well as from the legal mechanisms that codify aid workers as separate. In this way, the laudable purpose of the humanitarian endeavor serves to silence explanations that may attribute responsibility to aid actors themselves. These "silent" or hidden dimensions of cause, which I term "internal vulnerabilities," are underconceptualized and inhibit a more complete theoretical understanding of the causes and dynamics of violence. They are apparent in the reluctance to tarnish the hallowed image and admirable intentions of aid workers and agencies, exhibiting the "moral untouchability" and hierarchies of humanitarianism (Fassin 2010b), and in the tendency to foreground the objects or recipients of aid while neglecting the actions and lifestyles of the givers of aid and their attendant practical and ethical implications (Fechter 2012; see also Autesserre 2014). For a sector that depends on the generosity of donors to support their work, this image is valuable; the cost of a tarnished reputation can be significant. The result is the maintenance of a public silence about the internal vulnerabilities that contribute to security incidents and an analysis that sees aid actors as outside of and not embedded within the complex and interdependent worldwide system of actors and relationships.

The roots of this exceptionalism are manifested through an examination of dichotomous and competing visions of aid. These binaries serve as heuristic devices (as opposed to absolutes) to capture archetypal discourses and images that describe how the essential character of aid is framed as a matter of either principles or politics, and how the aid system is depicted as instrument of empire or tales of rescue. Aid workers themselves typically are characterized either as heroic-mythical figures or greedy neocolonials, when in fact they are ordinary people. In addition, aid agencies must navigate between an idealized and informal past, which is often set in contrast to an institutionalized and professional present.

In particular, I explore how the aid world and its commentators have accepted certain explanatory discourses of the violence as social fact. The humanitarian exceptionalism narrative explains both the prevalence and the persistence of certain causal explanations, which in turn privilege security-management responses based on separation and fortification. The discourses of principles and politics and of empire and rescue encapsulate the externally focused factors that have dominated the theoretical framing of the causes of violence against aid workers. These discourses emerge from the dominance of certain disciplinary lenses, particularly that of political science, in explaining attacks against aid workers. These lenses privilege the primacy of politics in relation to humanitarianism and the changing context within which humanitarian actors operate. In this literature, violence against aid workers figures as part of the changing context, but is often seen as epiphenomenal. Together these lenses hamper attempts to develop a more nuanced and complete theoretical understanding of the violence itself and to unpack some of the resulting ethical dilemmas inherent in the system. A full accounting of causes requires interdisciplinary analysis.

In giving voice to the competing images of aid workers and aid agencies, I render visible the silent, internally focused dimensions and make possible a more complete theoretical understanding of the causes and dynamics of violence against aid workers and agencies. It is precisely because of the growth and power of the humanitarian system and the dominance of "security," particularly in a post-9/11 environment, that these issues deserve further scrutiny. Indeed, the ways by which aid agencies provide security implicitly communicate the values inherent in the system. Thus, through a narrow focus on violence against aid workers and responses to security concerns, we gain insight into the broader aid system as a whole.

Aid in Danger, then, conveys the need to reckon with two intertwined challenges, namely how to deliver aid in perilous and fluid settings, and how to hold fast to the fundamental ethos of humanitarianism. Examining the aid system through an analysis of security incidents offers a new interpretive lens on humanitarianism and aid. It suggests pathways to reform the current system that reflect and sustain the relational basis of the endeavor and thereby hold the aid industry more accountable to the fundamental principle of humanity.

A Relational Approach

The antidote to exceptionalism, I suggest, lies in a *relational* approach to humanitarianism that sees aid as embedded within an interdependent system of actors and actions, which both remedies the theoretical silencing of certain causes and suggests a way forward in reforming the system. The relational approach is best embodied in the principle of humanity.[2] In a relational approach, however, this concept of humanity is tempered by the notion that humans are social beings who exist within a complex web of interdependent and often unequal relationships. For humanitarians, these relationships involve, among others, co-workers, local and national officials, donors, belligerent forces, host populations, as well as the recipients of aid. A relational approach forces critical scrutiny upon the relationships that aid actors create and neglect, which, in turn, demands attention be paid to the internal vulnerabilities, and not just the external threats, that must be part of a full accounting of the complex causes of violence against aid workers and agencies.

The relational and compassionate mission of aid is epitomized in the early stories of modern humanitarianism and in the founding of the ICRC along with its cousins in the world of relief and development organizations. For most aid actors, the core principles of impartiality and independence are the foundation upon which to build and preserve the relationships that enable a humanitarian response to have meaning. Service to suffering humanity, understood and acted upon without regard to constructed markers such as race, religion, clan, or class, should remain at the core of humanitarian action.

It is precisely the relational nature of aid that is absent from discussions about humanitarianism and the aid system. Placing the relational character of aid work at the center of thinking about security and security management will transform the latter. Such re-centering enables the development of a nuanced and complex explanatory framework of the causes of violence and suggests an alternative lens through which to assess security responses based upon the principle of humanity. Analyzing the causes and dynamics of conflict and intervention in this manner offers a way to recast humanitarian action and aid work more generally within an interdependent and complex set of relationships, actors, and actions. Moreover, in doing so, I am making a normative argument that providing aid in danger can serve to challenge and counteract the dynamics of violence that cause suffering in the first place: By reaffirming the inherent value of individuals through a relational approach to aid and security, it is possible to interrupt the cycle and ameliorate the effects of violence.

Such re-centering would also address the unfortunate fact that some current approaches to security management are undermining the core principle of humanitarian aid. The typical post-9/11 responses of fortification and separation as means of addressing the dangers of the work are part of the problem, in that the securitization of aid and the militarization of humanitarian security are not geared to addressing the root causes of the violence aid workers experience. Moreover, the physical and emotional distances they embody serve to further undermine the relational foundations of aid and feed the narrative of humanitarian exceptionalism. Rather, fear and the anxiety to provide security of a certain kind, at all costs, are displacing humanitarian principles when humanitarian principles, including their relational orientation, should be guiding approaches to providing security.

The chapters that follow contextualize the problem of aid workers and agencies as targets of violence, deconstruct the competing discourses and images of aid, critique and expand the rhetorical and explanatory frameworks commonly used to explain the violence, and offer recommendations based on a more realistic and nuanced analysis. Given this analysis, I contend that the humanitarian response has been hijacked and that aid agencies have lost their way. The goal of the reforms I propose, then, is to place security in service of humanity. In turn, this requires taking seriously a relational interpretation of humanitarianism, its principles, and its implications for action. Reclaiming humanity makes it possible to counter exceptionalism and assert an alternative vision of humanitarianism more consistent with its founding principles.

Genesis and Organization

This book is the culmination of over a decade of research about violence against aid workers. First motivated by the question of effective protection of aid workers (Fast 2002, 2007) and experiences as an aid worker, consultant, and researcher, my inquiry expanded over time to the causes of violence against aid workers. In particular, I found perplexing the question of why some organizations experienced security incidents and others did not. In exploring that question, it became apparent that some answers gained explanatory traction while others remained in the shadows, neglected or underemphasized in the dominant narratives reported by journalists and internalized by academics, commentators, and aid workers themselves. The chapters that follow are an attempt to understand why this is so.

In writing this book, I have been influenced by hundreds of conversations with aid workers and NGO security officials in the field, at conferences, and at NGO security-management seminars and workshops over the past decade.[3] I cite some of these conversations explicitly in the text. Beyond my own experience, the book is based on data I collected more systematically through three research projects. The first project, funded by the U.S. Institute of Peace, involved a survey of aid workers about their perceptions of the threats they face (Fast and Wiest 2007) and semistructured formal interviews. The interviews, conducted primarily in 2006 and 2007, took place in Boston, Geneva, London, and New York with academic experts, aid workers, aid policy experts, and security directors/managers of NGOs, UN agencies, and international organizations, such as the ICRC. The interview protocol included questions about interpretations of humanitarian principles, the challenges to and evolutions in humanitarianism, and their influence on conceptualizations of the causes of security incidents and on security management. To maintain confidentiality, I cite these individuals in the text by category (e.g., aid worker, aid official, security director) and provide additional detail only as relevant to the point I am making. A list of these interviewees appears in the Acknowledgments.

A second, related piece of research, for which I conducted fieldwork in the occupied Palestinian territory, was published as one of a series of case studies for the Humanitarian Agenda 2015 (HA2015) project of the Feinstein International Center at Tufts University. The HA2015 project examined four challenges to humanitarian action: the universality of humanitarianism, terrorism and counterterrorism, coherence (referring to linkages between humanitarian and political and military agendas), and security issues. For this research, I conducted semistructured interviews on these four topics with aid workers from NGOs, UN agencies, and other international organizations, and with two focus groups of Palestinians living in Bethlehem about their perceptions of aid and aid agencies (Fast 2006).

A third project examined how NGOs conceptualize and implement acceptance, a consent-based approach to security management. The project, funded by the U.S. Agency for International Development, used a collaborative learning approach and involved aid workers and security personnel from thirty-seven NGOs. Save the Children served as the primary implementing agency. The project involved two daylong workshops (one in Geneva and one in Washington, D.C., in fall 2010) with headquarters-level security managers and directors; a week-long training of national and regional staff of international and national NGOs from Kenya, South Sudan, and Uganda; and field research in these three countries in April 2011. Three teams of researchers, for which I was team leader in South Sudan, conducted semistructured interviews with NGO staff, members of international organizations, and local officials and organized focus groups of beneficiary and nonbeneficiary communities to explore perceptions and the relationships between aid agencies and communities (see Fast, Patterson, et al. 2011 on South Sudan; Fast, Freeman, et al. 2011 and 2013 on acceptance).[4] The third research project proved especially influential in shaping my overall argument and discussions of security management.

My starting assumption is that aid agencies and the security managers, directors, and field officers, as well as the human resources and other staff charged with security, are generally doing their best to manage security and risk in fluid, often dangerous circumstances. Some manage better than others. Yet it is impossible to protect against or prevent all incidents. Individual aid workers, and the strategies they consciously or unconsciously choose to cope with the danger, moral dilemmas, and suffering they witness and experience, are not to blame for the incidents many unfortunately experience, nor are the capricious circumstances of context uniquely responsible for the violence. Security managers and aid workers themselves are often acutely aware of the complexity of cause.

With this in mind, the following chapters hold up a mirror, with which individual aid workers, agencies, commentators and academics, and the system as a whole can examine and reflect on their analyses, actions, and inactions. In challenging the exceptionalism that characterizes much of the humanitarian discourse, I contend that aid workers and agencies need to go deeper in their analysis of the patterns and causes of the violence that afflicts them and hinders or forces the closure of their operations; in their self-understanding and reflection, refined by a sober analysis of the inescapably political dimensions of their various presences on the ground; in their self-scrutiny, especially of the character and architecture of their on-the-ground presence, as reflected in the behaviors and attitudes of aid workers as well as in agency policies, operations, and infrastructure; and finally in their responses to situations unfolding in a setting affected by local, regional, and global dynamics, at least some of which are beyond their control. The key will be to discern which events are within their control, how to influence events that can be influenced, and how to respond to those that cannot be shaped.

Two sets of questions serve as organizing frames for the book. First, why are aid workers and agencies attacked? What do we know about this type of violence, and how do we explain it? Second, what are the mechanisms of protecting aid operations and aid workers, and what are the (unintended) consequences of employing these mechanisms? The answers to the former address the analytical challenges of aid in danger, which feature in Chapters 1 to 5. Replies to the latter appear in Chapters 1, 2, and 6, which lay out the practical and operational challenges and implications of my analysis.

Chapter 1 contrasts three stories of aid in danger: the bombing of the UN headquarters in Baghdad, Iraq, in 2003, which served as a watershed for the fortification of aid; the murders of seventeen national staff members of Action Contre la Faim in Muttur, Sri Lanka, in 2006, which illustrate the public silencing of internal vulnerabilities; and the mythical origin stories of modern humanitarianism from the nineteenth century, which showcase its compassionate and relational foundations.

Chapter 2 describes the practical and analytical challenges of contemporary humanitarianism, which appear in the stories of Baghdad and Muttur and underscore the need for a multidimensional analysis of the violence. This analysis lays the foundations for an analytical framework that recognizes the complete landscape of cause. This framework, outlined in the chapter, encompasses the structural and global to the personal and relational dimensions and embeds humanitarian actors within the systems they inhabit, thereby transcending the bifurcated analytical perspectives that too often characterize conceptions of the causes of violence against aid actors.

Chapter 3 pokes holes in the accepted wisdom about violence against aid workers, providing a historical analysis of the danger of working in war zones that debunks the myths of the inviolability of aid workers and the recent genesis of targeted attacks. It scopes the dangers that aid workers face and describes the evidence base in order to expose the gaps in our collective knowledge and to illuminate the ways in which existing evidence helps to create social fact and supports the underlying assumptions of exceptionalism. Together Chapters

1, 2, and 3 set the stage on which competing visions of aid, and the causes and responses they champion, are enacted.

Chapters 4 and 5 analyze why aid workers are attacked, lay out the central discourses, perceptions, and rhetorical constructions of the causes of violence against aid workers and agencies, and construct a foundation for the notion of a "humanitarian exceptionalism" on which conceptualizations of causes and responses are built. Chapter 4 sketches competing discourses of aid: humanitarian action as principled or political, and aid as extension of empire or as embodying a tale of rescue. These constitute the macro-level explanations that dominate the collective discourse and emphasize external threats. Chapter 5 discusses competing images of aid seen through the lens of the players in the aid drama: aid workers, seen as both inheritors of confining mythologies and ordinary people, and aid organizations caught between an informal and idealized past and an institutional and professional present. The images constitute the micro dimensions of cause, or the internal vulnerabilities that usually reside in the shadows. In both chapters, I return to the theme of exceptionalism and begin to build the case for a relational approach.

The penultimate chapter deconstructs the paradigms of security management, framing the conceptualization of security as a challenge to the aid system and a clarion call for reform. This chapter begins with a description of the evolution of security management, including the professionalization and fortification of security-management strategies. It explores the three basic paradigms—the assumptive, legal, and operational—of providing protection for humanitarians, examining the implications and unintended consequences of employing these measures and how they emerge from the competing visions, and contrasts each with a relational approach. The first, the assumptive mechanisms, frames a normative argument and relies upon the symbols and principles of humanitarianism and the protective qualities of outsiderness to render humanitarians inviolable from attack. The legal mechanisms are both customary and codified, such as UN Security Council Resolution 1502, which declared attacks against humanitarian workers a war crime, the Geneva Conventions, and the 1994 Convention and 2005 Optional Protocol on the Safety of United Nations and Associated Personnel. The third, the operational measures known as deterrence, protection, remote management, and acceptance, capture the practices that most organizations employ in the field. In remaining tied to the assumptions of exceptionalism, I argue, aid agencies privilege certain kinds of professional knowledge and expertise and contribute to the fortifications of the aid enterprise that further separate the givers of aid from those who receive it, which undermines the fundamental compassionate and relational nature of humanitarianism. Instead, I propose that aid agencies must embrace a relational approach that counteracts the unintended consequences of the fortification of aid and supports rather than undermines the fundamental purpose of the humanitarian endeavor.

In the concluding chapter, I offer recommendations for recapturing the original ethos of humanitarianism. The conclusion revisits the theme of exceptionalism, describes a typology of danger, and reviews the multiple dimensions of cause. Finally, it reiterates the implications of a relational analysis for systemic reform of the humanitarian enterprise in recommending reforms designed to harness both the symbolic and real power of humanitarian principles while encouraging practical approaches by which to analyze and address internal vulnerabilities *and* external threats.

CHAPTER 1

Three Stories of Aid in Danger: From Baghdad and Muttur to Solferino

The history of humanitarianism is peppered with incidents of violence against aid workers and aid delivery. The deadliest and highest-profile security incidents, however, have occurred since the mid-1990s. Two of these, the bombing of the United Nations headquarters in Baghdad, Iraq, in 2003 that killed twenty-two people and the murder of seventeen staff members of Action Contre la Faim in Muttur, Sri Lanka, feature in this chapter. Together these and one other earlier story compose three stories of aid: one of the challenge of providing security in environments rife with violence, one of the dominant discourses that explain the causes of security incidents, and a third that encapsulates the founding values of contemporary humanitarianism.

As two of the most lethal examples of violence against aid workers, the events in Baghdad and Muttur are not illustrative of the more typical and everyday incidents in scale or type. They nonetheless demonstrate the complexity of security incidents that compel a closer look at causes, responses, and the power of the humanitarian exceptionalism narrative. Each is emblematic of the analyses that tend to dominate contemporary security challenges, in which security management is portrayed as a choice between constructing a fortress or relying on the protection assumed from the principles and symbols of humanitarianism. In these analyses, the causes of incidents are represented as the result of politicized aid and thereby mask internal vulnerabilities. Therefore, they typify the central tendencies and tensions explored throughout the book. Neither story, however, is as simple as it might first appear.

The contrasting story of Solferino, which ends the chapter, is about a clarion call for action and of the compassion and perils that marked early humanitarianism. The efforts of Henri Dunant, the most famous humanitarian at Solferino, as well as those of his contemporaries, Florence Nightingale and Clara Barton, embody a tale of mercy in the face of suffering. Dunant and the others who assisted him performed acts of indiscriminate compassion that deliberately bypassed politics and nationality. These acts offer an alternative vision that, at the same time, demonstrates the motivating myth of the contemporary humanitarian endeavor and is often lost in its modern performance.

Bombing in Baghdad: A Story of Blame and Bunkers

At 4:28 P.M. on the afternoon of 19 August 2003, the driver of a flatbed truck loaded with approximately one thousand kilograms of explosives raced down an access road in Baghdad to a catering college between a hotel and a hospital. His target was the Canal Hotel, the site of the UN headquarters in Iraq. A split second after the "screeching and tearing of metal," a massive explosion shattered glass, leveled the building, and caused the concrete ceilings and floors to pancake and collapse on top of each other, killing, wounding, and trapping those inside under piles of rubble (Independent Panel 2003, 14). The explosion left a crater large and deep enough to fit a small car and rained debris for five square miles around the blast site (Power 2008, 483). The bomb scattered and destroyed vehicles in the compound, and damaged the adjacent hospital, wounding some patients inside.

Despite the heroic efforts of rescuers, the blast killed Sergio Vieira de Mello, the UN secretary-general's special representative (SRSG) to Iraq, fourteen of his international and Iraqi UN colleagues, and seven others. A further 160 people were wounded, some severely, in the attack. It took several days to establish the list of dead and wounded, owing to inconsistencies in records of the numbers and names of those in the Canal Hotel at the time of the bombing and to a lack of preplanning that would have established points of assembly and contact to determine names, injuries, locations, and other pertinent information (Independent Panel 2003).[1] Ramiro Lopes de Silva, a survivor of the blast who was the UN humanitarian coordinator for Iraq and the designated official for security, recalled, "We were always told, 'Move in, don't move out.' Because out was where we thought any explosion would be. When the explosion happened inside, we had no plan. We were lost. We didn't know what to do. If we had ever thought that such an attack could occur, and if we had planned to respond to such level of emergency, the UN would not have been in Baghdad" (as quoted in Power 2008, 463).

The rescue scene was chaotic and mostly unorganized, without a centralized authority or a designated coordinator for the rescue operation. Rescuers lacked first-aid supplies and heavy equipment to remove debris and enable them to reach the survivors. American military engineers eventually arrived with excavators and drills, but "even then they were not directed either to the rear of the building or inside, where their mobile equipment might have been of use" (Power 2008, 473). Iraqi fire trucks also eventually reached the Canal Hotel compound, but the trucks were empty, having been looted of equipment (476). Most important, the rescue effort lacked lumber to help stabilize the area in which Sergio Vieira de Mello and Gil Loescher, the only individual in de Mello's office to survive the bombing, were trapped.[2] Instead, rescuers had to improvise with unlikely but available rescue equipment—a curtain rope and a handbag—in their attempts to free the two men (Power 2008, 488).

The UN remained in Iraq after the attack. According to UN security protocol, only the UN secretary-general possesses the authority to declare a phase 5 security situation, which constitutes the highest security level in the UN system and requires a full withdrawal of all international staff.[3] For over two months after the bombing, Kofi Annan, the UN secretary-general in 2003, declined to declare phase 5 for Iraq, despite the objections of many advisors. In justifying his decision, Annan and other senior UN officials cited de Mello's death and the desire to honor his last words, his memory, and his life's work for the UN.

Many criticized the decision, particularly in light of additional attacks that occurred in September: gunfire around the perimeter of the Canal Hotel on 13 September and a car bomb explosion on 22 September in a parking lot near the Canal Hotel that killed a UN security officer and two Iraqi policemen (Independent Panel 2003). Thus, the UN headquarters remained in the Canal Hotel complex, with more security personnel and additional measures in place to address some of the security lapses existing before the bombing. By mid-September, however, the number of international UN staff in Baghdad was reduced to sixty-one, and by early October it numbered between two and three dozen in the entire country (Independent Panel 2003, 16).

As families, friends, UN staff, and aid workers near and far buried and mourned their loved ones and colleagues, the fallout began. Iraq in 2003 epitomized the contest over protection and rescue, both central to the case of the Baghdad bombing. The U.S.-led Coalition and the UN traded veiled accusations of neglect and accountability, while the Americans and the Iraqis shared conflicting responsibilities and lacked clear lines of authority (Power 2008; see also Anderson 2004). Prior to the U.S. invasion, the Iraqi government had provided adequate protection for the UN mission (Independent Panel 2003, 7). Yet in occupied Iraq, the U.S.-led Coalition authorities dismantled the police and the military, the Iraqi security institutions that could have provided protection. Samantha Power points out that the UN relied on the host government for protection, yet "when it came to rescue in Iraq, it was unclear just who constituted the 'local authorities.'" The U.S. Army in Iraq was geared to war and security, not rescue. Thus, the chaos of the rescue efforts owed partly to the "multiple, dueling command structures and improper planning that gave rise to insufficient capacity" (Power 2008, 480).

The violence in Iraq against aid workers and aid operations affected agencies beyond the UN. In September 2003, approximately two hundred foreign relief agencies were operating in Iraq. After the bombing, NGOs in Iraq dramatically changed their security stances, adopting lower profiles and removing the logos and flags from their vehicles, compounds, and project sites (Carle and Chkam 2006; Vick 2003). Then on 27 October 2003, attackers set off four bombs in a coordinated attack during Ramadan. One of the bombs, using explosives packed into an ambulance, exploded outside the Baghdad offices of the International Committee of the Red Cross (ICRC).[4] In the following months, security deteriorated dramatically for civilians, including aid workers, when a wave of kidnappings and killings of aid workers swept through the aid community. Many organizations pulled out of Iraq altogether because of the security situation.

An al-Qaeda-affiliated organization, the Abu-Hafs al-Masri Brigades, claimed responsibility for the attack (Independent Panel 2003). In January 2005, a man named Awraz Abd Al Aziz Mahmoud Sa'eed, also known as al-Kurdi, confessed to helping plan the attack on behalf of the leader of al-Qaeda in Iraq, Abu Mussab al-Zarqawi. Authorities had arrested and detained al-Kurdi on other charges. Al-Kurdi reportedly had earlier gained entry into the Canal Hotel complex and decided that the access road offered the best opportunity for an attack. He was apparently unaware that the SRSG's office lay directly above the access road, even though the SRSG was the target of the attack (Power 2008, 513–516). According to al-Kurdi, who was present when al-Zarqawi explained the reason for the attack to the bomber, "Al-Zarqawi told him [the bomber, Abu Farid al-Massri] that al-Qaeda's decision-making council had ordered the strike because a UN senior official was housed there who, in al-Kurdi's words, was 'the person behind the separation of East Timor from Indonesia and who was also the reason for the division of Bosnia and Hercegovina'" (Power 2008, 514).

In elaborating on the reason for the attack, al-Kurdi mentioned the UN sanctions and "injustices and various occupations and foreign troops using the UN resolutions . . . against Muslim people under the name of the UN" (Power 2008, 515). Al-Kurdi pleaded not guilty in an Iraqi court, claiming a legitimate right to resist the occupiers of the country. He was convicted and executed in July 2007.

The Response: Investigations and Security Management in the Aftermath of the Bombing

In late September 2003, Kofi Annan appointed Martti Ahtisaari, the former president of Finland, to lead the first independent panel to investigate the incident. The four-member panel conducted interviews with UN and non-UN staff and officials in Iraq and elsewhere, and examined relevant documents in its investigation. It released the Ahtisaari Report one month later, concluding that "the UN security management system failed in its mission to provide adequate security to UN staff in Iraq" (Independent Panel 2003, i). The panel found "dysfunctional" security-management systems and a lack of accountability on the part of those making decisions about security. Specifically, it cited the absence of a security assessment before the return of UN staff to Baghdad in early May, the failure to develop and implement evacuation and contingency plans in the event of an attack, and noncompliance with minimum-security procedures and standards, all in contradiction to UN security protocols at the time.

The Ahtisaari Report cited the rush to return to Baghdad, largely the result of pressure from member states, as a primary reason for the security deficiencies. Upon the UN's return "security issues," the report observed, "became entrenched in bureaucracy in relation to budgets and methods of acquisition of materials." It continued, "The number of professional security officers was not sufficient to respond to the heavy and administrative workload, and there was an attitude, at least within some agencies, that security was an inconvenience best avoided" (Independent Panel 2003, 17). The investigation determined that some UN agencies disregarded and exceeded the numbers of personnel allowed in country and did not maintain lists of all in-country staff, lists that would be needed in the event an evacuation was necessary.[5]

Furthermore, the report identified crucial lapses in security measures, such as the lack of blast-resistant barriers, unguarded entrances to the complex (such as the access road that passed directly underneath the SRSG's office), and the absence of a defensive perimeter or a protective film on the windows. All of these measures could have saved lives or minimized the injuries that the survivors sustained. According to two UN doctors present at the explosion, flying glass accounted for up to 90 percent of the injuries from the blast (UN Secretariat 2004, 16). The Ahtisaari Report called for a more "robust security management system with adequate disciplinary measures to counter non-compliance," the promotion of accountability for security at all levels, more and better risk analysis, and a significant increase in the resources available to protect staff (Independent Panel 2003, 26).

To follow up on the Ahtisaari Report's recommendations and to determine responsibility and accountability for the security failures, a second independent panel conducted an "investigative, independent audit" of the roles of individuals and UN entities in the attack (UN Secretariat 2004). Gerald Walzer, a former deputy high commissioner for refugees, chaired the four-member panel, which released its report on 3 March 2004. The Walzer Panel examined several of the key omissions and security lapses, including the blurred chains of command and accountability, the decision to return to Iraq on 1 May, the absence or inadequacy of perimeter defenses, warning signs, and the lack of numbers and lists of staff members in Baghdad and Iraq at the time of the bombing. The report corroborated the findings of the Ahtisaari Report, labeling the security management of the Canal Hotel compound as "seriously deficient and lacking cohesion" (UN Secretariat 2004, 15). In particular, it criticized the "excessive delay" in the building of the perimeter wall around the Canal Hotel compound and the "dereliction of duty" that characterized the absence of blast film on many of the building's windows (UN Secretariat 2004, 16, 18; see also 15–19). Contractors had started, but not completed, the construction of the wall, which in any event was not built to protect against explosion. Members of the security team had identified the need for blast film on the windows in late May, yet three months later much of the building lacked this protective film, despite an offer from the World Food Programme to pay for the film and assist with its procurement.

Furthermore, the security-management plan lacked contingency plans to deal with a bombing. The Walzer Panel admonished the UN Security Coordinator, the Designated Official, the Security Management Team, and the SRSG himself, who "failed to respond" to the warnings and security risks in Baghdad and who "steadfastly maintained the view, despite the rapidly deteriorating security situation, that the *UN was protected by its neutrality and its humanitarian mandate* and that the staff and its installations would not be directly targeted" (italics added).[6] The panel concluded that implementing the recommended security measures would have saved lives (UN Secretariat 2004, 11–12) and called for a "culture of security within the Organization" (UN Secretariat 2004, 31).

The investigations themselves resulted in the firing or resignation of UN security officials, including Tun Myat, the head of the Office of the UN Security Coordinator (UNSECOORD) at the time of the bombing, and disciplinary measures against several other staff members, such as Ramiro Lopes de Silva, the humanitarian coordinator in Iraq and the designated official for security, as well as the chief administrative officer and building manager. Following the completion of the second investigation, Annan asked for and received a General Assembly appropriation to strengthen and reform the UN security system. UNSECOORD became the UN Department of Safety and Security (UNDSS), a centralized and unified security body for the entire UN with an under-secretary-general who reports directly to the UN secretary-general. UNDSS subsequently hired more professional field security personnel and a new director, Sir David Veness, a veteran of Scotland Yard.[7] It also developed and instituted minimum operating standards for security (MOSS) for all UN subcontractors and partner agencies in an attempt to standardize and increase the levels of security, an evolution strongly influenced by the experience of the Baghdad bombing.

The Lessons of Baghdad

Many observers, especially within the UN system, refer to the attack as the "UN's 9/11."[8] The reference conveys a comparison to both the tactical similarities of the attacks (suicide bombing) and their seismic impact. Just a week after the bombing, the UN Security Council adopted Resolution 1502 on the Protection of United Nations Personnel, Associated Personnel and Humanitarian Personnel in Conflict Zones. The resolution called upon all parties to respect international law and "strongly condemned" the attack and all such attacks "knowingly and intentionally directed against personnel involved in a humanitarian assistance mission or peacekeeping mission undertaken in accordance with the Charter of the United Nations which in situations of armed conflicts constitute war crimes" (UN Security Council 2003).

To commemorate the one-month anniversary of the Canal Hotel bombing, Kofi Annan stood beneath the damaged UN flag from Baghdad and grieved the UN's "loss of innocence" in the attack (as quoted in UN News Service 2003). The evident deliberation of the attack caused UN officials and others to lament the loss of the protective value of the UN flag.[9] The discourse decrying the disappearance of the invisible-yet-protective aura of the flag and symbols of the UN illustrates the humanitarian exceptionalism narrative, which marks aid workers as different and therefore exempt from the surrounding violence. With UNSCR 1502, policymakers essentially codified this narrative into international law.

The bombing of the Canal Hotel left its mark on the UN as an institution, on its staff members, and on its security-management system. In a manner similar to the U.S. reaction after 9/11, the UN reacted to the Canal Hotel bombing in a way that privileged, almost exclusively, military responses, such as fortification and other hard security measures. The Ahtisaari Report concluded, "The level and military nature of the threats against the United Nations . . . demonstrate the urgent need for a more *forceful* approach to UN security," and recommended that UN activities, regardless of type, occur "only with security and *deterrence* capabilities appropriate to protect its staff and premises" (Independent Panel 2003, 22, italics added). Numerous critics and commentators point to the Baghdad bombing as a moment of paramount importance in the fortification of the UN security footprint, pointing out that "risk comes with the territory and will be greatest precisely where the United Nations presence is needed most" (Malone 2004, as cited in Stoddard and Harmer 2006, 32–33). Dissenting voices did speak out. Kieran Prendergast, a senior UN official, argued in favor of withdrawal: "'The UN has not been able to establish a differentiated brand,' he argued. 'If a fortress is required to ensure security, why be there?'" (quoted in Power 2008, 503).

The UN security profile in Baghdad, as a soft target with inadequate security measures or protections in an active war zone, contrasted with the bunkerized, "hard-target" profile of the U.S.-controlled Green Zone. At the same time, the political functions of the UN forced an association with the U.S.-led Coalition and the "war on terror" agenda. The UN's activities and mandate in Iraq comprised both humanitarian and political functions. Indeed, UN Security Council Resolution 1483 (UNSCR 1483) specified a prominent role for the UN in the humanitarian response and in reconstruction as well as in the "restoration and establishment of national and local institutions for representative government" (S/RES/1483, 22 May 2003). In addition, Resolution 1546 linked the humanitarian and security functions of the UN and other actors to the Multi-National Force in Iraq (S/RES/1546, 8 June 2004; see also Hansen 2007b). The mandate from UNSCR 1483 placed the UN in direct contradiction to its specified phase 4 security level, a level allowing only essential emergency humanitarian or security personnel to remain in Iraq, especially given the deteriorating security situation at the time (UN Secretariat 2004).

The legal and political contexts of the UN bombing reveal the complicated and contradictory nature of managing security for UN staff. As a global body composed of member states and with agencies that operate in war zones, the threats the UN encounters are uniquely shaped by these realities. Its responses are constrained by the nature of the institution and the perspectives of its member states. In turn, its size and dominance as an aid actor limit the parameters of action for non-UN actors.[10] The foundational and other relevant documents—the UN Charter, the 1946/1947 conventions on the Privileges and Immunities of the United Nations and of the Specialized Agencies, and the 1994 Convention on the Safety of UN and Associated Personnel— all identify the host state as the primary guarantor of security for UN staff and premises. In most places, therefore, the primary although not sole responsibility for security rests with the local authorities. For situations of occupation, as in Iraq in 2003, the 1907 Hague Convention and the Fourth Geneva Convention place responsibility for law and order and the protection of civilians in the hands of the occupying authorities.[11] In the case of Iraq, the U.S. Coalition forces were the occupying authorities. Several UN Security Council Resolutions reiterated these specific responsibilities.[12]

On paper, the roles and responsibilities related to security were clear. The on-the-ground reality, however, significantly muddied these waters, in terms of responsibility for security as well as in trying to simultaneously uphold an identity of the UN as an independent and a politically associated actor. The rising unpopularity of the occupation created a situation in which segments of the Iraqi population saw Coalition forces as illegitimate. For the UN, therefore, associating too closely with the Coalition represented both a potential threat to security and a political burden. Thus, the dual humanitarian and political functions of the UN in Iraq clashed and created an identity crisis: de Mello and others viewed the UN as an impartial and independent actor, separate from the Coalition forces. The location of its headquarters outside the Green Zone and the decision to remove the visible U.S. military protection from around the compound (Independent Panel 2003, 11) represented deliberate choices to distance the UN from the Coalition. This distance, they hoped, would help to maintain the UN's independence and promote its impartiality. Later investigations criticized de Mello and others for the belief that these choices and the separation they implied would serve to insulate the UN from attack. The Walzer Panel asserted, "It is, therefore, fair to say that this false sense of security was a state of mind that was shared by all the senior UN political and humanitarian staff in Iraq" (UN Secretariat 2004, 11).

Thus, the UN mission delicately balanced on a tightrope of conflicting identities; that is, it attempted to maintain a self-defined but illusory notion of independence and impartiality in the face of perceptions of the UN as a politicized and tainted actor, all the while trying to serve two demanding masters. On the one hand, a fortified security stance with U.S. and Coalition soldiers protecting the UN compound offered a "hardened" or deterrent approach to security that seemed to clearly associate the UN presence in Iraq with the politicized agenda of nation building. The attempt to escape this "guilt by association" and to foster an image of an independent and impartial actor ultimately proved unviable as a security approach.

The debate about an appropriate UN security stance symbolizes these conflicting identities, with their diverging expectations and approaches to providing security. As the Ahtisaari Report observes, "The argument of distancing the United Nations from the occupying forces in order to enhance its neutral image is relevant only to the extent that the UN benefits from such an image in the first place and also has a security alternative" (Independent Panel 2003, 23).

Since the Baghdad bombing, a fortified presence has characterized most UN missions, especially in the most dangerous countries. The bombing presaged the shift toward a more "risk-averse" and visibly fortified UN security-management posture and heralded the development of safety and security-management standards that have subsequently shaped the operational procedures of many international actors in war zones.[13] The two investigations into the bombing aimed to establish responsibility—and even to lay blame—for the lapses that failed to prevent the tragedy. Their findings led directly to changes in how security management functioned and how it was institutionalized within the UN system. Therefore, the bombing and resulting investigations served as watershed events in security management in the early 2000s, signifying the institutionalization of security management and reinforcing its professionalization.

These developments were well under way by the first anniversary of the bombing, when the UN Staff Association issued a statement opposing the return of UN staff to Baghdad unless and until security conditions and measures improved. Some of the more subtle effects of the primacy of security and its standardization, however, became apparent only later. "MOSS has made our defences more visible, which triggers hostility," in the words of one UN official. "The aim to be close to the people is hampered by barricades, even if some [of the barricades] are fully justified." According to another UN official, "Post 9/11 there is a fortress mentality. That we are aloof and arrogant and separate will cost us. They will get you if they want to, but we have become complacent with barricades."[14] The barricaded and separate compound, in other words, came with tangible physical and psychological costs.

The fortification of security management among aid actors has been led by and is most visible for the UN. Its tentacles extend beyond the UN and affect the operations of non-UN humanitarian actors, exerting pressure on others to harden their own security stances and to avoid becoming "soft targets" that are comparatively easy to attack. While some agencies have bought into the MOSS standards and protocols, others have chosen to establish sharper distinctions from the UN and its operations, affecting how they deploy staff in the field, how they look, and how they operate.[15]

These decisions closely mirror debates about the purpose and principles of humanitarian action. According to one view, humanitarianism is and should be impartial and independent, dedicated solely to the basic survival needs of ordinary Iraqis. Another sees the humanitarian response as part of a broader strategy or set of initiatives, indeed as an integral element of a more explicitly political agenda. For the former view, a security-management strategy dependent upon bunkers and armed guards is inconsistent with notions of impartiality and independence, because such a strategy aligns humanitarianism with explicitly military and political agendas. For the latter, the degree of separation and the boundaries between political or military action and humanitarian action are less important, both in terms of function and of the image an organization projects to those around it. Although in either case humanitarians have been and will continue to be targeted, these views delineate the parameters of appropriate security-management approaches.

The lessons of the Baghdad bombing ultimately relate to the reaction to security incidents. The urgency of an immediate response to the tragedy and the very public nature of the attacks, and later of the UN's failures, drove the security stance the UN adopted as well as the search for responsibility and accountability. This search placed blame on individual and even institutional failures and resulted in a profound shift that signaled the demise of the symbolic yet assumed protection of emblems and principles. This, combined with the UN's size and importance as an aid actor, defined the parameters of its response that, in turn, limited the response of other actors. As a consequence, the pendulum swung in another direction, away from the assumed protection of the flag and laurel of the UN and toward the professionalization and standardization of security management and the reactive fortification of aid actors. This pendulum swing, however, came at the cost of cementing the physical and psychological separation of aid actors from the populations they are mandated to help and, ultimately, of undermining the motivating ethos of humanitarianism.

Tragedy in Muttur: A Story of Politics and Misguided Policies

A second watershed event occurred in Sri Lanka on 4 August 2006. On that day, seventeen local staff members of the NGO Action Contre la Faim (ACF, Action Against Hunger) were killed at the ACF office compound in Muttur, Sri Lanka. All but one of the ACF staff members killed was Tamil and between twenty-four and thirty-six years of age. ACF and others named the deaths, which occurred during a resumption of fierce fighting between government and Liberation Tigers of Tamil Eelam (LTTE) forces, a war crime. The murder of the seventeen staff members marked the single largest loss for one organization in the history of aid work up to that time, surpassing the UN losses in the Baghdad bombing in August 2003, and equaling the seventeen UN staff from multiple UN agencies who later lost their lives in the Algiers bombing of December 2007.[16]

The secessionist war (1983–2009) between the primarily Sinhalese Sri Lankan government and the separatist Tamil group, the LTTE, displaced hundreds of thousands and killed between 80,000 and 100,000 people. The response to the war pitted aid agencies against the government, with each viewing the other with suspicion. The government accused international aid agencies of favoring the Tamils or supporting the LTTE. Meanwhile, one anonymous aid worker in Sri Lanka charged, "We are seeing a conscious and concentrated effort to make sure there are no international NGOs operating in any areas where there are military operations. There are two explanations. The benevolent one is that the government doesn't want NGO workers in the line of fire. The malevolent one would be they don't want eyes and ears" (Senanayake and Sengupta 2006).

This period was particularly lethal for aid workers. The Consortium for Humanitarian Agencies reported thirty-three Sri Lankan aid workers missing or killed between January 2006 and July 2007, with little or no progress in the investigations into their deaths (Integrated Regional Information Networks [IRIN] 2007c). Numerous national staff members working for aid agencies, including the ICRC, Caritas (the relief and development agency of the Catholic Church), CARE International, and local partner organizations, died in the fighting that later culminated in the end of the war.[17]

About the "heinous and barbaric" crime committed against ACF and the "whole international community," ACF writes,

> Although the crime was perpetrated within the context of the conflict between government forces and rebels troops (during what is now known as the "Muttur battle"), these deaths cannot be considered collateral damage; the 17 workers were intentionally executed, most of them execution style—by a gunshot to the head—on the premises of an international non-governmental organization while they were clearly identified as humanitarian workers. The 17 workers were specifically and deliberately targeted, shot in the head, execution style, on the premises of an international non-governmental organisation while they were clearly identified as humanitarian workers. (ACF International 2008, 8)

Rightly, most attention in the immediate aftermath focused on the alleged and actual perpetrators and the violence in Muttur leading up to the crime. Media reports highlighted the escalation in fighting, the "targeting" of aid workers and aid delivery, the execution-style killings, and the tension between aid groups and the government (Biggs 2006; Ganguly 2006). The ACF internal dynamics and decision making prior to the murders, in contrast, received comparatively little attention in public accounts of the incident. Yet organizational dynamics played a role in the tragedy. These included some dubious decisions by inexperienced managers, principally the decision, in spite of the fighting, to send the local Tamil staff (none of whom were from Muttur) into the city and without any expatriate staff who, by their presence, might have offered protection.[18]

As for the perpetrators, a local human rights group published a report on the massacres, blaming the Sri Lankan government and linking the massacres to the earlier deaths of five Tamil students in January 2006. The report names one member of the Muslim Home Guard and two police constables, indicating that these individuals carried out the killings in the presence of the Sri Lankan Naval Special Authorities and with prior approval of superiors in Trincomalee (University Teachers for Human Rights [UTHR] 2008). Scandinavian ceasefire monitors from the international Sri Lanka Monitoring Mission also blamed the government for the killings (Apps 2007a).

The actual motive for the killings remains unclear, although the UTHR report alleges one of the killers had sworn revenge for the death of his brother, who was killed by the LTTE, and that he led those responsible to the ACF compound on the pretext of it being an LTTE base. Given the politicized nature of aid in Sri Lanka, the fact that the ACF staff remained in Muttur after most civilians and other aid agencies had evacuated raised suspicions about why they did not evacuate earlier (UTHR 2008).

The Response: Accusations and Explanations in the Aftermath of Tragedy

The first anniversary of the ACF deaths reinvigorated the escalatory cycle of accusatory statements between aid agencies and the government. Government officials called Sir John Holmes, the UN under-secretary-general for humanitarian affairs at the time, a "terrorist who supported terrorism" and blamed ACF for its negligence, which they claimed led to the deaths of its local staff members. Meanwhile, aid agencies and officials such as Holmes criticized the government for its lack of progress in the investigations (Apps 2007b). That the killings took place in the context of significant tensions between aid agencies and the government highlights the role perception plays in creating insecurity and how politicization overshadowed other factors related to the incident.

The ACF investigation, published in June 2008, castigates the Sri Lankan government for its ineffectiveness in investigating the killings. It focuses only on the three official government inquiries into the killings: the judicial procedure at the Magistrate Court, a complaint at the Human Rights Commission, and a presidential Commission of Inquiry. The report chronicles a "flawed police investigation and judicial process" (ACF International 2008, 20) in the initial investigation; a lack of impartiality, independence, and transparency in the various inquiries; and political interference that stymied attempts to discover who was responsible and why. ACF withdrew in June 2008 to protest the Sri Lankan government's foot-dragging in effectively investigating the deaths and prosecuting those responsible (ACF International 2008). In June 2009, an official from the Sri Lankan rights panel indicated the panel members had concluded the investigation but declined to give any details.[19]

These accusations and incidents played out against a backdrop of politicized humanitarian action and animosity between the Sri Lankan government and aid groups. In the 1990s, partly as a result of donor pressure, many humanitarian actors shifted their focus from exclusively humanitarian work to incorporate human rights and peacebuilding agendas into their programming.[20] To local critics of the humanitarian presence, this shift in emphasis merely confirmed negative perceptions of NGOs (Goodhand and Lewer 1999), which spiked with the arrival of the "second tsunami" of international agencies after the December 2004 Indian Ocean tsunami. The confluence of events led many (Sinhalese) Sri Lankans, both official and unofficial, to view the involvement of Western humanitarian agencies with increasing suspicion. The critics were convinced that humanitarian actors entertained other, hidden agendas and quietly or even directly supported Tamils and the LTTE. These suspicions, in turn, were manipulated in order to call into question the effectiveness and appropriateness of assistance and to advance the goals of the government as well as its critics. Moreover, they signaled a failure on the part of humanitarian actors to effectively communicate messages about their mandates, activities, and goals (Harris 2007).[21]

These tensions reflect competing views of the roots of the Sri Lankan conflict as "domestic terrorism" on the one hand, and repression of a minority population on the other. In choosing to implement programming designed to promote peaceful relationships between conflicting communities, donors and relief-and-development NGOs aligned themselves, in the eyes of the government and Sinhalese majority, with the LTTE secessionist aspirations and against the Sri Lankan state. The net result was a tightened regulatory and operational environment for humanitarian and other actors (Harris 2010).[22]

The mixed-and-murky motives, questionable security procedures, and impunity for those responsible that surrounded the deaths and subsequent investigations illustrate the complexity and perils of contemporary aid work. The deaths of the seventeen ACF staff members were framed as part of the resurgent fighting and politicized nature of aid work in Sri Lanka. These undoubtedly contributed to the tragedy. Muted, if not silenced, in the narratives that characterized the incident were the internal ACF dynamics and their role in the tragedy. The event illustrates the hidden, internal vulnerabilities that often get lost in discussions of cause, especially in the context of politicized aid.

The published ACF report itself does not contain an analysis of the organization's own (in)actions, policies, and/or procedures in relation to the crime. Certainly, the government of Sri Lanka would have seized on and used any such admission as proof of ACF culpability in the subsequent ping-pong match of accusations and counteraccusations. The reputational and legal risk to ACF from a public admission of this sort likely would have proved significant. Nevertheless, the Sri Lankan government and others privately and publicly criticized ACF for its internal failings and questionable security-management decisions and procedures, including its failure to withdraw its staff from Muttur, despite ongoing fighting in the area, prior to the attacks (see Apps 2007b).

The Lessons of Muttur

The ACF case highlights how organizational dynamics and the politicized character of humanitarianism *together* facilitated the conditions that culminated in the tragic deaths of the seventeen staff members. The tragedy of the ACF murders also illustrates two divergent tendencies that plague explanations of the causes of violence against aid workers. On the one hand, the overarching and dominant discourse concerns the politicization of aid and how the use of aid in service of political agendas creates the conditions leading to the targeting of aid workers. This is also the discourse that dominates newspaper stories, the Internet, and academic commentaries about this type of violence.

On the other hand, in my conversations over the years with aid workers, security directors, and other experts about the causes of violence against aid workers, they frequently mention individual behavior or organizational lapses in security as contributing or causal factors when explaining the violence. Although they readily cite the politicization of aid, changes in the post–Cold War or 9/11 era, the availability of small arms and light weapons, criminality, or polarized dynamics between Western and Muslim countries, internal vulnerabilities such as individual behaviors and organizational policies and decisions figure prominently in the discussion as well. According to one aid expert, "There is a great disparity between international organizations and local populations, with their [the internationals'] lifestyle and big cars. . . . By local standards, internationals live extravagant lifestyles. They stand out. . . . It is semicolonial." According to another security expert, "Some of us don't behave well. . . . There is a lack of sensitivity and appreciation for other cultures." Such insights led one security director to observe, "Most security incidents are preventable at the organizational level. A dangerous environment, malaria, dehydration, criminal violence, random violence—these are mostly avoidable."[23] These internal vulnerabilities, however, are virtually absent in academic or policy literature discussions of the causes of violence against aid workers; thus, they are invisible.

When these factors do enter into the public discourse, they are usually linked to postincident investigations framed in terms of responsibility and accountability, as with the independent panels investigating the Baghdad bombing, or linked to exposés and lawsuits. Each of these sensationally renders visible the internal vulnerabilities, with associated goals of establishing responsibility and blame or of seeking redress. For instance, Sharon Commins was kidnapped and held, together with her Kenyan colleague Hilda Kawuki, in Darfur, Sudan, for three months in 2009. Commins has publicly decried the security lapses of her organization, the Irish aid agency GOAL, and its failure to evacuate her prior to the kidnapping, despite a shooting incident that had occurred several weeks before she and her colleague were kidnapped.[24] Another aid worker kidnapped in Darfur (Flavia Wagner) sued her employer, Samaritan's Purse, for "intentional, grossly reckless and negligent acts of misconduct." These acts include employing a "novice" security manager, failing to provide adequate training, and ignoring the warning signs of an increased risk of abduction for foreigners living in South Darfur.[25]

What explains this discrepancy? Like the discourse about the demise of the protective symbols and emblems in the wake of the Baghdad bombing, the politicization discourse exceptionalizes aid workers as actors in a context, implying they are somehow separate from the surrounding violence. In other words, their principles and the purpose of their work should have set them apart. Yet the aid workers killed in Sri Lanka, like many of those who are killed or kidnapped around the world, were national staff (Sri Lankan Tamils). While they worked for a humanitarian agency, their individual identities reflected the politicized ethnic identities of the Sri Lankan conflict. In this, they were anything but exceptional. Moreover, the scale of the tragedy, with seventeen dead from one organization, reversed the all-too-frequent omission in the foreign media of the deaths of national staff members. Thus, the deaths of seventeen national staff warrant significant media attention, yet the death of one national staff member rarely does, offering proof of the paradoxical hierarchies that govern the aid world. In these ways, the public renderings of the Muttur tragedy portray the dominance of external threat over the actions or inactions of the aid organizations and aid workers themselves, as well as the humanitarian exceptionalism that characterizes understanding of and responses to violence against aid workers. In short, these are the lessons of Muttur.

Expanding the Explanatory Discourse

The role of self-generated or internal vulnerabilities points to the importance of looking beyond the immediate and raises questions about aid agency decision making as a hidden though crucial piece of the puzzle. It also begs the question of why such factors do not receive more analytic consideration. While politicization undoubtedly plays a role in violence against aid workers, the following vignettes illustrate the all-too-frequent kinds of incidents that are buried in the security reports of aid agencies, regardless of whether or not they uphold the humanitarian principles of humanity, impartiality, neutrality, and independence. These stories counterbalance the well-publicized events and narratives of the Baghdad bombing and the ACF murders. All three are actual happenings, with some elaboration for narrative purposes and names and details changed to protect the identity of the victims.[26]

Vignette 1: Organizational Management and Personnel Conflicts

In West Africa, Joe, an international staff member of a large international NGO, discovers that Ahmed, a key national staff member, has failed to account for a large sum of money collected as part of a revolving loan-fund payment. Joe is devastated, because he has worked closely with Ahmed over several years, considers him a friend, and trusts him with significant financial and programmatic responsibilities. Joe discusses the matter with his in-country superior, Anna, and they decide to suspend Ahmed from his duties for one week pending investigation of the incident. Together Joe and Anna confront Ahmed and give him a suspension letter. Ahmed protests the language in the letter, but Joe and his superior assure Ahmed that he is not yet accused of wrongdoing. Over the next week, Joe conducts an investigation and submits the report to Anna, who will present and discuss the report with Ahmed the following Monday.

The next morning, a Sunday, Joe informs Ahmed that Anna would like to meet with him on Monday afternoon. Later that day, Ahmed returns to the office asking to talk with Joe and Joe invites him in. Ahmed closes the door, which locks automatically, behind him. Ahmed then demands to see his personnel file. Joe refuses, explaining it is confidential. Ahmed becomes angry and yells, "I'm not going to let you ruin my life!" Pulling out a knife, he lunges at Joe. Joe raises his hand to protect himself, and the knife slashes his hand. They continue to struggle, and the commotion draws the attention of neighbors and the one other staff person in the office on that Sunday. The group eventually breaks down the locked door and comes to Joe's aid. Joe is shaken and wounded, although not severely. They report the matter to local authorities.

Vignette 2: Reckless Behavior

Karen, a young, beautiful, and single female international staff member, arrives in a war-affected South Asian country to work for an aid organization.

She is looking to expand her horizons, excited about seeing new places and meeting new people. The landscape, culture, and people captivate her. Karen loves her work and enthusiastically explores the country. At a meeting one day, she meets a charismatic man named Arun, and they engage in lively conversation. He is a frequent traveler, and they discover a shared love for places near and far. They meet again and a mutual attraction develops. Arun takes Karen to out-of-the-way restaurants, wooing her with delicious food and drink. He is married, but tells her he doesn't love his wife.

Karen writes home, telling her friends and family about the new man in her life, with her excitement and happiness apparent. She falls in love with Arun and begins to socialize less with her friends and colleagues in order to spend more time with him. As time progresses, Karen realizes she knows very little about him indeed. Arun is a businessman and obviously wealthy, but the exact nature of his business is never discussed. Like some businessmen in the country, he travels regularly with a bodyguard and in a lightly armored vehicle. Despite her unease, their liaison continues, since Karen realizes she is in love with him and cannot imagine ending the affair. Her friends and colleagues are worried about her and grow increasingly so, even going so far as to talk to Karen's superiors about the potential risks of her affair with Arun.

One sunny afternoon as Karen is returning from lunch and crossing the road back to her office, a dark-colored four-wheel-drive vehicle with tinted-glass windows careens around the corner, one window rolled down. She is gunned down outside her office and dies en route to hospital. The local and then international media pick up the story, reporting another aid worker killed in the line of duty. The media reports blame her death on the militarization of humanitarian assistance, how aid is manipulated for political purposes, and how this compromises the independence and neutrality of humanitarians. The aid worker, the stories claim, died because the local population no longer sees assistance as neutral or impartial. Karen's colleagues and the word on the street tell a different story: Her liaison with the businessman led to her death. Arun's rivals killed her to punish him for a deal gone bad.

Vignette 3: Localized Grievances

In a town in a southern African country, religious dynamics played out to the detriment of one organization's security when a demonstration against the rendition of five Muslim teachers resulted in a stone-throwing attack on an NGO office. Other NGO offices remained unaffected. Was this an incident of "international religious terrorism"?

The organization's investigation into the attack revealed local, popular misconceptions about the agency and its work. The local community perceived the NGO as a "Christian charity," despite its secular mandate. The NGO employed only two Muslims in an area of the country where Muslims constituted 70 percent of the population. The NGO rented its office from the Catholic Church, and its staff—Christians from the capital city in a country that is, as a whole, majority Christian—openly propagated their beliefs in the office, with Christian posters and other religious adornments on the office walls. Furthermore, the NGO operated no projects in the town itself; all of its project work occurred in neighboring villages. As a result, the local community knew little about what the NGO did or why its staff drove around in marked vehicles (and not motorbikes, which were more common), with no visible projects or clear positive impact on the town or its citizens.

Together these factors created the perception of a Christian agency operating in a majority Muslim area, with little benefit to the local population. This set the stage for a local confrontation (the stone-throwing attack), isolated in itself, but also vaguely inspired by national and even global dynamics (Christian-Muslim tensions). The investigation concluded that the agency needed to address local perceptions of the organization, make its local workforce more representative of the population in the project area, and reach out to the community to increase its acceptance and security.

The incident itself illustrates the mutually reinforcing nature of local perceptions and global dynamics, and the ways in which organizational decisions play into these dynamics.

The Lessons of the Three Vignettes

These three vignettes about a disgruntled staff member, risky individual behavior, and discordant aid agency versus community perceptions of the organization and its purposes could have taken place anywhere. What is notable about these three vignettes is their unremarkability. Devoid of specifics about location or context, the main characters and basic circumstances are transmutable from one context to another. Only the second is fatal; the first and third vignettes typify the more ordinary and everyday types of violence that most aid workers experience.

The story of reckless behavior elucidates the role of Karen's behavior in creating vulnerabilities for herself and the risk that may transfer to the employing organization, particularly for agencies working in violent contexts. Attributing causation to the external threat, such as the militarization and manipulation of assistance, allows the agency to sidestep legal and even moral responsibility for its inaction in dealing with the situation. Yet blaming Karen for her choices is equally futile. People and organizations frequently do make mistakes. More often than not, mistakes remain near-misses or nonevents. That individuals pay for mistakes with their lives is indeed a tragedy, regardless of why. In moving forward, understanding what happened and how to prevent it in the future will be of more use than blaming those involved for their contributions, whether large or small, to the violence. While it is not possible to eliminate all risk, frank discussion of the ways that individuals expose themselves (and others) to risk and violence must be part of the overall explanatory picture.

The first vignette, about the desperation of an employee seeking to avoid exposure and the ramifications of corrupt behavior, exemplifies the ways in which the desperation that characterizes many humanitarian emergencies may elicit extreme acts. It also illustrates the potential risks inherent in human resource decisions, particularly in contexts of excessive inequality or places where the fault lines of conflict correspond to ethnic or other societal cleavages. The third vignette is fundamentally about the need to educate and engage the community and the ways in which perceptions affect the security or vulnerability of an organization.

All three vignettes exemplify the complexity of cause that is absent from mono-causal explanations, whether they derive from external threat or internal vulnerability. Instead, the interdependence of and interaction between factors better explain the violence. Moreover, the three tales point to the value of interpreting events in light of the relationships embedded within the aid system—between aid agencies and the communities in which they work, between colleagues, and between expatriate aid workers and host populations, or even between the wounded and those offering care. The following stories, those of Solferino and other early examples of altruistic acts on the battlefield, offer an interpretation of humanitarianism that reclaims these relational aspects of the humanitarian endeavor.

The Founding Story of Solferino: Humanitarianism as a Compassionate and Relational Act

The origins of modern humanitarianism are nestled in the simpler story of Henri Dunant at Solferino, Italy, a tale with near-mythic status that stands in stark contrast to the complexities of contemporary aid work. In June 1859, Dunant, a Swiss businessman, followed the trail of Napoleon III, to whom he wished to speak about a business deal (Moorehead 1998, 6–7). Dunant paused in his journey in time to witness a bloody battle in Solferino between the French and Austrian armies and its immediate aftermath that cost the lives of thousands of people. "Whole divisions threw off their knapsacks in order to be able to charge the enemy more freely with fixed bayonets," wrote Dunant in *A Memory of Solferino*. "As one battalion is repulsed, another immediately replaces it. Every mound, every height, every rocky crag, is the scene of a fight to the death: bodies lie in heaps on the hills and in the valleys." He continued, "the soil is literally puddled with blood, and the plain littered with human remains" (Dunant 1986, 19, 20).

His memoir recounted the valiant yet painfully inadequate efforts of the medical personnel assigned to treat the wounded and dying. At that time, armies located field ambulances and first aid centers well behind battle lines and marked them with a black flag (or else with a variety of country-specific symbols and flags) raised high enough to be visible. Even so, these flags did not provide any measure of protection. Armies "tacitly agreed that no one shall fire in their direction. But sometimes shells reach these nevertheless, and their quartermaster and ambulance men are no more spared than are the wagons loaded with bread, wine and meat to make soup for the wounded" (Dunant 1986, 39; see also Benthall 1993, 141). The wounded either walked of their own volition to these centers or porters transported them on stretchers. The less fortunate died where they fell. As a measure of the pitiful emphasis armies placed on treating their wounded, David Forsythe reports that European military forces engaged more veterinarians for their horses than doctors for their soldiers (Forsythe 2005, 15).

Confronted with and horrified by the gruesome sights, the "fearful stench" of the dead and dying, and the lack of water and basic medical care for the wounded, Dunant felt compelled to respond to the suffering of his fellow human beings. He organized relief efforts in the surrounding villages, enlisting the help of the villagers of Castiglione to care for the wounded from all sides. They lay on straw beds in hospitals, churches, monasteries, barracks, private houses, and in the streets and courtyards (Dunant 1986, 55). Dunant persuaded a group of women to help dress wounds and provide food and water. The women of Castiglione, he wrote, "seeing that I made no distinction between nationalities, followed my example, showing the same kindness to all these men whose origins were so different, and all of whom were foreigners to them. 'Tutti fratelli,' they repeated feelingly" (Dunant 1986, 72). In Castiglione and elsewhere, volunteers took on many tasks, organizing into auxiliary groups to receive and distribute supplies and provide care.

In Brescia, where he went after leaving Castiglione fully spent from his efforts, Dunant wrote letters to soldiers' families and distributed tobacco and pipes. With his actions, "Dunant established some of the fundamental ideals and methodologies of humanitarianism. He negotiated access, he chose to act impartially, he used his position of neutrality, and he organized civil society in a voluntary, non-coerced fashion" (Walker and Maxwell 2009, 22).

At the end of his treatise about his experiences in Solferino, Dunant outlined a vision of an international relief society of trained volunteers to provide assistance and solace to the wounded. He lamented the lack of such a force: "Oh, how valuable it would have been . . . to have had a hundred experienced and qualified voluntary orderlies and nurses!" And he asked whether it would be possible "in time of peace and quiet, to form relief societies for the purpose of having care given to the wounded in wartime by zealous, devoted, and thoroughly qualified volunteers" (Dunant 1986, 102, 115). To do this, he called for a "congress to formulate some international principle, sanctioned by a Convention inviolate in character, which, once agreed upon and ratified might constitute the basis for societies for the relief of the wounded" (Dunant 1986, 126).

Although Dunant's work at Solferino and his clarion call to establish relief societies to care for the wounded are lauded as seminal in the early history of modern humanitarianism, the efforts of two of his contemporaries, Florence Nightingale and Clara Barton, are equally impressive. In 1853, the British government asked Nightingale to organize a group of nurses to care for soldiers in the Crimea. The conditions she and her nurses encountered were appalling, with overflowing sewers and dead rats sharing space with the wounded, who were "themselves plagued by fleas, lice, bugs and maggots." With mops, disinfectant, and hard work, she and her nurses imposed order, hygiene, and cleanliness. She became a quartermaster for the British army. As a result of her efforts, where the "wounded and sick were brought in dressed in rags; they left the hospital with clean clothes, drinking cups and knives and forks." Casualty rates from sickness subsequently declined dramatically (Moorehead 1998, 31, 32).

Half a world away, Clara Barton, a nurse and the first president of the American Red Cross, was involved in the American Civil War. She provided food and supplies to the wounded, much as Dunant had done at Solferino. Her exploits, "her sense of outrage, her determination and her competence" became the stuff of legend. She accompanied the Union forces, providing medical care and making food from biscuits, water, and sugar for the wounded. Her work took her to the frontlines of battle, where she had the sleeve of her dress torn by a bullet, and a man for whom she was caring died in her arms (Moorehead 1998, 36). After the war, she eventually met some of the founders of the Red Cross and became a crusader for the U.S. ratification of the First Geneva Convention and the establishment of the American Red Cross.

The time was ripe for efforts to rein in the worst excesses of war. Dunant traveled around Europe publicizing his book, which was published in 1862. He was an "idea entrepreneur" (Forsythe 2005, 15). Several other prominent Geneva citizens received Dunant's book and endorsed its ideas, among them other founders of the ICRC, General Guillaume Hénri Dufour and Gustave Moynier (first president of the ICRC). They, together with Dunant, Dr. Louis Appia, and Dr. Théodore Maunoir, formed the International Committee for Relief to the Wounded, the precursor to the ICRC. The men organized an international meeting in October 1863, to which sixteen states sent delegates. Those present adopted a final resolution that established volunteer committees that would prepare for relief in times of peace and that would assist but not replace army military authorities. Members of the committee would wear a distinctive armband of a red cross on a white background (Moorehead 1998, 13–22).

The work of these men led eventually to the signing of the First Geneva Convention of 1864, the forerunner of the Geneva Conventions of 1949 and a legal complement to Dunant's plea to inject some humanity into the scourge of war. In August 1864, the Swiss Confederation hosted a diplomatic conference. Again, sixteen states sent representatives. The treaty they drafted included provisions for the care of wounded, regardless of nationality, and the neutrality of ambulances, military hospitals, and their personnel. "And since neutrality clearly depended on being able to recognize them," Caroline Moorehead writes of the treaty, "a red cross against a white background . . . was to be accepted as the universal emblem for all medical people and places, whether on a flag or as an armband. From now on the words 'Red Cross' were increasingly used when referring to the new movement" (Moorehead 1998, 45; see also 38–48). The twelve nations that signed the convention, known officially as the Geneva Convention for the Amelioration of the Condition of the Wounded in Armies in the Field, also became the first twelve national Red Cross societies (Walker and Maxwell 2009, 23).

The 1864 Geneva Convention birthed the emblem of the Red Cross. Prior to 1864, a variety of flags and symbols designated medical services on the battlefield. The adoption of the Red Cross emblem changed this, creating, in theory at least, a universally recognized symbol protected under the law. Unfortunately, misuse of the emblem has an equally lengthy history. It was replicated and placed in private homes and made into banners in the Franco-Prussian war (1870–1871), and again in the 1875 Balkan wars, where the Muslims associated the emblem with the symbols of the Christian Crusaders. The latter association eventually led to the adoption of the Red Crescent (Moorehead 1998, 66, 125–126). Over one hundred years later, the misuse continues. For instance, it was placed in shop windows in Liberia in 1991 and used to disguise the transport of weapons in war in the former Yugoslavia in 1991–1992 (Benthall 1993, 142–143). The red cross also liberally marks first-aid and medical products, a use prohibited by international law, even if not always judiciously enforced.[27]

The First Geneva Convention and the founding of the ICRC foreshadowed other efforts to limit warfare in the latter half of the nineteenth century, such as the Brussels Document of 1874, the Oxford Manual on War of 1880, and the Hague Conferences of 1899 and 1907, all of which sought to place limitations on the conduct of war (Slim 2007, 17). In this way, efforts to limit the excesses of war occurred concurrent with efforts to provide assistance in the midst of war. Dunant's legacy includes the founding of the ICRC, with its work to protect and provide humanitarian assistance to those affected by war and internal violence. The ICRC's role as guardian of international humanitarian law and provider of humanitarian assistance in war is built on the first and subsequent Geneva Conventions.

The principles that guide the work of the ICRC and compose the core principles of humanitarian action are *humanity* (the irreducible, inherent dignity of the human being), *impartiality* (providing assistance proportional to need and without discrimination based on identity, religion, nationality, or any other characteristic), *neutrality* (not taking sides in a conflict), and *independence* (autonomy of action).[28] Early on in the ICRC's history, however, Gustave Moynier, the first president of the ICRC, proposed the following principles for the movement: foresight (preparing in advance for providing relief), solidarity (that the Red Cross societies assist one another), centralization (one society per country), and mutuality (care for all, regardless of nationality, a forerunner of impartiality) (Walker and Maxwell 2009, 23–24). The Red Cross movement adopted its current seven principles in 1965 (Forsythe 2005, 29).

Reclaiming Humanity

Humanitarianism, in its essence, is about relieving the suffering of and protecting those trapped in the vortex of violence or swept up in nature's wrath. Belligerents often use humanitarian aid as a crutch or as a weapon to advance their cause. Humanitarians are often those most likely to stay and the last to leave, a result of their dedication to helping others in life-and-death situations. At times, the presence of humanitarian actors curbs the worst excesses of violence against war-affected populations. Their presence in these situations involves risk, a steady companion of aid workers since the inception of modern humanitarianism. The risks they encounter are both physical and psychological. Dunant described the "canteen women" of Solferino, who were "often wounded themselves" or even killed while helping to assuage the thirst of the wounded soldiers (Dunant 1986, 32).

The access of humanitarians to the front lines means that they are among the select few outsiders to witness atrocities directly, lending moral authority to their voices when they speak out and generating publicity when they are attacked. Attacks against aid workers, whether targeted or not, therefore not only pose a risk to aid workers but also can dramatically affect the civilian populations they assist. Violence against aid workers and aid agencies threatens lives and impedes the ability to provide lifesaving assistance to victims; as a result, needy populations go underserved or unserved. Sustaining a compassionate and relational presence in the face of attempted manipulation by one, both, or all sides to a conflict is precisely where courage and risk come in and where providing aid includes an element of danger.

Dunant's actions on that day in Solferino represented a response to the inherent humanity of those suffering. They were classic altruistic acts. His vision and the core principles of humanity, impartiality, and operational independence and neutrality have remained foundational, at least in rhetoric if not always in practice, for those engaged in humanitarian action.

The continuity of principles extends to other realms as well. Humanitarians, operating in greater numbers and in increasingly dangerous circumstances, still work on or just behind the battlefields, providing medical care for the civilian and military wounded along with food and shelter to those affected by war. Their work remains fraught with ethical dilemmas and existential danger even as the contexts in which present-day humanitarians work differ dramatically from those of the founders of the modern humanitarian movement. One wonders what Dunant and his contemporaries might think of today's aid world, with its dozens of donor states, interagency coordination mechanisms, and operational sectors (e.g., camp management, water and sanitation, health); the hundreds of thousands of aid workers and hundreds of agencies, many of which control multimillion-dollar budgets, that provide assistance; and the profession's standards of care and conduct. Doubtless, they would support some developments and eschew others.

The vision that drove Dunant and others was of humanitarianism as a compassionate act in service to the humanity of others, ignoring the fault lines of battle. Similar motivations drove the founding of contemporary aid organizations and have sustained their growth and longevity. Yet it is precisely this vision—of humanitarianism as a compassionate and *relational* act—that is in danger of being lost in the scuffle to provide security for those civilians working on the front lines of battle. Somewhere between the battlefields of Solferino and Baghdad's Green Zone, aid work stopped being exclusively about serving and protecting people in need.

As a principle, *humanity* is related to the inherent dignity of the person and the right to life. It is thereby tied to the equality of individuals and the integral nature of protecting civilian populations to humanitarian assistance. Although Jean Pictet, architect of the modern-day Red Cross principles, labeled humanity the essential principle "from which all other principles are derived," he did not define it beyond claiming its "special place because it is the expression of the profound motivation of the Red Cross" (Pictet 1979a, 135). As a legal framework, "humanity law," encompassing international humanitarian, human rights, and criminal justice law, emphasizes the "protection and preservation of persons and peoples" in situations of violence that has, over time, restricted state sovereignty and the use of force (Teitel 2011, 13).

As a formative or operational humanitarian principle, however, humanity has received comparatively little attention. Robin Coupland, an ICRC field surgeon and advisor, observes that the principle can refer to either the collectivity of human beings (all of "humanity") and a behavior or sentiment (being "humane"; Coupland 2001, 2003; see also Laqueur 2009). Its opposite, inhumanity, is perhaps more instructive, since it is more clearly defined in international law, and it is possible to identify the absence of humanity as sentiment in acts of inhumanity. Coupland suggests humanity "arises from and signifies restraining the capacity for armed violence and limiting its effects on security and health" (Coupland 2001, 988; see also Glover 2012). In articulating the unique value of the principle of humanity, Hugo Slim (1998) argues for application and ownership of humanity beyond the humanitarian community, precisely because of its prophetic power to restrict the excesses of war. The desire to help and protect civilians suffering the malevolent effects of violence is what motivates the choice of many humanitarians to do the work and put themselves in harm's way.

On the surface, humanity is the least controversial of the four core principles of humanitarian action—humanity, impartiality, neutrality, and independence—and holds primacy as a space of common ground among a diverse set of aid actors. Paradoxically, however, humanity's acceptability means it is often lost as an orienting or operational principle. Providing aid is therefore in danger of becoming something other than the indiscriminate act of compassion on the battlefield that the founders of modern humanitarianism enacted. Regardless of whether an agency claims solidarity or neutrality, or operates from a faith-based or secular perspective, humanity can serve as an orienting principle for the provision of humanitarian assistance.

Humanity's meaning and application, however, are not without controversy or paradox, nor is its compassionate essence always entirely laudable (Feldman and Ticktin 2010a, 2010b; Hyndman 2000). In fact, humanity enacted as charity is often predicated on hierarchy, where those of higher status and means give of their excess to those with less, and thereby incur obligations on the part of the latter to the former (Laqueur 2009; see also Mauss 2011). In the foundational stories, humanity referred primarily, even exclusively, to wounded soldiers, thus reflecting the reigning European prejudices of the day (Barnett 2011) and its changing meaning over time.[29]

In deconstructing humanitarianism, Didier Fassin (2010a; 2012) refers to the affective dimension of humanity (humaneness) and its affirmation of similarity between individuals ("mankind") and arguably of connection as humanity is enacted in response to suffering. In doing so, he highlights the "hierarchies of humanity" that emerge in the "politics of life" of the modern humanitarian response: a hierarchy that values soldiers' lives over those of civilians, the "freely sacrificed lives of aid workers" set against the lives of the populations engulfed in the violence, and the lives of expatriate over national staff members (Fassin 2012, 227). In critiquing the inequalities of the hierarchy, he affirms the exceptional and problematic nature of aid workers in relation to other players in the humanitarian drama and within aid agencies themselves. In this way, Fassin (2010a) highlights the tension between humanity's universalism and its particularism, where its aspirations are universal yet its enactment is rooted in inequality and difference, which are invariably particular (see also Malkki 1996). Others interrogate the universal and particular aspects of humanity with reference to "enlarging the circle of moral inclusion" (Feldman and Ticktin 2010b, 4; Laqueur 2009; see also Benhabib 2004).

In arguing for a relational approach to humanitarianism, I am proposing a reassertion of humanity as the central orienting principle. What, exactly, does humanity mean, given the tensions highlighted above? Humanity, as I conceive of it here, best embodies the universal inherent dignity and equality of the person spelled out in the preamble of the Universal Declaration of Human Rights *and* the possibilities for a compassionate and empathic response to the suffering of another. Qualifying the inherent dignity and equality of the individual is a relational interpretation, which sees individuals as social beings. This, in turn, recognizes the interdependent relationships inherent in humanitarian work and offers an antidote to the exceptionalism that too often characterizes the humanitarian endeavor. Following those who contrast humanity's universalism and its situated applications, I delineate the tensions that arise from an exclusive interpretation (humanitarian exceptionalism) and suggest a relational, intersubjective interpretation of humanity as a way of further extending the boundaries of inclusion *and* a pathway to reforming the humanitarian system. Therefore, a relational approach is both normative and analytical in its application.

Employing a relational, intersubjective (Benhabib 2004) approach suggests revisiting the response to the Baghdad bombing in light of the negative, if largely unintended, consequences of emphasizing fortresses, standards, and professionalization that result in greater separation from the populations in need of assistance. Reclaiming humanity calls for a better accounting of the internal vulnerabilities of the Muttur tragedy, which are embedded in the decisions of the organization and the relationships inherent in humanitarian work, that compose a central dimension of the causal picture. Such an approach suggests that the pendulum has swung too far in one direction and necessitates a correction that reclaims the virtues of the act of being with and accompanying people in their suffering, an act at the very heart of humanitarianism.

Perhaps most important, reasserting humanity not only offers a prophetic call against the excesses of war, as Slim suggests, or as a restraint on violence, as Coupland observes, but also *radically undermines the dominant dynamic of violence*, which relies upon dehumanization and the denial of the humanity of the "other" to sustain it. Humanity is at once aspirational (yet to be enacted) and pragmatic (offering guidance). While this conception may seem somewhat naïve and may not reconcile the inherent hierarchies delineated above, at the least reclaiming humanity will force aid agencies to recognize and grapple with the tension and inequalities that do exist and with the ways by which the everyday practices of aid define its meaning. It thereby helps to move the enterprise as a whole toward a vision that affirms the connectedness and equality inscribed in humanity as a guiding principle, both internally within organizations and externally in their relations with others suffering, living, and working in the areas in which they operate. In reasserting humanity as the core motivation and principle, aid agencies profess a distinctive model of operating that climbs out of the morass of exceptionalism and reclaims compassion as a central orienting feature of humanitarianism. Furthermore, it offers the possibility of a humanitarianism more consistent with the principles that it espouses.

CHAPTER 2

The Twin Challenges for Contemporary Humanitarianism

Both the Baghdad bombing and Muttur tragedy occurred in the years following the terror attacks on the World Trade Center in New York and the Pentagon on 11 September 2001. More broadly, writers, social scientists, theorists, and theologians, among others, have analyzed and written about the profound cultural shift and pervasive sense of fear that marks the Western post-9/11 world (Bauman 2006; Altheide 2002; Bader-Saye 2007; Amis 2008). The prominence of global terror, especially after the September 11 attacks and the war in Iraq, the discourse of the "war on terror," and pervasive government responses to terror all feed the beast of fear.[1] Those of us living in the West live with constant reminders of the threats we face: insurance agencies remind us to buy insurance in case of the unexpected, weather experts warn us to prepare for "catastrophic" floods and hurricanes, the global financial meltdown has "decimated" pensions and assets and uncertainty dominates future economic scenarios, security guards search us and our belongings in buildings and airports, and disembodied voices in airports remind us not to leave our bags unattended or that airports are operating at "threat level orange." Fear, or reminders to be fearful, permeates our modern existence.

The publicity that accompanies terror attacks reinforces the discourse of fear at a societal level (Altheide 2002; Bauman 2006). The repeated reminders of potential terror or other attacks perpetuate this discourse and create an individualized sense of fear that "I" will be attacked or that "our" way of life is in danger of imminent and violent destruction. They reinforce the notion that violence is ubiquitous, and therefore all we can do is hunker down and protect ourselves from those who wish us harm. The Obama administration's moratorium on the use of the "war on terror" language has moderated some of the polarization of the George W. Bush era, but the entrenched perceptions and enemy images of the years immediately following 2001 remain strong in places such as Pakistan and Afghanistan, where security concerns for humanitarians are prevalent and immediate. Given how pervasive and multisectored the discourses of fear have become, it is thus not surprising that a similar affliction befell many in the humanitarian community.

It is against this backdrop that the amalgam of the practical and analytical challenges of understanding aid in danger, both described in this chapter, is revealed. The practical challenge fundamentally concerns the most effective strategies of protecting aid workers and maintaining access to beneficiaries in the contemporary world, where discourses of fear and terror are prevalent and pernicious. The violence that befell aid workers in Iraq and Afghanistan in the early 2000s, in particular, shifted the terms of the debate around security and security management. It entrenched humanitarian exceptionalism and the fortification and professionalization of security management and drew humanitarianism further away from its relational core. In seeing the causes of violence in all their complexity and in challenging humanitarian exceptionalism, however, an alternative vision begins to emerge.

The related analytical challenge arises from the persistence of the external-threat discourse as the primary, or even sole, explanation for incidents such as the Muttur tragedy and the Baghdad bombing. A broad-stroke analysis of incidents consistently dominates and interprets incidents through a political lens, downplaying how individual or organizational actions might have played a role. These explanations privilege the political context, thereby framing the overall analysis for the violence in terms of external threat. Thus, *context* serves as a convenient and easily accessible hook for the violence aid workers experience and builds momentum for the exceptionalism narrative. While context is no doubt important, it is not everything—and in some cases, it is not decisive.

The tenacity of the external-threat discourse arises from a reluctance to publicly delve into factors that point toward aid agencies and aid workers and that inevitably raise questions of blame and responsibility. Using the example of the Baghdad bombing, I describe various explanations for the attack and the ways in which they illustrate the competing tendencies to look internally (emphasizing blame) or externally (toward terrorism) to explain the causes of violence. Individually, the internal-vulnerability and external-threat explanations are lacking and impede understanding. Moreover, the hunt for blame in the Baghdad bombing highlights the tension between the immediate need to react to an act of violence and the need to understand and address the underlying causes. Out of these tensions emerges the need for an analytical framework that recognizes the multiplicity of causes.

In the final section, therefore, I present an interdisciplinary analytical framework that examines multiple dimensions of the causes of violence and uncovers invisible internal vulnerabilities even as it acknowledges external threat. The framework embeds humanitarian actors in an interdependent and complex system of relationships and actions. In doing so, the framework helps to reappropriate a relational perspective that challenges humanitarian exceptionalism, accounts for the interactions that characterize humanitarianism, and offers a way forward in the face of the analytical and practical challenges of aid in danger. Such a lens helps to facilitate understanding and addresses the vexing discrepancy illustrated by the Muttur tragedy and the vignettes of the previous chapter: that aid workers and humanitarian security experts highlight the role of internal vulnerabilities, yet these, unless framed in terms of blame, are usually downplayed or even absent from public discourse.

The Practical Challenge: Security and Risk Management in the Age of Terror

For the humanitarian community, after September 11 a primary challenge and identity crisis for humanitarian action emerged in relation to the "global war on terror," particularly in relation to operations in Iraq and Afghanistan. For those inside and outside the humanitarian community, the numbers, targets, and intentionality of the attacks on aid workers made Afghanistan and Iraq especially troublesome. Between October 2001, the beginning of the U.S. bombing, and April 2008, 114 aid workers (national and international) were killed and forty-one kidnapped in Afghanistan. UN, International Committee of the Red Cross (ICRC), and NGO national and international staff died, and the scope of the attacks left aid workers reeling and large swathes of the country inaccessible to most aid agencies. Between January 2003, the start of the U.S.-led war, and April 2008, fifty-four aid workers were killed and twenty-six kidnapped in Iraq.[2]

The deaths of humanitarian colleagues in Iraq and Afghanistan, especially during 2003–2004, spurred existential questioning among NGOs and other international actors. Why are we here? Do we stay, and if so, how can we operate within the constraints of ensuring our staff are safe? The number and degree of severity of security incidents escalated over time, sending warning signals that feature more prominently in hindsight. For example, the August 19 attack did not occur out of the blue. Between 1 June and 19 July 2003, fifteen security incidents affected the UN. In the days immediately prior to the bombing, UN security management received credible reports of an imminent bomb attack in the area, and the daily security updates revealed a dramatically deteriorating security environment (Independent Panel 2003; UN Secretariat 2004). Two additional major security incidents occurred in September. After the second of these, the UN security team in Iraq again issued a unanimous recommendation for phase 5, which UN Secretary-General Kofi Annan rejected until 30 October, three days after the explosion outside the headquarters of the ICRC on 27 October (Power 2008, 507).

The lack of a clear and pressing humanitarian crisis in the early stages of the war in Iraq, in particular, made the question of whether to operate in Iraq even more perplexing, as the humanitarian needs post–U.S. invasion never reached anticipated levels (de Torrenté 2004a). The media attention on Iraq (and Afghanistan for that matter) made it difficult for agencies not to be present. Even so, the level of danger and needs that never materialized combined to create an exodus of agencies from Iraq in late 2003 and 2004. Those that remained chose to dramatically lower their profiles or operate with more militarized protective and deterrent security measures (Carle and Chkam 2006; Hansen 2007a). These responses led to the bunkerization of the humanitarian community, especially the UN, and the push in some of the most dangerous countries to manage by remote control—where agencies partially or completely withdraw (expatriate) staff from high-risk areas and operate either with only national staff or through local partners.

For the UN in particular, the bombing of the Canal Hotel in Baghdad played a seminal role in cementing a "fortress mentality." One UN staff member remarked, "After 9/11 and Afghanistan, things changed. But there was more of a change after the Baghdad bombing," marked by the "approach of building fortresses."[3] Another observed that "more armored vehicles, flak jackets, and walls mean more expenditures. . . . Security is becoming systematic and conservative."[4] One aid expert suggested, "The UN is inhibited by the security culture that emerged versus the actual threat."[5] The UN experience in Iraq tainted its approach elsewhere as well as the perceptions of risk and threat for humanitarians more generally, crystallizing the power of the insecurity discourse.

The prominence of these deliberate attacks on aid workers within the context of the "war on terror" starkly underscored the danger and stimulated a debate, particularly related to the prevalence and degree of the changes, about the changing nature of violence and humanitarian action. Antonio Donini observes, "Humanitarian action seems to be taking place in an increasingly murky landscape beset by manipulations and tensions between policy choices and even philosophies of humanitarianism" (Donini 2003, 8). The debate pits those who believe Iraq and Afghanistan typify the future against those who believe they are atypical. Underlying this debate is whether the changes of the post-9/11 world are entirely new or new only in degree (for more, see, e.g., Donini, Minear, and Walker 2004; Hoffman and Weiss 2006; Barnett and Weiss 2008a; Barnett 2011).

One argument extends the claim that the core principles of humanity, impartiality, operational independence, and neutrality that underpin humanitarian action are eroding in the face of new challenges, through the securitization of aid, in which humanitarian assistance becomes enmeshed within a security agenda, and through the militarization of aid, with its increasingly blurred boundaries between civilian and military actors. In particular, much has been made of the polarization of the world into those for and those against "fighting terror" and the consequent "loss of humanitarian space." According to an extensive consultation with the humanitarian community, this results in two concerns: the "malaise in the humanitarian community and the *uneasy sense that the community is caught up in a chain of events over which it has no control*" (Donini, Minear, and Walker 2004, 191, italics added). This view, therefore, emphasizes an increasingly chaotic operating environment characterized by targeted violence against aid workers, as exemplified in Iraq and Afghanistan.

In contrast to the view that represents Iraq and Afghanistan as harbingers of a new and dangerous era of humanitarianism, another view sees the challenges of Iraq and Afghanistan as an intensification of dilemmas humanitarians have faced for decades. Therefore, Iraq and Afghanistan, while dangerous and thus crucial to understand, do not portend an ominous future for all humanitarian emergencies. As contexts for humanitarian action, they are not necessarily reflective of or generalizable to other contexts. Instead, Iraq and Afghanistan represent the more violent fringes. Proponents warn against the "Iraqisation of assistance,"[6] in which agencies operate only by remote control or from behind fortified bunkers. This argument contends humanitarians must return to narrowly defined core principles as opposed to expanding or adapting the principles to reflect changing circumstances.

Of importance, the focus on targeted violence against aid workers in these contexts precipitates other, more subtle repercussions. During this period, the discourse about the deliberate targeting of aid workers gained traction to the neglect of other explanations. The repeated and deadly targeted attacks on aid workers in Iraq and Afghanistan after 9/11 and the pervasive reporting primarily on fatalities and kidnappings of aid workers mirrored the societal discourse of a generalized need to be fearful. A growing literature brought home to aid workers the proliferation of incidents and underlined the nefarious targeting of aid workers. Although much of the debate surrounded the changing context for humanitarian action, security incidents were portrayed as a seemingly inevitable consequence of the new environment. Examining such trends, Greg Hansen wrote in 2007, "Since 2004, there is a much stronger tendency among international humanitarian staff (as well as among donors and policymakers) to treat insecurity in Iraq as a nebulous, generalized, persistent and insurmountable challenge, rather than as a series of serious incidents, each of which can be analyzed, placed into (often localised) context, and used as a spur to adaptation" (Hansen 2007b, 53). The incidents prompted existential crises among agencies about their work and the apparently inevitable trade-offs between their responsibilities to their staff and those to the people they serve.

The preoccupation with severe violence (kidnappings, severe injury, and death) and the deliberate targeting of aid workers exaggerate existential threats and help foster a climate of fear. Focusing primarily on the severe incidents obscures the less violent incidents that aid workers around the world are more likely to experience on a daily basis, just as emphasizing the intentional nature of these more violent incidents magnifies the sense of being a target. Both further enshrine the notion that "they" are out to get "us," thereby dividing the world into us against them, good versus evil.

In analyzing media coverage of crime and violence, American sociologist David Altheide points out the bias in crime coverage that privileges the more severe crimes (i.e., homicides and assaults), even though individuals are far more likely to experience burglaries, which rarely rate news coverage. This bias has produced a "discourse of fear," the "pervasive communication, symbolic awareness, and expectation that danger and risk are a central feature of everyday life" (Altheide 2003, 10). The discourse of fear represents only the beginning, as its social consequences are myriad. As Altheide writes,

> It is not fear of crime, then, that is most critical, but rather what this fear can expand into, what it can become. Many changes in social life suggest that we are becoming "armored." Social life changes when more people live behind walls, hire guards, drive armored vehicles (e.g., Sport Utility Vehicles), wear "armored" clothing (e.g., "big soled shoes"), carry mace and handguns, and take martial arts classes. The problem is that these activities reaffirm and help produce a sense of disorder that our actions perpetuate. We then rely more on formal agents of social control to "save us" by "policing them," the "others," who have challenged our faith. (Altheide 2003, 19)

The mechanisms of social control and armored living are replicated in the aid world, especially in the most dangerous places and to a lesser extent in the safer countries. NGO security protocols establish curfews to regulate the movement of personnel. In some cases, they admonish staff to avoid certain neighborhoods and hangouts. UN field security trainings replicate such advice regardless of context. "By outlawing walking around or engaging with local people," Mark Duffield writes, "the exercise reinforces dependence on the organization while emphasizing the danger of the streets. Repeated on the CDs in different scenarios, the main response to the pervasive threats faced by aid workers is to encourage *isolation* and *risk aversion*" (Duffield 2010, 462, italics in original).

Whether a result of living behind walled compounds or a result of the increasingly expert and professional world of aid, expertise, living standards, and experience serve to separate aid workers from beneficiaries. In order to counter such forces, the NGO and humanitarian security sector must work to expand diversity among individuals and approaches and to maintain the flexibility and adaptability that safeguard a contextual and nuanced approach to security. The question must not pit these options—relationships or professionalism, hardened or consent-based security-management approaches, flexibility or standards—against one another. Instead, the question should be how to recognize the tensions between them, all the while holding fast to the relational ethos of humanitarianism. The practical challenge, therefore, is how to manage security given that the most dangerous outliers of Afghanistan and Iraq—which emphasize chaos, uncertainty, and fear and characterize aid workers as prominent and sometimes-lucrative targets—tend to dominate the landscape.

Many aid workers believe that something fundamental to the aid enterprise has been lost in contemporary humanitarianism. Indeed, given the physical and emotional separation that results from the fortification and professionalization of security management, and the undercurrent of fear that permeates the most dangerous contexts and that seeps into the less risky places, the pendulum has swung too far toward professionalism and fortification. The principle of humanity, and its respect for the myriad relationships that define humanitarianism, offers a counterbalance to the fortification and professionalization that characterize the current aid system. The challenge for the future is to recapture the relational ethos that drove the early humanitarians while recognizing the reality of growth and the complexities inherent in providing aid in contexts of insecurity.

By reclaiming humanity as the central principle, by returning to Solferino as touchstone and guide, and by laying claim to an alternative vision that resists the temptation to fall prey to the seductiveness of the terror discourse and the assertion that Iraq and Afghanistan represent the dominant landscape of humanitarianism, it is possible to begin to dismantle these tendencies. Indeed, the story of Muttur reminds us that the politicized discourse of aid cannot fully explain everything that resulted in the deaths of the ACF staff members. While reasserting the principle of humanity may not definitively solve these vexing issues, it does offer a set of parameters within which to navigate the practical challenges of humanitarianism that are fully consistent with its values and principles.

Furthermore, any satisfactory explanatory scheme of violence against aid workers and aid delivery must integrate the external cultural, social, and political structures and patterns, on the one hand, and the responsive and proactive actions and behaviors of the aid workers and agencies, on the other. In short, understanding the multidimensionality and mutually reinforcing nature of violence against aid workers and agencies offers both a way out of the impasse presented by currents of fortification and professionalization, and a pathway forward that reinstates humanity as the essential purpose of aid.

The Analytical Challenge: Blame Versus Understanding

Samantha Power's biography of Sergio Vieira de Mello offers a vivid and detailed description of the precedents, human stories, and aftermath of 19

August 2003. She portrays a scene of chaos, where no one actor—and certainly not the UN, with its leader and many of his colleagues trapped in the rubble of the Canal Hotel—took control of the rescue operation. In doing so, she reflects the conviction that if only someone had taken charge, if the equipment that was there had been appropriately deployed, de Mello (and others) might have been saved. De Mello was alive and coherent for three hours after the blast, talking with nearby rescuers in the early hours. As the minutes and hours stretched on, however, he gradually lost strength. In Power's account, the disappointment and indeed outrage of the survivors is palpable, underscoring the impact of the event on the victims and their loved ones, and the profound sense of vulnerability and frailty it evoked in the survivors. Their grief, loss, guilt, and anger and the stories of rescuers and survivors of the blast raise questions of cause and, by extension, of blame: Why did this happen? Who is responsible? With the costs so exorbitant and its organizational missteps laid bare in the rubble and exposed in the press and subsequent investigations, the quest to lay blame began. "Senior UN staff in New York were naturally caught up in a blame game that intensified with time," she writes. "All-knowing analysts in the United States, Europe, and the Middle East pointed to the ominous warning signs that Vieira de Mello and other UN officials missed. The consensus view was that the UN had been naïve in viewing itself as untouchable and in failing to appreciate just how hated the organization was in Iraq, owing to sanctions, weapons inspections, and (thanks to Vieira de Mello's high-profile intermediary role) its association with the Governing Council" (Power 2008, 505).

Power's description of the Baghdad bombing reflects an inherent tension between blame and understanding, particularly acute in explaining attacks on aid workers. The Baghdad bombing was a headline-grabbing tragedy, and the challenges that it exposed are multiple. The diverging opinions about causes and how to respond or to manage security in such contexts expose rifts that emerge from competing visions of humanitarianism. The exposure of the UN mission's lax security procedures and precautions reflected its internal vulnerabilities and is linked to efforts to attribute responsibility, and also blame, for the lapses in security that failed to prevent or protect. Set against the contrast of the heavily U.S.-guarded Green Zone, the UN functioned as a "soft target," its accessibility and political and media prominence combining to create an appealing target. Others pointed outside the UN to its tainted history in Iraq as setting the stage for the attack: UN control over much of the Iraqi oil revenue for over a decade, the corruption of the UN

Oil-for-Food program of the 1990s, and the hardship that UN sanctions created for many in Iraq. These combined to create a perception among many Iraqis that the UN served as a U.S. proxy and that its humanitarian efforts were neither neutral nor impartial but instead constituted a vital part of the U.S. war effort. By this logic, the UN could be interpreted as a "legitimate" target because of its association with the U.S. mission.

The question of what motivated the carefully planned attack on the Canal Hotel bears directly on thinking about how to prevent such attacks. If attacking the UN was simply a softer alternative to attacking U.S. Coalition forces, a security-management approach relying upon "hardening the target" would have made the attack more difficult and might have prevented or minimized its impact. The words of the attacker, al-Kurdi, indicate the UN was specifically targeted. On the other hand, attempts to address the UN's history and change the perceptions of Iraqis might have eliminated support for or perhaps even prevented the attack. For various reasons, the UN failed to address key vulnerabilities that might have saved lives.

In the case of the attack against the UN in Baghdad, the discourse of "terrorism" offered a convenient externally focused explanatory hook. It is shortsighted, however, to focus solely on this fact. "Terrorism" itself is a complex phenomenon cloaked in an ideologically charged term that lacks explanatory power.[7] Yet it does have extraordinary power nonetheless—the power to inspire institutions to react in certain ways that carry with them intended and unintended consequences. In the post-9/11 context, the polarizing discourse of "terrorism" evokes fear, violence, and intimidation, and rewards the perpetrators with the power to wreak havoc in an otherwise orderly world (Asad 2007). It privileges a militarized, reactionary response: To fail to respond suggests a weakness of resolve and capacity. The incendiary acts of terror, moreover, foster a pervasive sense of victimization and provoke an immediate and forceful response.

In the quest for understanding, several insights emerge from the Canal Hotel bombing. To focus on a solitary cause, whether terror or organizational deficiencies, is to lose sight of the many other factors that together constitute a "terrorist event." With regard to the UN bombing in Baghdad, these factors included inadequate and dysfunctional security systems, negative perceptions on the part of Iraqis that hindered the ability to make necessary distinctions and create useful alliances, and inadequate sharing of information regarding the security threat and dynamics of insurgent groups. Taken together, these and other factors engendered a perfect storm.

It is precisely an understanding of this bigger, more complex picture that could have increased the effectiveness of violence prevention. Yet the discourse of "terrorism" often sets the tone, as it did in Baghdad, and results in a sapping, rather than an enhancement, of coping resources.

At another level, it is possible to assail the deficiencies in the UN security-management system. Given the high-profile and tragic nature of the Baghdad bombing and of the UN as an institution, it was impossible to avoid public and independent scrutiny. Indeed, the two independent panels analyzed the failures of security management with the aim of establishing responsibility within the institution itself. However, for most security incidents, such as that of Muttur, this type of attention is ephemeral or altogether lacking. Inadequate and ineffective policies and procedures, both of which are linked to the sustainability of the agencies themselves, are related to liability concerns. The reputational costs of organizational shortcomings, such as corruption within agencies themselves, individual violations of social norms, or deficiencies in organizational policies or decision making, are potentially severe. A tainted reputation undermines the public's trust in the agency and how it operates, detracting from its ability to raise funds or to hire new staff members. It is thus in an agency's interest to keep these factors largely hidden and absent from public discourse. Consequently, the emphasis on external threats is convenient because it obfuscates the reputational and liability costs of bad policies or inappropriate behaviors. Aid agencies therefore have perverse incentives to hide these factors from public scrutiny.

The reluctance to publicly name the self-generated, internal vulnerability to violence—whether individual actions or organizational decision making—against aid workers is rooted in the "moral untouchability" of humanitarianism and an understandable discomfort with "blaming the victim." Both impede our ability to understand and prevent future incidents. The "untouchability" of humanitarianism stems from its status as a "morally prized social activity, precisely because those activities involve persons and institutions believed to be above suspicion because they are acting for the good of individuals and groups understood to be vulnerable" (Fassin 2010b, 37). This complicates any investigation into the causes of violence, since to identify the internal vulnerabilities challenges the moral status of humanitarians and humanitarianism.

The search for blame likewise complicates the moral and ethical picture. Raising the specter of individual actions that might directly or indirectly lead to security incidents appears akin to blaming the victims of such violence. The reluctance to blame the victim is particularly acute in incidents involving interpersonal violence. In investigating the safety issues facing anthropologists doing fieldwork, Nancy Howell identifies a similar dynamic. She writes, "More than other hazards, interpersonal assault and threat are touchy subjects for anthropologists, calling into question the relationship that the fieldworker is supposed to establish with colleagues and with the subjects of his or her study, as a matter of professional competence" (Howell 1990, 89). By way of illustration, she discusses the 1931 murder of a young female graduate student studying Apache sex life. A member of the research team, in describing what happened, suggested that the graduate student's research topic and the different cultural mores and norms that govern relationships between sexes contributed to the circumstances that led to her tragic and untimely death (Opler 1987, as cited in Howell 1990). Howell then questions to what extent anthropologists "*take the blame* for what goes wrong in the field, or whether others are seen as independent agents who might be held responsible" (Howell 1990, 94–95, italics added).

Like anthropologists, aid workers, and especially expatriate aid workers, often work in cultural contexts radically different from their own, and sometimes knowingly or unknowingly violate cultural mores. In the event that personal behaviors or actions lead to a security incident, to what extent is the aid worker "responsible"? Returning to Karen's story from the previous chapter, a similar question would ask to what extent Karen's actions contributed to the circumstances that resulted in her untimely death. To blame Karen, or any other victim or survivor, is inappropriate and misinformed; ultimately, responsibility rests with the perpetrator. Yet to attribute her death solely to the lack of neutrality or impartiality of aid, as did media reports of her death, is equally erroneous.

Remaining silent about the internal vulnerabilities, including individual and organizational actions, permits the maintenance of "public secrets" (Taussig 1992, as cited in Green 1995, 119), known within the humanitarian community but not outside of it, about why aid workers are killed, kidnapped, or otherwise harmed. Theoretically, the invisibility of internal vulnerabilities reflects a tendency to "foreground the 'other'"—the recipients of aid—in the analysis of relief and development aid that concurrently renders the aid givers invisible. This, in turn, inhibits open debate about the ethical and moral conundrums of providing aid (Fechter 2012).

Failing to acknowledge the "public secrets" related to the causes of violence leaves aid workers and agencies invisible as agents of change and allows the silence to continue. Not acknowledging the full spectrum of causes, moreover, puts others in danger by painting a distorted and even self-interested picture of why the violence is happening. As one UN official put it, "We are dishonest in some cases. This results in more people getting killed. If we understood [the causes of violence] better, people might be more careful. . . . We need to be professional in how we deal with incidents, in terms of public exposure and dealing with family members."[8] This silence inevitably complicates any attempt to fully understand the complexity of factors involved in aid worker victimization, since the full story is rarely straightforward and clear. Agencies and individuals do make mistakes, and in dangerous places, the price is sometimes tragically high. These concerns dramatically complicate an understanding of violence against aid workers and the issue of humanitarian security.

A Way Forward

Concerted attention to the multiplicity of factors that contribute to a security incident is crucial in advancing our understanding of violence against aid workers and agencies and in moving beyond a perspective that privileges external threat or that remains fixated on blame. Toward this goal, in this section I propose an analytical framework that advances a relational approach. It applies an interdisciplinary lens to examine the multiple and mutually reinforcing dimensions that cause violence against aid workers and aid agencies. Such a framework can better answer the question of why some are attacked and others are not, thereby generating new avenues for investigation. In proposing this framework I have three goals in mind: first, to challenge the axiomatic discourses that attribute the causes of violence first and foremost to the political context and external threats; second, to challenge the humanitarian exceptionalism that conceptualizes aid workers as separate from the conflict systems in which they operate and isolated from the people they help; and third, to reassert humanity as the central guiding principle of humanitarianism, thereby recognizing the relational character of the endeavor. My approach is instrumental in nature, precisely because my ultimate goal is to help safeguard aid workers.

The framework I outline below places a relational approach, and therefore humanity, at the center of aid work. Doing so weakens the dynamic of violence and reestablishes a relational character to the humanitarian endeavor that is so often missing from the discussion. The framework conceptualizes aid agencies and aid workers as responsible for their own actions and the image they project, rather than something that others foist upon them. At the same time, it recognizes the importance of context and the dynamics at work in the world today. Such a framework helps to hold agencies and individuals accountable for their actions and undermines humanitarian exceptionalism while not discounting the role of the political or social context. The framework conceptualizes aid workers as embedded within institutions, which are themselves embedded within a conflict system and within global dynamics and relationships.

Many prominent scholars have studied violence (e.g., Arendt 1970; Burton 1997; Galtung 1969, 1990; Rapoport 1995; Staub 1989; Tilly 2003; Kaldor 2006). In elucidating this framework, I draw explicitly on two scholars, one of conflict and its transformation (John Paul Lederach) and the other of violence (James Gilligan). Both scholars interpret conflict and violence as relational acts that are embedded in social structures, and recognize that understanding the root causes of violence is crucial to its transformation. They have influenced my thinking about the dimensions of violence and their interdependence, and about the importance of an analytical approach that sees violence as relational and lodged within social processes.

The first, John Paul Lederach, is a conflict-transformation scholar-practitioner with decades of experience in protracted conflicts around the world. Lederach has written extensively about the approaches and strategies needed to transform conflict from destructive to constructive processes of change (Lederach 1995, 1997, 2005). He proposes four dimensions of change: the personal, relational, cultural, and structural (Lederach 2003, 24–27). Together these comprise the core elements of conflict transformation, each of which functions as a location and space for change. The effect of conflict on individuals and their cognitive, emotional, perceptual, and spiritual lives preoccupies the personal level. The relational level refers to changes in "face-to-face relationships," the power dynamics, the extent of interdependence in the relationship, and the "expressive, communicative, and interactive aspects" of conflict (Lederach 2003, 24). The structural level examines the patterns of conflict and their effects on the social, economic, and political structures and institutions. Finally, the effect of conflict on identity issues and cultural patterns and processes appears at the cultural level.

Bringing the perspective that it is possible to effectively address the causes of violence against aid workers only by understanding the factors that give rise to violence, Lederach's framework offers multiple and mutually reinforcing levels at which to analyze contributing factors and dynamics. He sees actors and processes as mutually influencing and argues for the need to address conflict at multiple levels, since the "presenting issues," the triggers of violence or the factors that move a conflict from latent to overt, are embedded in other levels and dynamics. To effectively transform the conflict and identify platforms for constructive change, he advocates looking at each of the levels to understand how it interacts with conflict processes and dynamics. Thus, any analytical approach to the issue of violence against aid workers and aid delivery must examine the system as an interdependent whole and treat aid workers as part of the system, rather than as separate from the conflicts in which they work.

In Lederach's view, constructively transforming conflict inevitably requires attention to responses and consequences, a theory-of-change approach. Applying this perspective to the issue of violence against aid workers, therefore, forces an examination of the effects of security-management strategies on aid itself *and* as crucial ingredients to reforming the aid system. As a consequence, his model notes the importance of action at any level in addressing the causes of violence and of the generative potential of relationships as spaces for change. The interdependent whole explores the contributions of each level to the entire picture, examining not only the tensions between the levels but also their complementarities.

The second scholar is James Gilligan, a psychologist who spent many years working in the Massachusetts prison system, interviewing and interacting with violent offenders, many of whom committed gruesome murders. Gilligan analyzes the causes of violence, arguing that truly understanding why violence happens is imperative to its prevention. Moreover, the way we define cause shapes our responses (Gilligan 2000). In his view, murder in the United States and most Western countries is defined as aberrant and the appropriate response, therefore, is to lock murderers away to isolate them from potential victims.

Like Lederach, Gilligan conceptualizes violence as embedded in social processes. He challenges perspectives on violence that rely on blame as opposed to understanding, and analyzes violence as tragedy, as opposed to pathos or morality play (Gilligan 2000, 94–95). Pathos denies human agency by framing violence as natural disaster or "acts of God," while morality plays reduce it to good versus evil, ignoring the complexity of violence and its antecedents and consequences. Framing violence as tragedy allows us to acknowledge the destructiveness of violence for all involved, victims as well as perpetrators. Gilligan argues that even the most "irrational" and seemingly inexplicable acts of violence are symbolic and have meaning to perpetrators. In other words, all violence is rational in the minds of the offenders.

Gilligan's analysis serves as a reminder of three insights relevant to the causes of violence against aid workers and aid delivery: the situatedness of violence, the importance of understanding over blame, and the need to view violence from a relational perspective. First, Gilligan provides a lens on violence not commonly used or understood within the aid world. He reminds us of the situatedness of violence by focusing on its psychological and situational circumstances as well as social, economic, and political factors, without neglecting more local and individual explanations. Thus, his perspective affirms the external threats—the global context and conditions within which humanitarians live and work—while simultaneously emphasizing the organizational decisions and policies and individual risk taking that may increase the likelihood of violence.

Second, Gilligan's analysis of the causes of violence is an attempt to *understand* the roots of this violence and, hence, to more effectively prevent its occurrence and recurrence. In his view, shame is at the root of violence. He separates understanding from blame and judgment of perpetrators in an effort to uncover the causes of violence and generate more effective responses to prevent violence. Indeed, he writes,

> Moral approaches to violence do not help us to understand the causes and prevention of violence; and what is worse, some of the moral assumptions about violence actually inhibit us in our attempts to learn about its causes and prevention. The most popular moral ways of thinking about violence lead to the mistaken conclusion that to understand violent behavior is to excuse it; or as the French proverb puts it, *Tout comprendre c'est tout pardonner*, to understand all is to forgive all. (Gilligan 2000, 24)

This is not to imply that he condones the actions of these violent murderers, for he does not. Instead, his focus on tragedy, as opposed to pathos or morality play, places individual acts of violence within a broader context and acknowledges the suffering on all sides. This perspective challenges the unwillingness to tarnish the myths of humanitarianism on the one hand and, on the other, the unwillingness to accept the power of humanitarian actors in an effort to understand the full range of causes.

Pathos and morality-play interpretations obscure the roles of others in the causes of violence, a third insight from Gilligan's analysis. In focusing entirely on blaming the perpetrator and his (or her) evilness, we fail to examine the societal and cultural factors that create the conditions for violence and ignore our own role and responsibility for maintaining and even benefiting from those conditions. In Gilligan's words, "For the tragedy of violence involves not just victims, but also victimizers. What we need to see—if we are to understand violence and prevent it—is that human agency or action is not only individual; it is also, unavoidably, familial, societal, and institutional. Each of us is inextricably bound to others—in relationship. All human action (even the act of a single individual) is relational" (Gilligan 2000, 7).

While social, political, or economic factors undoubtedly motivate violence against aid workers, focusing exclusively or even primarily on these causes obscures the role of other factors. While individuals within the humanitarian sector do acknowledge these factors, the dominant discourses tend to overlook them. Gilligan offers an alternative strategy: to examine these factors, without emphasis on blame, but instead with a focus on understanding as the key to prevention. In highlighting the importance of the internal vulnerabilities as causes of violence against aid workers, the purpose is not to attribute blame or responsibility but instead to promote self-reflexivity in order to fully understand why the violence occurs and to develop more effective responses in preventing it or mitigating its effects.

The idea of blame in relation to violence against aid workers is complicated, with implications for how aid actors respond to violence, how aid is characterized in the public imagination, and to whom explanations for the violence attribute responsibility. These elements, in turn, shape the dominant discourse about violence against aid workers. Placing violence in a broader context allows for an understanding of the internal vulnerabilities that underlie the violence, without blaming the victim.

Internal vulnerabilities		External threats
Personal/individual	← → R E L A T I O N A L ← →	Cultural/metanarratives
Structural/organizational		Structural/humanitarian or aid system
Hidden narratives		Dominant narratives

Figure 1. An Embedded Framework of Violence Against Aid Workers and Aid Delivery

Based on these insights, I propose a framework of the causes of violence against aid workers and aid delivery that offers multiple and interrelated dimensions for analysis (Figure 1). The framework facilitates the analysis of the competing visions of aid and their implications for our understanding of causes, as explored in the chapters that follow. The framework corresponds roughly to Lederach's four dimensions, although I divide the structural level into two dimensions, one referring to aid organizations and the other referring to the aid system, and I represent the relational level as connecting all dimensions.

On the left are the internal vulnerabilities, akin to Lederach's personal and structural (referring to the organizations) levels, which highlight those factors related to individual behaviors and organizational actions and decisions that are most often hidden from public scrutiny. On the right are those factors that dominate explanations of causes in the literature. These correspond to Lederach's structural (referring to the aid system) and cultural levels. Linking the sides is the relational element of causation, referring to both the interactions between dimensions and their interdependent nature.

While not all dimensions are important in every case, the framework points to the importance of avoiding a singular emphasis on one dimension over another, since "causes" of violence can originate in any one of the four quadrants. Notably, the left side of the matrix also denotes the external threats over which agencies exert the least amount of control, in contrast to the right side, representing the internal vulnerabilities, over which individuals and agencies have the greatest degree of control.[9]

None of the four aforementioned dimensions on its own can definitively explain the violence that aid workers experience or that affects aid delivery. The relational dimension points to the mutually reinforcing and constituting nature of these dimensions, and calls for an accounting of the ways in which perceptions enter the lexicon of causes of violence against aid workers and aid delivery. The relational dimension accounts for how local communities or other actors perceive humanitarian actors and actions and for the interplay between individuals and their environment and between aid agencies and the populations they serve. Thus, for local populations to see multiple aid agency vehicles at the local bar, which is also the place where prostitutes hang out, sends messages about the values of aid actors, which may be in tension with local values. This dimension examines the power dynamics inherent in the aid system, such as the differential pay and benefits or access to resources afforded to the international development set as opposed to the "immobile onlookers" of the aid industry (Duffield 2010, 457). The relational dimension sits at the intersection of the personal, structural, and cultural dimensions, highlighting the ways in which individuals, organizations, and global issues shape the perceptions of local communities and vice versa (see also Lynch 2011).

In highlighting the interconnectedness of the various factors, the relational dimension brings the discussion of violence against aid workers and aid delivery closer to the notion of violence as tragedy. Therefore, it moves the explanatory framework away from blame and toward agency and action. Applying this framework helps to identify the interconnectedness of the personal and structural/organizational levels, while at the same time underlining the need to consider the mental and emotional well-being of aid workers. Such considerations help to contextualize the actions and reactions of both agencies and individuals, while not absolving them of responsibility for these actions and reactions. Therefore, the framework endows rights, demands accountability, and recognizes the interconnectedness missing from an approach that attributes causes to one explanation.

Conclusion

The pragmatic and analytical challenges of providing aid in danger demonstrate the need for a different approach, one that aims to understand the causal dimensions of violence against aid workers and aid delivery in all their complexity, and that moves beyond responses that blame the victim, corral aid workers behind gated communities, or rely on the magical properties of the symbols and emblems of humanitarianism for protection. Following in the footsteps of others who have moved beyond the dualistic categories of political/apolitical, or the consequentialist (do no harm)/deontological (Dunantist) ethical frames, suggesting these are not necessarily helpful (Rubenstein 2008; Barnett and Snyder 2008), I argue for a relational lens (Tilly 2003) to analyze the causes of violence against aid workers and aid agencies. This lens challenges the assumptions of humanitarian exceptionalism that conceptualize aid workers as outsiders who are separate from the conflict systems in which they operate and the people whom they help, and that view aid workers as a special category of civilians deserving attention and protection. It calls for a willingness to make the hidden causes visible, to challenge the powerful, axiomatic discourse of external threat, and to debunk the myth that violence against aid workers is a recent phenomenon. In doing so, I am moving beyond deliberately stereotypical dichotomies and seeking a middle ground that is more nuanced and reflective.

Unfortunately, a faulty or incomplete analysis of the causes of violence against aid workers can lead to a misguided response, with real and existential consequences for aid workers in the field. Much like spectacular and tragic organizational accidents (Reason 1997), rarely if ever is an incident attributable to a single, dominant cause. In addition, because the ways in which individuals and agencies respond to such events derive from their understandings of the context and the cause(s), it is imperative to truly and fully understand the complexity of the causes. Anything less constitutes a disservice to those who dedicate their lives to humanitarian work.

CHAPTER 3

The Dangers They Face: Understanding Violence Against Aid Workers and Agencies

On 6 December 1936, Italian airplanes bombed the city of Dessié/Dessye in north-central Ethiopia for over an hour, raining bombs onto ambulances and the Tafari Makonnen American hospital displaying the Red Cross symbol. The International Committee of the Red Cross (ICRC) promptly lodged a protest, one of many provoked by one or the other side in the 1936 Abyssinian War between Ethiopia and Italy.[1] The Italian government's reply, transmitted via the Italian Red Cross, claimed ignorance of the presence of the American hospital. This and other attacks on ambulances and medical facilities bearing the Red Cross symbol exposed the dangers of working in the midst of an active war zone.

Such attacks convinced Sidney Brown, the chief Red Cross delegate in Ethiopia, and others that the Italians deliberately targeted the Red Cross emblem. One cable from an official of the Ethiopian Medical Service to the ICRC read, "My tent and my aide's tent with all my medical supplies and other stuff blown up though bearing large Red Cross markings.... Wake up Geneva as is evident Italians making special target any red cross" (Moorehead 1998, 308, 310). The ICRC lost several delegates during that war, including a doctor killed during an attack on Addis Ababa and the driver of a clearly marked Red Cross ambulance.[2] These bombings and the death of the ICRC delegates are early instances of targeted violence against humanitarian emblems. They suggest that, despite assertions to the contrary, targeted attacks against humanitarians and their symbols are not a new phenomenon.

What kinds of dangers, specifically, do aid workers face, and why do attacks happen? Aid work is inherently risky business and aid workers have long been targeted. Few, if any, dispute the risks involved. Books celebrating aid workers' experiences, many of which contain stories that document the dangers of their work, regularly appear in bookstores (Danieli 2002; Bergman 2003; Cain, Postlewait, and Thomson 2004; Burnett 2005; vanOrden 2008). Although they tell compelling and often heartrending stories, the books capture only moments in time and chronicle selected individual experiences and perceptions. The more infamous of them, by conforming and contributing to mythical images of aid workers and aid work, sensationalize incidents of violence as part of the adventure and appeal of such work.

In doing so, these narratives reflect a tendency to portray insecurity and targeted violence against aid workers and aid delivery as relatively recent phenomena, thereby emphasizing the changes in the post–Cold War and post-9/11 eras and exhibiting the short-term memory that often afflicts the humanitarian narrative. This portrayal neglects a historical and analytical perspective that situates the occurrence of security incidents within the "ordinary" context of humanitarian work in violent conflict settings. This is compounded by a dearth of data about violence against aid workers, without which it is impossible to accurately estimate trends prior to the latter half of the 1990s, and by an emphasis on only the most severe violence, which results in injury, kidnapping, or death. While living through violence should be anything but normal, the risk of targeted and random violence has characterized humanitarian work since its very beginnings. It is, unfortunately, not unusual; rather, in some war zones, it more closely resembles the routine state of affairs.

This chapter challenges the entrenched notion that violence against aid workers is a new and particular characteristic of the post-9/11 context, and identifies the gaps in our collective knowledge about the dangers aid workers face. In narrating some early stories of security incidents, the first half of this chapter demonstrates that security has long been an issue for humanitarian actors. In doing so, it debunks the myth that incidents have only recently become an issue, thereby correcting humanitarianism's ephemeral memory and conforming to more recent analyses that place humanitarianism in a broader historical context (Barnett 2011; Donini 2012).[3] Moreover, in delving more deeply into the shooting of a Red Cross plane during the Biafran War (1966–1970), the complex interplay of factors and underlying issues that characterized even the early years of contemporary humanitarianism becomes apparent. The incident is easy to interpret using a political lens only, yet to do so misses other contributing factors. As one aid expert opined, "It is important to look at how security concerns arise in the first place. The tendency is to start with aid and then see security as an externality that disrupts or doesn't disrupt the delivery of aid. Instead we need to look at how intervention [aid] impacts the problem [security]."[4] In this way, the early examples identify danger as a corollary of the humanitarian endeavor across time and demonstrate the complexity of the causes of violence as a continuous thread through such action.

Likewise, when interpreted with a necessary degree of caution, the empirical evidence summarized in the second section of this chapter offers insight into some general patterns of violence against aid workers over the past fifteen years. The absolute numbers of incidents of violence are increasing, yet so are the numbers of aid workers. While important, these data are instructive more for the knowledge gaps they illustrate than for providing conclusive answers to questions about the dangers and causes of the violence. The basic statistics provide a starting point but suffer from methodological and definitional challenges that result in three shortcomings, each of which I explore in this and later chapters: aggregate data that obscure differential risk, a focus on fatalities and severe violence that magnifies the perception of risk and privileges reactive responses, and a dearth of information about *why* security incidents occur. The evidence, therefore, is not sufficiently robust to "test" causal explanations, nor is this the goal of presenting these data. The available empirical evidence does not definitively support the persistent and axiomatic discourses of external threat, such as the instrumentalization of aid, the changing nature of armed conflict, and the blurred lines between military and civilian actors, that have taken hold to explain the increase in attacks across contexts.

Taken together, these discussions uncover the ways in which the discourse of recent and prevalent danger has seeped into the humanitarian psyche and support the concept of humanitarian exceptionalism. Discussions of the risks that have long characterized humanitarianism and of the range of incidents and gaps in our collective knowledge serve as reminders of the importance of a clear assessment of existing dangers, which include but are not limited to severe violence. In turn, the chapter underscores the perspective that sees the relationship between violence and humanitarianism post-9/11 as new only in degree and thereby challenges interpretations that see the violence that characterized Iraq and Afghanistan as harbingers of a diffusely dark and dangerous future for humanitarians.

The Long View

> It was not until the American-led wars in Afghanistan and Iraq that the UN and other aid agencies began to be deliberately hunted down.
> —"More Dangerous to Work Than Ever," *Economist*, 20 November 2004

Relief workers disappeared and died in the line of duty long before the appearance of humanitarian security manuals or the twenty-first-century wars in Afghanistan and Iraq. As early as the 1920s, Clayton Kratz, a volunteer with the nascent relief and development organization Mennonite Central Committee (then known as the Mennonite Relief Unit), disappeared in Ukraine. After local authorities arrested him, he was not heard from again (Hiebert and Miller 1929). Nor was disappearance the only threat to humanitarians. Seventy-eight members of the Japanese Red Cross died during the Russo-Japanese War of 1904–1905 (Moorehead 1998, 156). Over the decades, various issues of the *Revue Internationale de la Croix-Rouge* (*RICR*, *International Review of the Red Cross*) have paid tribute to delegates who died in the service of the ICRC. These include one ICRC delegate killed in Katanga, Zaire, in December 1961 and two delegates killed in Biafra in a targeted attack.[5] The *Revue* also mentions the deaths of two Save the Children Fund staff members in a land mine explosion in Nigeria near Enugu on 29 July 1968, during the height of the war in Biafra.[6] In addition to those who died from the 1930s through the 1960s, the *RICR* mentions one delegate wounded in a land mine explosion in 1966,[7] two delegates wounded in an incident on the Allenby Bridge in January 1968,[8] and two Yemeni guards wounded in an attack on a clinic in Sana'a, Yemen, in March 1968 (Comité International 1968b, 236). Their mention in the annals of the *RICR* pays tribute to their sacrifice and illustrates the risks of the work.

The bombings during the Ethiopian-Italian War threatened the lives of ICRC delegates and their patients, as well as medical services and supplies, prompting an early version of what would now qualify as a security-management protocol. The bombings motivated the ICRC, in 1936 in conjunction with the Swiss army, to test the emblem's visibility from the air. The results influenced later decisions about the size and placement of the emblem (Comité International 1936c).[9] An ICRC commentary in the same year explored the security precautions necessary to mitigate the impact of aerial bombardments for hospitals. It suggested a series of measures, including guidelines for the construction, preparation, and practice of evacuation drills, use of gas masks, and education of all staff to reduce the impact of aerial attacks upon hospitals (Alter 1936).

Despite some targeted killings and kidnappings during this time, security incidents were "limited, isolated, and without patterns."[10] When they featured at all, they appeared in the literature about operations in the early years of humanitarianism largely as anomalies. These incidents served as signs of the risks that accompanied humanitarian work but did not define the work in the same manner as today. In this way, danger was part of the "ordinary" or expected context of much of the work, even though serious security incidents did indeed happen.

The secessionist war between Nigeria and the self-declared state of Biafra between 1966 and 1970 marked the first war in which Red Cross personnel, as opposed to the emblem, were deliberately targeted. The ICRC lost fourteen delegates in Biafra, including two shot by a Nigerian officer during an attack on a hospital.[11] Jean Pictet, commenting on these deaths in October 1968, remarked, "Our times are marked by a hardening of hearts and declining of international morality. . . . If one day the protective value of the Red Cross emblem should be doubted . . . the world would have regressed a hundred years" (as quoted in Moorehead 1998, 626).

In the history of humanitarian action, the size and importance of the Biafran aid operation mean it is well documented, in terms of both the "politics of aid" and security incidents. As such, it is a useful illustration of the complex causes of violence against aid actors. The crisis in Biafra unfolded in a highly politicized environment not unlike that of conflicts today; in particular, it was marked by global media attention and tension between Christians and Muslims. As the first "media war," it brought the suffering of Biafrans into the living rooms of those in Europe and North America and marked the founding or coming of age of numerous humanitarian organizations, including Médecins Sans Frontières (MSF) and Concern (now Concern Worldwide).[12] At its height in 1969, the Biafran relief airlift constituted the largest humanitarian operation since the 1948 Berlin Airlift (Walker and Maxwell 2009, 46–48; see also Barnett 2011, 133–147 on Biafra). The ICRC's monthly budget for its operations in Nigeria/Biafra was almost triple its annual budget before the war (de St. Jorre 1972, 248; Benthall 1993, chap. 3). At the height of the war, the ICRC employed 240 people in the Nigerian federal territory alone (Moorehead 1998, 619).

As both a political and humanitarian crisis, Biafra exemplified a humanitarian "Sophie's choice." The delivery of aid prolonged the war and thus the suffering of many Biafrans, while it also saved many from death by starvation. In particular, outside support for the Biafran cause proved crucial in the face of the blockade that the Nigerian government imposed on the secessionist region. Outsiders provided sustenance for Biafrans as well as material and financial support for their leaders. Early on, the Biafran government realized the power of the media and the images of starving and emaciated Biafran children, and even hired a public relations firm to advance its cause. These images translated into material and financial support.

The Catholic and Protestant churches sided firmly with the Biafrans, opting for solidarity as a defining principle, and banded together under the name Joint Church Aid (JCA). The JCA brought in food (and sometimes weapons) on its relief flights from the Portuguese island of Sao Tomé to the only functioning airstrip in Biafra at Uli.[13] The JCA and ICRC relief flights occurred at night to avoid attacks by Nigerian air force planes enforcing the blockade that prohibited day flights. The relief flights provided convenient cover for the arms shipments that also arrived at the airstrip at Uli, since it was impossible to tell the difference between the planes and their cargo in the dark. The foreign currency the churches brought into and exchanged in Biafra allowed the Biafran government to purchase these weapons in the first place (de St. Jorre 1972, chap. 9).

From the perspective of the Nigerians, the relief operations and night flights provided crucial assistance for Biafrans. They thus prolonged the war and solidified the Nigerian government's perception that aid agencies sided firmly with the Biafran cause. The Biafrans, for their part, welcomed the assistance and did not want to allow day flights, since this would remove the "shield" of relief flights as cover for the planes flying in weapons. Moreover, they feared that any food aid or medicines originating in Nigeria were poisoned (Yancho 2005). So the night flights continued and federal Nigerian planes regularly bombed the Uli airstrip, sometimes killing and wounding those on the ground and substantially increasing the danger for the relief airlift.

Reports differ slightly on the numbers of pilots and crew who died during the war, ranging from twenty-five (de St. Jorre 1972, 329) to twenty-seven, with sixteen planes shot down by December 1969 (Yancho 2005, 164). ICRC documents reveal multiple incidents of bombings of hospitals and attacks on planes by the Nigerian federal forces as well as airplane crashes that occurred in the process of delivering assistance.[14] The most dramatic security incident occurred in June 1969 when a Nigerian plane, flown by an English pilot, shot down a Swedish Red Cross plane, killing four people on board.[15] According to one source, a daring raid by Swedish pilot Count von Rosen (who also worked for the relief operations) in May 1969 against Nigerian aircraft on the ground had destroyed and damaged several aircraft and threatened to alter the balance of power in the war. In retaliation for the attack on Nigerian planes and thus on its sovereignty, the Nigerian leadership demanded that a Biafran plane, carrying relief or weapons, be "forced down so that it could be examined and Nigerian sovereignty be seen, by the whole world, to be respected" (de St. Jorre 1972, 331). The downing of the Swedish Red Cross plane occurred just two months later. International condemnation was loud and swift. The Nigerians justified the attack by claiming the plane was carrying weapons for the Biafran side.

This event almost ended the Biafran airlifts entirely and certainly provoked soul-searching among those involved in the relief flights. The ICRC, true to its mandate and principles, worked on both sides of the conflict until the Nigerian government expelled the ICRC senior delegate, August Lindt, in mid-1969 and revoked its permission for the ICRC to coordinate the international relief efforts. The Nigerian government's refusal to allow the ICRC to fly at night and the Biafran government's refusal to allow it to fly during the day prevented the organization from providing assistance to either the Nigerians or the Biafrans. In taking a stance informed by the principles of neutrality and impartiality, the ICRC decided to withdraw and turned over its operations to the Nigerian Red Cross.

By contrast, the churches and missionaries used solidarity to justify their support for the Biafrans. In doing so,

> the ICRC had opted for the path of legality, the Churches, less encumbered by sets of rules, precedents and international obligations, chose defiance and the airlift went on. Given the Protestant and Catholic Churches' deep missionary commitment in Biafra—the most in-

tensely "missionised" part of Africa—it is difficult to see how they could have acted otherwise. Their *local* interest dictated that they should defy the Federal [Nigerian] government, whereas the ICRC's *international* responsibility had, with a similar cogency, demanded that it should be obeyed. (de St. Jorre 1972, 249, italics in original; see also Comité International 1969f, 1969b)

Despite the intensely politicized environment in Biafra, the reasons for attacks on aid workers and operations, engendered in part through the actions of the agencies involved, are not reducible solely to politics. Less sensational factors, such as hunger and crime, also played a role. Once on the ground the supplies acted as a magnet for attacks from local populations and criminals. According to one relief worker,

The attacks on the lorries between the airport and our central store became more determined. At first, villagers and local people would try to jump on to the back of a moving lorry, cut down the barrier and throw something off on to the road. When we put the lorries into convoys, a log would be rolled across the road in front of the last one in order to cut it off from the rest. As the attacks became more subtle so we tightened our security, until finally we came in March [1969] to an armed hold-up organised by the sort of black marketeers and deserters that every war produces. (as quoted in de St. Jorre 1972, 240)

The fact that people were hungry motivated these types of attacks, as did the value of relief supplies on the black market.

Moreover, to focus primarily on politics neglects the crucial role of individual actions and autonomy in the Biafran drama. John de St. Jorre, a journalist, wrote about many of the colorful personalities involved in the war and the relief operations, including the mercenaries and foreign pilots, such as Count von Rosen. Von Rosen and others flew concomitantly for the war effort and the humanitarian effort.[16] Their exploits for the relief airlift as well as for the Biafran War effort not only undermined any claim of neutrality for the relief effort but also blurred lines between military and civilian action. De St. Jorre suggested that the unspoken code and economic motives of the mercenaries for keeping the Uli airstrip open prolonged the night-flying operations and minimized casualties, since the pilots knew one another and did not want to shoot down each other's planes.

In short, security incidents in Biafra included myriad motives, from economic to political. Some attacks were opportunistic or criminal in nature, while hunger and deprivation motivated the local populations' attacks on food convoys. For others, however, the ways in which the relief collided with politics compromised the security of aid workers. Personalities and aid flights played a significant role in the conflict and its outcome, and the actions of individuals influenced others' security as well. The food and material support from the humanitarian airlift provided crucial support for the Biafrans. Much of the humanitarian operation played politics and called into question the neutral and impartial nature of the assistance. The dual role of some of the pilots, such as Count von Rosen, who flew for the Biafrans *and* the ostensibly neutral humanitarian airlift, the mixed cargo of food and weapons on some of the JCA flights, and the use of the Uli airstrip for both humanitarian and material (e.g., military) support blurred the lines between relief and war support.

Were aid workers and agencies deliberately targeted? In some instances, they were. One could argue at least that the partial stance of some of the agencies and the dual roles of some key actors as humanitarians and activists transformed them from neutral actors to supporters of one side and thus an understandable target in the context of war. Indeed, the Biafran case demonstrates how tenuous the line between relief and support for a war effort can be, and illustrates the complexity of causes that has long characterized violence against aid workers and aid delivery.

How Dangerous Is It? The State of Empirical Evidence

Since the mid-1990s, the number of acts of severe violence—kidnappings, killings, and serious injury—against aid workers has climbed, as much as 92 percent between 1997 and 2005 (Stoddard, Harmer, and Haver 2006), and an additional 89 percent from 2003–2005 to 2006–2008 (Stoddard, Harmer, and DiDomenico 2009).[17] In 2009 and 2010, the total number of attacks declined by 26 percent from their peak in 2008 (Stoddard, Harmer, and Haver 2011; see Table 1). Even as the absolute number of incidents has increased dramatically, the numbers of relief and development workers in the field

Table 1. Absolute Numbers of Aid Workers Killed, Injured, or Kidnapped, 1997–2012

	Number killed	Number injured	Number kidnapped	Total
1997	39	6	28	73
1998	35	15	18	68
1999	33	15	20	68
2000	57	23	11	91
2001	27	20	43	90
2002	38	23	24	85
2003	87	49	7	143
2004	56	46	23	125
2005	54	96	23	173
2006	87	87	66	240
2007	87	87	46	220
2008	127	91	60	278
2009	107	95	94	296
2010	72	86	87	245
2011	86	127	95	308
2012	66	114	91	271
Total	1,058	980	736	2,774

Source: Aid Worker Security Database, https://aidworkersecurity.org/incidents/report/victims, accessed 23 September 2013, data verified to end of 2011.

have similarly risen. As a result, the *rate* of fatalities among aid workers remained relatively stable between 1997 and 2005, the earliest years for which systematic data exist (Stoddard, Harmer, and Haver 2006; see also Rowley, Crape, and Burnham 2008; Sheik et al. 2000).

Between 2006 and 2008, the global rate of severe incidents of violence against aid workers increased. This change was largely due, however, to the dangers humanitarians faced in the three most dangerous countries, Afghanistan, Somalia, and Sudan, which accounted for over half (60 percent) of the overall increase in absolute numbers of incidents. With these three hot spots removed from consideration, the overall rate for attacks against aid workers actually *decreased* slightly over time, from 2.7 per 10,000 in 2003–2005 to 2.4 per 10,000 in 2006–2008 (Stoddard, Harmer, and DiDomenico 2009, 2–4).[18] A further decrease from 2008 to 2010 appears largely as a result of aid agencies withdrawing from the most dangerous places as a result of insecurity, leaving few or no aid workers to attack (Stoddard, Harmer, and Haver 2011, 2).

While violence against aid workers is a burgeoning field of study, two primary challenges—reliable data and definitions—and their associated issues continue to plague empirical research about the type, severity, circumstances, and causes of violence against aid workers, and result in significant knowledge gaps.[19] First, many of the individual studies emphasize the difficulty of collecting reliable information on this topic. Research relying solely on media reports is biased, although in predictable ways (Abbott 2006). Attacks against national staff, incidents involving gender-based violence, and incidents not involving fatalities or kidnapping are consistently underreported. Nevertheless, media reports remain an important source of information.

Comparable and complete data from humanitarian agencies themselves are similarly difficult to obtain for a host of reasons, including liability, privacy, and reputational concerns. Although some agencies and coordinating bodies have improved data collection about safety and security incidents and track incidents of all types and degrees of severity,[20] other agencies languish behind in their efforts and lack basic statistics about incidents or even numbers of employees (national and/or international) in a particular country or worldwide. Sharing incident information across organizations is improving yet remains far from perfect.[21] Incident investigations are still shrouded in secrecy, making detailed causal comparisons and aggregations across incidents difficult if not impossible. Those that do reach the public domain serve as evidence in lawsuits or are featured in sensationalized exposés of individual or organizational negligence or misconduct.

The dearth of consistent and reliable data on the number of aid workers within a given context or organization complicates efforts to calculate *rates* of incidents (i.e., the so-called denominator issue, in which the number of incidents, the numerator, is divided by the number of aid workers, the denominator). This information is critical for determining whether security incidents have increased relative to the numbers of aid workers, and whether the situation has worsened over time. In this case, the dearth of data has research as well as practical implications:[22] the Independent Panel report on the UN Baghdad bombing highlighted discrepancies in staffing totals that complicated rescue efforts (Independent Panel 2003). These lacunae limit attempts to gain a comprehensive and accurate sense of the problem. The difficulties of data collection have led researchers to concentrate on establishing a baseline of the easiest-to-collect incidents. This has necessitated an approach focused on fatalities and severe violence along with the general trends related to such violence.[23]

Definitional Conundrums

Another significant challenge to existing research and documentation is the lack of consistency in definitions, notably of what is a security incident and who is an aid worker. Each organization defines security incidents and collects information using criteria that reflect its own purposes and goals (e.g., the type of information it collects about staff, liability and insurance factors, and agency risk thresholds).[24] Research studies often diverge on terminology (e.g., intentional violence and whether it includes or excludes events such as land mine explosions) and differ on whether to include safety incidents (those related to accidents or illness) in addition to security incidents (those resulting from violence) (Martin 1999). This hinders attempts to determine whether aid workers are targeted in increasing numbers and with increasing severity. This, in turn, affects the conclusions and confounds comparison across studies.

Defining who counts as an aid worker is particularly nebulous. In tabulating incidents and fatalities, the answer to the question is crucial in establishing the extent of the problem. The bombing just outside the ICRC headquarters in Baghdad in October 2003 killed twelve people, two of whom were ICRC-employed guards (ICRC 2003; Waddington 2003). Obviously, this was a security incident, yet counting fatalities of aid workers related to this and other incidents presents a definitional conundrum. Early security research, training, and management efforts, for instance, often ignored national staff in favor of international staff (InterAction 2001; Buchanan and Muggah 2005). Likewise, it was not clear whether the deaths of private contractors delivering food for the UN World Food Programme (WFP) should be counted among fatalities of aid workers. Under its mandate, WFP contracts with private companies to deliver food. If private contractors deliver items of an exclusively humanitarian character and work for an aid agency, they should qualify as aid workers, regardless of their temporary or permanent, contractor or consultant status. Indeed, one ongoing study of violence against aid workers includes contractors in its fatality and incident counts (Stoddard, Harmer, and Haver 2006, 2011; see also Stoddard, Harmer, and DiDomenico 2009).

Relying on media sources compounds this issue further, since media reports often collapse "foreigner" with "aid worker" or use the term "humanitarian" to cover a variety of actions and motives. For example, the headlines about the November 2005 kidnapping of four volunteers with Christian Peacemaker Teams (CPT) in Iraq referred to the four as "aid workers," "human rights activists," and "peace workers," and sometimes all three in one news report.[25] Although CPT volunteers are typically foreigners and share the values and principles of some aid actors (e.g., solidarity with local populations), they are neither humanitarians nor development workers. The kidnapping of twenty-three South Koreans in Afghanistan in July 2007 is a similar case in point, with media reports referring to them both as "aid workers" and as "missionaries."[26] Even sources devoted to compiling basic information and statistics about aid worker fatalities fall victim to this definitional imprecision. In a blog source listing aid worker security incidents, a headline reads "American Aid Worker Dead in Benin," yet the details indicate the woman killed was actually a Peace Corps volunteer.[27] These discrepancies contribute more generally to existing perceptions about danger and aid workers and point to the need to scrutinize sources and definitions and to establish standards for data collection.

Some uses of the term "aid worker" are simply imprudent; other instances portend injurious effects. Media portrayals sometimes use the cloak of "humanitarian" to disguise murky motives and questionable actions, rightfully sparking the ire of the humanitarian community because of the potential ramifications for security, reputation, and even an agency's permission to operate in a country. In a story that appeared in the *Washington Post* in early 2009, David Matthews wrote about his childhood friend, Stephen Templeton, and their trip together to South Sudan. The story portrayed Templeton as a humanitarian "on a mission" to document underground water sources for a local NGO and its international partner Catholic Relief Services (CRS). The story itself focuses on Templeton's actions in Sudan, which included offering military advice to local commanders, ostensibly the real motive behind his mission. Templeton's actions, Matthews writes, crossed an invisible line and called into question his status as a self-described "humanitarian" (Matthews 2009). The story elicited a reply several days later from Ken Hackett, then the president of CRS, that emphasized the humanitarian principles of neutrality and impartiality that are essential to "deliver aid effectively and protect staff," and clarified that CRS "never directly contracted the services of Mr. Templeton" (Hackett 2009).

It is stories like these that have led to accusations of humanitarians spying for government or other actors, with or without cause. For instance, CRS collaborated with the U.S. CIA and U.S. forces in helping Vietnamese refugees flee to South Vietnam in the mid-1950s (Barnett 2011, 147). One aid worker, also suspected of being a spy while working in the Caucasus region, offered the following explanation for these suspicions: "We are not perceived as impartial, especially in a part of the world where conspiracy theories abound."[28] In 2005, the Russian Federal Security Service charged that NGOs, among them the British aid agency Merlin, had helped foreign governments' intelligence services weaken Russian influence within the states of the former Soviet Union (Walsh 2005). In Darfur in 2009, the Sudanese government accused aid agencies of spying and providing information to the International Criminal Court.[29] In some instances, the security-related information that agencies collect, such as maps listing different types of security incidents (e.g., crime, cross-fire incidents, or land mines and unexploded ordnance) or conflict- or actor-mapping assessments, can arouse suspicion.[30] In Kosovo in the early 1990s, two CARE Canada employees were arrested and charged with spying after authorities discovered maps and other paraphernalia used for intelligence gathering in their vehicle.[31] These types of accusations are not reserved only for humanitarians, but plague those in other fields and activities, such as journalism and anthropology, as well.[32] Although aid agencies generally eschew affiliations with the intelligence community, these incidents illustrate the potential security risks of such accusations.

The most notable security incident resulting from the perceived collusion of humanitarians and intelligence work is the case of Fred Cuny, a celebrated yet controversial relief worker. In early April 1995, Cuny disappeared in Chechnya together with his translator, his driver, and two Russian Red Cross doctors. News of his disappearance was splashed across the front pages of major newspapers and shocked the aid community. His disappearance prompted a manhunt that involved diplomats, the American and Russian intelligence communities, military and rebel forces, family members, international organizations, a psychic, as well as tens of thousands of dollars. Their central yet unfulfilled goal was to find Cuny and his team and discover who killed them and why (Anderson 1996).

Cuny was a veteran relief worker who had worked in and on multiple disasters over more than three decades. He got his start in international relief working in Biafra in 1969 and soon after started his own company, called Intertect. Cuny and his unconventional approach to relief work generated controversy within the aid community. He was clearly comfortable working closely with the military, at a time when such associations were unusual and even suspicious: "Fred Cuny was . . . a man working at the murky confluence of humanitarian assistance, diplomacy, military operations and intelligence—the disaster specialist who in northern Iraq, to cite but one example, could commandeer United States Army helicopters to shuttle Kurdish guerrilla leaders across national frontiers" (Anderson 1996). He was a rogue in the relief world, an adventurer who gained the ear of the American foreign policy establishment yet did not hesitate to boldly criticize policies. Epithets described him as "big," "charming," or "Texan." Fred Cuny got things done, by using unconventional approaches to restore water and gas to Sarajevans during the siege in 1992 and by promising American military protection to deliver aid to and orchestrate the return of Kurdish internally displaced persons during Operation Provide Comfort in 1991. Cuny's creativity and lack of convention, however, incurred a cost: "In Chechnya, Cuny combined multiple roles that are usually separated among several institutions in a division of labor. . . . Centralizing all these tasks in his own person, Cuny lost the protection that derives from dividing labor among many others" (DeMars 2001, 206).[33]

Speculation about the reasons for Cuny's disappearance centered on his outspoken denunciations of Russian conduct in its war in Chechnya and on allegations that he was a spy. Prior to his disappearance, Cuny had published an article in the *New York Review of Books*, titled "Killing Chechnya," that denounced Russian brutality (Cuny 1995).[34] He also had met with policymakers in Washington to discuss the war. In Chechnya, he worked for the Soros Foundation, which funded "Cuny's ever-more famous—and ever-more risky—guerrilla-style relief projects" (Anderson 1996). His purpose and activities in Chechnya—to negotiate a ceasefire between Russian and Chechen forces and evacuate civilians trapped in the capital—coupled with his style and partiality defied the parameters of a traditional humanitarian approach and fed suspicions that he worked as a spy.

A more significant issue, however, relates to who is a "humanitarian" and who is an "aid worker." Though the two terms function as synonyms in common parlance, in fact they are contested and often ambiguous terms in the literature. One vision of "humanitarians" argues for a strict and narrow interpretation of the term, using it to refer exclusively to individuals working for agencies that deliver lifesaving assistance and protection according to the guiding principles of humanitarian action: humanity, neutrality, impartiality, and independence (see, e.g., Terry 2002; de Torrenté 2004b; Pictet

1979; Plattner 1996). "Aid worker," on the other hand, is a broader category that includes humanitarian as well as development workers and others in the aid industry. Similarly, "aid agency" refers to humanitarian agencies as well as multimandate (e.g., relief and development) agencies, such as Save the Children, CARE, or Oxfam, and UN family agencies that provide emergency assistance, such as the Office for the Coordination of Humanitarian Affairs, the WFP, the United Nations Children's Fund, and the United Nations High Commissioner for Refugees. The security-related implications of these narrow and broad visions of humanitarianism are treated in the chapters that follow.

Findings and Their Shortcomings

These caveats aside, existing research and documentation indicate that the absolute number of violent incidents against aid workers is increasing around the world. Moreover, separate analyses of this violence reveal the following general patterns. First, Africa is the place where the most aid workers die, an unsurprising outcome given the higher numbers of aid workers there (Abbott 2006; Rowley, Crape, and Burnham 2008).[35] Second, traveling to and from project sites, which carries an associated threat of ambush to aid workers and especially to the drivers of the vehicles, appears as a significant risk across studies (King 2002a, 2002b; Stoddard, Harmer, and Haver 2006; Rowley, Crape, and Burnham 2008; Stoddard, Harmer, and DiDomenico 2009). Third, more national staff lose their lives than international staff, although some evidence suggests the rates are increasing for international staff as well (Stoddard, Harmer, and DiDomenico 2009; see also Sheik et al. 2000; InterAction 2001; Barnett 2004; Buchanan and Muggah 2005; Rowley 2007; Stoddard, Harmer, and Haver 2006, 2011; Wille and Fast 2013). Finally, in the majority of studies on violence against aid workers, intentional violence emerges as the leading cause of death (above 50 percent) (Sheik et al. 2000; King 2002a, 2002b; Rowley 2005; Abbott 2006; Rowley 2007; Stoddard, Harmer, and Haver 2006, 2011).

While these studies provide important jumping-off points, the findings present a skewed and partial picture of the violence, doing little to illuminate the underlying causes of the violence or to answer why some agencies are attacked and others are not. Thus, the statistics are more important for what they obscure rather than for what they illuminate.

Their shortcomings are threefold. First, most studies analyze counts, rates, risk factors, and trends about who dies, where, and in what types of incident. Much of the data are presented in terms of aggregated and global numbers, rates, and trends. Aggregated data about who dies and how many are dying obscure the differential risks, linked to internal vulnerabilities, that staff and agencies face in particular contexts. Where in a country an organization operates, for instance, might increase or decrease risk. Likewise, an individual's job affects risk, since field staff members are more likely to encounter violence than those in office positions.[36] Although global trends mask the fact that the majority of incidents occur primarily in a handful of countries, some sources assert the threat is increasing (e.g., UN 2003), and a *global* trend analysis over time suggests that *overall* severe incidents are rising and surpassing the increasing number of aid workers. Collapsing data and treating organizations, individuals, and countries as the same, despite differences in context, organizational mandate, operating style, and position within an organization, obscures potentially decisive risk factors, factors that are hidden from view with a singular focus on external threat.

Together, these facts point to the need for disaggregated and contextually specific data and to the inadequacies of relying on conclusions based on global as opposed to context-specific trends, such as attributing an increase in the numbers of incidents to greater politicization of aid. Aggregated and global numbers are helpful in raising awareness about the scope of the problem but are less helpful in identifying why it happens or what specifically to do about it. Indeed, we have little to no information about how security-management measures might mitigate threats and decrease risk, or how these measures might diminish the numbers of incidents in a particular context. On a positive note, the overall decrease in severe incidents, when the three most dangerous countries are removed from consideration, suggests a less gloomy picture overall, raising doubt about whether the extremely dangerous contexts foreshadow a globally bleak and highly risky future. It also suggests that agency responses to security challenges are having a positive effect.

However, more information is needed regarding the effectiveness of specific types of security-management approaches and strategies in increasing security for aid agencies (Fast et al. 2013). Lack of knowledge about what works and why privileges those mechanisms that provide clear steps and guidelines for implementation, such as "hardening the target" or deterring attacks. Unfortunately, these same mechanisms may or may not effectively protect across different contexts and circumstances. While hardening the target might have mitigated the impact of the UN Baghdad bombing, such measures might not have helped Joe or Karen, whose stories appear in the vignettes in Chapter 1.[37]

Moreover, a lack of or decrease in violent incidents does not necessarily signal that a country or region is less dangerous. A small or decreasing number of incidents can also reflect the absence of aid workers. As one aid expert suggested, "There is a decrease in incident statistics when in fact the violence increases, especially for civilians. But there is no one to report the incidents. Insecurity causes evacuation of staff to safe areas, so there is less reporting on incidents, when in fact violence has increased."[38] Chechnya in the late 1990s is a case in point, as most aid agencies withdrew their personnel after the assassination of six ICRC delegates in December 1996 and the spate of kidnappings that followed. Similarly, the expulsion of sixteen aid agencies in March 2009 from Sudan meant fewer aid workers in Darfur. Although some of these agencies returned to Darfur, the total number of aid workers killed, kidnapped, or severely wounded decreased after that time.[39] Any decrease in absolute numbers or rates of incidents must be interpreted with this in mind and not simply attributed to an improved security situation, even if the latter is partially responsible. Thus, the absence of aid workers and agencies can paradoxically point to high levels of danger and hindered access to vulnerable populations just as it lowers the numbers of incidents. Even so, one important explanation for an increase in attacks is related a higher tolerance of risk among aid agencies and to increasing pressure to "stay and deliver" in the most dangerous contexts (Egeland, Stoddard, and Harmer 2011; see also discussion in Wille and Fast 2013a). How much risk is too much? Indeed, the picture is more complex than simple reports of increased numbers of incidents, targeted or not, might suggest.

Second, fatalities and severe incidents are clearly just the tip of the iceberg. The disproportionate, though understandable, focus on severe incidents privileges the extreme, accentuating the most dangerous contexts such as Afghanistan, Iraq, Sudan, or Somalia as well as the mortality rates of aid workers, which are tragically high. The severe-incident rate for aid work ranks it among the five most dangerous professions in the United States (Stoddard, Harmer, and Haver 2006, 4). Privileging the extreme, however, results in several unintentional effects. The aggregate statistics can obscure the fact that each death, kidnapping, ambush, or other violent incident represents a person and countless other affected lives. Prior experience of violence, in turn, appears to heighten the perception of danger that an individual feels, regardless of how dangerous a particular country might actually be (Fast and Wiest 2007). At the same time, the emphasis on fatalities and severe incidents feeds into a narrative of aid workers as under siege from external attack, magnifying the perception of danger and its associated fear, even if counting these incidents is easier and more reliable because of the accessibility of the data that do exist. This can promote a knee-jerk reaction—we are targeted—that makes measured and thoughtful responses more difficult or that suppresses more creative and adaptive responses (see also Hansen 2007b). This commonsensical, although potentially counterproductive, outcome increases the likelihood of seeing risk, threat, and danger everywhere.[40]

Indeed, the emphasis on fatalities tends to shift the data in favor of violence and away from other types of risk that represent more prevalent threats overall. Research studies, training, and reports tend to focus on the "sexy security aspects, such as kidnapping or bombing," according to one security director, when in fact he reported having "more security problems with high criminality and road safety."[41] In some cases, such "lesser" incidents presage the more severe. Warnings and threats of violence preceded the UN bombing as well as the kidnappings of Sharon Commins, Hilda Kawuki, and Flavia Wagner in Darfur in 2009. With hindsight, of course, these warnings magnify in importance, pointing to the need for more attention to the lesser security threats that plague the daily lives of aid workers. In short, having a more complete picture of the range of the types and the severity of security incidents suggests a more nuanced situation than the headlines imply. There are indeed greater risks of various types for aid workers, and understanding the nature of risk is critical.

The majority of that risk, as mentioned, derives from intentional violence. Studies that have examined both morbidity and mortality, however, point to safety incidents as being more significant (Ryan and Heiden 1990; Lange, Frankenfield, and Frame 1994; Martin 1999; Peytremann et al. 2001). Rowley, Crape, and Burnham (2008) examine morbidity (hospitalizations and evacuations) and mortality (deaths) for all causes, including safety issues such as accidents and illness, and conclude that intentional violence is the greater threat to aid workers, precisely because it is often lethal.[42] Nevertheless, this does point to an important discrepancy: incorporating illness (e.g., evacuations and missed work days) into the overall picture tends to reduce the importance of violence for mortality figures.

This supports the claim that the research emphasizes severe incidents and fatalities over the more common lesser threats that more aid workers face. Security managers and directors corroborate this observation, since some maintain that vehicle accidents and illness represent a larger proportion of overall incidents and thus a bigger issue for security management.[43] Liability and publicity concerns, however, may be responsible for skewing these results in favor of reporting safety incidents and not security incidents (King 2002b), even though security incidents, especially fatalities, receive more media attention.

Third, despite advances in our empirical knowledge, the "why" question remains difficult to answer. Aside from a few notable exceptions, the studies reviewed above do not focus on the causes of violence against aid workers, making it difficult to assess the validity of claims about causes and trends. The most comprehensive study to date claims that commonly cited contextual factors, such as the intensity of the violence, the presence of military forces, or global terrorist movement cells, have no statistically significant impact on fatalities and severe violence against aid workers in the six most dangerous countries (Stoddard, Harmer, and Haver 2006; see also Metcalfe, Giffen, and Elhawary 2011). Yet media stories and academic commentaries continue to cite these factors in explaining the violence.[44]

If such contextual factors have no impact on aid worker fatalities and if other "deep causes" are virtually absent in the research, then it is difficult to assert conclusively *based on empirical evidence* that these contextual factors significantly affect overall aid worker security (Fast 2010). Accurately assessing the intentionality of the act remains a vexing research problem, especially because talking to the perpetrators is seldom an available option. At the very least, such explanations fail to answer why some agencies are attacked and not others that operate in close proximity.

Evidence suggests politically motivated crimes occur with increasing frequency, although the actual motives for these crimes remain murky at best. Politically motivated attacks, such as those that interfere with the delivery of aid in order to send a specific message or gain leverage, contrast with economically or criminally motivated attacks, where the assets, not the people or the act of delivering the aid, represent the primary motive. As one security expert asserted, these assets are often targeted: "We are there with vehicles and valuables. We are attacked because of what we have, not what we do."[45] Politically motivated attacks, however, can encompass everything from specific targeting of individual aid workers or agencies to generalized attacks against the aid community and remain an aggregate category, making it difficult to discern why one organization is targeted over another or to distinguish between motives. Even with such aggregate categories, the intentionality of or motive behind the attack is apparent only in approximately half of the known incidents.[46]

When combined with evidence that 60 percent of the overall global increase in severe violence between 2006 and 2008 was due to incidents in three countries, this suggests that the increase overall appears to be driven by particular contexts in which the global and local interact in explosive ways. This does not necessarily portend dramatic changes for aid workers and their operating environments outside of these most dangerous places and serves as another reminder of the complexity of cause.

Conclusion

Clearly, aid work is a dangerous and stressful profession. Though prominent as explanatory devices, globally aggregated statistics or generalized explanations, such as the changing nature of violence and warfare or a worldwide increase in attacks over time, cannot fully capture the complexity of context and its interaction with the perceptions and actions of aid agencies and aid workers themselves, as the Biafra case demonstrates. Consequently, these explanations miss the organizational and individual factors—the internal vulnerabilities—that could help to unpack differential risk. Although the evidence does not definitively support the decisive role of context or external threat as causal explanations, it is likewise impossible to assess the role of internal vulnerabilities. Thus, the paucity of these data hampers attempts to discern between competing explanations for the violence.

At the risk of sounding redundant, what the data are able to "prove" is not the point here. Instead, these data and their shortcomings illustrate the gaps in our knowledge and beg the question of why particular explanations persist in public discourse about the violence. At the same time, the spotlight on fatalities and other incidents of severe violence has drawn attention away from the less dangerous but more commonplace and ordinary threats, such as job stress, traffic accidents, and crimes such as mugging and burglary. Moreover, this spotlight helps to magnify perceptions of a diffusely, increasingly dangerous operating environment and supports the assumptions of exceptionalism. In short, to better understand the causes of violence, it is imperative to look beyond implicit assumptions and globally relevant interpretations of cause, since appropriate and effective responses to the violence must build on a complete understanding of threat, risk, and risk management.

In the pages that follow, I explore these issues in more detail through four sets of competing discourses and images of aid. These discourses, in Chapter 4, encapsulate the dominant externally focused explanations for security incidents, while the images, from Chapter 5, uncover the internal vulnerabilities rooted in individual and organizational actions. The discourses and images as I frame them—as politics/principles and empire/rescue, and as mythical aid worker/ordinary individual and informal and idealized past/institutional and professional present—share an either/or stance: either aid workers are mythical superheroes or everyday Joes or Janes (or Mohammeds or Azizas, for that matter); either aid agencies are above reproach for the work they do or are excoriated for not having already achieved the end of poverty; either they are faulted for not being neutral and admonished for even thinking they could be or they are criticized for engaging in political, neocolonial projects aimed to make "them" look or act like "us." Although the either/or images never fully capture the complexity of aid or aid workers, I use them as heuristic devices to illustrate a larger point about the inability of mono-causal explanations to answer why aid workers and aid agencies are attacked. Moreover, they illustrate how each privileges certain approaches to security management.

The politics-and-principles and empire discourses, explored in the following chapter, capture the powerful and axiomatic explanations for violence against aid agencies and aid workers, particularly those relating to the politicization, militarization, and securitization of aid, that privilege the fortification and professionalization of security management and that dominate discussions of cause. These discourses, however, fail to recognize the role of individual and organizational actions as causal contributions to the violence that afflicts aid workers, factors that must appear in a full accounting of causes. The final discourse of the following chapter, that of rescue, illustrates the ways in which the "moral untouchability" of humanitarianism (Fassin 2010b) perpetuates the public silence about these dimensions. This untouchability manifests as the humanitarian exceptionalism that informs the legal and assumptive paradigms of security management explored in Chapter 6.

The competing images of Chapter 5 elucidate the internal vulnerabilities, or the intentional and unintentional ways in which aid workers and aid agencies contribute to or detract from their own security. These images are captured as the mythical aid worker and ordinary figure, and the informal past and the institutional and professional present. In uncovering the contributions of internal vulnerabilities, it is possible to better understand the causes of violence and the interdependent web of actors, actions, and relationships. This, in turn, opens the door to more effectively addressing the range of causes and to reclaim humanity as the central principle of humanitarianism.

CHAPTER 4

The Dominant Explanations: Competing Discourses of Aid

Violence against aid workers complicates where and how humanitarians operate and whom they can help. In some cases, violence blocks access to vulnerable populations. Security concerns, including fatalities of UN civilian international staff and peacekeepers, caused the United Nations to withdraw all international staff from Somalia in 1993. For many years after, the UN operated humanitarian and other programs remotely from Nairobi, with periodic visits to Somalia from international staff. It did not announce plans to return to Somalia until August 2010 (Hassan 2010). Similarly, the 2008 International Criminal Court (ICC) indictment of Sudanese President Omar Bashir for war crimes in Darfur caused the United Nations, for fear of reprisals, to pull its nonessential staff from the country. In March 2009, after the ICC issued an arrest warrant for President Bashir, the Sudanese government barred thirteen international and three national agencies from operating in Sudan, accusing them of helping the ICC in its investigations.[1]

In Sri Lanka, for weeks before the end of the fighting between the Liberation Tigers of Tamil Eelam and the Sri Lankan government in May 2009, the aid community called for a temporary cease-fire to allow trapped civilians to escape and sought permission to enter the war zone to provide assistance and care for the wounded. No permission was granted. Even after the fighting ended, bureaucratic obstacles such as visa rules and other restrictions impeded agencies' access to the camps. Sri Lankan officials complained that they did not want "journalists and others [to] go there to treat these people as if they were animals in a zoo" (Wax 2009) and that aid agencies wanted to use "'luxury vehicles,' which generated dust inside the camps."[2]

As aid is one of the first and sustained points of contact between the rich West and the ordinary "rest" (Easterly 2006), its implications are political and therefore controversial. The combination of scale of need, size of aid operations, and violence forces the question of how to balance the safety and security of staff with the needs of vulnerable populations. In a war zone—whether Dunant's Solferino, the battle-weary towns and beaches of Sri Lanka, or fortified Baghdad—the definition of humanitarian assistance is contested, as is the corresponding question of who delivers it. How one answers these questions reveals an allegiance to either a broad (politically engaged) or narrow (neutral, impartial, independent) vision of aid. The competing discourses of humanitarian aid revolve around *principles* and *politics*. Likewise, the aid system is cast as a metanarrative of *empire*, in which humanitarians are pawns or tools, or as a tale of *rescue* with heroes and villains. The discourses described here are not mutually exclusive, and each is partly a caricature. I frame them as opposing discourses in order to highlight the operational and conceptual differences in views of aid and of security risks.

Key themes in this discursive universe are blame, power, and context. The discussion of the available concepts of aid draws from an extensive literature that is rooted primarily in political science and international relations and that therefore privileges politics and the changing context of aid in a state or system-level analysis. In emphasizing context as the primary explanatory variable, violence against aid workers is epiphenomenal—a seemingly inevitable feature of the changing context in which aid workers operate. These competing views serve as interpretive lenses through which to scrutinize the meanings and connotations of aid and humanitarian assistance, as construed in today's globalized security context. Together these discourses capture the persistent explanations for violence against aid workers and agencies that dominate most analyses. By exploring these discourses, it is possible to demonstrate how the information to which we pay attention shapes conceptions of the causes of violence against aid workers and agencies and privileges responses that further separate aid workers from those they help.

What remains implicit and therefore unchallenged is how the two sets of competing discourses promote the logic of humanitarian exceptionalism and preserve the invisibility of the internal vulnerabilities that contribute to the insecurity aid workers experience. When the mere act of providing mercy is seen as a sufficient condition to ensure the security of humanitarians, aid workers are set apart from other actors. In focusing primarily on external, context-generated threats, their own actions and the ways in which their actions influence the contextual dynamics remain outside the scope of discussion. As acknowledged earlier, the veracity of claims about the effects of external threats is not the central issue. These explanations remain potent and persuasive, even if they also remain, as yet, empirically unproven across time and location. Instead, these explanations have achieved the status of axioms, thereby constituting generally accepted social facts and obviating the need for closer scrutiny. In neglecting other factors, the dominant explanations reflect the disciplinary bifurcation of causal explanations and Didier Fassin's observation that humanitarianism "tends to elude critical analysis" (2010b, 36). By contrast, an interdisciplinary and multidimensional analytical approach transcends this tendency, recognizing the interdependence of the dimensions and clearing the pathway for a relational analysis of and approach to humanitarianism.

Some explanations for violence against aid workers locate its causes in the compromise of the principles of neutral, impartial, and independent humanitarian action. Such explanations serve the purpose of humanitarians who argue for clearer separation between humanitarian action and broader political and military aims since, the argument goes, such separation will make them safer. Those who espouse an integrationist perspective, which sees humanitarian assistance as part of or integral to a broader agenda, argue the opposite: that humanitarian aid must occur under the umbrella of nation building, because only with better security (provided by military forces) can aid workers safely assist the local population. Thus, egregious attacks against humanitarians, whose presence and purpose are altruistic, must be countered with forceful responses, as the Ahtisaari Report concluded after the 2003 Baghdad bombing.[3] It is these forceful responses that further separate humanitarians from the recipients of their assistance.

Note that both of these approaches to aid set humanitarians apart from other actors, albeit in different ways. Likewise, the rescue discourse exceptionalizes aid workers and, by extension, aid agencies by idolizing their heroic acts, while the empire discourse replicates arguments that attribute violence to the contagion of insecurity that characterizes militarized and securitized aid. Neither of these discourses challenges the fundamental premise of exceptionalism, that providing for the basic needs of others should separate humanitarians from others. Moreover, in eliding critical analysis, these explanations undermine a humanity-based approach that requires attention to the role of internal vulnerabilities in creating security incidents.

Humanitarian Action: Politics and Principles

While the birth of modern humanitarian action coincides with the 1949 Geneva Conventions, its roots extend back centuries, prior to the codification of international humanitarian law and as far back as ancient Egypt and China (Walker and Maxwell 2009, chap. 1). These roots grew into three branches of inherited humanitarian tradition regarding the goals of aid: *containment* (to safeguard security or economic status), *compassion* (to alleviate suffering), and *change* (to work for social justice). These branches in turn represent the diversity of motives and agendas that compose a humanitarian response (Walker 2007).[4]

A parable neatly illustrates their contradictions: One day, villagers living by a river's edge discovered a person, barely alive, floating in the river. They nursed him back to health, but over the following weeks and months and years they discovered more and more bodies in the river. Unable to help or save them all, the villagers helped those they could and provided a decent burial for those they could not save. The storyteller named these actions in response to immediate need, "acts of mercy." However, he admonished, it is important to figure out why people end up in the river in the first place. Addressing these causes, he said, are "acts of justice."[5]

The parable encapsulates the debate over whether humanitarian action should be "principled" or "political." Interpreting humanitarianism exclusively as acts of mercy reflects a narrow definition of humanitarianism as a principled or "purist" approach to delivering assistance.[6] Rejecting this definition as too narrow, unrealistic, or otherwise problematic, however, invites the questions of whether and how to weigh and address the causes of the situation and the consequences of aid, in order to pursue justice alongside mercy.[7] In contrast to the "emergency humanitarians" who respond to the symptoms of the disease, the "alchemical humanitarians" work to address the root causes of the disease (Barnett 2011), or at the least they explore how to engage in a political context without being partisan (O'Brien 2004). Expanding the definition to incorporate acts of justice inevitably brings the politics of aid to the forefront.

The politicization of humanitarian assistance, in turn, raises the specter of using humanitarian assistance in service of other agendas. Not least, governments use humanitarian aid as an alternative to making the more difficult commitments and trade-offs involved in crafting political solutions to protracted conflict. In short, the competing discourses are framed around principles and politics. One perspective emphasizes the distinctiveness of humanitarians, thereby weakening any analytical approach that sees aid actors as embedded within and not separate from the system in which they operate, and the other brings humanitarians closer to the political and military agendas that characterize the violent environments in which they operate. Both, as a result, undermine a relational approach.

The Who and What of Humanitarian Assistance

Is humanitarianism defined by *what* it is or by *who* delivers it, regardless of whether it is "tainted" with the agendas (and finances) of governments, the military, or NGOs? This question and its related suppositions constitute a central debate within humanitarianism. How one answers this question defines the parameters of humanitarianism and implicitly shapes discussions about violence against aid workers. Competing views about the primacy of principles or politics, in turn, inform divergent approaches to security management. The conflicting approaches to UN security management in Iraq in 2003, described in Chapter 1, illustrate these divergent perspectives. Sergio de Mello believed in the impartiality and neutrality of the UN as an institution, even as the Security Council mandate and the perceptions of many Iraqis conflated the UN's humanitarian and political activities. His understanding of the UN's work as impartial and independent informed his decision to distance the UN from the U.S. mission and actions in Iraq and to refuse protection from Coalition forces, a decision that reflected the assumption that these principles made the UN less of a target and therefore safer. This decision, he hoped, would signal an unwillingness to compromise these principles and more visibly associate the UN with the United States and its (political) war aims.

Humanitarian assistance, according to the Institute of International Law (IIL), "means all acts, activities and the human and material resources for the provision of goods and services of an *exclusively humanitarian character*, indispensable for the survival and the fulfillment of the essential needs of the victims of disasters" (as quoted in Mackintosh 2007, 117, italics in original; see also O'Connell 2002). Several elements stand out in this definition. First, the "essential needs" clause limits the type of goods and services and emphasizes the urgency of assistance. This relates more to the "what" of humanitarian assistance, where survival needs define the meaning of lifesaving assistance. Second, the "exclusively humanitarian character" clause precludes other primary agendas, including the provision of goods and services for any purpose other than saving lives. In short, this clause hinges on intent. Humanitarian assistance is not to be confused with other agendas. By eliminating actors with mixed or ulterior motives, this definition delineates the "who" of humanitarianism.

A general consensus exists about the definition of *what* humanitarianism is. The common understanding affirms lifesaving assistance, or providing for the basic survival needs, such as water, food, and medical assistance, of people in crisis. Likewise, proper sanitation reduces the risk of disease transmission that can wreak havoc on already weakened bodies thrust together in close quarters, such as refugee or internally displaced person camps. Narrowly defining humanitarian assistance in this way limits the range of humanitarian activities, creating an exclusive niche for humanitarian actors and privileging acts of mercy. This conception falls within Walker and Maxwell's *compassion* tradition.

Such a narrow definition suggests humanitarianism should not be confused or aligned with other goals or types of assistance, such as development or peacebuilding, which are inherently political projects because of their association with a liberal peace agenda and the goal of social transformation. These other endeavors are not lifesaving in the short term but rather are focused on longer-term goals of reducing poverty and creating opportunities and choices. Such activities fall instead within the *change* tradition. In this way, the manifestation of humanitarianism as a compassionate and apolitical response to human suffering is akin to a narrow definition of humanitarianism, while the broader definition collapses the compassionate with the change and containment traditions.

Similarly, the military and government entertain larger and conflicting agendas. The purpose of the military is to defend the state and fight wars in service of the national interest, and the purpose of government is to protect and advance the national interest and, in a democratic society, to serve its citizens. Thus, a state's provision of humanitarian assistance becomes a means in service to a larger end (e.g., the national interest or national defense) and falls within Walker and Maxwell's *containment* tradition.

In violent conflict contexts, military actors often provide assistance or relief for other purposes, such as boosting morale among the troops or winning the "hearts and minds" of the local population. These alternative agendas disqualify military actors from consideration as impartial, neutral, or independent humanitarian actors,[8] despite the responsibilities of belligerent parties as defined by international humanitarian law (IHL) to provide or facilitate humanitarian assistance in situations of armed conflict or occupation. While the military may possess a comparative advantage in logistics and equipment (though not necessarily in cost), its purpose for providing assistance is never exclusively humanitarian. In this way, the assistance from military actors fails to meet the criteria of the above-mentioned IIL definition of humanitarian assistance and contravenes a principled approach, since such assistance is not independent or neutral and may or may not be given based on need and without discrimination.[9]

Going deeper into the definition raises questions about whether lifesaving assistance is just about sustenance. Kate Mackintosh, an IHL advisor to Médecins Sans Frontières (MSF), emphasizes the importance of the impartial nature of the assistance, meaning its distribution without discrimination and with regard to need. She concludes that protection *and* assistance for civilians and combatants alike define humanitarian aid (Mackintosh 2007, 116–117).

The inclusion of a protection agenda regained momentum following criticisms in the 1990s of the "well-fed dead" of Bosnia and Rwanda, where people might have received aid but received it in time to be slaughtered by those intent on killing them.[10] In short, the *what* of humanitarian action is lifesaving assistance, which entails the protection of life, health, subsistence, and physical security (Darcy and Hofman 2003; Kent 2003; see also Paul 1999; Bruderlein 2001; Minear 2002; Inter-Agency Standing Committee 2002; Slim and Eguren 2004; O'Callaghan and Pantuliano 2007) or physical protection and the securing of the rights of noncombatants via nonmilitary means (Hoffman and Weiss 2006, 2).

Defining *who* engages in humanitarianism, in contrast, is fraught with controversy. The classicist or "Dunantist" view of humanitarian action assumes respect for the four primary principles of humanitarian action—humanity, impartiality, and the operational principles of neutrality and independence—as the defining characteristics of the "who" question. Thus, humanitarian action stands apart from and is extraneous to a conflict, and the principles of neutrality, impartiality, and independence preserve this separation.[11] Jean Pictet, the architect of the seven fundamental principles of the International Committee of the Red Cross (ICRC), differentiated the substantive principles—humanity, and nondiscrimination and proportionality, which together compose impartiality—from the derived principles of neutrality and independence. The derived principles allow the ICRC to "put the essential principle [humanity] into action and enable us, without deforming them, to translate the substantive principles into factual reality" (Pictet 1979a, 136). He thus organizes these principles in hierarchical fashion, placing humanity and impartiality at the top and framing neutrality and independence as means necessary to achieving the essential principle of humanity.

The Dunant-inspired ICRC is the quintessential "purist" humanitarian actor.[12] International organizations such as the ICRC and a few other actors that operate in accordance with these four principles fall within the purist tradition. Their mandate is to deliver neutral and impartial humanitarian assistance and protection. This is not a task for governments or military actors, who are neither neutral nor independent. Indeed, these "impure" actors often defy the fundamental principles in service of their own agendas. A Colombian soldier's use of the Red Cross emblem in the rescue of Ingrid Betancourt and fourteen other hostages in July 2008, for example, violated the Geneva Conventions. It also rendered the work of the ICRC more difficult, because of this violation of the ICRC's principle of neutrality and because of the misuse of the Red Cross emblem, which is defined and protected under IHL.

Even as the definitions of these broad principles are generally accepted, the specific principles that individual actors espouse vary widely. The Red Cross NGO Code of Conduct in Disaster Response spells out a series of maxims of assistance delivery and their practical implications. Many of the major NGOs providing relief assistance have signed onto the code. While avoiding explicit references to humanitarian principles, the code's self-enforcement calls on agencies to provide assistance based on need and without discrimination, to not "further a particular political or religious standpoint," and to "endeavor not to act as instruments of government foreign policy" (International Federation of the Red Cross and Red Crescent Societies 1997, principles 2–4). Even so, aside from a few notable exceptions, most relief and development agencies have jettisoned neutrality and its attendant controversies in favor of the clarity and less controversial nature of impartiality, delivering assistance according to who needs it most and without regard for identifying characteristics, such as ethnicity or religion. In the eyes of the purists, it is not the role or responsibility of humanitarians to decide who is "right" or whose cause is more or less just; these labels rarely belong exclusively or neatly to one side, and any resulting affiliation violates the principle of neutrality.

Attempting to marry humanitarian relief with other goals of peace and stability, known as the coherence or integrated agenda, subsumes mercy under justice, forfeiting the immediate goal of saving lives for an unknown future benefit. As Nicolas de Torrenté, former director of MSF-US, writes, "The implication of the coherence agenda is that meeting lifesaving needs is too limited in scope, and that the principles of impartiality, neutrality and independence that have typically characterized humanitarian action should be set aside in order to harness the 'higher' goals of peace, security, and development" (de Torrenté 2004b, 3). Instead, the purists who uphold the principles of neutrality, impartiality, and independence choose to provide only lifesaving assistance, to maintain open lines of communication with all sides, to not take sides, and to assess needs and deliver proportional assistance without discrimination, even if this incurs trade-offs (see Magone, Neuman, and Weissman 2011).

In contrast, the "Wilsonians," or political humanitarians, openly acknowledge the political elements of humanitarian aid. They concede the impossibility of preserving the perception of neutrality and reject the notion that humanitarian action can exist separate from politics. Instead, they argue that the humanitarian project is inherently political, since to provide assistance to "save the lives of the neediest in conflicts" is a political decision designed to send a political message. Eschewing partisanship with political actors is the goal over and against the idea of remaining apolitical or politically disengaged (O'Brien 2004, 31). Humanitarian aid, proponents argue, is inherently political, because governments and belligerents use it to gain support from the people or to advance a particular cause or agenda.

To claim neutrality, by contrast, is to traffic in self-deception. Operating in conflict zones or polarized contexts means that assistance to one or both sides inevitably raises the ire of the belligerents and invites charges of "helping the enemy." Thus, this perspective suggests it is impossible to maintain a truly neutral stance, as the classic principles would dictate.[13] Even worse, in situations of genocide the refusal to take sides is tantamount to condoning and even supporting those who commit genocide.[14] Political humanitarians reject neutrality as a guiding principle, preferring instead to emphasize impartiality and independence.

Even within this camp, gradations exist. Thomas Weiss differentiates between "minimalist" and "maximalist" political humanitarians, based on the extent to which they engage political questions and on their respect for the four fundamental principles of humanitarian action. "Minimalists," he writes, "aim to 'do no harm,' whereas maximalists have a more ambitious agenda of employing humanitarian action as part of a comprehensive strategy to transform conflict" (Weiss 1999, 3).[15] The Do No Harm approach (Anderson 1999) and other efforts to improve the accountability, efficiency, and effectiveness of humanitarian relief, such as the Sphere Project (2000), have gained widespread acceptance, while the integrated mission agenda or "whole of government" approaches, promoted primarily by governments and the UN, are met with varying degrees of skepticism precisely because of their comprehensiveness and the extent to which such approaches blur political and humanitarian aims.

Others engage more deliberately in the political realm and adopt "solidarity" as their defining principle, arguing that to be effective is to act in solidarity with one side or to advocate on behalf of the voiceless. Solidarity implies taking the side of the poor or oppressed, or of particular categories of people, such as war-affected populations, usually in service of a broader aim of peace or social justice and equality (Minear 2002, 79). Norwegian People's Aid, for example, takes an explicitly solidarist stand. It argues, "To respond properly, it is important to analyse the political and social factors behind suffering, and to understand the impact of assistance. It is important to see organisations as political and social actors: whoever controls and distributes resources in a society marked by scarcity, conflict, injustice or oppression plays a political role. Choices about whom to help, where to help and what to do to help will have an impact on society beyond direct project results" (Bjoreng 2003, 10). Those who have adopted an explicitly partial or solidarist approach are fewer in number, and tend to include faith-based agencies. Most aid agencies, especially those with roots in North America, fall within the political humanitarian camp, leaving only a few truly purist organizations.[16]

Obviously, whether an actor respects the core principles is not the only issue. To further complicate matters, if one neighbor provides assistance to another, is this not humanitarian assistance? Or, if one government provides such assistance to another government, as in the case of the 2004 tsunami, is this not humanitarian assistance? What about those working for human rights; is this not humanitarian as well? More important, why does this matter? The answers to such questions determine who or what deserves the label "humanitarian." Some believe that these conundrums are purely theoretical, with minor consequence for actual on-the-ground assistance, since it is the perceptions of belligerents and those caught in the crossfire that matter and not the definitions. Yet these labels do matter, particularly with regard to security.

The labels matter because these competing views have defined the dominant discourses about targeting and the causes of violence against aid workers. Thus, assumptions and assertions about the causes of violence against aid workers have entered the discussion about humanitarian action and aid work more generally via the politics-and-principles debate. Notably, such discussion prioritizes a macro-level analysis focused upon the politicized nature of the aid system itself, the changing nature of warfare, and the distinctions between military and civilian actors. Indeed, many of the arguments about why humanitarian actors are targeted or killed and injured are implicitly or explicitly tied to the various principles and used to justify one vision, political or principled, over the other.

Both images share a basic assumption that politicization—the instrumental and manipulated use of humanitarian assistance—has made aid workers targets of violence. They suggest that it is precisely the context of aid, its politicization, and the corresponding loss of impartiality, independence, and neutrality that result in the targeting of aid workers. Assertions about insecurity and the demise of various principles reflect these assumptions. In one analysis, the authors argued, "The causes of the conflict become confused with international geopolitical agendas. One consequence is the increased targeting of aid workers by combatants" (Adams and Bradbury 1995, 33–34). According to another, "The refusal to acknowledge explicitly the political function of relief in conflict situations contributes to the maintenance of violence, playing into the hands of the powerful, while the politicization of humanitarian assistance, through selective provision and the militarization of delivery, increases the security threat to agencies" (Macrae and Zwi 1994, 30). Accompanying this doctrine is the corollary that violence against aid actors constitutes an exception to a more "normal" state of affairs, illustrative of the exceptionalism narrative and the notion, described in the previous chapter, that this type of violence is a relatively new phenomenon.

Aid workers are threatened and sometimes killed because states (or warring factions, whether secular or religious) manipulate aid, or because they are in various ways dependent upon or implicated with these state or factional forces. Certainly, there is more than a grain of truth to this analysis; humanitarian workers are often targeted for political reasons. This analysis, however, should not obscure the actual complexity of the causes of security risks to aid workers. Unfortunately, the politics-and-principles debate, and the assumptions about and conceptualizations of cause that derive from it, do not subsume the full range of causes. Moreover, this preserves the invisibility of internal vulnerabilities as contributory mechanisms.

A systemic, relational analysis calls for closer scrutiny of these vulnerabilities, not only of external threats. The explanations of the politics-and-principles image, therefore, suffer two shortcomings. The first relates to the assumption that violence against aid workers is primarily due to the instrumentalization of humanitarianism and the compromise of humanitarian principles, and the second to the assumption that these explanations locate aid workers external to the wider system of conflict within which they operate, thereby supporting the narrative of humanitarian exceptionalism.

Humanitarian Principles and the Instrumentalization of Humanitarian Action

Upholding or compromising the humanitarian principles of neutrality, impartiality, and independence serve as powerful explanations of the causes of violence against humanitarian actors. Not remaining neutral in conflict makes humanitarians a target, even as the political machinations of aid make neutrality almost impossible to uphold. According to one security director, "The rejection of humanitarian action... makes us potential targets. Big states have instrumentalized humanitarian action."[17] When aid actors apply the principle of impartiality, conflict parties may interpret the provision of assistance to the "enemy" as support for enemy aims and goals (thereby voiding the protection that may have derived from remaining extraneous to the conflict). This support, then, makes those providing the assistance a potential target of violence.

Upholding the principles of neutrality and impartiality paves the path to vulnerable populations and exposes humanitarians to the front lines, where violence is most virulent and aid workers are least safe. Likewise, compromising the principle of independence, related to funding and advocacy, may be perceived as siding with one actor or cause over another. In all cases, applying or compromising the principles (whether self-generated or externally imposed) is linked to insecurity.

Of all the humanitarian principles, neutrality is the most controversial. It is especially relevant in situations of war and violent conflict, since by definition it requires at least two opposing sides. The Red Cross defines neutrality as follows: "In order to continue to enjoy the confidence of all, the Red Cross may not take sides in hostilities or engage at any time in controversies of a political, racial, religious or ideological nature" (Pictet 1979b, 6). In his commentary, Jean Pictet elaborated upon this definition, suggesting that neutrality is both military and ideological. It requires discipline and a refusal to judge. It is "essentially a negative idea: one is neutral who does not take sides in a conflict." Pictet himself labeled neutrality as a derived as opposed to a core principle of humanitarian action (Pictet 1979b, 52ff.).

The cornerstone of neutrality is the notion of humanitarian assistance and action as separate from explicitly political action because of a principled refusal to take sides. In choosing to interact with all sides, humanitarian actors maintain their apolitical and outsider stance. Those eschewing neutrality instead argue that assistance is political precisely because it alters the balance of power by introducing resources into the conflict, by supporting a status quo that inherently favors one side, or by using aid in service of an agenda other than simply "mercy." This remains true even in the face of inaction.

The challenges to neutrality that drive the politicization and instrumentalization of aid are multiple. States use humanitarian assistance as a foreign policy tool, substituting such assistance for more decisive diplomatic or military engagement, as in Rwanda in 1994. Their assistance allows states to be seen as doing something even if the assistance is akin to putting a Band-Aid on a hemorrhaging wound. In other cases, states wishing to avoid controversy provide humanitarian assistance in lieu of development aid, which typically requires more stability or recognition of the legitimacy of rebel movements, as in South Sudan in the 1980s and 1990s (Macrae et al. 1997). Using aid for political purposes, such as "hearts and minds" campaigns to win over local populations, using the military to distribute aid, providing aid to allies over enemies, or tying aid to peace processes—all practices that undermine the neutral, impartial, and independent basis of humanitarian action—are perceived as serving a particular Western liberalization agenda (Macrae 1998; Bouchet-Saulnier 2001; Duffield 2001; Fishstein and Wilder

2011; Donini 2012). In other cases, such as the Biafran War in the 1960s or Sudan and Somalia in the 1980s and early 1990s, critics charged that humanitarian assistance prolonged or exacerbated the violence (de Waal 1997; Vaux 2004). Involvement in politics undermines the untouchability that derives from neutrality, thereby making aid workers targets of attack.

In earlier years, the politicization/instrumentalization debate was most often framed in either/or terms: aid is either principled or political. More recently, these either/or arguments have gained less traction within the scholarly and practitioner humanitarian community, in recognition of the fact that even the purist actors must have a healthy respect for the political dimensions of aid (see, e.g., O'Brien 2004; Barnett 2011). Over time, the debate has evolved, from politicization and instrumentalization in the 1990s to militarization and securitization in the 2000s and the coherence/integration/"whole of government" perspective that unites humanitarian with political objectives.

The latter view posits that aid is more effective if all government and other actors work together for a common goal or agenda. The integration and coherence agendas link political and humanitarian activities and endanger neutral or independent aid.[19] Within the UN, for example, the under-secretary-general for humanitarian affairs, also known as the emergency relief coordinator (ERC), is the head of the Office for the Coordination of Humanitarian Assistance (OCHA). The ERC reports to the UN secretary-general, a political position. In most countries, OCHA is housed within and reports to the political arm of the UN.[18] Similarly, the "One UN" pilots in countries like Rwanda and Mozambique unite UN humanitarian, development, and environmental programming under one leader with the aim of enhancing UN systemwide coordination. Likewise, participation in the "cluster system" forces more coordination between aid actors of all stripes and persuasions working in a cluster (e.g., water, sanitation, and health), and limits the possibility for neutral or independent action. As of 2008, the integration policy applies to all "conflict and post-conflict situations where the UN has a Country Team and a multi-dimensional peacekeeping operation or political mission/office, whether or not these presences are structurally integrated" (UN Secretary General 2008).

The militarization and securitization of aid provide additional fodder for explanations of the causes of violence against aid workers. A common refrain is that the blurred lines between civilian and military actors make it difficult to distinguish between the two, thus making civilians, including humanitarians, targets of belligerents. Underlying this assumption is the idea that military actors are legitimate targets of violence and that civilians are not. Correspondingly, aid workers should be exempt from violence precisely because they are civilians. Defining who is a civilian, however, is fraught with controversy, even as it remains a cornerstone of IHL (Slim 2007). Practically speaking, Laura Hammond (2008) points out that the "blurred lines" argument underestimates the intelligence of belligerents and civilians, since it assumes they are too ignorant or naïve to know the difference. In reality, she argues, they know exactly who they are targeting and do it anyhow.[20]

The rise of "militarized charity" blurs the distinctions between soldiers and civilians even further, with an assumption of a consequent risk for humanitarian actors. One author opines, for example, that the battlefields of contemporary conflict on which both soldiers and humanitarians operate "now encompass villages and terror tactics [that] draw no distinction between soldier and civilian." She continues, "This is evidenced by the rapid increase in the number of aid workers killed in combat zones" (Lischer 2007, 101). This is especially true in contexts like Iraq and Afghanistan, where aid agencies have legitimately accused coalition and International Security Assistance Force military forces of encroaching on "humanitarian space" by distributing aid when out of uniform and releasing from planes yellow-packaged cluster bombs that resembled the yellow food packets they also dropped.[21] The moral and practical dilemmas of the association between military and aid actors are widely debated in the field (Gordenker and Weiss 1990; Smith 1993; Mackinlay 1993; Slim 1995b; Whitman and Pocock 1996; Roberts 1996; Moore 1999; Weiss 2004). In general, most aid agencies believe that associating with the military compromises their impartiality or neutrality and, for some, raises questions related to their mission and ethical stance.[22]

In other cases, it is the humanitarians themselves who initiate and support the links with military actors, most clearly in the case of armed escort. In Rwanda, in the early fall of 1994, the security situation in the refugee camps proved so precarious for aid workers and refugees alike that military protection became necessary (Borton, Brusset, and Hallam 1996, 53–57). In fact, virtually all humanitarian and development actors have, at one point or another, resorted to the use of armed, often private, security forces (Stoddard, Harmer, and DiDomenico 2008). One agency's decision to use armed protection has implications for all agencies operating in the same area (Van Brabant 2000, 81), because it makes those who choose not to tread this path "softer" targets. This "soft target" argument often drives the adoption of fortified security-management strategies.

In other cases, military escorts for humanitarian assistance have provoked a violent reaction, as parties to a conflict interpreted the armed escort as a challenge to their authority (Anderson 1999; Van Brabant 1998, 118–119). The ICRC, for example, uses military escort only in locations with high levels of banditry or criminal activity. While some have advocated for the use of private or volunteer security forces (Stein 1998; Vayrynen 1999; Bryans, Jones, and Stein 1999), more often than not this topic has generated diverging opinions within the humanitarian community (see, e.g., Van Brabant 2000; Inter-Agency Standing Committee Working Group 2001; Slim 2001; Barry and Jefferys 2002).

Neutrality is traditionally interpreted as remaining apolitical. Some, however, think more in terms of "operational neutrality," where neutrality is not an end in itself, but is instead a means of ensuring access to those in need of assistance (Humanitarian Policy Group [HPG] 2007). In this way, ensuring the security of aid workers and aid delivery becomes the flip side of access to civilian populations.[23] Conceptualizing security in this way emphasizes the importance of negotiating with military actors (whether rebel, military, or other irregular forces) to gain access and of the role of neutrality in gaining this access, denial being more likely if a humanitarian actor is perceived as taking sides.

In short, the stated assumption is that the principles of neutrality, as well as impartiality and independence, separate aid workers from military actors and nonhumanitarian agendas and provide consequent protection from harm.[24] "We associate with the military and therefore are perceived as less impartial," said one aid worker, "which makes us less secure, which increases the need for protection."[25]

Whereas neutrality refers to the humanitarian's independence from political or partisan affiliations, impartiality, defined in terms of proportionality and nondiscrimination (Pictet 1979a, 136), dictates that humanitarian assistance must go first to those in greatest need, regardless of their affiliation (or lack thereof) with any political party, movement, or other group. Impartiality describes the humanitarian attitude toward those who gain as well as those who lose in conflict settings, especially when civilians are targets. Acting impartially in a world where civilians are targets and where helping any side is often construed on a battlefield as providing direct support to the enemy, entails risk and serves as an explanation for why humanitarians are targets of violence. In this way, discussions of impartiality have generated implicit and explicit assertions about the factors that lead to violence against aid workers and agencies.

These factors relate to civilians as targets and to interfering with who gains and who loses in conflict settings. In a context where violence against civilians is a widespread weapon of war, offering protection and assistance may be construed as a partial act that makes aid workers and agencies themselves targets of violence, since belligerents often construe civilian populations as supporting one side or another. In doing so, the logic implies, aid workers lose any protection that might have arisen from remaining external to the conflict. Attempting to protect civilians inevitably allies the protector with one or more parties in a conflict, possibly even making the protector a central player in the eyes of the conflict parties. In this way, insecurity for those providing assistance and often for all other actors in the same area grows. Minear and Weiss, writing in 1995, asserted this connection:

> As those under fire have found themselves in more desperate need of mercy from the outside world, those seeking to provide assistance have more frequently come under fire themselves.... Those who work for the Red Cross or the United Nations often are denied their right of access, harassed and held hostage, injured, and killed. Long-established symbols no longer command automatic respect or assure implicit protection. In many conflicts, relief convoys have been hijacked or blocked, drivers wounded or killed, and emergency assistance activities commandeered or shut down. International humanitarian actors suffer indignities differing only in degree from those experienced by distressed civilian populations. (Minear and Weiss 1995, 3)

Implicitly recognizing this assertion, the UN Security Council included acts of violence against the provision of humanitarian assistance as a war crime (UN Security Council 2003).

The targeting of aid workers helping civilians is especially complicated when fighting forces are less disciplined or lack an organizational hierarchy. With regular forces, negotiating access with the commanding officer is more likely to trickle down the chain of command. Irregular forces, particularly those that use child soldiers, are often less disciplined and less observant of the rules of war, thereby increasing the risks for civilians and aid workers. Less discipline for fighting forces often translates to increased danger for humanitarian actors, since they must educate and negotiate with multiple actors, and a centrally negotiated access agreement is unlikely to hold among all factions. This, in turn, complicates efforts to negotiate for safe access, since contexts with undisciplined, unorganized, or predatory nonstate actors are most dangerous for humanitarians and civilian populations. These circumstances compose the most challenging security-management contexts.[26]

Indeed, all too often security concerns, including men and women with guns, prevent access to civilian populations, with the consequent risks that derive from attempting to circumvent this denial or otherwise negotiate access. In many contexts, the widespread availability of conventional weapons—small arms and light weapons[27]—hinders access to vulnerable populations or increases the danger and the lethality of crime and banditry (see Muggah and Berman 2001; Muggah 2001; Muggah and Batchelor 2002; Beasley, Buchanan, and Muggah 2003), and creates insecurity for aid workers.[28]

In fulfilling their mandate to provide assistance, aid agencies often interfere with the winners and losers in conflict settings and with the economic agendas of war and insecure environments (Berdal and Keen 1997; Berdal and Malone 2000; Nordstrom 1997, 2004; Collier 2000; Taylor 2002; LeBillon 2000, 2005). In providing such assistance, aid actors introduce new resources and assets that can provide tempting and valuable targets. In fact, violence provides the opportunity for groups to further their economic fortunes through a variety of means, such as pillage, protection money, trade, labor exploitation, land, and stealing aid supplies (Keen 1998, 15–17; 2000). Pillaging is symptomatic of a weak chain of command and a lack of discipline, and further supports cycles of violence as underpaid or undisciplined soldiers use pillage for pay or to supplement their meager incomes. This increases the levels of insecurity for humanitarian actors, because their aid supplies become profitable targets of attack (Anderson 1999, 64; see also Prendergast in Smock 1996). Such criminality is a significant security issue for aid actors. According to one security expert, "For belligerents, it comes down to criminality and opportunity or if there is something to be gained—money, resources, reputation."[29] Another links security incidents to economic factors, suggesting some incidents are perpetrated by those who "are not paid well, since if they are not paid well, they attack."[30]

Anderson (1999), however, makes a strong case for the micro-factors of the behavior and actions of individual aid workers and organizations—what she labels the implicit ethical messages—as contributing to the potential for violence. Ransom payments for kidnapped foreigners, some of whom are aid workers, provide a lucrative source of income and increase the danger for others. Recognizing this effect, most agencies state they do not pay ransom, even though stated policy and actual practice do not always coincide. In some cases, governments or family members pay the ransom. According to some estimates, al-Qaeda in the Maghreb received up to US$70 million in ransom payments between 2003 and 2010, and al-Qaeda affiliates received US$25 million in ransom payments from seven Western governments between 2008 and April 2010 (Walt 2010). Observers labeled the Taliban's claim of responsibility for the deaths of ten staff of the International Assistance Mission in Afghanistan in August 2010 as "opportunistic," since the Taliban appeared more focused on kidnapping aid workers as a source of income than on killing them.[31]

While operational neutrality and impartiality are crucial for gaining access to vulnerable populations, the ability of an organization to demonstrate and maintain independence (or at a minimum, the perception of independence) is evidence that the organization is not tainted by nonhumanitarian agendas or by serving as a puppet for other political actors. The principle of independence, linked to autonomy of action (Plattner 1996), often revolves around funding, since reliance on one major donor, such as a government, risks limiting an organization's freedom of choice about where and how to operate and casts doubt on the ability of agencies to maintain an independent, neutral, or even impartial stance. The advocacy issues and positions humanitarians adopt are perceived as signs of independence or a lack thereof. Funding for humanitarian assistance, decisions about advocacy and public statements, and multiple mandates all compromise or support an organization's independence, and therefore can be linked to whether or not an organization is a target of violence.

Some organizations benefit from a strong individual donor base of support and rely less on government-funded projects and priorities. In 2009, for example, approximately 86 percent of MSF revenues came from private sources, giving the organization more flexibility in how and where it responds to emergencies.[32] The ICRC accepts funding from multiple governments (as well as private donors) on the condition that it retains complete independence and discretion in all its operations. It is precisely this independence that led the ICRC to decline in August 2011 to deliver food assistance in Somalia on behalf of the UN or other agencies in response to the drought and famine. Al-Shabaab, the Somali militant group controlling portions of southern Somalia where the need was most acute, had previously banned the World

Food Programme from accessing areas under its control. In a news conference, then ICRC President Jakob Kellenberger explained the decision as follows: "The ICRC is an independent agency, for reasons you'll understand, for its protection.... And I think that's important for its perception, for its personality, especially in delicate contexts like this" (as cited in Miles and Lough 2011).

Other agencies have similarly attempted to decrease their dependence on a single donor by diversifying their revenue sources. Nonetheless, governments and the UN remain by far the largest donors for the majority of NGOs. For some organizations operating in Iraq and Afghanistan in 2003 and 2004, their funding from the U.S. and British governments proved a metaphorical minefield as they struggled to juggle risks to their reputations and public images with organizational alliances and donor priorities.[33] Other U.S., UK, and European NGOs chose not to accept U.S. or UK resources for their work in Iraq or Afghanistan in 2003 and 2004 in order to maintain a more independent stance there, a choice reminiscent of that facing U.S. NGOs operating in Vietnam in the 1960s and 1970s and in Central America in the 1980s. Perceptions, therefore, are linked to security: "The extent of your success in getting people to perceive you as neutral is key, fundamental to whether you are secure. This will determine your security."[34]

The dilemma of when, where, and how to speak out about injustices and abuses that aid workers often witness is a corollary manifestation of an organization's independence. It is also the source of much debate within organizations. Several doctors working in Biafra for the ICRC in the 1960s felt handicapped by and morally outraged at their inability to speak out about what they saw. In response, they founded MSF and emphasized the idea of witnessing and speaking out against abuses.[35] While not all welcome relief agencies' forays into advocacy and expanded mandates (e.g., African Rights 1994), many agencies have embarked on advocacy campaigns of multiple stripes, usually related to an issue or policy, or have spoken out more generally against abuses and direct or structural violence inflicted on the populations they serve.

For example, Catholic Relief Services, a relief and development NGO, cited advocacy efforts supporting the cessation of hostilities in Sierra Leone as part of its peacebuilding activities (Catholic Relief Services 2000, 8). Agencies such as Oxfam and MSF have taken on advocacy activities as one component of their organizational mission. In some cases, these advocacy and information campaigns are related to particular countries, while others are devoted to particular issues, such as the "One" campaign to eradicate world poverty, fair trade advocacy, campaigns to control or limit specific weapons (land mines, cluster bombs, or the "Control Arms" campaign), MSF's public campaign for more accessible medicines in the South, or the ICRC's "Healthcare in Danger" campaign. The campaigns take the form of public education through donor appeals, websites, policy briefs, and advocating specific policies to legislative bodies. In many cases, campaigns are a primary mechanism that agencies use to raise awareness about global issues of structural injustice.

What is less clear is the extent to which advocacy campaigns are linked to insecurity. In a 2007 study on neutrality in Darfur, the Overseas Development Institute examined the relationship among advocacy, operational programming, insecurity, and humanitarian access and concluded, "Advocacy by operational aid actors is frequently juxtaposed with programming, with speaking out weighed against potential costs to programmes, staff and beneficiaries. This relationship between advocacy and access and security appears to have been an important determinant in the quantity and quality of advocacy efforts on Darfur" (HPG 2007, 2). The policy brief mentions administrative or bureaucratic hassles that plagued organizations, especially those engaged in advocacy efforts for Darfur, and that the period of more frequent administrative hassles coincided with a period of heightened levels of violence against aid workers. This insecurity has affected the humanitarian community in Darfur, and these levels of insecurity appear to have influenced the advocacy work of organizations.

In other cases, it is host-government intimidation or intervention that limits advocacy work. This has occurred in Uganda, for example, where government intimidation limited the advocacy work of NGOs in relation to civilian protection issues (O'Callaghan and Pantuliano 2007, box 3), and in Darfur, where the Sudanese government accused and expelled relief organizations after the indictment of Sudanese President Bashir in March 2009. One organization's expulsion from Darfur was linked to its gender-based violence programming, since President Bashir's indictment for war crimes included the use of gang rape.[36]

Clearly, the security implications of the politics-and-principles debate are not confined to the conceptual or "academic" realms. At the root of the debate is the gradual erosion of the principles of neutrality, impartiality, and independence that safeguard the mercy-oriented nature of humanitarian assistance. An organization's stance in relation to these principles generates operational implications, including how agencies respond to security issues, such as whether they shun or (reluctantly) embrace armed protection. Each of the principles incurs costs of some kind. The moral and security questions that many agencies have about neutrality and its benefits have marginalized neutrality as a widely affirmed principle, whereas the costs of impartiality appear to be ones that agencies are willing to bear because of impartiality's traction as a core principle of humanitarianism and its value as an operational principle. Asserting and demonstrating independence buttresses an agency's claims of an apolitical agenda. The actual security benefits of such stances remain, as yet, empirically unproven.

Nevertheless, these axiomatic discourses, rooted in the central debates of humanitarianism, compose the primary explanations for the violence aid workers face. They are indeed important. Unfortunately, they neglect other contributing factors and the constellation of dimensions as an interrelated whole. As the dominant framing of security issues, this debate supports an analysis of humanitarianism that remains focused on itself as separate from conflict and the centers of power and as isolated from the recipients of the humanitarian act.

Preserving the Logic of Humanitarian Exceptionalism

As framed by the politics-and-principles debate, attacks against humanitarians are seen as egregious precisely because they happen to those who are supposed to be "outside" of the violence: humanitarians are neutral, independent, and impartial and therefore not "of" the violence. In making claims about their good works in their fund-raising or other publicity efforts and in their assertions that they do not take sides, do not serve foreign policy agendas, and make decisions based on need alone, humanitarians make normative claims that set them apart. These claims conserve the foregrounding of humanitarians as purveyors of assistance over and against the recipients of such assistance and the system as a whole. In invoking a narrow definition—that mercy is the domain of the nongovernmental and of a select few actors—humanitarian actors implicitly argue for the preservation of "humanitarian space" and for their unique role and separate realm of influence (physical and symbolic; see EU Commission 1998; Slim 2003; Yamashita 2004; Wagner 2005; Sida 2005; Hilhorst and Jansen 2010). At its most cynical, this argument preserves humanitarian territory in asserting a monopoly on mercy and, furthermore, in asserting that the association of mercy and compassion with justice taints mercy with other agendas.

In advancing these arguments, humanitarian actors are essentially claiming that acts of mercy (and the humanitarians who perform them) are somehow different and special—that they are exceptional—and therefore deserving of and following a separate set of rules—that they are exceptions.[37] This difference mandates an inviolability and protection from violence and its perpetrators. The dominant discourse of the politics-and-principles debate usually supports the basic assumptions of humanitarian exceptionalism. The skeptics answer that humanitarian action, notwithstanding the ICRC credo, is *not* impartial, neutral, or independent and that this makes humanitarians an unsurprising target. In reality, however, the situation on the ground is more complex than such stark attitudes convey.

Indeed, humanitarian exceptionalism remains a powerful notion. Taken a step further, as they are when humanitarians invoke and extend the principles to the realm of security and protection, these claims imply humanitarians are therefore deserving of a morally justified immunity that derives from this exceptionalism. Even the language of targeting is normative language; the phrase "targeting of humanitarian actors" and the press releases and media stories that usually follow violence against aid workers suggest a taboo against attacking or killing aid workers. A taboo, in turn, implies socially or culturally prescribed prohibitions against certain actions and endows the subject of the taboo with sacred value.[38]

Most commonly, the exception is presumed to derive from the principles of humanitarian action, but even those who espouse an integrated approach appear to assume that acts of mercy, which provide life-sustaining assistance, should offer a degree of protection from attack. This is precisely the idea that Kenneth Anderson explores in relation to the UN missions in Iraq and Afghanistan in 2003 and 2004.[39] He suggests that "humanitarian inviolability" rests on the pillars of neutrality and impartiality. In Iraq, however, the UN claimed neutrality but simultaneously engaged in nonneutral actions, thus rendering moot the notion of humanitarian inviolability in the eyes of Iraqis and the terrorists who attacked the UN and occasioning an "intellectual and moral crisis" about the idea of and justification for inviolability (Anderson 2004, 42). He, like others, points out the inconsistency between claiming neutrality to support inviolability and claiming political and nonneutral goals: "The U.N. and international NGOs cannot have it both ways in Iraq—committed to values and yet neutral—as suits their purpose for that moment" (Anderson 2004, 74).

Whether the humanitarian principles ever conferred inviolability on humanitarian actors, however, is open for debate. The principles have not granted the ICRC immunity from attack, despite its steadfast promotion of and adherence to the humanitarian principles. One study demonstrated that certain organizations working on both sides of the conflict (akin to neutrality) experienced a greater degree of risk than those that did not (Fast 2002, 2007). Acts of goodwill, altruistic intentions, and the emblems and symbols of the humanitarian world do not function as magic shields, nor should humanitarian principles provide an automatic pass into the realm of inviolability. Humanitarian principles have value in and of themselves and with respect to their ability to facilitate access to vulnerable populations, regardless of their actual or supposed security benefits. In short, humanitarian principles should be upheld and protected because of their intrinsic value and not with regard to how they may create a more secure operating environment. Clearly, security management must be among an aid agency's priorities, but relying on principles to provide security is not the answer.

Acts of mercy are important in their own right and deserve a literal and metaphorical space apart. While acts of justice cannot and should not be neglected, to judge the effectiveness of humanitarian action based on its contribution to addressing the causes of injustice is to forever condemn it to the realm of the ineffective and disingenuous. Applying metrics of social justice and equality, commensurate with acts of justice, to actions designed only to provide life-sustaining assistance means acts of mercy will always come up short.

Nevertheless, mercy and justice are intimate relatives, and humanitarian actors must be sensitive to the possible unintended consequences of performing acts of mercy without considering their potential for exploitation. In some cases, the ironic effect of humanitarian compassion could be the exacerbation of injustice, the legitimation of questionable actors, or the bolstering of the unjust structures that required the acts of mercy in the first place. It is precisely these effects that cannot be set aside, the integrationists argue, and that have prompted intense discussion among the purists. Most humanitarians are all too aware of the ways in which others manipulate aid and compassion (see, e.g., Donini 2012).

The framing of this debate pits one side against the other, ignoring areas of common concern between the purists and the integrationists. Transcending this debate, therefore, requires a different set of analytical lenses. In this regard, humanitarian actors must indeed be politically savvy, aware of the broader context within which they operate, and self-reflective of the ways in which their actions feed into or interrupt politics as usual. In doing so, they adopt the rudimentary elements of a relational approach, which attributes agency to aid actors and credits them with the ability to define (or at least to influence) how they are perceived. Such an approach sees humanitarians as embedded within, as opposed to separate from, the conflict system and questions the assumptions of exceptionalism even as it affirms the value of humanitarian principles.

Aid: Empire and Rescue

The debate about politics and principles concerns the concept of aid, its definition, and how it is delivered. While both sides in the debate recognize the essential validity of humanitarian action, the competing discourses of empire and rescue challenge and reify, respectively, the aid enterprise. This section, therefore, touches on issues of the power and legitimacy of the aid system, the metanarratives of aid, and the construction of images and discourses within the literature, much of which falls roughly under one vision, empire, or the other, rescue.

Critics of aid, on the one hand, tend to reflexively cast aspersions on aid and its purpose, manifestations, or associations. This discourse portrays the aid system as a Western invention and puppet, blindly carrying out the policies of Western cultural and political empires or as suffering from corruption, mismanagement, or plain incompetence (see Stirrat 2008). The "public, hierarchical, and institutionalized" nature of humanitarian governance manifests certain qualities of empires, such as paternalism, and some members of the enterprise willingly engage in a symbiotic relationship with modern-day empires (Barnett 2011, 8, 221–222). In all these ways, aid is both empire and tool of empire.

On the other hand, the discourse of "aid as good" tends to portray aid and aid workers within the particular narrative structure of the fairy tale (Benthall 1993), constructing a story that features heroes who work within the aid system and externally located villains. The villains are ruthless dictators or power-hungry rebels abusing their people, or corrupt governments exploiting their people and misusing wealth and thereby confining people to poverty and desperation. In this metanarrative, the aid system is beyond blame and aid workers appear as saviors and heroes who, against the odds, rescue the victims of structural or direct, physical violence.

Both views of aid inform implicit and explicit understandings of the causes of violence against aid workers. With a big-picture focus on the overall system of aid, the empire discourse either ignores security issues or exhibits a similar tendency to the politics-and-principle debate and locates causes within the externally generated politicization, militarization, and securitization of the aid system. The rescue discourse, by contrast, construes aid workers and agencies as blameless, thereby bypassing critical analysis and illustrating the power and untouchability (Fassin 2010b) of humanitarianism. Both help to clarify the reasons why internal vulnerabilities remain hidden.

Aid and Empire

Where tales of rescue present a simplistic description of the aid system, the empire discourse is more complex. It depicts the aid system itself as an empire, but also as a tool of empire, often characterizing aid as bad or harmful. In the portrayal of the aid system as itself an empire, pragmatic critiques prevail. They portray aid, particularly development assistance, as inefficient and corrupt and as a means of promoting dependency. The issue of violence against aid workers does not figure in this discourse. In the portrayal of the aid system as a tool of empire, aid is associated with a Western, neocolonial, militarized, or securitized agenda that belies its original goal and is biased toward continuing Western dominance (Donini 2010). As such, it reproduces the same explanations for violence against aid workers and agencies as the politics-and-principles debate.

Both depictions share a fundamental skepticism of aid, its efficacy, and its contributions to addressing basic needs, eliminating poverty, and creating a foundation for sustainable development or sustainable peace. At their extreme, these critiques argue for the abolition of the entire system or, at the least, a fundamental reorientation of the system or industry as it is currently organized. Although my focus and that of much of this literature remain on providing aid in contexts of violence, many of these sources critique the aid system writ large, including the development enterprise.

Indeed, the portrayal of aid as inefficient or counterproductive to its stated aims is a recurrent theme in the literature. Polemics about the aid system abound, often written by former aid workers themselves who gradually become jaded and disillusioned or by journalists observing one emergency response after another (Hancock 1989; Maren 1997; Polman 2010). Other more thoughtful critiques have deconstructed the aid industry, analyzing its shortcomings and offering pathways for reform (e.g., Terry 2002; Bornstein and Redfield 2010; Barnett 2011). Many of these charge that assistance usually only reproduces the very inequalities and injustices aid is supposed to address in the first place, particularly in violent contexts, by feeding into corrupt systems or by undermining existing coping mechanisms (Shawcross 1984, 2000; Harrell-Bond 1986; de Waal 1997, 2005; on development aid, see Crewe and Harrison 1998; Moyo 2009).

Others make a direct link to societal violence. Peter Uvin, for example, in a detailed and pointed critique of development aid in Rwanda prior to the 1994 genocide, argues that "the way *development* was defined, managed, and implemented was a crucial element in the creation and evolution of many of the processes that led to genocide" (Uvin 1998, 3, italics in original). He questions the development enterprise, asserting that its projects and advocates colluded with the structural violence that existed in Rwanda. This structural violence and its processes of inequality, exclusion, and humiliation, together with a pervasive and virulent racism, combined to generate genocide.

These critiques highlight a fundamental paradox inherent in the aid industry: that it is an industry vested in its own existence despite stated goals to "eliminate poverty," thereby ending the need for its services. Meanwhile, the humanitarians who provide life-sustaining assistance simply move from one crisis to the next. The existence of aid organizations and the livelihoods of aid workers, consultants, and contractors all depend on the aid industry itself, placing them in the paradoxical position of working themselves out of an often-lucrative job. In this conception, aid—whether relief or development—represents an empire that is devoted to its own perpetuation, rather than a service industry devoted primarily to the needs of its clients, beneficiaries, or participants. Thus, mercy, compassion, and altruism are indelibly tainted with self-interest.

The critiques of aid that emphasize inefficiency and corruption, therefore, are directed at the system or empire, and question the nature of the system itself and whether reform is even possible. At minimum, they highlight the fundamental paradoxes inherent in the humanitarian empire. Aid workers are professionals and experts, who know what is in the best interests of those they help. This expertise, in turn, creates a physical and emotional distance between the helpers and the helped. It is these characteristics that reek of paternalism and the excesses of empire (Barnett 2011). The distance inherent in the notion of empire and the professionalism of the expert helpers likewise conforms to the exceptionalism narrative.

A different set of critiques concerns the idea of aid as the benevolent yet manipulative tool of empire. In this vision, aid serves a particular agenda as a popular and sometimes-devious puppet manipulated by its master, the West. Western governments, with real and perceived self-interested agendas, finance aid operations, and aid agencies, in turn, are often (rightly or wrongly) associated with these agendas. In the words of one security director, "Humanitarian action is perceived as Western, financed by big states. This makes us potential targets."[40] David Rieff's analysis of Afghanistan exemplifies this perspective and its connection to attacks on aid workers. Rieff wrote,

> After the bombing began, it almost immediately became clear to what degree [the Taliban] associated the NGOs with the great Western powers that financed them. It is not simply that foreign workers from groups like the IRC, Oxfam, MSF, and the others were expelled. Their offices, and those of the UN agencies, were targeted by Taliban fighters in Afghanistan and pro-Taliban mobs in Pakistan. For them, there was no distinction between the Western relief agencies and the U.S.-led coalition that was bombing Afghanistan. (Rieff 2002, 250–251)

The provision of humanitarian, reconstruction, and development assistance in the wake of the "war on terror" and the reconstruction of Iraq and Afghanistan has clearly added significant fuel to this association. In writing about the 2003 Iraq war, Arthur Helton and Gil Loescher reported that Andrew Natsios, the head of the U.S. Agency for International Development (USAID) at the time, indicated that NGOs interested in obtaining funding from the U.S. government "should emphasise their links to the Bush administration" (Helton and Loescher 2003).[41]

This linkage between foreign policy aims and assistance is a recurrent and controversial theme. Former Secretary of State Colin Powell infamously claimed NGOs acted as "force multipliers" for the U.S. military in Iraq, serving as an "important part of our combat team." His statements explicitly linked these sets of actors and their aims (Powell 2001). Nor is this only a President-Bush-era trend. In April 2009, Richard Holbrooke, President Obama's special envoy to Afghanistan and Pakistan, claimed that 90 percent of the American intelligence about Afghanistan came from aid organizations, thereby linking aid organizations and U.S. intelligence-gathering activities (Burns 2009). More recently, the controversy resurfaced with regard to "branding" of assistance with USAID logos, "From the American People," in Pakistan after the 2010 flooding, where incidents of violence against aid workers have been increasing.[42] Such statements and actions in Iraq and Afghanistan undermine the safety and security of NGO and other civilian actors (de Torrenté 2004a).

In this discourse of empire, violence against aid workers and organizations unfolds within the dynamics generated by global trends. Part of this discourse is related to "terrorism" and "counterterrorism" measures and the rise of global terror networks. Humanitarian security concerns, then, become symptomatic of the "culture wars" pitting the (Christian) West versus Islam, ongoing terror and counterterror operations, and the inequalities between North and South that plague our world. Aid workers are attacked because they represent Western/Christian interests and values or because they have more than those around them.[43] These threats gained in prominence and frequency with the wars in Iraq and Afghanistan and their centrality in the American "global war on terror."

In some cases, these terror networks have specifically targeted humanitarian actors, and the UN in particular. News reports from 2007 asserted that the al-Qaeda network placed a price on the lives of both Kofi Annan, the former UN secretary-general, and Lakhdar Brahimi, a former UN special envoy to Iraq and Afghanistan (Lynch 2007; Deen 2008a). Kemal Derviş, former head of the UN Development Programme, reportedly admitted to al-Qaeda threats against the UN in six countries, including Algeria, where a bomb decimated UN headquarters and surrounding buildings in Algiers on 11 December 2007 and killed at least thirty-seven people (Deen 2008b). The investigation into the Algiers bombing revealed a pervasive sense among United Nations personnel that perceptions of a "pro-Western" or "anti-Muslim" agenda hinder their work and threaten their security (Independent Panel 2008).[44]

A related component is the securitization or militarization of aid through the merging of the aid, development, and security agendas. The U.S.-led military interventions in Iraq and Afghanistan in particular have created unprecedented linkages between military and humanitarian actors, especially at the operational/field levels, and the proliferation of private security actors further complicates this equation (see Avant 2005). The Provincial Reconstruction Teams in Afghanistan and Iraq that bring together military and security experts with development workers have been controversial in the humanitarian community for precisely this reason (Agency Coordinating Body for Afghan Relief 2002, 2003a, 2003b; see also Fishstein and Wilder 2011).

On the one hand, military commanders argue the humanitarian and reconstruction activities are crucial to maintaining morale among their troops, winning the "hearts and minds" of the people, and providing "force protection" for military actors.[45] Critics charge that these types of activities blur the lines between humanitarian and military activities, especially when soldiers out of uniform provide assistance (Cater 2002) or when NGOs take advantage of military personnel and equipment to carry out their own programming. Statements by military commanders precisely illustrate the concerns of aid workers. According to now-retired Canadian Lieutenant-General Andrew Leslie,

> It [civil-military cooperation projects] is critical, because by spending money on infrastructure, we show the locals that we are making their lives better. What they care about is security, water, food and shelter. If we can help them with those elements, they will see that we are a positive force, not just another invader. Then, when hostile elements try to kill some of the locals or some of us, perhaps the people we've helped will think twice before letting them. So, it's a force protection issue, as well as a desire to do good. (Department of Foreign Affairs and International Trade 2003)

The general's remarks are yet another example of the kind of statement that contributes to blurred lines between civilians and combatants in conflict zones. Humanitarian and aid actors have reacted with dismay and vehement objections, charging that the increasingly blurred lines between military and civilian actors in conflict zones raise the risk for humanitarians. In a January 2003 policy brief, for example, CARE International in Afghanistan argued that Coalition forces should refrain from engaging in reconstruction activities because it "distracts attention from their security role, risks undermining government capacity, and may put communities and civilian assistance workers at risk" (CARE International 2003). In this, CARE advocated against blurring the lines between military and civilian actors (O'Brien 2004).

In cases where the hardened military targets are difficult to attack, the logic dictates, perpetrators turn to the softer targets that are usually civilian or humanitarian. Furthermore, tainting humanitarian assistance with military objectives—as is the inevitable result of military forces engaging in humanitarian work—challenges the independent and impartial basis of traditional humanitarian assistance. It is not clear, however, to what extent this matters to those who receive assistance. One study of aid in Afghanistan suggested communities cared more what type of assistance they received (and that it came at all) than who—civilians or military forces—provided it (Donini et al. 2005).

On the other hand, aid agencies are adopting more military language and strategies. Aid agencies hire "heads of mission" and work in "operational theaters" or have "operational sections" that carry out "plans of action" (Abu-Sada 2011). Taken to their extreme, protective and deterrent measures result in "bunkerized" agencies whose compounds more closely resemble military fortifications rather than centers providing humanitarian aid. Alternatively, organizations operate by remote management, resulting in "stealth" or "clandestine" operations that provide resources to communities but are without the visible branding that usually accompanies aid projects. Humanitarians critique others, especially military actors, for not respecting humanitarian space, yet in many places NGOs fortify their compounds and appear little or no different from those from whom they attempt to distinguish themselves.

As Alexandre Carle and Hakim Chkam observe in relation to humanitarian actors in Iraq from 2003–2006, "Finding a balance between putting appropriate protection measures in place and giving outsiders the impression that something is being 'hidden' or 'guarded' is not easy.... Those who have opted for visible protection usually also accommodate a deterrence strategy. It must be noted that a high-profile security set-up increases the insecurity of immediate neighbours and antagonizes the population" (Carle and Chkam 2006, 19). Moreover, they point out that NGO security is "militarized" in the detailed reporting of the activities of the Multi-National Force, and "not tailored to the holistic approach to security" that humanitarian actors require (Carle and Chkam 2006, iv, 13–14).

Unfortunately, the militarization of security is not confined to the most dangerous contexts. Mark Duffield refers to the "fortified aid compound" (primarily of the UN) in Sudan and South Sudan as the "defining feature of the architectural peace dividend." These compounds, often grouped together in particular neighborhoods in Juba and Khartoum, resemble the gated communities of the West, with high walls and razor wire to keep out unwanted intruders. The compounds are often self-sustaining, with electricity, water sources, medical supplies, food, fuel, and spare parts stockpiled within compound walls, along with sophisticated telecommunications equipment that maintains the possibility of communication well beyond the borders of the country. Some facilities in the more rural areas offer exercise and leisure activities in addition to housing and dining facilities, much like the self-sustaining bases of foreign militaries. Duffield states, "In considering these structures, it is legitimate to ask what sort of impression they make on the public and, not least, those aid beneficiaries that agencies claim to empower and better" (Duffield 2010, 466, 467). Thus, it is not only military actors that contribute to the porous boundaries that ostensibly separate civilian from military actors; the aid community, through some of its practices and security-management strategies, inadvertently dismantles these boundaries itself.

At a deep level, the increased use of military actors in the provision of assistance and the challenges of providing assistance in the context of ongoing counterterror operations are manifestations of problematic linkages between aid and security (Cortright et al. 2008; Lynch 2011). Duffield critiques this agenda, arguing that it is based on the social exclusion of underdeveloped states and their large populations from the global capitalist system. The aid-and-security agenda that now predominates is premised on a "fear of underdevelopment as a source of conflict, criminalised activity and international instability," which has created a humanitarianism designed to prevent and mitigate violent conflict (Duffield 2001, 7). In other words, the merging of development and security is driven by fear and a need to create boundaries that exclude and keep the unstable, underdeveloped world from infiltrating the "ordered" and stable world. Poverty and violence thus become inextricably intertwined in the public imagination. In embracing a humanitarianism that departs from a singular focus on saving lives and relieving suffering, humanitarians have adopted a social transformation agenda that not only abandons its core principles but also further solidifies existing inequalities. This, in turn, provides a compelling explanation for the violence against aid actors.

The militarization and securitization of aid promotes a world where the compounds sequestering aid actors resemble those of military or private security actors, where relief and development assistance are framed in the service of national security, and where military commanders control billions of dollars destined for relief and development (see DuBois 2011 for an MSF perspective on this issue). In such a world, profit and empire, rather than principles, figure centrally in the provision of mercy. This contrasts with the altruistic motives and principles that have long defined humanitarian acts in the popular imagination.

Aid as Rescue

Since the Biafran War in the late 1960s and especially after the dawn of the "CNN effect," media reports from war zones and of emergency operations have become nearly instantaneous. Humanitarian operations generally rate as newsworthy, since for viewers at home they promote the sense that "something is being done." Relief and development organizations often facilitate media access to their operations and to suffering civilians in war zones; reporters tell the stories of war-affected populations, aid workers, and aid operations. This, in turn, provides free publicity for aid agencies and their work, which often translates into increased donations and support. The close relationships between aid workers and journalists and the common experience of working in war zones has meant that reports of aid worker deaths and injuries capture headlines with increasing frequency. This is true especially when the reporters and the aid workers share common experiences, since such stories offer an immediate connection with the readers and viewers back home.

For the most part, the relationship between aid agencies and the media is symbiotic (Ross 2004). Although most portrayals are sympathetic, not all are uncritical. Some intrepid reporters have uncovered circumstances of mismanagement, abuse, and manipulations of donor trust and funds (see, e.g., *Chicago Tribune* 1998). In general, however, the images in the media reports usually follow the script of the mythical or superhero aid worker who offers succor and empathy or otherwise rescues the victims of disasters and war. In this way, aid workers and their work or sacrifices offer a hopeful counterpoint to the depressing stories of atrocity that dominate the "if it bleeds, it leads" headlines.

In December 1996, for example, six ICRC delegates in Chechnya were shot in the early hours of morning while sleeping in their beds. Newspapers eulogized the dead and carried sensational headlines of aid workers "killed in cold blood" (Reeves and Bellamy 1996) and "slaughtered as they slept"

(Topouria 1996). Other stories referred to the perception of increasing danger, with headlines like "Red Cross Nurses Serve Under a Frail Emblem" (Forbes 1996), "Relief Missions More Risky Than Ever" (Appleby 1996a), and "Relief Workers Losing Their Bystander Status" (Saffron 1997).

The headlines seem to have changed little over time. After the murders of ten staff members of the International Assistance Mission (IAM) in Afghanistan in early August 2010, media stories carried similar headlines: "Slain Aid Workers Were Bound by Their Sacrifice" (Dewan and Nordland 2010) and "Dead Aid Workers Knew Risks but Loved Afghanistan" (CNN Wire Staff 2010). The executive director of the IAM, Dirk Frans, refuted the idea that the team members were "saints," highlighting instead their dedication as "selfless professionals willing to spend their lives and energy in a meaningful way" (International Assistance Mission 2010a).

This relationship between the two—media and aid—magnifies the power of the media and aid organizations in determining which stories get told, how they are told, and who appears as victim or as victimizer. In his book about disasters and the media, Jonathan Benthall deconstructs the images and narratives put forward in news reports and television stories in particular. Benthall's analysis does not aim for cynicism. Instead, he writes, "The agencies depend on the representations to publicize both the need and the relief. . . . When one wants to tell a story, it is hard to avoid certain stylistic constraints. The listener needs a way into the story" (Benthall 1993, 190).

Although his analysis is twenty years old, the story lines of today share the same basic structure. Many of these narratives, he asserts, follow the basic formula of a fairy tale. Fairy tales are stories of good versus evil in which heroes and villains battle for supremacy. The heroes, aided by "magical helpers" or "magical objects," triumph in the end, though not without adversity, and the story finishes with a moral or lesson. Drawing on Vladimir Propp's classic deconstruction of the *Morphology of the Folktale* (Propp 1968), Benthall describes the cast of characters in the predominant disaster narrative. The main characters are the "traveling hero" (the aid worker) and the "villain" (the despots and warlords who oppress their people). In those cases in which a villain is absent, a "dispatcher" notices the bleak conditions that give rise to the need for relief assistance. The "donor" provides the "magical agent" or "helper" that proves indispensable in allowing the hero to triumph, in this case, Benthall proposes, Western abundance and technology. The "false heroes" are the imposters who set up fake charities, the incompetents who send expired medicines or inappropriate donations to disaster zones (e.g., high-heeled shoes to women in refugee camps or winter boots to tsunami victims in tropical climates), or the corrupt officials who siphon off assistance destined for the needy.

The final character is the "princess," a "person of rank and/or charisma who intervenes and rewards" (Benthall 1993, 189). In the early 1990s, Princess Anne, then the president of Save the Children–UK, served as a real and figurative princess. Obvious modern-day equivalents are movie stars like Angelina Jolie, George Clooney, and Don Cheadle; opinion leaders and activists like Wangari Maathai and Jane Goodall; and artists and writers like Bono, Yo-Yo Ma, and Paulo Coelho, who advocate for various issues and causes.[46] Together these characters provide a familiar and predictable narrative that engages and draws in the consumer of the media report.

The images that many aid agencies use in their publicity and advertising are another element of the depiction of aid as rescue. Denis Kennedy examines the "faces" of the aid industry, quite often homeless refugees, starving children, or helpless mothers, and the ethical implications of the ways in which these images are used to "produce and disseminate images of human suffering" (Kennedy 2009). He argues that the images that aid agencies use in their fund-raising campaigns function to "bridge the distance" between giver and receiver, thereby encouraging individual donors and solidifying independence from institutional donors and priorities. Yet, he asserts, "fundraising images evoke and reproduce in unique ways what has been called the 'humanitarian narrative': helpless victims are confronted by localized problems to which only the aid organization in question can respond. Images thus reflect both the perceived identity of the victim, and also the heroic and action-oriented self-conceptions of humanitarian organizations" (Kennedy 2009). The images used in fund-raising drives frequently endow victims with needs but an inability to act, thus depriving them of voice and their essential dignity as human beings (see also Hyndman 2000). These images and the narrative they promote, therefore, play into the rescue discourse, allowing humanitarian agencies to enter the scene as heroes out to help the needy victims in a predictable story line. In this way, the mythical aid worker is projected to a systemic level, with aid agencies serving as the mythical heroic agents.

The implications of aid-as-rescue in relation to security are twofold. First, this discourse endows the aid agencies (and aid workers) that function as heroes in the story with virtually unchallenged ethical and moral legitimacy. They are doing good, acting as underdogs in standing up against the villains and the powerful and advocating for and serving the vulnerable. In the simplistic world of the fairy tale, they can do no wrong precisely because they are the heroes. To depict them in all their complexity would tarnish the reputation of the hero and detract from the story. The result? Since rescuers cannot be in any way responsible for the tragedies that may befall them, they achieve near mythical status in the public imagination. Thus, the way the story is told creates and bestows power and legitimacy.

The rescue story is a familiar one and, as Benthall argues, gives listeners immediate entry into and identification with the story. In this rendering, the legitimacy of aid agencies derives from where they work (war zones), the context in which they work (self-sacrifice to help others in very difficult conditions), what they do (good), and whom they help (the most vulnerable). The founding stories of aid agencies add to this powerful elixir, endowing organizations with grassroots connections and altruistic motivations.[47] Aid agencies benefit from this message, as it serves to bolster their appeal and provides a degree of immunity from criticism. It also elevates concerns about reputational risk and ensures that the consequences of a fall from grace, if or when it happens, are even more disastrous.

Second, aid-as-rescue facilitates a simplistic understanding of the causes of both violent conflict and violence against aid workers. The discourse is uncomplicated, drawing the world in categories of good and evil, black and white, with no shades of gray. It promotes a simplistic understanding of the causes of violence that disavows the complex reality of providing assistance in the midst of conflict or disaster. Furthermore, the victims in the story are its driving force, yet they have no substantive role. They are "other." They fade into the background, becoming nameless and faceless characters in the story. The central protagonists in the story are the heroes, followed by the villains, donors, and princesses, with little attention to the deindividualized victims who are in need of assistance (see also Fechter 2012).

In categorizing people as innocent (e.g., aid workers providing lifesaving assistance) or guilty (e.g., those committing violence against aid workers or innocent civilians), these stories make implicit moral judgments about blame and responsibility. These judgments conform to the morality-play narratives of violence that Gilligan (2000) disparages for their power to impede understanding. It is more difficult to blame the "donors" (the Western public) or those sent to help (the aid workers) than it is to blame the perpetrators/villains with power and guns (governments and armed insurgents) or even the nameless and faceless victims of violence (the war-affected populations) for any shortcomings or failures in the story. As consumers of the rescue discourse, readers want to blame the "guilty" rather than recognize an ambiguity that may expand their categories and assumptions.

Yet it is precisely these "innocent and valiant" aid workers who bear the burden of the collective response. These protagonists act in "our" name. Indeed, humanitarian action relieves the moral conflict and discomfort that those of us sitting on the couches feel when watching all-too-frequent television reports about violence, starvation, and famine in far-off places. For the privileged, it is comforting to donate money to assuage guilty consciences about the bad things that happen to other people. Jenny Edkins powerfully illustrates this notion using a 1994 cartoon titled "International Community" by Steve Bell.[48] In the image, a figure in a darkened room cradles a brightened television set that pictures a curled-up, obviously lifeless figure on a roadside. Of the cartoon, she writes, "We are watching, helpless to prevent, yet implicated. Not only are we unable to stop the tragedy, we are unable to comfort its victims" (Edkins 2000, 115). In general, people do not want to blame or attribute any kind of responsibility to those who assuage our collective conscience about not doing more to mitigate the suffering of others. This discourse perpetuates simplistic explanations that avoid consideration of any factors that might lay a semblance of responsibility at the feet of the heroes.

Conclusion

The competing discourses of politics and principles share the assumption that humanitarian aid is legitimate and generally positive, even as the extremes diverge on whether a broad-and-integrated or a narrow-and-principled interpretation of humanitarian action is more effective. The empire and rescue visions differ on this issue, with the former questioning aid's essential contribution to society and the latter uncritically accepting the aid discourse. In their various guises, the debates about principles and politics, on the one hand, and about the metanarratives of empire building and heroic rescue, on the other, have dominated the literature about humanitarianism for more than two decades. These debates have constituted the primary vehicle through which the causes of violence against aid workers are transported into the public sphere, defining the parameters of the conversation and rendering silent any discussion of internal vulnerabilities.

Underlying these prevailing explanations of the causes of violence against aid workers is the assumption that the politicization, militarization, and securitization of aid are the primary and appropriate frameworks of analysis. A view of aid as bad or evil is more apt to place blame on the flaws in the system, the inappropriateness of the aid, the incompetency or greed of those within the system, or the conflicts within the system. These flaws become sensationalized, in contrast to the view of aid as good, which shifts responsibility and blame to external causes. The alternative is to ignore the issue almost entirely. All points of view work to preserve the logic of exceptionalism.

Interpreting the causes of the violence that aid workers face through the lens of the instrumentalized nature of assistance perpetuates the public silence surrounding those causal explanations located in organizational dynamics or the individual actions of aid workers. Nor do these conventional discourses provide an explanatory model that views "macro" (the external environment) and "micro" (the internal dynamics of aid workers and the aid community) realities as interdependent. In short, the discourses of aid in this chapter present only one entry point for examining the causes of violence. A systemic perspective, by contrast, accounts theoretically for the full range of interdependent causes and helps to restore agency to aid actors in ways that allow them to help shape their own destinies.

CHAPTER 5

Explanations in the Shadows: Competing Images of Aid

In September 2000, three aid workers were killed in West Timor, Indonesia. An email sent by one of them, Carlos Caseres, just hours before he died, circulated over the Internet.

> I was in the office when the news came out that a wave of violence would soon pound Atambua. We sent most of the staff home, rushing to safety. I just heard someone on the radio saying that they are praying for us in the office. The militias are on the way, and I am sure they will do their best to demolish this office. The man killed was the head of one of the most notorious and criminal militia groups of East Timor. These guys act without thinking and can kill a human as easily (and painlessly) as I kill mosquitoes in my room.
>
> You should see this office. Plywood on the windows, staff peering out through openings in the curtains hastily installed a few minutes ago. We are waiting for this enemy, we sit here like bait, unarmed, waiting for the wave to hit. I am glad to be leaving this island for three weeks. I just hope I will be able to leave tomorrow.[1]

The email evokes a helplessness in the face of imminent, passion-provoked violence. Yet the deeply personal tone of the email serves as a reminder of the very human faces behind security incidents and the hazards and anonymity of relying solely on statistics to capture the essence of the problem. The aid world is a small community, and most aid workers have either experienced acts of violence themselves or know friends and colleagues who have.

Underlying the essence of the problem, however, are complex definitional issues of who is an aid worker and who are the institutional players involved in providing assistance. These definitional debates pepper the literature and mask an implicit struggle between competing images of aid actors. By deconstructing and demystifying aid workers and agencies, this chapter exposes the public silence surrounding the role of individual and organizational actions in security incidents and discusses how images of the personalities and institutions involved frame conceptualizations of the causes of violence against aid workers and aid delivery. This exposure challenges the dominant discourse of external threat and the concept of humanitarian exceptionalism and is integral to a relational analysis of the aid system that interprets violence against aid workers within the context of the protection of civilians.

Aid workers are both mythologized and ordinary, creating competing images of *mythical figures* and *ordinary people*. Similarly, aid agencies emerge from an *informal and idealized past* that has given way to an *institutionalized and professionalized present*, both time-bound images of what aid agencies should be. These conceptualizations, in turn, shape responses to the violence. Like the aid discourses of the previous chapter, none of these four "images" is mutually exclusive nor exclusively held. The images are archetypes, rooted in but not entirely reflective of reality. Two of these images (the mythical aid worker and the informal-and-idealized past) reinforce one another, and all four follow an evolution of the field over time. These caricatured images linger in the collective public imagination, as well as in the self-perceptions of the aid community itself. More important, the images complete the pictures of violence that remain absent from the public discourse about violence against aid workers, serving as heuristic devices that render the invisible visible.

This chapter first examines questions of who aid workers are and what motivates them to do this work, paying particular attention to how competing images of aid workers as mythical figures and ordinary people inform security issues. As heroic or self-serving figures, they either are devoid of responsibility or are to blame for what befalls them. Recognizing aid workers as ordinary people, however, endows them with agency and their actions with a complexity missing from other conceptualizations. The chapter then shows how the identities and characteristics of aid institutions are constituted through contrasting images of an informal and idealized past on the one hand, and an institutional and professionalized present on the other. In this discussion, I give particular attention to the ways in which organizational decisions, profiles, and programs, as shaped by these images, create vulnerabilities and security risks. By this analysis, I demonstrate the complexity and diversity of the humanitarian identity and institutions that actually shape views of the causes of violence against aid workers and what to do about them. In contrast to the discourses discussed in the previous chapter, the explanations of the causes of violence against aid workers and agencies that emerge from these images inhabit the private sphere, thereby remaining implicit or ignored. Emphasizing only these elements, however, privileges responses that serve to blame the victim or promote an inflexible bureaucracy, both of which ignore the crucial role of external context. Nevertheless, these images are central dimensions of the analytical framework that unmasks the role of individuals and institutions in order to understand the causes of violence.

In short, the chapter showcases the factors in the shadows that contribute to security incidents, demonstrating the role of internal vulnerabilities in a relational analysis and rounding out our collective understanding of the causes of the dangers that aid workers face.

Aid Workers: Mythical Figures or Ordinary People?

Contrasting images of aid workers are apparent in the stereotypical portrayals of their personal characteristics and the work they do. In the eyes of the Western public, aid workers are saints or altruistic heroes who risk life and limb to help others (and in the process, assuage the guilt of consumption-driven Westerners); they are modern-day Florence Nightingales, who forgo the privileges and comforts of home to serve others. From the perspective of critics, however, aid workers are self-serving neocolonialists who profit from the misery of the poor and vulnerable; they are thus deserving of the excoriating critiques the aid system often engenders. Stories with titles such as "Lives of the Saints" (Harr 2009) describe in vivid detail the characters in the drama: the "missionaries" compelled to help the less fortunate; the "madmen" and adrenaline junkies who shrug off or even solicit danger and quip that it is part of the job; and the "mercenary" characters, drawn by the lure of tax-free salaries with perks and hardship pay for the most dangerous locations. Aid workers themselves use similar labels: martyrs, misfits, and masochists (Smith et al. 1996, 398).

Like all images, these labels carry some basis in reality. Roderick Stirrat, an anthropologist, characterizes "mercenaries" as the development professionals and consultants, motivated by money and working for the better-paid international financial institutions and official governmental development agencies (such as the U.S. Agency for International Development or the UK Department for International Development). "Missionaries" refers to NGO workers, motivated by duty and obligation, and closer to the "real world" of the "grassroots." Stirrat argues these groups are similar in practice and goals, sharing a "common commitment and common goal: to produce the modern person in their own image" (Stirrat 2008, 416). These potent self-images, moreover, reflect the characterizations of the colonial administrators (now the "mercenaries") and missionaries (who remain "missionaries," though of the mostly secular NGO world) of the nineteenth and early twentieth centuries, who likewise shared common goals of modernizing and remaking, often through variations of a conversion experience, those they encountered. The "misfits," in contrast, are those who do not fit into their cultural milieu. They have been transformed by their experiences living and working abroad and have carved out distinct niches in their adopted countries that make it difficult to acculturate to life "back home." Underlying these characterizations are assumptions about motives and actions that, in turn, influence conceptualizations of the causes of violence against them.

Mythical Figures

The characterizations of aid workers are marked by a spectrum that plays purity of character against greed and unrealistic expectations against incompetence. At one end of the spectrum sits an image of the superhuman, mythical, saintly figure who travels to hot, dirty, and desperately poor places to work with the downtrodden and underprivileged. As early as 1990, Susan George profiled the "superhuman" aid worker:

> First they must take graduate degrees in social anthropology, geography, economics, a dozen or so difficult and unrelated languages, medicine and business administration. Second, at a slightly more practical level they must demonstrate competence in agronomy, hydrology, practical nursing, accounting, psychology, automotive mechanics and civil engineering. In addition, they must learn to give a credible imitation of saintliness and it would be well, if they could learn sleight-of-hand as well, since they will often be called upon to perform feats of magic. (George, as quoted in Slim 1995a, 110)[2]

Hugo Slim, calling for a reappraisal, asserted that the protective sheen of saintliness had faded, forcing relief workers to become instead "moral philosophers" who constantly make and remake ethical decisions about neutrality, solidarity, and the like. This reappraisal attributed new skill sets to the aid worker, such as conflict resolution, negotiation, human rights monitoring, media savvy, and country-specialist knowledge. Furthermore, Slim emphasized the importance of relationships with the local community, arguing that the defining characteristic of "good humanitarian practice must be the *depth* of commitment to and understanding of the communities with which they work" (Slim 1995a, 124). A more recent survey of aid workers identified a series of competencies focused on knowing one's strengths (resilience, integrity, time management, self-awareness), working with others (leadership, trust building, teamwork), and achieving results (problem solving, needs assessment, financial management) (Walker and Russ 2010, 34–38).

The attributes-based image affirms the fortitude required by living and working in situations of disaster and war. Many humanitarians exist in extremis, often working long hours and without adequate resources to respond to the overwhelming needs of those they encounter. They witness the neglect and brutality as well as the grace and care that human beings exhibit toward one another. They acknowledge that whatever they might be able to provide is likely not enough. Indeed, working in these conditions "does require that workers develop an emotional style of managing danger, witnessing unfair allocation of life-sustaining resources, and coping with both the admirable and distasteful behavior of the refugees, fellow relief workers, or themselves" (Smith et al. 1996, 398).

Even so, the work offers emotional rewards not available in many other professions. These rewards are often tied to what Michael Barnett terms humanitarianism's "transcendental significance" that manifests in the concept of humanity in particular. While noting the religious foundations of humanitarianism, he claims that "for many who staff secular agencies, humanitarianism is a way of both expressing and bringing into existence an international community" (Barnett 2011, 20).

Far less flattering portraits emphasizing greed and incompetence stand in stark contrast to the sympathetic portrayal of aid workers. At the core of these portraits are the discrepancies in wealth and privilege and the culture clashes that emerge when the aid world encounters "beneficiaries" and nonrecipients alike. While many shun the neocolonial image of the mercenaries and missionaries that Stirrat evokes, it lurks in the shadows of expatriate privilege.

"People think, 'I'm doing the humanitarian thing,'" remarked one aid expert, "but they are getting an international salary with perks, can be lifted out at a moment's notice, and take leaves back home. It is semicolonial."[3] The perks, which conjure up a colonial legacy, are both shunned and celebrated. For example, a poster advertising a gathering of expatriates in Kabul, Afghanistan, to commemorate the 2008 U.S. election featured "Flashy," a fictional character from a series of novels.[4] The poster for "Flashy's Bonfire Night" echoes nineteenth-century British colonial sensibilities, in which Flashman appears as a stalwart and smirking soldier wearing a blue uniform and lightly holding the hilt of his sword by his side. Sitting submissively on the floor and clinging to his lower leg is an exotic and scantily clad woman who looks as though she stepped out of a harem. Such images are offensive in many contexts, and especially so for the insensitivities they display in a Muslim country such as Afghanistan. The image harkens back to the colonial era, with an implicit reminder of its association with foreign occupation, domination, and privilege.

The perks of the aid world, set in contexts of poverty and scarcity, stand out. In the eyes of the poor recipients of humanitarian largesse, the expensive four-by-four vehicles with clunky antennas that mark the enterprise and the large houses foreign aid workers usually occupy are signs of the wealth and privilege of the humanitarian enterprise, wealth that shortchanges and passes them by. The vehicles and other trappings convey status and power. According to one security director in an African country, "We changed the vehicles we were driving because of the type of vehicles targeted. We took away the four-wheel drives. It was a status issue."[5] One writer focusing on security and the United Nations goes so far as to suggest, "Some United Nations personnel are now targeted simply because they work for the Organization. In some poor States, the United Nations is viewed as representing a superior economic class. This generates animosity among some local inhabitants and serves to justify in their minds taking United Nations property or attacking its personnel" (Arsanjani 1995, 118). Another author notes the "misleading expectations" that NGO involvement in a country often provokes:

> NGO workers, especially in capital cities, live like ministers or militia leaders: travelling in private vehicles, drinking in designated bars, eating special food, living in guarded houses, shopping in exclusive shops and establishing separate security procedures. These indicators of wealth and power are more visible to people in host countries than

caveats in texts about participation that they never see. The privilege NGO workers display reflects their position in the global economy, not the impact their assistance makes, and accepting benefits while denying responsibility creates tension in their relations with other people. (Marriage 2006, 222)

In contrast, the beneficiaries receive often-meager rations of humanitarian aid because the need is greater than the resources or live in tent cities with makeshift walls and roofs while awaiting more permanent shelter. The disparities in the access to resources and living conditions of aid workers and those they serve, and between the salaries and lifestyles of many national and international staff, crystallize an image of the "humanitarian international"—the "cosmopolitan elite of relief workers, officials of donor agencies, consultant academics and the like, and the institutions for which they work" as well as "journalists and editors who faithfully propagate the humanitarian worldview" (de Waal 1997, 4)—who profits from the misery of the poor.[6]

For communities seeking to improve their situations, the arrival, needs assessments, promises, and eventual departure of aid agencies occur with and sometimes without concrete improvements or programs. This reality signifies yet another way in which the rich of the world have failed their poor neighbors and may help to create the conditions for security incidents (Fast, Freeman, et al. 2011). Such impressions led the Afghan Minister of Planning, Bashar Dost, in March 2004 to publicly accuse NGOs and aid agencies of not doing anything to help the Afghan people and instead of using foreign aid for themselves. Dost charged, "I have yet to see an NGO that has spent 80 per cent of its money for the benefit of the Afghans and 20 percent for their own benefit. International NGOs get big amounts of money from their own nations just by showing them sensitive pictures and videos of Afghan people, and there are even some individuals who give all their salaries to NGOs to spend it on charity here, but [NGOs] spend all the money on themselves, and we are unable to find out how much money they originally received in charitable funds" (as quoted in Saeed 2004). Dost's critique must be interpreted in light of the politically charged atmosphere of foreign aid in Afghanistan and his desire to appeal to a domestic audience sympathetic to his assessment. It nevertheless conveys a sense of frustration with the inequalities and corruption that plagues some, though not all, aid projects.

The culture clash between aid workers and local populations often revolves around more and less permissive attitudes toward alcohol, sex, and gender roles, and how this positively and negatively shapes perceptions of aid workers. For devout Muslims and others, for example, the parties and socializing that draw the expatriate communities out of their compounds at night and on weekends reflect the excesses and moral vacuity of Western culture. Adding insult to injury, many of these soirées involve consuming copious amounts of alcohol in a bid to let off steam. One aid worker related the following example from Afghanistan: "Someone sent out an email that indicated that the aid community should be careful about loud parties. The assumption was that we'll have loud parties, and focused on how to hide this as opposed to the other way around—that we shouldn't have loud parties; that drinking, dancing, mixing the sexes is an appalling infraction in the eyes of many Afghans. They didn't get that this could cause resentment."[7] Noting that weekends are often a security manager's busiest times, one security director lamented, "Unfortunately a high number of security incidents seem to happen Friday night, and Saturday and Sunday morning."[8]

A 2009 documentary film featuring Médecins Sans Frontières workers in West Africa shows the medical team decompressing after a tough stretch of intense and difficult work and intrateam conflict by drinking and dancing in a hazy bar. The scene ends, leaving what happens next to the viewer's imagination. In reflecting on the evening, one doctor remarks the next morning, "I think it is having death all around us that makes us crave sex so much" (Hopkins 2009). Sex, in this instance, serves as a tangible reminder of life and its perpetuation, and as a coping mechanism against the death and destruction that often fill the team's days.

In other instances, the dangerous combination of power and scarcity easily leads to exploitation. A particularly explosive United Nations High Commissioner for Refugees and Save the Children report documented a pattern of abuse and sexual exploitation among aid workers and peacekeepers in West Africa. Refugee children reported that dozens of perpetrators—aid workers and peacekeepers—traded food, soap, medicine, and small amounts of money for sex (UN Office of Internal Oversight Services 2002).[9] Accusations of sexual exploitation have plagued UN peacekeeping missions in the Democratic Republic of Congo and Haiti as well.[10] Other aid workers are tempted by greed and the lure of easy money. One anthropologist's inquiry into shadow economies documents an incident of aid workers "carrying rocks," a reference to smuggling diamonds (Nordstrom 2004, 120–121). These public and other undocumented stories constitute the seedy underbelly of aid work, revealing the questionable and sometimes unethical behavior of aid workers and lending credence to critiques of the aid system as exploitative and predatory.

Other "offences" are less egregious but still not without effect. Even the seemingly innocuous issue of clothing can result in a culture clash. How aid workers, particularly women, dress and whether their clothing either corresponds to or offends cultural mores lies at the junction of gender and culture. For many, the motto is to dress like the locals. More modest dress, covering arms and legs, not only protects against sun exposure and insect bites but also avoids offending local sensibilities about exposing too much skin. Referring to Central Africa, one security director observed, "Some of us don't behave well. For example, women go without headscarves or dresses. There is a lack of sensitivity and appreciation for other cultures."[11] A female aid worker's choice to wear a headscarf in a Muslim country likewise demonstrates respect for the religious traditions of her host country. For other women, the choice to cover up in such a way violates deeply held beliefs about gender roles or implies submissiveness. Sleeveless shirts and short skirts might simply function as a way to stay cool in a hot climate, even though the choice not to respect local dress habits risks offending community members and leaders.

The actions and behaviors of aid workers in the office or at other points of contact can influence community members' impressions of them. In many instances, these choices and actions have security implications. Treating others in the office (from cleaners, maintenance staff, secretaries, and assistants to senior staff) with respect positively affects such impressions, just as acting out of arrogance, often linked to privilege, can lead to negative impressions. In South Sudan, one aid worker pointed out that national staff serve as important reputational interlocutors for aid agencies and that how they are treated affects their family and friends' favorable or unfavorable perceptions of their employing agency (Fast, Patterson, et al. 2011, 5). In many countries, Afghanistan and South Sudan among others, local populations have frequently complained about the dangerous and aggressive driving habits of foreigners, including aid workers and private security companies (Donini et al. 2005; Fast, Patterson, et al. 2011). NGO security directors acknowledge driving habits and incidents as significant security issues.[12]

Obviously each of these extremes—aid workers as mythical heroes or cosmopolitan and exploitative elites—contains nuggets of truth. Yet the reality is far more perspicuous: aid workers typically are ordinary people.

Ordinary People

Though often living in "exotic" locales, expatriate aid workers also live ordinary lives; they too go to work, raise families, and socialize with friends and neighbors. Their blogs describe the boredom, excesses, moral quandaries, and trivialities of daily life. Some offer insightful commentaries and analysis of the dilemmas of aid work or the vagaries of place. Others weave together the professional and personal, indicating the ways in which their public (i.e., work) and private lives are interwoven; they describe relationships, often with coworkers, and social occasions in anonymous detail. Some portray life as a kind of soap opera, thereby (inadvertently) feeding the perception of aid work as a world of excess and privilege.[13] The anonymity of many of the revelatory blogs enables the bloggers to take the private into the public realm while minimizing the negative repercussions for careers and reputations. Thus, although the blogs may expose the silenced factors that sometimes contribute to security incidents, rarely do they connect these to risk or to security management.

One's perspective about aid workers is undoubtedly influenced by one's billing as bystander, provider, or recipient of assistance. In a post about watching an interaction at an airport between a tourist and two aid workers wearing T-shirts imprinted with a relief agency logo—a story often repeated in airports around the Western world—one blogger wrote of his struggle to figure out why the tourist's affirmative reaction bothered him. The aid workers were returning to the United States from work in Haiti, after the January 2010 earthquake, and the tourist gushed praises, thanking them for the "wonderful thing they've done." The blogger wrote, "Our work makes a difference. But as people we're just as selfish and self-centered, ruthless, hardhearted, sometimes even as shallow and vane [sic], as *human* as anyone else. We're all broken. And we're definitely not noble" (Tales from the Hood 2010).

In reality, aid work is populated by all kinds: the thrill seekers, risk takers, and those who "go native," the naïve and the greedy, the idealistic and those out to take advantage, those who consider the work a calling or vocation, and others who think of it merely as a job, albeit a sometimes exciting one. Some are contracted or salaried and still others volunteer. Aid work has become a viable career path. Many are drawn to the work out of a sense of moral or ethical responsibility (the missionaries and martyrs), a sense of adventure (the madmen, misfits, or adrenaline junkies), the privilege and salaries that often accompany such work (the mercenaries), or some combination of the three. Some observers characterize aid workers, especially the expatriates, as "runners" escaping something or someone back home, or "seekers" of adventure and a sense of purpose (Harr 2009). As such, aid workers exhibit the altruism and good intentions of people wanting to help others, the adventure seekers drawn to a socially sanctioned and publicly admired adrenaline rush, and the disaster tourists gawking at or taking advantage of the downtrodden. In short, aid workers represent all types of people, from the extraordinary to the ordinary, and each with very human foibles and eccentricities.

The work itself is clearly enticing enough to attract and employ individuals in the tens of thousands.[14] Although the dominant (media) image of an aid worker is a white expatriate, the term "international staff" increasingly includes the Filipino working in Sudan, or the Kenyan working in Timor-Leste. Many expatriates—international staff hired abroad—are young, often relatively inexperienced, and idealistic, although mythical cowboys and experienced "old hands" still bounce from emergency to emergency and from agency to agency.

Most important, the vast majority of aid workers are "national" staff. The term refers to staff hired locally or within the country who are citizens, residents, or internally displaced persons of the countries in which they work. They are sometimes refugees from neighboring countries. Within some agencies, especially those with a development mandate, 90 percent or more of staff members are national staff. This preponderance of national staff is one of the more visible shifts in aid work over the past ten to twenty years, as agencies hire and promote staff either within a country or from the region. Thus, the image of the white, Western aid worker is no longer the true face of aid work.

In emergency contexts and specialist organizations, however, the proportion of international to national staff tends to be higher. The sudden onset of natural disasters and the dramatic escalations in violence create demand for quick deployment, which can translate into shortcuts in the pre-deployment training, orientation, and screening of staff.[15] Furthermore, it is often difficult to recruit qualified individuals for emergency situations, leaving vacant positions. One aid worker linked this to security issues: "Lack of staff is a security issue. Not filling a position is a security issue. If there aren't enough staff, security falls through the cracks. It took us eight months to recruit a security focal point. He was ex-army, and quit after two months."[16]

Another veteran aid worker pointed out that more operations require more staff, which has resulted in a corresponding decrease in the average age of aid workers. The younger staff "have less experience and are less realistic. They are goal-oriented but don't understand the context in which they operate." As for the older ones with more field experience, "they think 'I know everything.' There is complacency there."[17] One aid worker remarked, "There are mission junkies, who go anywhere and think, we've been through this before. They are desensitized so much [to danger] that they become a greater risk to themselves and others than the 'newbies.'"[18] Each creates corresponding security vulnerabilities.

Deployment in the riskiest countries, moreover, is often part and parcel of the expatriate humanitarian career path. The résumés of the most experienced read like laundry lists of disaster zones. One aid expert commented, "Some say part of the job is risk, but that you don't have to go to Somalia. But if you want a career out of it, you may need to go to Somalia."[19]

Somewhat surprisingly, very little research exists on the biographies or "life histories" of aid workers, although this is changing (Fechter and Hindman 2011; Bergman 2003). One qualitative study of forty-four aid workers traces three paths to aid work: the path of those whose interest stemmed from childhood and a desire to help others, of those whose gradual involvement occurred after exposure to poverty or disaster (personal or political) of some kind, and of those who turned to the profession after a "turning point or epiphany" of some kind.[20] The strong desire and tendency to want to help those less fortunate exists for both international/expatriate staff and national staff, despite the varied professional profiles of aid workers. Roth (2009, 9; 2011) notes that "while the respondents in the North tended to get involved after an illness, accident or break-up of a relationship, respondents from the South got involved after a political conflict in their country." The caricatures of the martyrs and seekers, it appears, hold some basis in reality, for both international and national staff.

The Stress of Aid Work and Its Security Implications

Regardless of aid workers' motivations for engaging in the profession, their work is taxing, both physically and emotionally, and even demoralizing, as they are often forced to decide who is most in need of assistance in the face of limited and finite human, material, and financial resources. The accumulation of everyday stressors, of trauma resulting from acute crisis, and of the various coping mechanisms aid workers employ is linked to security. The burnout rates of such demanding work are high, as are the psychological costs that result from aid workers' high-stress jobs and lifestyle (Cardozo and Salama 2002; Ehrenreich and Elliott 2004; McFarlane 2004).[21] Experts have long recognized the transfer of trauma and its psychological effects to counselors, therapists, and others in the helping professions. Psychologists refer to this as "countertransference" or vicarious or secondary traumatization.

Yet aid workers not only are at risk for vicarious trauma, many are traumatized themselves. The mental health repercussions of the violence that aid workers experience or witness can be dramatic. One retrospective study of posttraumatic stress disorder (PTSD) symptoms among 113 aid workers returned from the field found that 10 percent exhibited the full diagnostic criteria for PTSD and a further 19 percent reported symptoms in two or more diagnostic categories (Erikksson et al. 2001).

While the acute stress that results from the effect of safety or security incidents is more obvious, the sources of psychological distress are chronic as well. The stress accumulates over time and is rooted in the pressures of the job and the inherent moral dilemmas of aid work. Chronic stress affects judgment, which in turn can create vulnerabilities that may lead to security incidents. One aid expert observed that "most of the security incidents I have seen happen in offices where pressures are high. People are internally focused on programming issues, funding constraints, office politics as opposed to externally focused. They forget to look outside at the threats that exist."[22]

Ruth Barron refers to aid workers as "worker-victims," noting the tension between care for self and care for others. She writes, "With all the obvious victimization around them, worker-victims typically do not feel entitled to attend to or have others attend to their own needs" (Barron 1999, 156). Clearly, it is necessary to care for oneself in order to effectively care for others, but this may be perceived as hoarding resources or energy or receiving special treatment. Such exceptionalism—the aid worker as distinct and apart and the "weakness" of those not able to cope adequately—generates unease. It is implicitly rooted in a recognition of privilege, which manifests in the discomfort related to the parallel structures and resources for aid workers that separate them from the populations they help. Being seen as able to cope with whatever happens is paramount, and not being able to "take it" is equated with weakness, be it weakness of character, resolve, or commitment.

Inevitably, aid workers must live with the inescapable contradiction of participating in and simultaneously denouncing the "unfairness" of the allocation of resources. Barbara Smith and her colleagues observe that "relief workers generally reserve adequate supplies to sustain themselves and do not give the victims anything close to 'the shirts off their backs'" (Smith et al. 1996, 399). Care of self is necessary for them to carry out their work, but the moral dilemma this invokes induces guilt, since they often have resources or access to resources but never enough for all. Ironically, "It is people who maintain their own health who can look out of place and as if they do not care about the suffering around them," Smith and colleagues write, "because they are not joining in the self-destructive behaviors" (Smith et al. 1996, 414).

National and international aid workers face different stresses and security concerns, which change according to gender, age, and even marital status. National staff face unique security challenges owing to their social, economic, and political ties to the places in which they work.[23] For them the effects of natural disasters or war are intensely personal; it is they and their families, neighbors, and friends who directly experience the violence or lose their belongings and livelihoods in floods and earthquakes. In Haiti, for instance, many aid agencies lost staff members in the 2010 earthquake. Of those who survived, many had harrowing tales of escape or lost family members, friends, or colleagues in the disaster. In an emergency situation, these losses and their emotional toll add to the already high stress of an emergency response. As staff of agencies that enjoy a certain degree of influence and wealth in a country, national staff often serve as the first point of contact and are most exposed to those who wish to exploit this influence and wealth. Equally, the vulnerabilities of national staff resulting from a lack of social support networks or the different standards of conduct they experience when they move from one region of the country to another are easily overlooked (Rowley et al. 2011; Fast, Freeman, et al. 2011; Siddique and Ahmad 2012). For example, the location of headquarters, field offices, or jobs within an organization may force national staff to move from their home regions to another part of the country, dislocating their families or separating them from family and social support. For women, especially, finding suitable living accommodations can prove challenging.

One study of the personal and professional stresses and problems for national staff in Bangladesh chronicles the difficulties of accommodation, training and promotion, and financial hardships, among others. The study discusses poor salaries for national staff and the dearth of opportunities for additional training or promotion (Ahmad 2002). While their status as national staff gives them insider knowledge of the cultural rifts and conventions and thus some insulation from harm, this is not always the case. Indeed, the ethnic, tribal, or religious identities of individual staff members may either increase or decrease their risk, depending on the context. Moreover, the jobs they hold may increase their risk: "It is usually the driver, the guard and interpreter that get caught in attacks on vehicles," remarked one aid worker; indeed, national staff usually occupy these positions.[24]

For international staff, dislocation is a given. Compensation surpasses that for national staff, but other pressures of the job are similar. Short-term (six months to one year) contracts abound, and many aid workers jump from contract to contract and agency to agency.[25] Personality conflicts within the office, the unpredictability of many emergency contexts, long hours and few days off, and the isolation of living and working away from family and friends can magnify the stresses of the job.[26] In many emergency contexts, expatriate aid workers share work and living spaces, working in an office and sharing "guest houses," compounds with separated and common living space (e.g., kitchens, washing facilities, or gardens) that agencies rent to accommodate multiple staff members. Thus, the boundaries of their social, professional, and private lives are porous, and truly private time and space can be difficult to find.

The chronic uncertainty of the situation, coupled with the unfamiliarity of context, also creates a situation in which individuals experience a loss of personal control, a factor vital in positively assimilating difficult or traumatic experiences. This further complicates and impedes effective coping strategies (Barron 1999, 162) that lessen the negative ramifications of stress for productivity, effectiveness, and security management. One study found that work stress was the most commonly reported type of security threat and that respondents reported less dangerous threats in numbers that far exceeded the more dangerous ones (Fast and Wiest 2007). Indeed, as one handbook claims,

> The most stressful events in humanitarian work have to do with the organizational culture, management style or operational objectives

of an NGO or agency, rather than external security risks or poor environmental factors. Aid workers, basically have a pretty shrewd idea of what they are getting into when they enter this career, and dirty clothes, gun shots at night and lack of electricity do not surprise them. Inter and intra-agency politics, inconsistent management styles, lack of team work and unclear or conflicting organizational objectives, however combine to create a background of chronic stress and pressure that over time wears people down and can lead to burnout or even physical collapse. (Fawcett 2003, as quoted in Loquercio, Hammersley, and Emmens 2006, 5)

In addition to the well-known and documented effects of "culture shock" that accompany working in foreign environments, international staff may encounter "disaster shock" (Stearns 1993) as they witness the atrocities of war or the destruction of a natural disaster. They may also experience the incongruity between their own personal values and those of the organization that employs them (Fawcett 2003, as cited in Walker and Russ 2010, 29). These stresses, coupled with environmental and security factors, as well as program, organizational, and personal factors, can lead to excessive (i.e., dysfunctional) staff turnover in humanitarian agencies (Loquercio, Hammersley, and Emmens 2006).

As a result, the recruitment and retention of experienced aid professionals is a challenge for most agencies. Responses to stress play a prominent role in job performance, promotion, and security. In some agencies, some senior staff are now more willing to share their stories of harrowing experiences and how they did or did not cope well, proving that it is possible to succeed despite these experiences.[27] The focus on resilience leads to a profile of an aid worker as having the "right stuff" to manage trauma and stress and succeed in the job. Such a person should be resourceful; curious, and possessed of "intellectual mastery" and an "ability to conceptualize"; flexible, with a range of emotional experience; and gifted with a "need and ability to help others" as well as a "vision of a moral order" (Barron 1999, 151). Those without such resilience traits might employ less healthy coping mechanisms, such as heavy drinking or smoking, poor eating or sleeping patterns, or inadequate recreation. These self-destructive behaviors can increase risk and result in burnout or poor job performance. Not least, security incidents increase when put-upon aid workers take unnecessary risks or place others in difficult situations.

For many, stress, isolation, and the lack of support systems, exacerbated by a drinking culture among expatriates, can combine to diminish good judgment and put their own and others' lives in jeopardy.[28] One humanitarian security expert attributed the majority of an organization's security incidents to vulnerabilities related to "sex and alcohol."[29] While this assessment remains anecdotal and difficult to prove, potent combinations of promiscuous relationships, unprotected sex, and alcohol consumption are undoubtedly contributing factors to many security incidents. Similarly, long hours increase stress, as do the difficult living conditions (Hilhorst and Schmiemann 2002).

The commitment to mental health care, however, typically lags behind security in funding and human resource support, and often occurs only after crisis situations.[30] While these issues are now generally recognized, few organizations have deliberately instituted preventive measures to enhance mental health (McCall and Salama 1999; Ehrenreich and Elliott 2004), even as staff care is recognized as a crucial component of human resources management (Porter and Emmens 2009). Organizational neglect or lack of support can have devastating consequences.

Barbara Smith and her colleagues write of a UN field worker in the Middle East who was taken hostage and later experienced a downward spiral that left him suicidal, due in part to his agency's response to his case. They write,

> As a part of his treatment/rehabilitation program in his native country, his agency was asked to assign him to an office job at Headquarters. The request was turned down. He felt rejected and let down, became depressed and his condition worsened.... Unable to work, he applied for disability payments, but was turned down by his pension plan because his membership had not lasted long enough. Over time he had to sell his summer house, later on his house, and ended up poor. His depression deepened and he became suicidal. In the end, his national government had to approach the agency to negotiate a satisfactory financial settlement for him. (Smith et al. 1996, 421)

Cases of litigation are increasing, as families and former employees sue their employers for wrongful death or negligence (Kemp and Merkelbach 2011). The Sharon Commins and Flavia Wagner kidnappings mentioned in Chapter 1 are only two examples. In these cases, "duty-of-care" standards (referring to the responsibility to care for the mental and physical health of staff) gain in importance, as they become the benchmarks that courts use to determine liability and damages (Klamp 2007).

While the maladaptive coping mechanisms raise the more obvious security implications, mental health experts point out that some of the behaviors and actions of aid workers are in fact normal psychological responses to stress and trauma. Experts point to a variety of countertransference reactions (avoidance reactions, such as denial or detachment, and intrusive reactions, such as overidentification or guilt) as well as typical emotional coping mechanisms. Enmeshment reactions, referring to the ability to see things only in black-and-white categories, hostility and cynicism toward beneficiary populations, as well as self-destructive behavior and dissociative responses (suspension of reality) are all typical coping strategies.

The last two, in particular, have implications for security. The psychological mechanism of "downward comparison," a contributing factor to self-destructive behaviors, functions when aid workers compare their lot to that of those they are helping. Upon finding themselves better off, they do little or nothing to care for themselves. Thus, they fail to see how their own situations are preventable and within their control, even though the situation of the refugees or internally displaced person (IDPs) they are helping is beyond their control (Smith et al. 1996, 415). With dissociation, individuals may take exceptional risks rooted in a sense of invulnerability. In fact, "A mix of grandiosity, denial and dissociation can underlie a frequently seen sense of invulnerability to danger expressed by relief workers. Whereas in their home countries, these workers would wear seatbelts and drive carefully, they may do neither in the disaster setting. . . . Whereas in their home towns workers would take care to avoid dangerous neighborhoods, they may remain in an area known to be at risk for mortar attack" (Barron 1999, 161). Colleagues of Sergio Vieira de Mello, the veteran UN official who died in the Baghdad bombing, sometimes referred to him as "Teflon guy, since nothing bad seemed to touch him" (Power 2008, 254). He earned this moniker after repeated scrapes and security incidents that left him unscathed, including a dangerous backcountry trip on foot with few colleagues and without the benefit of radio contact with the UN base (he was meeting with key officials of the Khmer Rouge in Cambodia) (Power 2008, chap. 5).

A similar phenomenon is "danger habituation," where individuals become used to increasing degrees of danger. Their habituation to risk prevents them from recognizing the extent of danger in their context. Thus, the stress of the work and the context of severe hardship that many aid workers experience and the (sometimes maladaptive) coping mechanisms they employ remain potent factors in security incidents.

Accounting for Internal, Self-Generated Vulnerabilities

The "self-generated" risks—risks and vulnerabilities that occur as a result of the behavior and actions of individuals—described above are integral to the realities of aid work and security management. In myriad ways, the competing images and actions of aid workers, both good and bad, shape assumptions about security. The images illustrate the diversity and eclecticism of the workers as well as the complex intercultural and intra- and interpersonal dynamics that agitate in sometimes explosive ways. The diversity of aid workers underscores the necessity of disaggregation and of analyzing the differential risks that they face, whether driver or program officer, national or international, female or male, Christian, Hindu, or Muslim. Their personae and motivations may curtail certain behaviors or incite others, just as they will lead to different responses to the stresses of the job and context. These coping mechanisms, in turn, both facilitate and detract from effective risk management.

In reasserting humanity, with its emphasis on aid workers as social beings embedded in a complex web of relationships, these interactions and relationships must feature as one dimension in analyzing the factors that lead to security incidents. Individual actions, in some cases, end in security incidents, as in the Chapter 1 examples of Karen, the young aid worker in the second vignette, who engages in an illicit affair with a local power broker and is killed, or Ahmed, from the first vignette, who stabbed a colleague in desperation after being suspected of embezzling funds from the organization. Other self-generated risks may include arguing with or not obeying the orders of a pugnacious militiaman with a gun at a checkpoint or sporting sleeveless shirts or miniskirts, which might offend local customs and expectations of attire. While not all of these actions lead to security incidents, some do. Undue emphasis on these internal vulnerabilities, however, easily becomes construed as blaming the victim and thereby impedes understanding. Self-generated risks compose only one part, albeit an important one, of the overall picture of the causes and conditions related to security incidents.

Individual staff members, and expatriate staff in particular, are often seen as representatives of their organizations, and this representation extends beyond normal business hours. Thus, they can never leave their jobs or fully dissociate from their organizations. In these instances, the dividing lines between public and private blur. At home, wherever that may be, the actions of individual employees outside of office or work hours tend to remain in the realm of "private" and separate from the work life and reputation of the organization. These spheres conflate when living overseas, especially because of the blurred boundaries between expatriates' private and public lives. Back home, an aid worker might be robbed at gunpoint, injured in a car accident, or even killed in a drive-by shooting. He or she might feature in the media as a civilian, not necessarily as an aid worker, affected by violence. In these cases, such an event would figure as a security incident for an aid agency only if clearly and directly connected to the individual's work. For international staff, however, working abroad tends to come with agency-provided living quarters, and for both national and international staff, such incidents are typically attributed to their work. The issue is not so much that people break host country social or cultural mores, but that in the context of the disparities that exist and the conflated public/private spheres, these behaviors become vulnerabilities for the organization.

Moreover, the actions of individuals color how others are viewed. For example, expatriate aid workers seen frequenting nightclubs or engaging in illicit activities, such as illicit diamond trading, can tarnish the reputations of all expatriates in the eyes of the local community, particularly if these activities are seen as immoral, unacceptable, or culturally insensitive. Discrepancies in wealth and access to resources can also breed resentment and result in negative perceptions of aid and aid workers. This works both ways, as aid workers who see community members as corrupt or inefficient tar other community members and groups with the same brush.

In less visible but more insidious ways, these competing images underlie how we conceptualize security incidents. The image of aid workers as mythical heroes places them on a pedestal that isolates and (magically) shields them from the messy and complicated world in which they operate. It mutes voices of criticism, blame, or responsibility, or ignores examples that do not fit neatly within this story line. If faced with stories of individual neglect or culpability, this archetype makes it easy to brush off responsibility with a "boys will be boys"–type explanation. Similarly, when they do fall from their pedestal, as they sometimes do, the negative repercussions for the individual and, by extension, for the profession are magnified.[31]

In contrast, the critical image of aid workers is more apt to hold aid workers responsible for their actions and the security incidents that might result, or at the very least regards them as key players in the drama or set of ills that might befall them. This image tends toward blaming the victim. The underlying stresses or conditions of aid work and the psychological coping mechanisms of aid workers that might help to explain such behavior are tossed aside as irrelevant. Each image, therefore, privileges a particular way of thinking about the causes of violence.

Seeing aid workers as ordinary people, with career aspirations as well as personality flaws and gifts, suggests an alternative pathway that conforms more closely to a relational analysis. Ordinary people, as opposed to heroes or mercenaries, make mistakes and bad decisions that must be tallied in any accounting of causes. Aid workers must assume responsibility for these mistakes and decisions, yet this responsibility must also be mediated by the external context, particularly in places that blur the distinctions between public and private spaces and actions.

Security directors and aid agencies do recognize the importance of internal vulnerabilities and particularly the importance of individual behavior as causes of security incidents. Even so, the role of the individual in relation to safety and security is not necessarily inculcated among aid workers. According to one security expert, "In police and emergency professions, the first thing they teach you is your own safety first. This is not an attitude prevalent in humanitarians."[32] Attempts to address these internal vulnerabilities typically fall into two categories: personal security training and individual codes of conduct. Personal security training emphasizes how to "stay safe" in new or violent contexts. Training manuals and curricula typically identify dos and don'ts of behavior, roles and responsibilities, travel preparedness prior to and during a mission, cultural awareness, and how to deal with the unexpected. The more sophisticated preparatory strategies involve multiday or weeklong simulations of working in violent environments. Such training aims to make aid workers aware of the ways in which they are responsible for *and* able to effect their own safety and security.

Individual codes of conduct operate from an organizational level. They prohibit or regulate specific behaviors as ethical imperatives or as conditions of employment, and can be used to promote accountability to beneficiaries

(Humanitarian Accountability Partnership 2010). The Save the Children Staff Code of Conduct, for example, highlights power and trust as inherent aspects of aid work and specifies that abuse of that power and trust, particularly in relation to children, is unacceptable. Its standards include respect for others and the active promotion of the rights of children. It also recognizes that staff members represent the organization at all times. This representation is particularly visible when traveling or working internationally. The code states, "As a member of our staff, you are an 'ambassador' for us and will be seen by us and by others as a representative of the organisation both during and outside working hours" (Save the Children 2005, 1). The document indicates the code is binding and that the organization may take disciplinary action for violations of the code and its standards, up to and including dismissal and criminal prosecution, as warranted.

Likewise, the International Committee of the Red Cross's (ICRC) Code of Conduct for all delegates, consultants, and even family members of delegates outlines strict regulations for behavior that apply at all times while on mission, not simply during work hours. These rules are related to the organization's humanitarian principles and mission and recognize the connection between upholding these principles and the organization's image and reputation, upon which it depends to carry out its mission.

Such codes are important, particularly in setting ethical standards of conduct. It is less clear, however, to what degree these are consistently enforced at the various levels of an organization or are used as a reward or to sanction questionable or even egregious behavior. Nor is it clear that organizations identify such measures as integral to an overall strategy of risk management (Fast, Freeman, et al. 2011). Moreover, the codes of conduct usually remain part of the internal workings and policies of organizations. Greater transparency about the existence and content of these codes could function as an additional mechanism to promote accountability to beneficiaries and host populations precisely by rendering visible that which usually remains hidden.

While important, individual codes of conduct and personal security training must be interpreted within the larger context. On their own, these measures place the onus and responsibility for security on the individual, thereby downplaying the role of the institutional context and response. Nevertheless, these measures represent a crucial, if tentative, step toward a relational approach to security management that acknowledges individual action and responsibility and interprets this within a larger context, yet still shies away from blaming the victim. A relational approach, in addition, must include steps to address differential risk and the duty of care toward the mental health of both international *and* national staff.

Aid workers, however, are not the only players in the aid world. The organizations and institutions that employ them are also key actors in this drama.

Aid Organizations: The Informal and Idealized Past and the Institutional and Professional Present

In the decades since the Battle of Solferino and the signing of the Geneva Conventions, the number of actors providing humanitarian and development assistance has proliferated into the thousands. A dizzying array of motivations, philosophies, and missions animate these myriad actors, which range in size, budget, mission, and organizational structure. The broad spectrum embraces both secular and faith-based organizations; organizations that espouse the core humanitarian principles of humanity, impartiality, independence, and neutrality and those that do not; well-established organizations with multimillion-dollar budgets and hundreds or thousands of staff as well fledgling agencies with a few paid staff and legions of volunteers. Stories about their efforts appear regularly in the mainstream and independent media, especially in times of disaster. As a sign of their influence, the UN and relief organizations, such as the ICRC, Médecins Sans Frontières (MSF), and the American Friends Service Committee, have won the Nobel Peace Prize ten times since the Norwegian Storting (Parliament) awarded the first prize in 1901 to Henri Dunant and a prominent French pacifist, Frédéric Passy.[33]

Humanitarian actors in the twenty-first century occupy a prominent actual and symbolic place in the global system. Estimations of the number of aid workers indicate the population has exploded, from approximately 136,000 in 1997 (Stoddard, Harmer, and Haver 2006, 8) to over 290,000 in 2008 (Stoddard, Harmer, and DiDomenico 2009, 2), suggesting a growth rate of approximately 6 percent per year (Walker and Russ 2010, 10–11). Funding for emergency operations has expanded and, with it, the public profile and power of those providing assistance. From 1970 to 1994, the number of NGOs registered with the U.S. Agency for International Development jumped eightfold, from fifty-two to 419, and their revenues increased more than eleven times, to US$6.8 billion (Lindenberg and Bryant 2001, 4). All of the "big seven" American NGOs (CARE, Catholic Relief Services, International Rescue Committee, Mercy Corps, Oxfam, Save the Children, and World Vision) command large budgets and staff, often with multiple headquarters and offices located on several continents. Each of these solicits funding from individual and institutional donors.[34] The 2008 through 2010 annual budgets for World Vision International (WVI), the largest of these, exceeded US$2.5 billion. World Vision works in dozens of countries and comprises multiple entities—national offices and boards—coordinated by an international body (WVI 2008, 2009).[35] Where once organizations with the same name might have separately incorporated organizational headquarters in different countries, these national member organizations are merging to create bigger confederations and alliances. The International Save the Children Alliance, CARE International, Oxfam International, MSF International, and others are similarly organized into international confederations comprising national organizations and offices. Coordination mechanisms, such as the Inter-Agency Standing Committee (IASC) and the Steering Committee for Humanitarian Response, bring together humanitarian actors to discuss and advocate on issues of common concern.[36]

While funding for long-term development activities dominated until the late 1980s, James Fearon charts an upward trend in total emergency relief over time. The continued and dramatic increase in absolute terms is a puzzling trend in the face of declining numbers of refugees since the end of the Cold War. Fearon attributes this trend to a combination of factors: a more systematic counting of IDPs, whose numbers have risen since 1997; a shift in foreign policy priorities among donor governments to more humanitarian funding; and what he terms "task expansion" among NGOs, meaning that they are expanding the number and types of activities in which they engage (Fearon 2008). The donor community has similarly expanded, from sixteen government donors who responded to the Bosnian crisis in 1992 to more than ninety for the 2004 tsunami in Asia. The members of the Development Assistance Committee (DAC) of the Organisation for Economic Co-operation and Development (OECD) have traditionally dominated the humanitarian sector, providing the most funding.[37] This growth, however, exists in tension with the emerging role of non-DAC donors and the shift in priorities and perspective that this inevitably entails (Harmer and Cotterrell 2005; see also Benthall and Bellion-Jourdan 2003; Binder and Meier 2011).

The 2008 worldwide recession threatened this growth trajectory. The recession negatively affected revenues for most charities and NGOs. Some agencies sought new sources of revenue, looking to innovative partnerships and other ventures in order to expand and diversify their income. More commonly, charities instituted cost-cutting measures, from freezing hiring or wages or laying off staff members to slashing programs. Some expanded into private sector partnerships or courted celebrity endorsements to increase their public presence and fund-raising appeal. Others shifted their programs to sectors and regions of greatest need. Experts project these cutbacks will extend well into the future (IRIN 2009).[38] Although donations and funding are down due to the global economic recession, the number of aid workers and agencies is still greater than a decade ago.

The sector has changed in other ways as well. Many seasoned veterans of humanitarian crises around the world talk about the "good old days" when their jobs were simpler and less complicated. Aid workers from earlier eras speak of living "out in the bush" with the people or of the lack of bureaucratic constraints to their work that allowed not only more autonomy but also more creative and flexible responses. One veteran aid worker recounted, "Before satellite phones, agencies and people had more maneuverability. There is now more micro-management of humanitarian action, and security is a part of this, as is increased professionalism."[39] Another security director opined that "in the old days, people that wanted to do good just went out. Now the selection process is more strict and professional. People have to fit the profile."[40]

Nowadays, with some exceptions, it is rare for an agency to send a single foreign aid worker to live in a remote village to supervise or implement relief or development programs. An aid worker who lived in Darfur in the 1980s reminisced, "I was the lone expat in the village, far away from everything. We used local vehicles." He contrasted this experience with a recent trip to Katanga province in the Democratic Republic of the Congo, "a huge swathe of territory where only MSF is active. It is the old kind of humanitarianism, where you are living in the bush with limited access." In thinking about opening a new office, he remarked, "It is difficult because of the rules and regulations. You can't put staff in places without access—by road, plane, etc. You can't put someone alone."[41]

More often than not agencies employ national staff in positions that foreigners occupied in the past. UN missions come burdened with requirements for personnel, supplies, reporting, and funding, and NGO operations are similarly equipped and laden. Public and private donors and beneficiaries demand more accountability and oversight, and the proliferation of actors has created an intensely competitive environment. Early on, Bernard Kouchner, one of the founders of MSF, resisted such professionalization, denouncing what he called "bureaucrats of misery or technocrats of charity" (as quoted in de Torrenté 2007). The shift from charity to business model has emphasized the efficient delivery of goods and services, and some evidence suggests that beneficiaries of such assistance rue the corresponding move away from building relationships (Listening Project 2008; Anderson, Brown, and Jean 2012), or even time in the field (Autesserre 2014). One aid expert lamented, "If humanitarian action is about the expression of caring, then the increasing numbers of for-profit actors and the business elements are pushing the boundaries."[42]

The actual growth and expansion of power and influence is at the heart of the competing images of aid agencies: that of an informal, often idealized past versus that of an institutional and professional present. The former image is characterized as being composed of smaller and fewer organizations doing good by responding to suffering and acting as a counterpoint to the inhumanity of war. The latter image, by contrast, is characterized by a growth in numbers, wealth, and power, where aid is a business and reflects business priorities of expansion and brand recognition, and in which aid agencies constitute a powerful set of actors in the international system. The images reflect a tension over individual responsibility and the role of security management within the organization, such as whether security management should remain intimately connected to programming and be the responsibility of each individual, or should be designated as an area of expertise under the domain of the professional whose role is to ensure the security of the others (and who is easily blamed in the event a security incident occurs).

The Informal and Idealized Past

The founding stories of the large relief and development agencies frame the image of the informal and idealized past. These stories are usually anchored in a call to respond to suffering and extreme deprivation of those far away. In 1919, Eglantyne Jebb and her sister Dorothy Buxton formed the Save the Children Fund to raise money to send relief to children in Vienna, Austria.

Jebb wrote the Declaration of the Rights of the Child (the precursor to the 1989 Convention on the Rights of the Child), which the League of Nations adopted in 1924 and the United Nations adopted in 1959. The individuals who formed the Oxford Committee for Famine Relief in 1942, now known as Oxfam, organized to galvanize public opinion to lift the Allied naval blockade against occupied Greece and then to send food and other supplies to starving Greeks (Jones 1965). CARE, originally named the Cooperative for American Remittances to Europe, also has its roots in World War II. The organization sent packages of food, known as care packages, to survivors in postwar Europe.[43] Concern Worldwide, another NGO, was founded to respond to the war in Biafra/Nigeria in the 1960s.

These founding stories usually feature a few entrepreneurial and committed individuals organizing for change, which then grows into a movement to protest or advocate for certain policies or to assist those who are suffering and less fortunate. This altruism is a crucial ingredient that characterizes, sometimes with an inherent paternalism, both the individual aid workers and the aid agencies that employ them. These altruistic impulses motivate and enable them to persevere in difficult circumstances and in the face of the impossible list of skills that characterize the superhero aid worker.

In the early years of the modern-day humanitarian response, therefore, these neophyte organizations gained experience as they responded to successive wars. During the Cold War state actors operated behind the scenes to determine where, how, and how many relief actors operated in any given context. Relief work generally lacked a well-established imprint or set of common characteristics. Instead, the early responses of aid actors were marked by flexibility and adaptability to circumstances, but also by inefficiencies and a lack of reflexivity about the negative or unanticipated effects of aid or the wider context within which the distribution of humanitarian aid occurred. Aid actors expected risk and treated it an inherent part of the work. The more limited scope of aid operations and actors, by the standards of the largest of today's aid operations, and the concomitant independence of individual humanitarians in those early days meant that much of their work escaped widespread public attention and conversation.

In the image of the informal past, aid workers lived or stayed among the people they helped, working to improve the lot of those around them. They were, as the story goes, relatively unconstrained by instructions or guidelines from aid agency headquarters. In her history of the ICRC, Caroline

Moorehead traces the evolution of ICRC delegates from "witnesses and bystanders" prior to the 1936 Abyssinian War to participants in the "delegates' wars" that followed. Abyssinia/Ethiopia birthed the "modern delegate ... who, unlike his predecessors, saw his role as that of humanitarian actor, one able to influence events" rather than simply react to them. The ICRC delegates in this war were "obstinate, adventurous, dutiful, but ... also had strong views on the conduct of war itself. Because the distance to Geneva was so great, and communications so slow, there was no choice but to give them independence and power" (Moorehead 1998, 304). Thus, in the early years the effectiveness of the ICRC relied largely on the acumen, experience, and personalities of its delegates. ICRC delegates exercised near-absolute autonomy in their decisions, reporting back about their decisions and activities rather than seeking permission to act. In joining the ICRC, these men (for delegates in those days were primarily men) understood and accepted the risks inherent in their work.

In contrast, the humanitarian response to the civil war in Yemen in the 1960s marked "one, last old-fashioned war," after which ICRC delegates were never again "so isolated or so free." The advent of radio communications and televised images of humanitarian activities in the 1960s facilitated communication between field operations and headquarters, making Yemen the first ICRC operation in which field delegates maintained radio contact with ICRC headquarters in Geneva. These advances curtailed some of the autonomy of individual ICRC delegates who served after the civil war in Yemen. Several of the veteran ICRC delegates Moorehead interviewed expressed the sentiment that being a delegate in the 1960s was far better than being one in later years. She quotes one as saying, "We were sent off and we were free. We made the decisions" (Moorehead 1998, 598, 603).

At the forefront of the informal past is a picture of an individual foreign aid worker living in a remote village, far from roads and "civilization," ensconced in an unprotected hut in Africa or Asia and walking from village to village to meet with the locals and carry out programs. Deborah Scroggins, in her biography of Emma McCune, describes her as an aid worker consumed by her work and the cause of the South Sudanese.[44] McCune lived and worked in southern Sudan in the 1980s and early 1990s, married a Sudanese rebel, and eventually died in a car accident. Scroggins writes of McCune's life and job with UNICEF in the rebel-held town of Kapoeta, where she helped deliver supplies and restart schools in the south. Her relationships with the Sudanese people whom she helped and with whom she worked generated both controversy and admiration. McCune lived in a "bullet-scarred concrete house with a corrugated iron roof" (Scroggins 2002, 138) and later moved into a Sudanese *tukul* (hut) after her marriage to Riek Machar, a Sudanese rebel who became a vice president in the South Sudanese government after the 2005 Comprehensive Peace Agreement. She "went native," as the saying goes, gaining the love and respect of the Sudanese people in the process: "Emma's willingness to get out and walk from village to village won her respect from the southern Sudanese. Most *khawajas* [(white) foreigners] were afraid to be parted from their machines—their cars and their airplanes" (Scroggins 2002, 140).[45] The idea of "going native" resonates with both that of missionary work—helping and saving others—and the colonial impulses to civilize the "deepest, darkest Africa" of Joseph Conrad's *Heart of Darkness*. It is a largely unconscious, though potent, image.

The aid agencies, mostly NGOs, facilitate the work of the humanitarians, providing the organizational structure for the work. Relief and development NGOs in earlier years were fewer in overall numbers, were less bureaucratic, and had fewer staff members and less robust budgets at their disposal. In this way, aid was not quite yet an industry with its attendant bureaucracy and professionalized standards. In his analysis of the ICRC, David Forsythe characterizes the organization as "totally unprofessional" before 1970, and "highly professional" since that time (Forsythe 2005, 9). Mark Duffield characterizes the 1960s and 1970s as defined by "NGO voluntarism," in which the "organizational and personal ethos was that of symbolic identification with the world's poor through institutional frugality and denied personal consumption" (Duffield 2010, 464).

In the informal past, organizations had and needed the freedom to creatively adapt to circumstances, although without the standards of performance and levels of expertise of today. Still the needs outstripped available resources. The organizations offered low pay, which was partially offset by high job satisfaction.[46] The scarcity of resources meant that agencies provided less support, both technical and personal, to their employees. Less support meant more isolation. The challenges of communication gave the individual aid worker more autonomy and prevented regular, let alone daily, contact with headquarters. Without phone service or the technological advances of Internet access and email, they often could not or did not check in with headquarters in making decisions.

This image is at the heart of the idea of NGOs as closer to the people, the "grassroots," and therefore more able to know and deliver according to their needs. NGOs were seen as connected to the communities in which they worked, in part because many of them trace their beginnings to community activism and engagement. In this way, NGOs served as the institutional equivalents of the mythical aid worker. The idea of the smaller, flexible, and adaptable organization that is responsive to the needs of the suffering, war-affected population predominated and generated the notion that NGOs could correct the ills of large-scale, state-driven development.

The media stories and images of famine in the 1980s (and beyond), in which journalists reported on the efforts of aid agencies, buttressed this portrayal: the still photo of the white, Western, often female, aid worker with her agency's logo displayed on her T-shirt, providing supplementary feeding to an emaciated, often African, child while the mother looks helplessly at the camera, or the detailed descriptions of the swashbuckling flying doctors and pilots/adventurers ready to brave violence and uncertainty to care for the suffering and wounded (as an example, see de St. Jorre 1972, chap. 9). The Ethiopian famine of 1984 punctuated this portrayal. Referring to these images, Barnett writes, "Caught in the media's web, as well, were the image of heroic aid workers persevering against the odds, representing the conscience of the West. Aid now becomes a cause célèbre" (Barnett 2011, 156).

In this fictional world, security was not an issue. Indeed, adventure, voluntarism, self-sacrifice, and sometimes danger were intricately woven into the narrative. Aid work carried inherent risks, especially in war zones. Nevertheless, aid workers were seen as safe, largely protected by the people with whom they lived and especially because of the work they did or the services they provided. One aid worker who lived in Sudan in the 1980s called it "the worst man-made famine in history" but reported, "on the whole I felt safe from being white."[47] The dangers consisted more of bad roads and car accidents, insect-borne diseases, or the local wildlife. If working in a war zone, then the dangers, including the possibility of being caught at the wrong place at the wrong time, were just part of the job. In this way, security incidents were simultaneously anomalous and almost inevitable. If and when they occurred, they appeared isolated and irregular, even when targeting aid workers specifically.[48]

Few if any agencies devoted systematic attention to security management, protecting their staff, or ensuring that programming and services could continue in the midst of violence and chaos. Instead, many seemed to operate under an assumption of altruistic immunity,[49] an aura of invincibility rooted in the supposition that no one would intentionally attack someone there to help. The idea that an aid worker, providing much needed assistance, could be purposefully attacked supervenes such inviolability. Security, in short, does not feature prominently in this image; rather, risk was just part of the job.

The power of the vision of the informal past and its founding stories is rooted in the relational acts that drove and sustained acts of mercy and justice, including the compassion and drive that motivated the founding of many organizations and continues to capture the imagination of those who donate their money. This is what makes humanitarian action both ordinary and remarkable. It is ordinary in that it reflects a very human impulse and remarkable in the ways that it is institutionalized and scaled up to represent billions of dollars and the livelihoods of hundreds of thousands of people.

The Evolution of the Institutionalized and Professionalized Present

Cracks in the image of the informal and idealized past began to appear in the early 1990s, a decade that saw the proliferation of humanitarian actors, the dramatic growth of budgets, and the institutionalization of the field, including the shift from states as shadows to active partners (Barnett 2011, 168–169). Several factors combined to create unprecedented possibilities for expansion and the professionalization that have transformed the NGO sector. First, the recession of the 1980s forced the retreat of the public sector and the contraction of services. It simultaneously opened the door for the expansion of the private sector, to which governments devolved certain functions. NGOs stepped into the gap in the provision of social services around the world (Lindenberg and Bryant 2001, chap. 1).[50] In the 1990s, the overall amount of governmental funding for relief and development activities decreased, and governments channeled what remained through NGOs, much of it to relief assistance (Stein 2000). After the end of the Cold War and the eruption of identity-based conflicts around the world, funding for peacebuilding and conflict resolution activities in "postconflict" countries blossomed, causing one aid worker in Rwanda to observe that "everyone getting off the plane now in Kigali is doing conflict resolution. What we really need is some people doing agriculture and health."[51]

Second, the collapse of the Berlin Wall, ushering in the end of the Cold War and inaugurating the dawn of the "new world order," profoundly affected the environment in which aid workers operated. The end of superpower polarization brought about new possibilities for collaboration, just as violence engulfed Somalia, Bosnia, and Rwanda. These and other conflicts pushed NGOs to expand their operations into war zones and other dangerous places. The scale of subsequent humanitarian operations magnified the power and influence of humanitarian actors, while the proliferation of aid actors has dramatically complicated their operating environment. For example, between April and December 1994, bilateral and multilateral donors channeled US$1.4 billion through humanitarian agencies (Borton, Brusset, and Hallam 1996, 5; and Roberts 1996, 18 for figures and donors).

According to some analysts, it was precisely the ways in which the world powers, primarily the United States and the Europeans, used humanitarian assistance to cover for the absence of political involvement in these conflicts (e.g., Rwanda) and deployed the military to provide humanitarian assistance in others (e.g., Somalia) that undermined and eroded humanitarian principles of neutrality, impartiality, and independence. In short, humanitarian assistance became a substitute for decisive political action in response to emerging complex emergencies (Duffield 1997; Paul 1999; Borton, Brusset, and Hallam 1996). The large bureaucracies needed to manage these resources increased the anonymity of and sometimes generated hostility toward aid workers and agencies (Anderson 1999).

With expansion and exploding crises, scrutiny and criticism of humanitarian and emergency operations intensified. A darker side of humanitarianism surfaced. In particular, the monumental humanitarian response to the mass influx of refugees fleeing violence in Rwanda after the 1994 genocide engendered a crisis of conscience and principles for the aid community (Terry 2002; Joint Evaluation of Emergency Assistance to Rwanda 1996). The massive response focused on the refugee camps across the border in Zaire (now the Democratic Republic of Congo) that sheltered Hutu refugees who were fearful of retaliation by the advancing Tutsi-led Rwandan Patriotic Front. The genocide survivors (primarily Tutsi) who remained in Rwanda received little assistance in comparison. The perpetrators of the genocide sought refuge in the camps alongside their fellow Hutu. They controlled the camps and the distribution of assistance, leading to accusations of aid agency complicity in feeding the *génocidaires*. Even so, many aid agencies chose to continue delivering food and other necessities, arguing that not all in the camps were guilty of genocide.[52] Aid agencies were criticized for contributing to the overall dynamics and escalation of conflict in the region and for not speaking out against human rights abuses that eventually culminated in genocide (Uvin 1998).

Efforts at principled reform aimed to avoid the perpetuation of violence via the provision of charity and assistance. These included the Providence Principles (Minear and Weiss 1995, chap. 2) and the Mohonk Criteria for Humanitarian Assistance (Ebersole 1995). A group of agencies, under the leadership of the Red Cross movement, united to create a Code of Conduct for organizations working in disaster relief. The wide-ranging code affirmed the humanitarian imperative and the meaning of the principle of impartiality and called for agencies to refrain from espousing particular political or religious perspectives. The code also proposed principles to guide visual and fund-raising representations of disaster-affected populations (International Federation of the Red Cross and Red Crescent Societies 1997).

At about the same time, a *Chicago Tribune* investigation into the child-sponsorship practices of some relief and development NGOs revealed a series of disturbing discrepancies and misleading advertising practices. The resulting scandal rocked agencies that relied on child sponsorship for private funding (*Chicago Tribune* 1998). The expansion of the sector, coupled with the critiques and concrete examples of aid as wasteful, corrupt, and neocolonial that gained traction in the late 1980s and 1990s, combined to create momentum for stronger standards and accountability to constituents, supporters, and beneficiaries, and thereby to further professionalize the humanitarian and development sectors.[53] Indeed, some have characterized accountability as a missing principle of humanitarianism.[54]

Donor demands progressively became more stringent.[55] Within the aid sector, some observers pushed for principled reform to promote accountability and improve the practice of agencies operating in violent conflict environments. The Sphere Project, the Humanitarian Accountability Partnership International (HAP International), the Active Learning Network for Accountability and Performance (ALNAP), and the Good Humanitarian Donorship (GHD) initiative have emerged as important reform mechanisms over the past fifteen years. The Sphere Project, now located within the International Federation of the Red Cross and Red Crescent Societies, brought together a broad-based coalition of agencies to establish a charter and handbook specifying minimum standards for the provision of assistance. The Humanitarian Accountability Project, now HAP International, provides a voice for those on the receiving end of humanitarian assistance and promotes standards of accountability toward recipients. ALNAP, an initiative that followed the evaluation of international assistance to Rwanda, works to enhance learning and thereby improve the performance and accountability of humanitarian actors. The GHD initiative provides a platform for donors to promote common principles for donors that encourage more effective humanitarian action.[56]

Another initiative, the CDA Collaborative Learning Project's pioneering Local Capacities for Peace project, resulted in a series of case studies and eventually a book entreating agencies to "do no harm" (Anderson 1999). The do-no-harm approach emphasized the impact of assistance on conflict and suggested ways aid could reinforce the capacities for peace that exist in every violent conflict context. Using examples of the ways in which development and relief assistance can inadvertently cause or exacerbate existing conflict within societies, Mary Anderson argued for more attention to the mechanisms and results of providing resources to communities ("resource transfers") and the underlying values and messages of the ways in which agencies operate in areas of conflict ("implicit ethical messages"). Providing aid to only certain groups can increase tension between groups and deepen the fault lines that exist in societies, just as the different living standards and pay scales for national and international staff of NGOs send implicit messages that the lives of some (expatriates) are valued more highly than others (Anderson 1999, 58; see also Fassin 2012). A similar dynamic occurs if national staff are left behind to fend for themselves when violence explodes while expatriate staff and equipment are evacuated. In both cases, the differential equality of national versus international staff members raises ethical questions for agencies focused on humanity or social justice.

The net result of all of the above factors was a dramatic expansion and institutionalization of the sector during the 1990s. While many of these developments have improved the quality of the delivery of services that NGOs and other humanitarian actors offer, their effects are not entirely without controversy and complication (de Torrenté 2007). As large institutions with significant staff and budgets, these organizations have developed bureaucracies to govern their operations and must balance their own self-interests with those of the people they represent. These interests do not always neatly coincide. The perpetuation of the institution along with the salaries and continued employment of its staff members all depend on continued and consistent funding for development and disaster and emergency response projects. Ethically, agencies committed to alleviating suffering find it difficult to stand by (or to withdraw) and not help because of security concerns. Practically, not operating in some high-profile crises, such as the response to the Rwandan refugee crisis in 1994, the 2004 tsunami response, or the 2010 Haiti earthquake, can pose a significant challenge to an agency's ability to stay afloat. Many organizations depend on crises and the overhead costs they help to support in order to bolster their fund-raising capacities and to sustain their work elsewhere.

The system in which humanitarian agencies operate is one in which individual and institutional donors privilege and support specific projects for predetermined and often short periods of time, but not necessarily the people and systems, such as security management, that sustain them. This creates a marketplace that makes mismanagement and misappropriation of resources more likely (Cooley and Ron 2002). Indeed, in their analysis of the international response to the Rwandan refugee camps in 1994, Alexander Cooley and James Ron discuss the drive for funding in the competitive marketplace in which aid agencies operated. They suggest this contributed to the reluctance of aid agencies to speak out about the control Hutu militants exercised over the camps and the refugee population, and the corresponding insecurity for refugees and aid workers in the camps. This enabled the militants to co-opt the aid for their own purposes. A few groups chose to withdraw, among them MSF, but at a cost. As Cooley and Ron write, "MSF's experience is the exception that proves the rule: It was able to protest aid abuse only by opting out of the Goma contract system altogether. As long as relief groups remained embedded in Goma's competitive humanitarian market, institutional pressures forced them to tone down their criticism" (Cooley and Ron 2002, 31).

In some crises, such as the response to the Rwandan genocide or the Iraq war, humanitarian principles were at stake. For many agencies in Iraq, the dilemma forced a rude calculation between maintaining operational independence and staying out of Iraq—or at least not accepting U.S. or UK government funding. To accept funds from the belligerent governments made it impossible to remain neutral or independent and created a perception of complicity with or at least tacit consent for the goals of the "global war on terror." Nevertheless, choosing not to operate in a situation like Iraq carries its own ethical and practical dilemmas since "staying home is not a comfortable option for groups committed to the humanitarian imperative" (Minear 2003).

Similarly, with expansion NGOs often become larger, more hierarchical, and overall less participatory organizations. For organizations that espouse a mission of helping the needy and vulnerable, observers point out an increasing separation from the "grassroots." The most vociferous critics accuse them of acting more like businesses committed to never-ending growth than organizations committed to social justice or like institutions committed to their own survival and perpetuation rather than to the needs of those whom they purportedly serve. "The organizational apparatus needs to keep growing to support the growth of the system. It means growth of budgets," remarked one aid expert.[57] Another aid worker provided a similar analysis: "It is a humanitarian industry. Because of this, we are focused on function. NGOs . . . function like corporations. They sell a product and are concerned about the bottom line. They provide services, and need to get out there. It is not about quality or impact emphasis, or principles."[58] The industry aspect of humanitarianism manifests in efforts such as the establishment of the Sphere standards, one of the efforts to professionalize and standardize humanitarian services, which promote a business model of humanitarianism in which beneficiaries are consumers of services (Barnett 2011, 214; see also Anderson, Brown, and Jean 2012).

These contradictions also play out in terms of the qualifications of staff members. The myth of the informal past extols the benefits and commitments of volunteers, while the institutional present praises the expertise of the professionals. A series of blog postings debated this very topic: the professionalism and effectiveness of (unpaid or underpaid) volunteers and salaried individuals. In her blog, Linda Raftree caricatured the amateur as bumbling and ineffective, hindering the real work of aid, and the professional as stodgy and bureaucratic, impeding creative responses. Of those espousing the "amateurs are evil" perspective, Raftree writes, "In no other field are amateurs allowed to go in and muck around in other people's lives with no preparation and experience just because they have good intentions, so why are they allowed to barge into poor communities and bumble around just because they feel guilty about their own wealth and privilege or think it's their right to help?" (Raftree 2010; also Keizer 2010).

An inherent tension exists between a focus on the commitment of the people working for the organization as set against a focus on the services it delivers. In emphasizing the former over the latter, recipients deserve professional (read competent and expert) assistance and not simply good intentions and mediocre outcomes. A related tension exists between the increasing numbers of those who see humanitarianism as a career and those who value the volunteerism of many of the early aid organizations (de Torrenté 2007).

As aid agencies have grown and matured, they have moved closer to professionalization and career paths and away from volunteerism and charity. This translates also to the sought-after skill sets, which now emphasize technical expertise and experience over relationally proficient skills, such as empathy.

The professionalization of the humanitarian sector more generally has two implications. First, the humanitarian career path means that experience, models, and aid workers from one emergency context travel to others. Second, it has created a class of humanitarian/development professionals who are more comfortable moving from country to country than living in their countries of origin. These "third country nationals" are the "misfits" of relief and development work (Stirrat 2008). The global mobility of this class of individuals contrasts with the decreasing mobility of the local aid workers and the beneficiaries of assistance. Aid workers are, in Mark Duffield's words, "distinguished by their relative mobility and stasis. While those on international contracts are able to move and circulate, local aid workers, like beneficiaries, are also immobile onlookers trapped outside the archipelago's magical space of flows" (Duffield 2010, 457). Professionalization, therefore, functions to further solidify inequalities and separate aid workers from those they assist.

Taken to its extreme, the trajectory of growth and expansion highlighted in an unfettered, institutionalized present leads to a view of humanitarians as globalized, all-purpose providers of assistance—imperious, if not neo-imperial, humanitarian Walmarts (Hopgood 2008). This trend stands in tension with a prevalent self-defined identity of aid agencies, rooted in the founding stories of compassion and social change, as system outsiders representing a humane presence in an exploitative and warring world. Left hanging are questions of whether it is possible to professionalize acts of mercy or whether these aims are fundamentally contradictory. These developments threaten to move aid provision further from its essence as a relational act, informed by humanitarian principles, that made possible a view of aid work as the "beautiful human mission" (de Torrenté 2007, 15).

The Evolution and Its Implications for Humanitarian Security

The contemporary relief-and-development sector has fundamentally changed from the lean, grassroots organizations of the informal past to the large, professionalized confederations and alliances of today. These changes, however, are not universally welcomed. These two images represent a different vision of what the humanitarian and aid enterprise should be. In a relational approach, they deserve exploration as dimensions affecting the violence that affects aid actors. Those rooted in the informal past sit uneasily with the image of aid agencies as professional businesses, with the sizeable budgets and power of agencies, the extensive qualifications of staff, and the sophisticated marketing and glossy pictures this implies, all of which typify the "bureaucratized misery" that Kouchner decried. Such professionalism and power risks diluting the altruistic motives, grassroots activism, and creative spirit that motivated the founding of many relief and development NGOs.[59] Moreover, this professionalism further magnifies the inequalities and distance between the aid givers and aid recipients. Instead, those who value the informal past rest more comfortably with an image that assumes (whether true or not) shared values and a deep commitment to the cause and less comfortably with the contradictions and inequality implied in the wealth and power of an organization devoted to relieving suffering or promoting social justice and equality.

In reality, many agencies are caught between the two images, uncomfortably straddling or attempting to straddle these two worlds without losing the benefits of either. As Jonathan Benthall observed in 1993, "The most stressful tension in a Western humanitarian agency is between, on the one hand, the need to campaign and raise funds within the domestic context, and, on the other, the need to maintain an institutional ethos appropriate to the organization's 'deprived' clientele and the professional practice of the field personnel directly concerned with them" (Benthall 1993, 56). This remains true two decades later. Agencies struggle with cultivating autonomy *and* accountability, with delegating decision making to those in local context *and* meeting the accountability demands of donors and others. Agencies grapple with meeting a duty of care to their own staff members, cognizant of donors' wishes to assist vulnerable populations *and* not spending too much on "overhead," which is often how the cost centers for security and duty of care are categorized. They wrestle with ensuring institutional survival *and* meeting the needs of the less fortunate, without compounding existing inequalities between the haves and the have-nots. They weigh the benefits of a professionalized and technically skilled workforce against the less tangible attributes, motives, and relational skills that often characterize volunteerism. In short, agencies must balance an external focus on those they espouse to assist with an internal focus on the safety and security of their own staff and on their institutional health and perpetuation. They must balance the values of the informal past with the realities of the present, recognizing that the way forward lies in a both/and as opposed to an either/or conceptualization. These issues come to the fore in a relational analysis of aid and security, endowing aid organizations with agency regarding the ways that others perceive them and their own level of security.

A permanent feature of the present-day humanitarian landscape is security. An organization's profile—whom an agency hires and fires, its policies and procedures (or lack thereof), and the nature of its programs—affects how local communities and other stakeholders perceive it. These perceptions, in turn, exert a profound influence on an organization's level of security. How an organization chooses to manage security concerns is where the tensions come into play. For example, how agencies define the professional status and qualifications of those responsible for security is obviously pivotal in shaping their security-management approaches. Should security managers have responsibility only for security, separate from programming responsibilities, or should an individual hold responsibility for *both* security and programs? Should qualifications be oriented toward "hard security," relying on experience in the military or police? Should they be program defined, drawing on hard-won experience working in war zones or other emergency contexts? These decisions affect the ways in which security management is integrated into or separate from programming, as well as the default strategies those responsible for security might choose to employ.

The perceptions of an agency play an important role in security management (Fast, Freeman, et al. 2011; see also Abu-Sada 2012a, 2012b). The profile of an agency and the people it hires and even its pay scales may affect its level of security, as the composition of the staff and how it uses its resources, among other factors, send implicit messages about the underlying values of an organization (Anderson 1999; Anderson, Brown, and Jean 2012) and influence how the local community perceives an agency.

An NGO's hiring policies, or the combined hiring policies of the agencies working in a particular area, may privilege one group over another and feed into the systems of inclusion and exclusion already present in a society (Uvin 1998; Keen 1998, 2000). In Pakistan, the practice of providing jobs for outsiders as opposed to locals in the aftermath of the 2005 earthquake created resentment and led to security incidents (Wilder 2008). An in-depth study of the Pakistan earthquake response revealed an analytical discrepancy between global, external factors and those risks and vulnerabilities that derive from the agency's own actions or inactions: "While the main threat analysis of most international agencies continued to focus on external factors such as terrorist attacks, nearly all of the actual security threats and incidents proved to be related to internal factors having to do with perceptions of aid agency actions or inaction" (Wilder 2008, 7). In short, the analysis focused on global dynamics and did not take enough account of how local communities perceived the agencies and the agencies' own actions or policies.

Likewise, the actions of an individual or a small group have ramifications on organizational security. Indeed, many incidents involve employees of an organization. Inequality in compensation or differential treatment of employees, often between national and international staff, may cause resentment. Former employees with a grudge against the agency or a fellow employee for one reason or another perpetrate a significant number of security incidents, as the embezzlement example in Chapter 1 illustrates. An Office for the Coordination of Humanitarian Affairs (OCHA) situation report from Somaliland described a shooting incident in which an ex-employee wounded a program manager (OCHA 2008). News reports about the killing of ten aid workers in Afghanistan in August 2010 speculated about the involvement of an eleventh employee, who was spared from being killed (Partlow 2010).

In other cases, the activities of employees and NGOs lead to resentment or suspicion. Mokbul Morshed Ahmad reports suspicion as a "major problem" in Bangladesh, citing "many fake NGOs in rural areas who have cheated innocent clients. Crooks have formed cooperatives and embezzled the money" (Ahmad 2002, 187). Such activities can taint the reputations of all NGOs operating in the same region. The plethora of organizations can be confusing for community members who may fail to distinguish one organization from another. Many refugees in the camps in eastern Zaire in 1994 were unable to differentiate between the myriad aid agencies operating in the camps, instead referring to NGOs collectively as the Croix Rouge or Red Cross (Borton, Brusset, and Hallam 1996, 142–145).

As years of beneficiary interaction with NGOs have stretched into decades, communities have become more sophisticated—and, some might argue, more manipulative—in their expectations, assessments, and demands of NGOs, distinguishing one from another in a landscape where project sites, vehicles, and compounds sport organizational and donor signage like badges. Field research in East Africa suggests that beneficiary and nonbeneficiary communities are adept at differentiating between organizations, associating specific NGOs with the programs and services they do (or in some cases do not) deliver.[60] Organizations have recently begun to examine how others perceive them (Abu-Sada 2012a, 2012b) and what communities think about the aid system (Anderson, Brown, and Jean 2012), both crucial aspects of an analytical approach that sees aid agencies as embedded within a web of perceptions and relationships.

In some cases, the actions of one NGO spill over to affect the others and consequently affect the level of insecurity for other organizations.[61] In an East African country in the early 1990s, children at play would jump onto the aid trucks delivering food in the refugee camps. Eventually one child fell off one of the trucks, and the next truck in the convoy accidentally struck and killed the child. Several days later, a revenge killing took place. The driver killed in retaliation did not work for the NGO responsible for the convoy. What mattered was that an NGO worker was killed to avenge the loss of the child.[62] In this way, it is difficult, even impossible, to divorce the actions of one agency from those of another, just as the actions of an individual aid worker have an effect on organizational security (Fast et al. 2013).

The vulnerabilities and risk factors of individual employees provide opportunities and challenges for security management. Following the postelection ethnic rioting in Kenya in 2008, for instance, as a security precaution agencies deployed staff based on ethnicity. An Integrated Regional Information Networks (IRIN) report quoted an anonymous aid worker as saying, "One agency operating in the Rift Valley town of Narok has reported that the local community has refused to accept non-Maasai staff in the camps." In this situation, internationals proved more acceptable because of their lack of affiliation with any of the conflict parties (IRIN 2008a; Freeman et al. 2011). Similarly, an investigation of humanitarian action in Sudan suggested that Darfuri IDPs trusted expatriate staff more than their Sudanese colleagues because of their perceived neutrality and lack of bias regarding the conflict. This trust was not universal, however, as the report cited examples of resentment against expatriates for their lavish lifestyles and cultural insensitivity (Mowjee 2006, 7–14).

Such perceptions are not static, but instead evolve over time and place. After the 2005 earthquake in northern Pakistan, local, national, and international responses received high praise from the affected population. As the immediate relief phase ended and operations moved toward reconstruction, these initial feelings of goodwill dissipated, giving rise to significant tensions around the promotion of women's rights and religious values, in particular, and local perceptions of aid agencies and their work, in general. Consequently, after a period of relative security for aid agencies, the spring and summer of 2007 saw a sharp increase in attacks. Militants in northern Pakistan threatened and attacked NGOs that hired women, forcing the evacuation of a number of agencies (IRIN 2007b). A representative of an Islamic student movement highlighted religious and political tensions: "Apparently these NGOs come here to help us on different fronts, but their actual motives are different. They come here to protect and promote the interests of the West. They give our children toffees, but actually they strive to distance them from our religion. This is not acceptable to us. So we are not going to let these people turn our children into infidels" (as quoted in IRIN 2008b).

The religious affiliations of some faith-based agencies, despite assurances that proselytism is not part of their activities, clearly create tension and serve as an explicit rationale for attacks. In August 2010, Somali al-Shabaab insurgents expelled three faith-based agencies—World Vision, Adventist Development and Relief Agency, and Diakonia—on charges of proselytism. Al-Shabaab charged, "Acting as missionaries under the guise of humanitarian work, the organizations have been spreading their corrupted ideologies in order to taint the pure creed of the Muslims in Somalia," and al-Shabaab blamed the organizations for the "proliferation of corruption and indecency" (as quoted in Mohamed 2010). Similarly, in an early claim of responsibility for the deaths of ten medical team members in Afghanistan in August 2010 (later rescinded), the Taliban claimed the team members were spies and Christian missionaries and that this is why they were killed. Their organization, the International Assistance Mission, denied both charges even as it acknowledged the Christian identity of the agency.[63]

Notwithstanding the examples above, faith-based organizations do not appear to encounter higher rates of attacks than the aid community as a whole (Stoddard, Harmer, and DiDomenico 2009, 4). Security manuals recognize the importance of those an agency hires and fires as part of its security-management strategy for precisely this reason. Indeed, the profiles and overall composition of an organization's staff and their ethnic or religious backgrounds or genders are important in determining the level of risk an organization faces in a particular context.

Just as organizational identity affects an NGO's level of security, so does its programming. Whom it serves, where it serves, what it does, and how it conducts itself and its programming can all cause resentment and exacerbate tensions in communities, thereby setting the stage for security incidents. Agencies that implement human rights programming or fail to notify or consult about project locations and priorities may irritate local or national officials, just as women's rights and empowerment programs may butt up against local or cultural or religious customs and practices. In Uganda, one program officer suggested that gender-based violence programming required agencies to "be sure of your security" (Rowley et al. 2011, 5). Another aid worker related a story of working in West Timor, where his organization was attacked because of a perceived association with other organizations supporting unpopular refugee-return policies.[64] Agencies that promise particular services but then are unable to deliver them may stimulate resentment resulting in security incidents. Similarly, inconsistencies between real or perceived promises of services and actual service delivery may contribute to organizations' levels of insecurity (Van Brabant 2000). Refugees and IDPs may violently protest a sudden decrease in food rations in a refugee camp or a perceived imbalance in the amount of food that one group receives over another, especially if the changes are not accompanied with information or convincing explanations. One study that examined the characteristics of a select sample of NGOs and their relationship to insecurity found that organizations that carried out multiple types of activities and provided material assistance were more insecure than those that did not provide material aid (Fast 2002, 2007). These examples highlight the importance of assessing organizational profiles in relation to security management.

Conclusion

The discussion in this chapter confirms the existence, and indeed the importance, of the internal vulnerabilities related to individual behaviors and organizational policies and practices, even though they receive scant attention in the dominant discourses related to security. Adopting an analytical approach attuned to the interdependent and relational elements of causes treats these internal vulnerabilities as visible, not invisible, dimensions. In addition, implicit in the images of the mythical or ordinary aid worker and the informal past and the institutional-and-professional present are assumptions about how best to provide security for organizations and the individuals they employ.

The images of the mythical aid worker and the informal past rely on a variant of humanitarian exceptionalism, assuming protection derives from the good intentions of aid workers and organizations, the services they offer, and from the communities they serve. It builds on a self-image of altruistic immunity that assumes humanitarians are exceptions, because of their work and altruistic motives or because of the emblems and principles that characterize their work.

The dissipation of a taboo against attacking aid workers that many believed present until the mid-1990s has challenged this conception: grassroots connections, white skin, or "living with the people" do not automatically confer safety, nor does outsider altruism. In many cases, these communities are unable to protect themselves, let alone outsiders, from predatory violence. Remembering that aid workers are also civilians can help to disabuse us of the notion that certain characteristics or principles provide immunity from violence.

Agencies generally recognize that doing nothing about security management is no longer acceptable. Indeed, all InterAction members must agree to adhere to a set of minimum standards of safety and security to retain their membership. Yet how best to provide security remains challenging. Whether organizations that hire armed protection, provided either by military forces or private security companies, are more protected is a matter of debate. Armed protection nevertheless implies consequences for the security of other agencies, especially if local populations do not distinguish between NGOs. Providing armed protection for some NGOs and not others tends to increase the overall insecurity for all operating in a particular country or region. Likewise, inappropriate or inadequate security procedures, as in the lack of blast film on the windows of the UN headquarters in Iraq despite its inclusion in established security protocols, is as problematic as not having any security-management protocols. For liability and reputational concerns, agencies often downplay their own shortcomings or inadequacies, preferring instead to emphasize the external context of war and violence and the inevitable dangers of operating in these environments.

At the other end of the spectrum are overly strict security-management protocols of the inflexible bureaucracy. In the aftermath of the 2005 Pakistan earthquake, aid workers involved in the immediate relief efforts complained about restrictive security measures based on the perception, versus the reality, of a dangerous operating environment due to the presence of Islamic militants and terrorist organizations. Some expressed "concern that their inappropriateness and inflexibility could be costing lives," while others, especially in the UN system, simply violated established security protocols (Wilder 2008, 84).

To what extent do humanitarian principles of impartiality and neutrality provide protection or justify risk-taking behaviors? Does the end of altruistic immunity or humanitarian inviolability negate the value of relying on positive, strong, and stable relationships with community as a means of providing protection? The answers to these questions are not simple. Agencies must balance between the extremes of an informal past, in which security was ignored or was an afterthought, and an institutionalized present, in which security is the domain only of the professional and aid workers protest the dominance of security rules and regulations over humanitarian concerns.[65]

Aid workers, as I have suggested above, are often targeted because of the ways they are perceived: as the new face of colonialism; as rich, privileged, and often inexperienced Westerners seeking adventure; as new-age Clara Bartons providing solace or much-needed medical care; as agents of Western and Christian policies; or even as traitors to the "cause," whatever the cause may be. Yet to focus only on these dimensions is to promote an equally erroneous picture of why security incidents occur.

Aid workers and agencies possess only partial control over these representations. Global realities, the global context in which aid workers and agencies operate, taint even the most impartial or neutral humanitarian assistance. It is virtually impossible for any agency to be perceived as remaining neutral—"above" or "beyond"—with respect to the charged ideological warfare that engulfs so many regions and nations. Clearly, however, the composition of these representations is not entirely external, since an organization's policies and the behavior of individual aid workers color the picture. Individuals who respect cultural norms and mores and organizations that actively seek and maintain the consent of communities for their presence and activities can enhance a positive image, just as aggressive drivers in white Land Rovers with logos emblazoned on the doors or rude and disrespectful field staff demanding access can tarnish it. In these ways, the interdependence of the dimensions, which is inherent to a relational analysis, matters.

Unfortunately, some aid organizations and individual aid workers are remarkably unreflective about this image, their actions, and the critical role that together these play in influencing their personal or organizational security. Organizations do not make programming and other decisions in a vacuum. Indeed, the larger context of aid is impossible to ignore. The players in the aid drama are only part of the context, yet they and their behaviors are crucial elements of the overall picture of the causes of violence against aid workers and aid delivery. Largely absent from discussions of violence, these internal vulnerabilities inhabit the private conversations of aid workers and remain mostly invisible in the analysis of violence against aid workers and agencies.

CHAPTER 6

Coping with Danger: Paradigms of Humanitarian Security Management

The "technicals" of Somalia (pickup trucks mounted with guns used to protect relief operations in 1992 and 1993), much like the bunkerized "Green Zone" of postinvasion Baghdad in 2003, exist in stark contrast to the lack of protection for the aid worker living in a village in Africa or Asia or aid organizations in Iraq in 2004, operating in deliberate anonymity and without armed protection or hard security in an effort to blend in with their surroundings. Today, most agencies employ security measures that fall somewhere between these extremes. Ideally, the measures an agency uses to protect its staff and operations derive from a sound analysis of the context, vulnerabilities, threat levels, and the agency's risk threshold. What the extremes represent, however, are dichotomous approaches to security management. As such, they mark a dramatic shift from a time when the risks of aid work were downplayed or simply seen as part of the job, to an age in which security concerns figure in everyday conversations and govern discussions and decisions about where agencies can or should operate.

Clearly, security incidents of varying degrees are not unusual, nor are they always preventable. Some of the risks of aid work, such as ambush or attacks on the road, do indeed come with the job. The fact that many attacks are intentional forces a calculation about the costs for the aid providers as measured against the benefits for those in need. In short, the calculation begets a moral quandary between an organization's responsibility to its staff and its mission to reduce poverty, provide medical care, or assist vulnerable or needy populations.

This, in turn, generates the question of how to ensure access to vulnerable populations and also to ensure protection for the agency's staff, assets, programs, and reputation. The legal context and emblems and principles of humanitarianism factor into the equation, although primary are the policies, minimum standard operating procedures, and security-management approaches designed to mitigate risk, address extant threats, and protect the agency's personnel, assets, and reputation while ensuring program continuity and access. Therefore, risk and security are organizational management issues and are increasingly defined as areas of specialized and professional expertise. Security-management strategies employ a combination of measures that range from armed escort and "hardened targets" to consent-based approaches. Implicit in the ways that agencies manage security concerns are assumptions about the role of aid actors in responding to crises and the values and principles that inform such assumptions.

This chapter examines the ways in which aid agencies protect staff and programs, focusing first on the evolution of the organizational field (DiMaggio and Powell 1983) of humanitarian security. The evolution mirrors the trajectory of the aid system (described in Chapter 5) and culminates in a professionalized and standardized field of expertise. Next, I delineate three distinct models, undergirded by a set of assumptions, which I broadly refer to as three paradigms of managing security: assumptive mechanisms, the legal regime, and operational security-management approaches. These paradigms reflect the themes emerging from the competing visions of aid described in the previous two chapters, namely how they emphasize the dominant discourse of external threat and neglect internal vulnerabilities, function to anchor security management in a narrative of exceptionalism, and undermine humanity. I explicate each of these paradigms, beginning with the assumptive paradigm and then the legal protections and the operational measures, and contrast each with a relational approach to humanitarianism and security management. By uncovering their underlying assumptions, I build the case for a way of operating that supports, rather than undermines, humanity.

The assumptive paradigm, examined first, emerges from the rescue and mythical discourses and relies on principles, emblems, symbols, and the status of humanitarian workers. These "magical shields" fulfill a discursive function, since their actual protective benefits are limited; they nevertheless remain potent in the humanitarian imagination. The legal mechanisms, examined second, hold in tension the status of aid workers as civilians with that of aid workers as a special category of protected individuals. The resulting hierarchy of status draws on and reinforces the "mythical figure" images. These first two paradigms, to varying degrees, rely on the narrative of humanitarian exceptionalism that, I argue, must be demonstrated and earned. Instead, a relational perspective questions the assumed protection of "magical shields" and seeks to frame the legal and operational protection of aid workers within the broader framework of protecting civilians.

The final paradigm, operational security management, describes practical field-level approaches to providing security. Elements of these approaches are rooted in the competing visions of empire and the institutional present, finding their genesis in the professionalization and militarization of aid and their apogee in the professionalization and fortification of security management. Even so, the seeds of a relational approach are present, primarily although not exclusively in the consent-based approaches of acceptance and negotiation of access.

The chapter ends with a proactive call for a restoration of the relational basis of aid that draws authority from recognizing the embedded nature of humanitarian actors, that takes into account the full range of threat and vulnerability, and that questions exceptionalism. Calling attention to the broader trends in security management that undermine humanity may prevent their widespread institutionalization without recognition of their full impact.

The Evolution of Security Management

The trend, described in the previous chapter, to standardize and professionalize humanitarian agencies over the past two decades also characterizes the evolution of safety and security. Prior to the early 1990s, few if any humanitarian actors considered security management in a systematic way. Early security-management efforts focused largely on personal security training and critical-incident response, reflecting the interpretation of incidents as isolated and not widespread. Over time this has shifted, with the focus on individuals and the incidents affecting them giving way to a more sophisticated, organization-focused approach of risk or security management that emphasizes standards, professional expertise, and duty of care. Together these have fundamentally shifted the internal context for aid organizations, with ramifications for how and where they operate. With this approach, security management must be more than training, documents, and security manuals, all of which only scratch the surface. Instead, security management requires changes in organizational culture and a "mainstreamed" approach to addressing vulnerabilities and threats, an approach that integrates security management into all aspects of an organization's work. A more robust emphasis on security management as an integral element of aid efforts exists as a result.

The International Committee of the Red Cross (ICRC) led the way in advancing the notion of "humanitarian security," meaning how to protect humanitarian aid workers and agency assets (compounds, equipment, programs, and reputation) and maintain access. The rampant violence in Somalia prompted the ICRC to use, for the first time in its history, armed escorts and personnel—2,600 gunmen, in fact—to protect its compounds, convoys, and staff (Moorehead 1998, 685). The dangers of operating in violent conflicts such as Liberia and the former Yugoslavia and debates over the use of armed protection in Somalia in the early 1990s resulted in the creation of an ICRC security cell in 1993,[1] the first non-UN organization to do so.[2] The ICRC published its first personal security manual in 1999 (Roberts 1999) and developed a fictional location ("Jurassie") for a training simulation that mimics the dangers delegates experience in the field (Hockstader 1997). All newly hired delegates participate in this exercise.

Security challenges in Rwanda and elsewhere as well as the deaths of Fred Cuny and six ICRC delegates in Chechnya in 1996 marked a critical juncture for the humanitarian community. In December 1996, just days before Christmas, masked gunmen attacked the Red Cross compound at Novye Atagi, outside the capital Grozny, during the early hours before dawn. A perimeter fence and armed guards protected the ICRC compound itself. The gunmen's attack was well planned and intentionally aimed to kill the expatriate delegates. They shot seven expatriate delegates while they slept in their beds. Six died. The dead included five nurses, from Canada, Norway, New Zealand, and Spain, and a construction technician from the Netherlands.[3] The perpetrators used silencers, killing their victims at point-blank range. Survivors recounted how the attackers were completely silent, not speaking a word during the three-minute attack. Those who locked their bedroom doors escaped the massacre (Beaumont 1996, 3; Moorehead 1998, 682).

The ICRC delegate general for the region, who traveled to Chechnya immediately following the murders, wrote,

Although the ICRC has yet to receive any information on the findings of the investigation, it is clear that the murders were carefully planned. The assassins were familiar with the premises and were equipped with weapons designed for this type of operation. The attack was obviously aimed at the expatriate staff, since the two Chechen interpreters sleeping in the same building as the delegates were spared, and the two guards whom the assailants came across were struck but not killed. There is every indication that the intruders intended to murder all the expatriates at the hospital, but were interrupted in this grisly undertaking when the alarm was sounded. (Bugnion 1997)

Many delegates had observed hints of the changing context for humanitarian work in the Balkans and perceived the disappearance of a taboo against attacks on aid workers.[4] For the ICRC, the tragic deaths of their delegates (including three in Burundi in June 1996 and one in Cambodia in January 1997) constituted the "end of innocence" for the ICRC and a "turning point" in the way its delegates thought about their work. The awareness of changing circumstances and the self-reflection and soul-searching engendered by the tragedies gave new impetus to security management within the organization. That the ICRC was attacked proved especially disturbing, as it challenged the belief that those working in active conflict zones, guided by the principles of neutrality and impartiality, would not be attacked. In this sense, the murders were truly shocking.

The deaths and the circumstances of the murders grabbed media headlines and drew attention to the dangers of humanitarian work. Dozens of media outlets reported the killings and subsequent withdrawal of ICRC delegates from the country. Such reports emphasized the "new" risks for aid workers and alluded to the changed circumstances within which aid workers operated: "Today, with civil wars waged increasingly by well-armed, ill-disciplined militias oblivious to the Geneva Convention and acutely attuned to the Western media appetite for mayhem, there is a consensus that the banner of neutrality has been displaced by mounting anarchy" (Appleby 1996a). The reports referred to aid workers as "no longer untouchable" (Beaumont 1996), or to the "growing tendency to see relief workers as partisans, or to use them as pawns in a larger struggle" (Knox 1996). One Médecins Sans Frontières (MSF) employee stated in response to the assassinations, "There are no longer the same brakes on everybody. There used to be a fear that if you attacked one party, you might be invoking the reaction of someone very powerful. And that's no longer the case, because there is this international paralysis of will about coming to the aid of civilians in danger or aid workers in danger" (Appleby 1996a).

An in-depth investigative report about the murders describes the paradoxical goodwill and suspicion that the ICRC field hospital, the only one in the area, generated. The hospital had opened only several months before the attack, in early September. The ICRC chose the location, twenty kilometers south of Grozny, because of the absence of fighting and the presence of a compound easily convertible to a field hospital (Bugnion 1997). The delegates and the hospital provided much-needed health services in the midst of a war zone, yet few in the town "had any experience of a western-style charitable organization, and some were suspicious. In a place with virtually no formal employment, the Red Cross arrived flush with cash, equipment and four-wheel-drive vehicles. It began hiring people to work as drivers, guards, secretaries, cooks, cleaners, translators, assistants, technicians. By local standards, the monthly salaries of $150 to $300 were princely, and the competition for jobs was intense" (Hockstader 1997, 17). This competition drew in local power brokers, who vied to make sure the ICRC hired their people. The prominent Red Cross symbol offended some, including a Muslim guerrilla commander who saw it not as a symbol of neutrality but as a Christian symbol.[5]

Signs of impending danger included warnings from the mayor about hiring practices and from the guerilla commander about the insult of the Red Cross symbol (Saffron 1997; Appleby 1996b). Nancy Malloy, one of those murdered, wrote in letters home about the "climate of lawlessness" in Chechnya. Her letters narrated how a "man entered our compound with his armed guard to complain that we had too many crosses displayed" and how "two Red Cross administrators were kidnapped because a work contract was not given to their friends" (as quoted in Appleby 1996b). Kidnappings of staff and attacks on other international organizations,[6] as well as an armed incursion into the ICRC compound at Noyve Atagi on 24 November, occurred less than a month before the murders. The attack on 17 December was deliberate, efficient, and coordinated. Were it not for a single shot that apparently caused the perpetrators to flee, it could easily have resulted in more deaths among the other twenty ICRC delegates in the compound (Hockstader 1997).

Despite the deliberate and targeted attack, the actual motive remained murky. As with Fred Cuny's murder (described in Chapter 3), the Russians and Chechens blamed each other for the murders (Zaks 1996). ICRC delegates interviewed after the attack spoke of intensified security measures in response to the verbal and written threats that preceded the murders and their belief that the attacks were political, not criminal, in nature. "Nobody ever came to assassinate in such a cowardly fashion just because you didn't hire somebody," remarked one delegate. "It was four o'clock in the morning. The men wore masks or hoods over their heads and they went about very systematically killing people."[7] No one claimed responsibility for the attacks, and the true killers remain unknown. In November 2010, however, a former Russian Federal Security Service agent wanting to defect to the West confessed to his own involvement and that of a Russian Special Forces unit pursuing a group of Chechen fighters into the hospital. The murders, he claims, were a case of mistaken identity (Boyes 2010).[8]

Throughout 1997, another sixteen aid workers were kidnapped in Chechnya. Virtually all agencies operating there pulled out because of security concerns (Hansen 1997). Chechnya thereby disappeared from the list of the most dangerous places for aid workers, not because of the absence of a need for protection or assistance but because it was too dangerous to stay.

The shockwaves extended beyond the ICRC, lending new urgency to the need for better security management among humanitarian actors operating in war zones. The brutality of the murders and the target—the ICRC—galvanized the development of organizational policies and procedures around security management and the drive to professionalize NGO/humanitarian security as well. The 1990s saw the development of training curricula and security manuals, with many emphasizing personal and site security. The larger and better-funded agencies hired security managers or directors to mainstream security management. The UN moved from a small group of security officers in the Office of the UN Security Coordinator to what are now well over two hundred staff members in the UN Department of Safety and Security (UNDSS). Each UN agency staffs its own security-management team.[9] In 2002, the UN Office for the Coordination of Humanitarian Affairs Consolidated Appeals Process required agencies to submit safety and security plans with proposals.[10] These initiatives institutionalized security management.

Within the NGO community, InterAction, the membership consortium of relief and development organizations in the United States, led an initiative to develop a training curriculum for personal security and organizational security management. It featured topics such as context and threat assessment, image and acceptance, site security, abduction, land mines, and stress and security, among others (Working Group on NGO Security 1997). This curriculum became the basis for the widely used Overseas Development Institute (ODI) Good Practice Review 8 (Van Brabant 2000; revised as Humanitarian Practice Network 2010). The NGO Registry for Engineers in Disaster Relief offered one of the early personal-security training courses, building on and adapting the InterAction curriculum to reflect its accumulated knowledge. Other agencies produced their own manuals (e.g., Rogers and Sytsma 1998; Bickley 2003; International Federation of the Red Cross and Red Crescent Societies 2007), the first of which appeared in 1995 (Cutts and Dingle 1995).

In 2001, ODI, a leading think tank on humanitarian and development issues, produced a volume on mainstreaming security management within organizations (Van Brabant 2001) and in 2004, the European Commission's Humanitarian Aid and Civil Protection department produced a series of humanitarian security resources (Barnett 2004; Mayhew 2004) and made them freely available online in multiple languages.[11] Organizations have adopted procedures and standards and hired security directors at headquarters offices. The larger and better-funded humanitarian agencies, and even some of the smaller ones, also have one or more security professionals, often a mix of national and international staff, located at regional offices and in the field. Policies and training materials tend to emphasize threat and risk assessment. They provide less guidance for national staff practices and security awareness in relation to job descriptions (Rowley, Burns, and Burnham 2010).

Security responses, however, remained largely reactive—"knee-jerk reactions"—to incidents, and often involved withdrawal after significant events. According to one security expert, "We need a change in mindset. Security is not taken seriously without a serious incident."[12]

The Professionalization and Standardization of Security Management

The development and publication of security manuals, the subsequent hiring of the first security managers for major organizations and their operations, and the standardization of policies and procedures that began in the late 1990s and coalesced in the 2000s mark an important shift in the development of an organizational field (DiMaggio and Powell 1983) of humanitarian security. The field itself is a relatively small network, where most people know each other and move from one organization to another, as they do in the humanitarian sector more generally. Several mechanisms exist that gather together security directors to discuss issues of common concern.[13] An initiative to create a professional association of individuals working in the NGO security sector is gaining momentum.[14]

The advances in security management illustrate the attention that organizations give the threats against them and their attempts to deal with the uncertainties of operating in areas wracked by war, civil unrest, natural disaster, poverty, and crime. These changes are signs of the trajectory of growth, professionalization, and maturity in the aid industry. The benefits are many: greater accountability within the profession, the development of security-management standards, the evolution of approaches, and a seriousness that underscores the life-and-death nature of the work. Nevertheless, the tensions inherent in the growth of the humanitarian industry manifest in security management as well as through the professionalization and standardization of the field. The danger is that the maturation of the field will decrease diversity and result in an orientation toward preset standards and "personnel protection," in which security is an end as opposed to a means and the ultimate aim is preserving the institution and its reputation rather than enabling the delivery of assistance and preserving the underlying relational ethos of aid. From this perspective, the effects of maturity and professionalization are not universally beneficial, nor are standards universally accepted or welcomed.

The push to professionalize created a corresponding market for security professionals. Within the sector, a small pool of applicants exists for the increasing number of positions, and agencies struggle to recruit experienced and qualified personnel. The background, qualifications, and experience of many humanitarian security officers are similar, especially at the security director level. Many cut their teeth and gained legitimacy from experience in Pakistan, Somalia, Iraq, or Darfur, which constitute some of the most dangerous operating environments for humanitarians but are not characteristic of all emergency contexts. Many security professionals are North American or European men, although agencies do hire national staff as regional or field security officers. Aid agencies, however, often do not post these national staff outside their country of origin. The women who hold security director and security field officer positions are an even lonelier bunch.[15] Especially in the 1990s and early 2000s, the predominance of former military or police officers among the ranks of security officers and directors defined the field. Agencies, unsure of how to advertise positions and what qualifications to require for security officers and directors, relied on military or police experience and credentials to identify suitable candidates.[16] While those with extensive emergency experience also hold such positions, they are fewer in number. The most experienced aid workers, who have operational experience in multiple emergencies, are more likely older and have families whom they do not want to leave behind, or they leave the profession as a result of burnout or changing personal priorities. As a result, they may be less willing to serve in danger zones. The net result is a dearth of diversity in the profiles of security professionals.

Some question whether military or private security officials really can or do understand the humanitarian ethos. This is where the experience and qualifications of security professionals often diverge from those of their fellow aid workers with more extensive programmatic experience. According to one security director, "There is a cultural clash between the military and the humanitarians. They follow orders and we don't do that. . . . When they don't know what to do, they fall back on the chain-of-command approach. That doesn't work."[17] The divergence in language, professional values, mission, and mandate has proven the source of many misunderstandings and conflicts in field operations. In these cases, the divergent "assumptive worlds" (Docherty 2001, 155–157) of military or private security actors and humanitarians that help each group make sense of the uncertainty around them may also inhibit effective communication and understanding. Although it is possible to successfully bridge this gap, individuals with military, private security, or police qualifications will naturally rely on their training, experience, and background in developing security strategies, thereby privileging particular approaches—likely falling within the "hardened" approaches—to mitigating risk. In other words, they rely on assumptions based on the model of their past experience in determining how to respond in their current positions as humanitarian security directors or field security officers.

The debate over qualifications also plays out in terms of decisions about how to provide security. Those with specific security credentials are less likely to see professionalization as problematic, while those who want to downplay security or root it within programmatic approaches are more likely to see the specialization and emphasis on security as a hindrance. Among organizations, the organizational culture also affects whether security is lodged within programs, with field staff, or under the purview of security professionals. Some organizations delegate security management to their field staff, decentralizing decision making away from headquarters to those responsible for program management and administration at the country level. Others centralize security at headquarters, within a security office staffed by those with specific responsibility for safety and security. Both options generate challenges. While the former may delegate responsibility for security to all, leaving each to his or her own devices and coping strategies, the latter risks creating a security silo, where the security manager is blamed for shortcomings and incidents. As one security director put it, "People forget about vulnerability and think that threats just 'materialize.' They think that the security person comes in, does an analysis, and that 'you will tell me my problems.' But they mean external threat and not vulnerability."[18] These approaches, to some degree, reflect an acknowledgment of different organizational cultures, built over time and in response to organizational mandates and structures (Fast et al. 2013).

Staff turnover and organizational rotation schedules compound these tensions. Staff turnover within aid agencies engenders a loss of institutional memory that could help prevent future incidents; those departing take with them knowledge of the history of organizational involvement in a country or area of a country and the pitfalls and successes of the operation, both of which could have security implications. The turnover and relatively short rotations in a country tend to favor a sense of similarity and a superficial knowledge of a country; offices and hangouts may look similar from country to country, and expatriate aid workers often run into former colleagues or friends in a new assignment. As a result, "Reinforced by frequent staff rotations, aid workers are remote from, and often fearful of, the people they aspire to help" (Duffield 2010, 471).

Despite the move toward standardization and institutionalization, organizations exhibit a degree of heterogeneity in their management approaches, thereby demonstrating the diversity of and the lack of cohesiveness among aid agencies. Security manuals and the sharing of good practice in security management encourage standardization and cooperation, as do donor requirements, such as the establishment of the UN and InterAction Minimum Operating Standards for Security (MOSS) and the UN Saving Lives Together (SLT) initiative.[19] In some contexts, aid agencies have established security-coordination bodies, such as the Afghanistan NGO Safety Organization or the Gaza Strip NGO Safety Office, among others.[20] Although the U.S.-based InterAction has established MOSS for its membership, no common MOSS exists for other regions or membership organizations. The UN Menu of Options (related to security) for contracting agencies has evolved to become SLT, a framework emphasizing security collaboration among the UN, NGOs, and intergovernmental organizations like the International Organization for Migration. It is nonbinding, although it requires more funding for full implementation in the field.

The UN is the largest actor in emergency situations, in terms of both staff numbers and budget. Agencies wishing to subcontract for the UN, one of the largest partners and funders of NGOs in crisis situations, must ensure they comply with the UN security procedures and frameworks. Yet it is also one of the more risk-averse actors.[21] How the biggest actor copes with uncertainty can exert a powerful force, encouraging or even forcing others to mimic its strategies. Under the old UN-NGO security arrangements, UN-contracted agencies were not allowed to operate in UNDSS-declared no-go zones, locations designated as too insecure and where the dangers outweigh the benefits of operating. This policy was a source of tension between the UN and NGOs and a driving factor behind the creation of the newer SLT framework. In reacting to targeted attacks, such as the 2003 Baghdad bombing and the December 2007 bombing in Algiers, the UN has hardened itself as a target, employing more guards, building stronger and higher walls, and hiring private security (Lynch 2010). While this opens up space for NGOs to distinguish themselves from the UN in their physical security architecture, it can complicate efforts of other UN-contract agencies to use nonfortified security postures. The hardened security stance also transfers a degree of risk to the softer targets, where the "softer" targets are usually NGOs or organizations that have fewer human and financial resources and that are easier to attack.[22] Similarly, organizations with restrictive security standards will be unable to operate in the most dangerous areas. This helps to explain the "risk transfer" identified in studies of security management (Stoddard, Harmer, and Haver 2006; also Wille and Fast 2013b).

Likewise, the "acceptable risk thresholds" of individuals and organizations differ and fix the invisible scale that calculates risk against benefit and determines whether or not an agency might operate in a given context (Kingston and Behn 2010). In parts of Sudan and Somalia, for instance, humanitarian access is limited or nonexistent in large swathes of the country, reflecting the inaccessibility due to road or other conditions as well as the danger for aid workers. Aid agencies cannot justify the risk against the potential benefits of assistance missions.[23] Consequently, agencies have no sense of the needs that exist outside of the areas where they already operate.

In some cases, decisions to declare or respect "no-go" areas generate criticisms that "insecurity" is used to prevent access. One aid worker claimed, "Insecurity is a deliberate attempt to keep NGOs out of certain areas. This is not being tested. DSS [the UN Department of Safety and Security] declares an area a no-go zone, and doesn't push to see whether or not insecurity is present. The perception of insecurity is essentially creating a de facto deterrent from people going to a certain region."[24] Another aid worker charged that in Sudan, "security obstacles were cited as part of the reason why aid couldn't go to rebel-held areas," providing legitimacy for the decision. This contributed to perceptions of bias in the delivery of aid and undermined humanitarian principles.[25]

Moreover, it is difficult to get liability insurance for war zones, and ethically it is difficult to justify known and substantial risks to staff, even if individuals are willing to take the risk to help others.[26] Yet another aid worker charged that the costs of security have "mushroomed," and that many decisions are motivated by insurance and liability concerns. This, he proposed, is about "the politicization of security decisions, not about danger."[27]

Professionalization encourages the development of standards and qualifications as well as shared perspectives and practices. These undoubtedly contribute to the safety and security of aid workers. The danger is that professionalization and standardization stifle the creativity inherent in an interdisciplinary approach and thus further separate aid workers from those they are meant to help. These developments, in turn, can detract from the relational ethos of aid as an act of mercy in the midst of war and render the practice more bureaucratic and static as opposed to flexible and responsive to the suffering of others. One aid expert echoed this view: "We emphasize structure over values. The structures are overpowering and have stopped serving the needs of people."[28]

To remain true to its original purpose, humanitarian aid work cannot lose sight of its compassionate and relational beginnings as it moves forward into an uncertain future; the ways that organizations manage their security help to chart the path forward.

Protective Coloring, Humanitarian Inviolability, and Altruistic Immunity: The Assumptive Paradigm of Security Management

> For the first half century of its existence, the United Nations felt protected by its flag and the reality that it was a neutral, benevolent actor in world events. When United Nations personnel were directly targeted, it was generally viewed as an isolated event.
> —UN Department of Safety and Security website[29]

As this quotation illustrates, humanitarians for many years assumed that the principles of neutrality and impartiality or their skin color and foreign passports would protect them from attack, or that the symbols and emblems of humanitarianism and multilateral action, like the Red Cross or the UN flag, would be enough to insulate them from harm. The tale of one aid worker evinces the power of such mechanisms and of "protective emblems." The aid worker told me of a female African national staff person of the Red Cross who donned a cloth vest adorned with the Red Cross emblem as part of her work in a war zone. To identify an aid worker with his or her organization is common practice; many aid workers wear T-shirts or other clothing with organizational logos. The national staff person in question believed the vest was bullet proof, endowed with magical protective qualities, and because of the moniker of "protective vest," that it would help keep her safe in the field.[30]

To depend on emblems, flags, or passports for protection implies putting faith in a tangible yet apotropaic mechanism. In this way, these mechanisms serve a similar function to the "protective vest" with its magical qualities. And to some degree, they likely did. One UN aid worker with responsibilities for security in Sudan in the 1980s remembered, "The UN flag used to protect us.... We self-evacuated as field staff (we had no access to management in HQ to help make the decision). We made the decision to relocate, by boat. We passed by one faction of the SPLA. We weren't escorted, but they saw the flag and let us go."[31]

This assumptive paradigm of aid worker protection essentially relies on various types of "magical shields" endowed with the ability to protect aid workers. These range from the "protective colours of the endangered chameleon" (Slim 1995a, 123) to a "humanitarian inviolability" that derives from the principles of neutrality and impartiality (Anderson 2004). The protective colors that make aid workers sacrosanct come in the form of multicolored agency logos, the emblems of the Red Cross or the light blue laurel wreath of the UN, and the white, Western faces (and their foreign citizenship) that personify aid work. Each of these, it is assumed, provides some element of protection. Buttressing the protective coloring are the rescue discourse and the mythical images of aid workers and aid organizations that reify their altruistic endeavors and good intentions and brand them as revered outsiders. Likewise, aid workers and others see the humanitarian principles of neutrality, impartiality, and independence as providing or enhancing protection, based on an assumption that not taking sides or providing aid based on need distinguishes humanitarians from conflict parties or others who profit from war and violence. This thereby provides a measure of protection. These attributes and colors, in short, mark aid actors, and humanitarians in particular, as separate and somehow inviolable.

In contrast to the reality that those who profess allegiance to or are perceived as helping one side of the conflict or the other seem to be legitimate targets, humanitarians have traditionally conceived of themselves as immune from the violence surrounding them. The erosion of such mechanisms has featured in commentaries about violence against aid workers. According to one aid worker, "The principles have become eroded.... The Red Cross, the UN symbols have less value and respect than before. We have become agents of foreign policy rather than agents of help."[32] Louise Arbour, a former UN high commissioner for human rights, lamented in 2007 that "the blue [UN] flag is not any more the kind of protection that historically we assumed it was" (as quoted in CBC News 2007). Ten years earlier, commentators bemoaned the disappearing respect for the Red Cross emblem in Chechnya. After the deaths of the six ICRC delegates in Chechnya, one journalist wrote,

> They were vulnerable and visible, crisscrossing the Chechen roads in their gleaming white Toyotas, unarmed, without flak jackets or helmets. They relied on persuasion to get past obstructive soldiers and fighters, on walkie-talkies and satphones for mutual reassurance and location reporting, and most of all on the residual power of the Red Cross symbol. But even when it was becoming clear how little respect the cross really commanded, no one expected the cold-blooded murder of sleeping nurses in the dead of night. (Beaumont 1996)

These and other comments are often tinged with incredulity about who might want to perpetrate such attacks and why. According to those ascribing to this paradigm, the upward trend in attacks on aid workers signified the erosion of such mechanisms and a worrisome harbinger of deadlier times. The taboo against attacks on aid workers had disappeared.

Assuming Protection in the Age of Fear and Terror

While few agencies now rely solely on assumptive mechanisms, these mechanisms solidly underpin some of the dominant discourses about security and the causes of attacks against aid workers and aid organizations. The assumptive paradigm may not function in the absence of other operational mechanisms of protecting the helpers, yet it is present, if implicit, in statements that attribute responsibility for incidents to the blurring of lines between civilian and military actors. Underlying such a statement is the idea that if humanitarians mark themselves with distinguishing brands or emblems, then the attackers will know that humanitarians are civilians and are not part of the conflict environment within which they operate. While it is important to distinguish between the two, this does not provide protection. Given that civilians have consistently, over time, been deliberately and indirectly killed in war (Slim 2007), why should aid workers be any different?

The idea that the protective colors have ceased to function as such, the demise of the taboo against attacking aid workers, the erosion of a humanitarian inviolability, and the deliberate targeting and increased numbers of attacks against aid workers (regardless of the rate of attack) all contribute to a sense of uncertainty and fear about the shifting ground and rapid change in providing aid in dangerous places. All suggest that the violence is exceptional, a violation of an accepted order. Although the breakdown of the perceived taboo on attacking aid workers began in the 1990s, the very public, targeted, brutal, and frequent acts of violence against aid workers in places such as Iraq, Pakistan, or Afghanistan after 9/11 magnified this perception and merely confirmed the extent of the change and the unpredictability of violence. These factors contribute to and reinforce the notion of humanitarianism in crisis, a recurrent theme in the literature on humanitarianism since the mid-1990s (see, e.g., Uvin 1998; Moore 1999; Terry 2002; Vaux 2004; Barnett and Weiss 2008b). The sense of crisis heightens uncertainty, with the two locked in a mutually reinforcing cycle that raises questions about the nature of the enterprise and how best to respond in changing times.

The violence in Iraq in 2003 and 2004 proved particularly deadly for aid workers, magnifying uncertainty and challenging long-held assumptions about security. Only two months after the August 2003 Baghdad bombing, another suicide bomb killed twelve people in front of the headquarters of the ICRC in Baghdad. As one aid worker observed, "To hit MSF and the ICRC sends the deepest shock waves. If they hit an NGO associated with the US Department of Defense, it is almost local"[33]—the implication being that to hit a "local" target was expected, and therefore less newsworthy. The ICRC had withdrawn some of its international delegates earlier that year after an ICRC Sri Lankan water engineer was deliberately assassinated in July, a devastating blow to the organization. After the October bombing, it dramatically curtailed its operation and closed its offices to the public, leaving its national staff to operate by remote management from their homes and through the Iraqi Red Crescent. Nevertheless, Iraq remained an operational priority for the ICRC. Internal investigations into the bombing to better understand why it happened suggested the perpetrators deliberately targeted the ICRC, but not necessarily the symbol of the Red Cross. Instead, the attack was directed at the whole effort to reconstruct Iraq, with which the ICRC was seen to be associated.[34] Therefore, the general Iraqi population's level of acceptance for the ICRC and its mission was likely intact, but the same acceptance did not exist for the "war on terror"–associated agenda of reconstruction.

The kidnapping and murder of Margaret Hassan, the country director for CARE and a British and Irish citizen, in October and November 2004 occurred during a period of intense violence in Iraq, both among Iraqis and directed at aid workers and foreigners in the country. Hassan, with her long-term experience in and intimate knowledge of Iraq, was seen as untouchable or, at the least, less vulnerable than other expatriates in the country. According to the assumptive paradigm, Hassan's ties to the Iraqi community via her conversion to Islam, knowledge of Arabic, and marriage to an Iraqi, her work to help the Iraqi people, and her decades of experience as an aid worker should have protected her. Her kidnapping and killing provided a chilling message: "To scare people, you kill Margaret Hassan, who has lived in Iraq for decades, is married to an Iraqi, and speaks Arabic. Who else would you kill to make a more visible statement?"[35]

Her kidnapping and murder challenged the notion that "acceptance"—interpreted in the passive sense to mean that one's ties to the community and understanding of the context should, on their own, create consent for an individual's presence—could provide security. Her understanding of Iraq and its people, its culture, and its traditions undoubtedly contributed to her effectiveness as an aid worker, even if it did not ultimately protect her. Particularly for organizations applying an acceptance strategy, an often-unstated yet potent question is whether an attack signifies the failure of the organization to secure consent and acceptance, which thereby serves as an indictment of the agency and its mission.

Hassan's death illustrated the failures of the assumptive paradigm (as opposed to acceptance) and contributed to the dismantling of an image of aid workers rooted in exceptionalism: that aid workers are inviolable because of the principles they uphold, their knowledge of or connection to a context, or their outsider colors and affiliations. To function as an effective protection mechanism, however, acceptance requires consent not only from community members but also, and more important, from stakeholders who have the capacity and motive to harm aid workers or agencies. Thus, while some stakeholders may have accepted Hassan (and unquestionably did), this acceptance did not hold in other quarters of society. Her death, unfortunately, served as proof positive of the need to fortify and separate in order to stay safe.

Hassan's death sent shock waves through CARE as an organization and precipitated major changes in its security-management system. Her death and the organization's response revealed "serious flaws in the decision-making system as well as leadership issues among members of the confederation," including in competing lines of authority (or lack of authority) for safety, security, and decision making among various CARE organizational members. In response, CARE created a director for global safety and security, a position housed in the International Secretariat in Geneva. The director position retains the responsibility to develop and oversee security policies, to intervene in crisis situations, to coordinate between members as needed, and to refer any security matters to a board of appeals in cases where decisions might lead to breaches of security protocols.[36] These changes, in turn, necessitated a shift in organizational culture, which followed more slowly than mandated changes in policy. CARE closed its operations in Iraq following Hassan's death, acceding to the wishes she expressed in one of the last video statements broadcast on Al Jazeera (BBC News 2005).

Why was Hassan targeted? Multiple explanations for her disappearance and death exist, which illustrate the complexity of the causes of the violence that afflicts aid workers and aid delivery. One anthropologist propounds that Hassan was attacked *because* of who she was—a humanitarian—and that she was not, as popular myth proclaims, protected because of it. In other words, aid workers are attacked because of the powerful symbols they personify and represent. Hassan's murder, Laura Hammond writes, was a form of terrorism, with strategic and practical benefits to the attackers, designed to "instill fear in the public and doubts about the abilities of the state and its agents to provide protection" (Hammond 2008, 178). According to this interpretation, in murdering Hassan, her killers highlighted the violence in Iraq and simultaneously demonstrated the strength of the insurgency and the inability of the powers that be, in this case the occupation forces, to prevent such attacks. By beheading Hassan and thus challenging and subverting all she represented, they sent a disturbing and effective message that no one was immune, and certainly not expatriate aid workers with fewer ties to and less knowledge of the Iraqi people and context than Hassan. Hammond calls this "violence as performance," where "the objective of violence is not only to inflict harm on an individual or group (causing pain, suffering, or death may not even be a primary objective), but also to deliver a shockingly powerful message about the capabilities of the perpetrators to audiences that may be both near to and far from the site of the act" (Hammond 2008, 177–178). Indeed, Hassan's death received far more news coverage than the plight of the thousands of Iraqis who were kidnapped or killed around the same time, illustrating the exceptionalism that often characterizes violence against aid workers.

This interpretation, however, does not represent the whole story. Other murky yet hidden explanations both complicate attempts to interpret motives and illuminate the various factors contributing to such acts of violence. Hammond's analysis of Margaret Hassan's murder, for example, relies heavily on a news story citing commentary from a British Islamic radical activist named Anjem Choudary, who claimed that Hassan and other female aid workers were "legitimate targets" because they were helping the "occupying power" (McDonald 2004). While the explanation is plausible and demonstrates the theater value of violence against aid workers, it both conforms to the terror narratives prominent at the time and assumes that these claims were those of her actual kidnappers and killers. In reality, the motives of the perpetrators were likely more obscure. Investigations into Hassan's death revealed an alternative interpretation: that her kidnapping was a criminal act, motivated by ransom, and not connected to her work as CARE's country director.[37] In this way, her death, though tragic, was not exceptional in that it was consistent with the pervasive and horrific violence that afflicted civilians in Iraq at that time.[38] Hassan was targeted as a civilian, and not protected as an aid worker.

Similarly, although the Taliban initially claimed responsibility for the deaths of ten staff members of the International Assistance Mission (IAM) in Afghanistan in early August 2010, Taliban leaders later rejected this claim and offered condolences to the families of the team members. It appears instead that those responsible for the deaths were criminals, who targeted the team because they were foreigners, not because they were aid workers (IAM 2010b; IRIN 2010a; Clark 2010a, 2010b, 2010c). Both of these incidents—Hassan's death and the deaths of the ten IAM workers—represented opportunities for militants to claim responsibility and generate publicity to advance their cause, regardless of their actual involvement in the events. IAM curtailed its Eye Camp operations and revisited its security protocols as a result of the killings, but did not withdraw from Afghanistan (IAM 2010b). The fact that IAM did not leave testifies to the increasing sophistication of security management (that withdrawal is one of several options and not an automatic response) and the higher levels of risk tolerance, more generally, among NGOs working in insecure environments.

Unfortunately, a prominent lesson of the humanitarian experience in Iraq and Afghanistan following 9/11 seems to be that a security-management strategy that relies on consent for and "acceptance" of an agency's presence and work is not effective in the polarized context of the "war on terror," since those most "accepted," such as Margaret Hassan and the ten IAM aid workers, were no less immune to violence. Lost in the shuffle was the equally plausible lesson that acceptance must be earned from multiple stakeholders and sustained over time.[39] Instead, led by the UN, many agencies have institutionalized and professionalized security management, often relying on more militarized approaches. In the process, the implicit message is that of "personnel protection" as the more important aim. Curiously, while the deaths of Hassan and the IAM aid workers questioned the effectiveness and value of an acceptance approach, the failures of the protective and deterrent measures to protect aid workers often result in calls for more, and not less, hard security, revealing a higher burden of proof for the relationally based approaches such as acceptance. In these ways, the security agenda has trumped the relational ethos of humanitarianism.

The deliberate attacks against aid workers call into question the existence of a taboo against aid workers and the protective value of the emblems and logos. Instead, a more accurate question is whether the colors, emblems, and principles of the assumptive paradigm ever offered anything more than a false sense of protection. Instead, the assumptive paradigm fails to address the causes of violence against aid workers. In ascribing attributes and power to the principles and symbols of humanitarianism that they do not have, the paradigm undermines the actual value of the humanitarian currency.

Contrasting Approaches

The shared roots of the assumptive paradigm are grounded in and reflective of the heroic image and rescue story of aid work, and of a perspective that conceptualizes aid work and aid workers as exceptional and axiomatically separate. The roots of the paradigm are at once paradoxical and multiple, nurtured in the soil of humanitarian principles, the altruism of the founding stories, the traditional outsider status of humanitarians and humanitarian agencies, and even the convenient (if largely inaccurate) images of white aid workers generated for Western consumption. It is precisely these foundations that I seek to uproot with a relational analysis.

Humanitarians are visibly branded outsiders, drawing on the powerful message of humanitarianism and its principles of neutrality, impartiality, and independence that all assert a philosophical and sometimes physical separation from the parties and issues in a conflict or from others with a partial and therefore biased agenda. Because aid workers are not part of the conflict and because they are helping, they should not be attacked. They are alternatively immune or inviolable. Hassan's murder forces a reevaluation of this assumption, given that she likely was attacked because of her affiliations. Relying solely on such assumptions promotes passivity, where security is interpreted as being present until proven otherwise (i.e., an attack) and not necessarily proactively sought.

Humanitarian principles serve a vital function in relation to acts of mercy, as principles that govern the provision of assistance and thereby open the door to accessing populations in need. Therefore, they are valuable in and of themselves. The function of these principles, however, is not literally *protective*; principles do not, in and of themselves, protect humanitarians from harm. In guiding acts of mercy, the principles and their claims paradoxically separate humanitarians from those they are helping and from the conflicts in which they intervene—by not taking sides, by remaining independent from political and partial agendas, and by providing assistance based on need alone. They even uphold some of the inherent inequalities of the global system: by providing only lifesaving assistance, they do not challenge the status quo or support the aspirations of those working for social change (the critique of those advocating for acts for justice and not only mercy). At the same time, this separation detracts from the relational aspects of the work. It is for this reason and in support of a justice (as opposed to a solely merciful) stance that some agencies have chosen solidarity or accompaniment as their guiding principles in lieu of those of neutrality, independence, or even impartiality.

Demonstrating the principles in action, as opposed to merely stating their meaning and affirming their value, is more difficult and sometimes controversial or unpopular. It is, nevertheless, vital. This is also where the value and contributions of a relational approach become apparent. In their demonstration, the underlying tensions and inconsistencies of the assumptive paradigm fall into sharper relief. Asserting neutrality and impartiality often involves hiring staff from different social, religious, political, or ethnic groups in a country, in addition to expatriate outsiders. The white and Western image of some aid workers is precisely what many NGOs are working to correct by hiring more national staff and is what underpins reform efforts to decrease the Western imprint and practices of aid.

Ironically, the increase in national staff has diversified and arguably eroded the "protective coloring" of aid, since the vast majority of aid workers are citizens of the countries in which they work. In this way, strategic hiring reflects the "colors" of the context and affirms aid workers as embedded within the civilian population, both of which embody a relational approach. National staff face different risks as a result of their (assumed) partiality, and hiring in this way attempts to "balance" the overall risk even as it cannot address the differential individual risks. In this way, hiring staff is akin to developing "multi-partiality" so that everyone sees himself or herself in the agency, or at least sees someone "like me" in the agency and its staff composition. In making a decision to hire staff on this basis, an agency helps to reduce the internal vulnerability related to staff composition and thereby to prevent or minimize acts or threats of violence against the agency and its programs, reputation, or staff (Fast, Freeman, et al. 2011; Fast et al. 2013). The agencies' security strategies, from a relational perspective, must deliberately and proactively address differential risk.

The differing status of staff also elicits tension with regard to security-management policies and procedures. When violence erupts, the international agencies and international staff often depart, whether by evacuation or withdrawal. Outsiders *can* leave, regardless of whether or not they choose to take advantage of the option. Thus, the hierarchies that predominate in many agencies and in the aid system itself, between national and international staff, and even the special protections in international law for some categories of aid workers, extend such privileges. These privileges can be simultaneously a source of resentment among those who do not benefit from these advantages and of guilt on the part of those who benefit but recognize the inherent inequalities and wish these benefits extended to their less privileged colleagues.

The exceptionalism here is based on privilege and hierarchy, both of which are in tension with the relational basis of humanitarianism and the equality inherent in the principle of humanity. Implementing identical security-management policies for all staff, however, does not address the differential risks of staff or the practical realities of the situation, since evacuating national staff to another country may involve separating staff members from their families and might require entry or exit visas, which may be hard to obtain on short notice or for certain populations. Instead, a proactive engagement that involves all staff members in discussions about appropriate and effective measures that address differential risk is crucial. Such discussions must see all aid workers as embedded within webs of relationships that both protect and render them vulnerable.

While the assumptive mechanisms might indeed have offered a degree of protection, it is imperative to acknowledge the fundamental tensions these mechanisms create. This version of protective exceptionalism rests on a sense of privilege and paternalism that is incongruous with the relational roots, principles, and vision of a shared humanity that underpin both acts of mercy and acts of justice. The paradigm, as part of the analytical frame, also conveniently supports the dominance of external causes while neglecting internal vulnerabilities. It assumes that the power of symbols and colors will supersede circumstances and overcome individual or organization actions or inactions. The danger lies in this very *assumption* that the protective colors and logos provide protection, rather than in a multidimensional analysis of risk and vulnerability, an analysis that might have brought to the surface other reasons for attacks. To be true to and consistent with the relational interpretation of aid, humanitarian exceptionalism must be won and not be based on privilege, earned and not assumed or simply stated.

Paradoxically, some of the assumptive mechanisms also erode whatever protection such symbols and mechanisms may have afforded aid workers. Withdrawal sends the (unintended) message that targeting humanitarians will cause them to leave, leaving the perpetrators to continue their excesses against civilian populations with impunity and without being watched. Continuing aid operations in virtual anonymity, however, diminishes the protective and distinguishing value of humanitarian symbols. In operating invisibly, challenging or counteracting rumors and accusations that others may unleash—accusations charging aid organizations act as spies for foreign governments, that they are ineffective or corrupt, or that they are not doing anything to help the local population—becomes next to impossible. This is especially problematic and potentially dangerous if local communities hear that NGOs are receiving money, but see no evidence of how the money helps them. According to one security director, "There is a tendency [of NGOs] to reduce the visibility of what they do and then the population doesn't understand. It is good to be discrete but make sure people know what you are doing. This is a tough balance. You pay a price because you are not visible—you are seen the same as everyone else but you might be targeted because of your visibility."[40]

The emblems and logos of aid work are externally directed. Agencies use logos and brands to visibly encourage differentiation between organizations, and presumably, their staff educate local populations about an organization's uniqueness among agencies in the same operating context. Aid organizations post signage with their logos or emblems at office compounds and on vehicles, and create websites to convey information about what it does, why, and where. In emergency contexts, some agencies go to great lengths to emphasize distinction. In Angola in the 1990s, for example, MSF went so far as to paint a pink stripe on its vehicles to differentiate them from UN and other white four-wheel-drive vehicles on the roads.

Distinction, however, is not the same as protection. Seeing emblems as protective inherently assumes that people value the presence and activities of the organization in question (Fast et al. 2013). One security director opined, "The protection is not from the emblem but what's behind it," observing that an emblem's protective value is related to behavior and action.[41] Without emblems, however, people are left to wonder what happens behind walled compounds or what agencies are actually doing that contributes to the well-being of the population, as in the vignette about localized grievances in a southern African country (see Chapter 1). Without such markers, the local population is left with fewer clues to figure out the benefits and services that the organization offers.

Thus, the demise of the power and value of the assumptive mechanisms is not entirely externally generated. Both options—using or not using emblems—assume each strategy offers a measure of protection. The power of the assumptive mechanisms lies in the intangible factors—their psychological value as a symbol of humanity and the value of mercy—rather than an actual protective value. A relational approach interprets the symbols, flags, and colors of aid in this light and examines the vulnerabilities of all aid workers in light of the specific context in which they operate. This requires an analysis of the interactions of aid workers as integral to and not separate from the conflict environment and the aid response.

The Law as Protection: The Legal Codification of Humanitarian Exceptionalism

> It is essential to frame the context in terms of numbers of civilians who die (much higher) and numbers of aid workers who die (much lower). Otherwise it is almost immoral to devote this much attention to the issue [of violence against aid workers]. We choose to put ourselves in harm's way. Civilians don't.
> —Aid expert[42]

Various legal mechanisms to protect humanitarians exist within international law, both customary and codified. These protections derive primarily, though not solely, from the law regulating armed conflict and war and specifically from "Hague law" (the laws of war), "Geneva law" (protection of persons), and international criminal law. Therefore, the protections reflect the violent context within which humanitarians operate. The Geneva Conventions and Additional Protocols offer humanitarians protection by virtue of their status as civilians, not because of their status as humanitarians. Several mechanisms offer more specific protection, including the 1994 Convention and 2005 Optional Protocol to the Convention on the Safety of United Nations and Associated Personnel, the 1998 Rome Statute (which established the International Criminal Court, or ICC), and UN Security Council Resolution 1502. In addition, the 1946 Convention on the Privileges and Immunities of the United Nations criminalizes attacks on UN property and premises. Article 2, Section 3 declares UN premises "inviolable," but the treaty makes no reference to UN personnel.[43] This and other legal instruments put responsibility for the protection of aid workers in the hands of states, which in many contexts is inadequate. State compliance in relation to prosecuting perpetrators or even in complying with responsibilities under the various conventions can break down, especially in violent contexts.

Increased attacks against UN peacekeepers prompted the passage of the 1994 Convention on the Safety of UN and Associated Personnel (hereinafter the 1994 Convention).[44] Many hailed the 1994 Convention as a step forward, and its passage generated extensive analysis of its implications for the protection of humanitarian actors and in relation to international humanitarian law (see especially Bloom 1995; Bouvier 1995; Bourloyannis-Vrailas 1995; Arsanjani 1995). An Optional Protocol to the 1994 Convention was adopted on 8 December 2005 and entered into force on 19 August 2010, the third anniversary of the Baghdad bombing and also World Humanitarian Day.[45] The Optional Protocol extends the scope of the 1994 Convention beyond UN operations to maintain international peace and security for those circumstances in which an "exceptional risk" exists, including for those operations that involve emergency humanitarian assistance and peacebuilding, as well as the delivery of development or political assistance.

The 1998 Rome Statute also provides some protection, as it labels "intentional attacks" against personnel, assets, and installations of humanitarian assistance missions as war crimes and defines as a crime the "improper use of a flag of truce, of the flag or of the military insignia and uniform of the enemy or of the United Nations, as well as of the distinctive emblems of the Geneva Conventions, resulting in death or serious personal injury" (Rome Statute Article 8(2)b(vii), as cited in Higgins 2003). UN Security Council Resolution 1502, passed after the August 2003 bombing of the UN headquarters in Baghdad, reaffirms existing legal protections and obligations and does not offer any new protections beyond those of the Geneva Conventions and Additional Protocols, the Rome Statute, and the 1994 Convention.

It does, however, broaden the scope of persons to include "humanitarian workers" as well as UN and associated personnel (Suttenberg 2005).

The legal mechanisms adopted to provide protection for aid workers highlight the conundrum of definitions and the challenge of determining who is covered under the law. Specifically, the various legal mechanisms create a hierarchy of differential protection that exceptionalizes certain categories of aid workers, providing the most protection for UN and associated personnel. In doing so, they highlight the tension between protecting aid workers and the populations they assist and codify the internal hierarchies that characterize the aid system, both within agencies (between national and international staff) and within the system itself (between different aid actors). This is a manifestation of the inclination to characterize aid workers as an exceptional population.

Exceptionalizing Aid Workers

The 1994 Convention, at least until the Optional Protocol entered into force in 2010, offered protection only for UN and associated personnel and for peacekeepers in particular. Its scope of application was limited to UN operations and situations of "exceptional risk." For the purposes of the convention, UN operations were defined as missions established by a "competent organ" of the UN and under UN command and control. Thus, any mission under the command of individual states or intergovernmental bodies, even those with Security Council authorization, fell outside the scope of the convention (Bourloyannis-Vrailas 1995). Either the Security Council or the General Assembly could declare situations of "exceptional risk," which would also mean the convention would apply. This is an inherently political action, however, since most governments would vehemently protest such a designation referring to the situation in their respective countries. In the treaty deliberations, some delegations expressed reservations about this "trigger mechanism," since the declaration forces troop-contributing countries to justify placing their troops at such "exceptional risk" (Bloom 1995, 623n9).

Furthermore, if UN personnel engaged in combat operations, the convention no longer applied. In this case, the laws of war and Geneva Conventions came into play. Evan Bloom attributes this to the need to preserve the applicability of the laws of Geneva. He writes,

One important reason for this was to avoid undermining the Geneva Conventions, which rely in part for their effectiveness on all forces being treated equally. It was widely held that the new Convention should not criminalize attacks on UN forces engaged as combatants in an international armed conflict, as this could (by making the very act of waging war against the United Nations a criminal offense, and thus favoring one side over the other) lessen the willingness of opposing forces to adhere to the laws of war. (Bloom 1995, 625)

The Optional Protocol to the 1994 Convention, passed in 2005, expanded the scope to which the 1994 Convention applied, but it maintained the original definition of "protected personnel," meaning UN and associated personnel (Mackintosh 2007, 124).

As a result, the strongest mechanisms offering legal protection do not apply to all aid workers. The 1994 Convention and the Optional Protocol apply to only two categories of personnel: UN personnel working for a UN operation (and other UN personnel working in the area of such an operation) and "associated personnel," which includes non-UN staff, but only those who are in a special contractual relationship to the UN. A contractual relationship, by its very nature, implies a degree of UN influence over the activities of non-UN agencies involved in the operation (see Bloom 1995, 624; Bourloyannis-Vrailas 1995, 565), something that independent humanitarian actors prefer to avoid.

Analysts assailed this deficiency, pointing out that perpetrators do not necessarily distinguish between various types of UN personnel (hence the extension of protection to all UN personnel in the same area) or have knowledge of the contractual status of non-UN entities. Nevertheless, in negotiating the 1994 Convention, such arguments did not hold sway over those states that, based on claims that universal criminal jurisdiction represents an infringement of state sovereignty, objected to the broader definition, which they were willing to permit for peacekeepers but not for UN activities in general (Bloom 1995, 624). In expanding the scope of coverage to include associated personnel, the Optional Protocol stretched the coverage of the convention to include humanitarian, development, and peacebuilding operations, but this protection does not extend to humanitarian or other actors that are not in a contractual relationship with a UN operation. In other words, it too offers no protection to independent humanitarian actors.

For independent humanitarian actors, a problematic linkage to the UN exists for agencies that receive UN funds, operate under UN contract, or sign on to UN security protocols. This linkage is not only perceptual and operational, but legal as well, with attendant implications for how and under what legal regimes prosecutions of perpetrators of crimes against humanitarian personnel are possible. Given the integration agenda of the UN, however, whereby its humanitarian and political functions are united in policy and in practice, some humanitarian actors and NGOs are hesitant to formally associate or contract with UN agencies, for fear of compromising their neutral or independent stance and therefore their ability to operate. This is especially troublesome in contexts where the UN is particularly politically active or has deployed peacekeeping forces.

Under these laws, personnel of the United Nations family receive the most comprehensive legal protection, and staff of NGOs, especially those vigorously asserting their independence, are mostly left to their own devices. Ironically, the very elements that might make them targets of violence (e.g., nationality) also offer protection, while the principles of independence and neutrality offer scant legal protection. In analyzing the various mechanisms of legal protection for humanitarian actors, Kate Mackintosh, international law advisor for MSF, concludes: "Members of independent humanitarian organizations have less protection, legally speaking, than most of them probably think. Two key features of their work—their neutrality and their independence—as well as practical steps they take to implement these principles, actually serve to place them outside much of the protection afforded to either civilians or medical workers assigned to a party to the conflict" (Mackintosh 2007, 129). For example, whether the conflict is international or internal changes the nature of the protection. In international conflicts, additional protection accrues only to "enemy nationals" (citizens of enemy states) or those without diplomatic representation. In other words, legal protection in international conflicts is based on nationality under the Geneva Conventions.

Humanitarian organizations, however, often send nonenemy nationals to work in active war zones to preserve, reinforce, or create the perception of neutrality or, at the least, minimize the risk of targeted attacks against these nationals. For instance, some NGOs avoided sending Americans to work in Iraq. Ironically, these very practices diminish the legal protection the Geneva Conventions offer to aid workers. The protection for humanitarians is actually greater in noninternational/internal conflicts. In these conflicts, legal protection is based not on nationality but instead on the civilian character of humanitarians and specifically on their status as "persons taking no active part in the hostilities." If a serious violation occurs, those responsible could be prosecuted for war crimes and held criminally liable (Mackintosh 2007, 120).

A similar paradox exists in relation to armed escort, one of the mechanisms that many aid agencies have used in violent contexts such as Iraq, Afghanistan, Somalia, or northern Uganda at the height of the conflict there. Common Article 3 of the Geneva Conventions, which stipulates a minimum set of protections that apply to all armed conflict, requires a "nexus between the crime and the armed conflict in order to bring the act within the scope of international law" (Mackintosh 2007, 121). This can occur if a perpetrator perceives the victim to be helping the other side. Armed escort, particularly from parties to the conflict, may brand humanitarians as doing precisely that, while at the same time it may also breach the principles of independence or neutrality. Indeed, the risk for humanitarian organizations lies in the association with those who escort them, which raises the paradox of increasing their vulnerability to targeting while simultaneously providing legal protection (Mackintosh 2007, 122).

In certain cases, additional protection derives from the emblems and symbols used to distinctly identify the actor associated with the emblem. The ICRC and the International Federation of Red Cross and Red Crescent Societies (IFRC) benefit from additional protection related to the Red Cross emblem. Under the Geneva Conventions, the emblem—and its sister symbols of the Red Crescent and the Red Crystal (see Additional Protocol III to the Geneva Conventions)—covers the activities of the ICRC, the IFRC, and the national Red Cross societies. States party to the Geneva Conventions are responsible for regulating the use of the emblem, which refers primarily to medical care for civilians and wounded combatants. Facilities, services, and those providing such care are protected through the use of the emblem under the conventions.

While the Red Cross emblem is protected under international law and its misuse is a breach of international law, abuse of the emblem has a long history.[46] The blue laurel wreath of the UN is also protected under international law, but the logos and brands of other relief and development agencies do not have equivalent legal status. As a result, protection of these two emblems is specific and does not extend to the logos of NGOs, which they use to "brand" programs, activities, and even staff members, and to provide a visible way of distinguishing one agency and its activities from another.

The 1994 Convention likewise established the importance of emblems as distinctive features and links identification to intention. The convention defines an intentional attack as related to knowing the victim is associated with the UN and not simply an attack due to negligence (Bloom 1995, 626–629). Article 3 of the 1994 Convention requires identification of military and police personnel and their means of transportation, and documentation of UN association even if this documentation is not immediately visible. Bloom writes,

> This provision balances the desirability (including from the point of view of establishing intent under the Convention) of having covered personnel clearly identified as associated with the United Nations or the operation in question, and concerns expressed by the UN Secretariat that in some situations wearing the UN symbol might lead to an *increased* risk of attack. It was the clear intention of the negotiators that the wearing of identification by the victim not be a prerequisite for the criminal liability of a defendant. (Bloom 1995, 628; see also Bourloyannis-Vrailas 1995, 569–570)

This point is important, as it allows the UN to contextualize its security-management approach, by either clearly identifying or removing identifying markers depending on the context and level of risk without compromising the available legal protection.

In some cases, compliance with legal instruments, politics, and humanitarian security collide. For many organizations, including the UN, field security training is compulsory and employee benefits are contingent on compliance with security-management protocols. Failure to comply could result in loss of benefits or limited liability for the organizations in the event something does go wrong (see Duffield 2010, 463). Living in Israel, for instance, is often part of security-management policies and procedures for international staff of organizations working in the West Bank or Gaza Strip. For those married to Palestinian spouses without permits to live in Israel, this elicits an inherent contradiction: risk losing one's benefits or maintain a separate residence from one's family. In the case of the UN, this issue is a legal one, since the 1946 UN Convention on Privileges and Immunities exempts UN employees and spouses from immigration restrictions (see discussion in Fast 2006, 25).

For all its value, legal protection offers no clear and practical solution to the issue of violence against aid workers and aid agencies. Law regulates the behavior of those who respect it and sets standards of acceptable conduct in a society. For those who do not respect the law, it specifies sanctions. Punishment, therefore, is understood as a preventive strategy. It remains up to states to investigate, arrest, and prosecute those responsible for attacks; this is often lacking. In an address to the Security Council regarding the safety and security of UN and associated humanitarian personnel, former UN Deputy Secretary-General Louise Fréchette reported that between January 1992 and February 2000, 184 UN staff members died in the line of duty, of whom ninety-eight were murdered. Yet, she admonished, in only two of these cases had the authorities arrested and consequently convicted the persons responsible (UN 2000). Not much has changed over time, as many of those responsible for acts of violence against aid workers remain at large.

While not necessarily existentially important to or protective of aid workers, the legal protections do establish rules of behavior and provide a mechanism for determining right and wrong. In the case of attacks against aid workers, the various conventions clearly spell out the moral unacceptability of such actions. In this way, the most important contribution of the 1994 Convention is its stance that attacks against UN and associated personnel are indeed unacceptable, a perspective clearly evident from the passage of the convention and its goal of providing justice for those who are attacked (Bourloyannis-Vrailas 1995, 589).

Contrasting Approaches

Existing law dedicated to protecting the helpers, aid workers, and peacekeepers thus offers better protection for UN staff, including peacekeepers, and employees of UN-contracting organizations. The emphasis on the UN as a body of member states privileges state-centric mechanisms of protection, leaving nonstate actors such as NGOs out of this equation. This hierarchy highlights some of the inherent tensions of aid work. Contracting with the UN often involves de facto participation in an integrated mission or, at a minimum, a perceived association with the UN. This, in turn, may compromise an organization's ability to maintain a principled stance with an independent, impartial, or neutral profile.

A separate but related issue is whether humanitarians deserve special status or specific legal protections by virtue of who they are or what they do. As a principle, humanity affirms the inherent dignity of the person and the right to life and is therefore linked to the protection of civilian populations. As civilians, all aid workers in situations of armed conflict are protected under the Geneva Conventions (Mackintosh 2007). Special legal designations separate aid workers as a category from a general category of civilians. Creating special categories of civilians builds a hierarchy of individual value and can weaken the legal protection for civilians more generally.

At a deeper level, this humanitarian exceptionalism values the lives of some over others, a perspective that violates the universal equality of basic human rights and the principle of humanity. As one aid expert suggested, "The security of civilians—what we work out for ourselves is the same as protection for civilians. . . . We cannot pursue these separately."[47] Violent attacks against aid workers occur, yet so do attacks on the civilians they are there to help; the latter often do not receive comparable outcry for the equally despicable atrocities committed against them.

The legal codification of protection is often motivated by acts of violence against aid workers, particularly in the case of UNSCR 1502. The paradox is thus: "At the same time, many in the humanitarian community are wary of appearing to ask for 'more' protection than the civilian population affected. In the words of one aid worker, 'Why should we get more protection than other civilians just because we decide to go to dangerous areas while they have no choice?'" (Mackintosh 2007, 123). The occurrence of violence against aid workers, though tragic, is no different or less complicated than violence against civilians more generally.[48] In this way, it is lamentably unexceptional.

This points to an alternative approach, one emerging from a relational perspective that more explicitly frames the protection of aid workers within a broader framework of protecting civilian populations (Slim and Bonwick 2005; O'Callaghan and Pantuliano 2007). For example, such an approach could, at a minimum, establish better linkages between civilian-protection and security-management teams, or it could even incorporate security management within a broader civilian protection unit. A related advocacy campaign could exhort for legal protections that are consistent with equality of all civilians and remind states of their duties to protect all civilians. In addition, framing protection in terms of access and aid delivery provides a natural bridge between aid workers and aid recipients as civilians and helps to downplay the disproportionate emphasis on aid worker fatalities, kidnappings, and injuries as well as to undermine the internal and external hierarchies implicit in the narrative of humanitarian exceptionalism.

A related legal and moral development concerns organizational policies and practices of duty of care, the responsibility to care for the mental health of staff who experience or are affected by security incidents. For many organizations, the need to hire and retain qualified staff informs this duty of care, but the emphasis also derives from an obligation to support staff members who face difficult and trying circumstances, including security incidents, that exert a heavy toll on their emotional and physical health. The effects of security incidents are related not only to the humanitarian operation and an organization's ability to respond to emergencies, but also to the physical and psychological effects on the staff themselves.[49]

Early mental health interventions took the form of the Critical Incident Stress Debriefing (CISD), commonly used in the helping and rescue professions more generally to help individuals process the mental and emotional effects of a critical incident. While helpful, the problem with the CISD as a sole or primary intervention is that for all but those directly affected, it is business as usual. This short-term and isolated intervention does not take account of the broader and less immediate impacts of an incident on the organization's programs or operations, the long-term specific or cumulative effects of the incident on an individual, or its ramifications for colleagues, friends, and family members as well as an agency's—or a group of agencies'—operations and programs. Moreover, such interventions do not address the chronic stresses of aid work.

Addressing the mental and emotional effects of such work must become part of an overall "protection" landscape, in which agencies consider the physical and psychological health of their staff.[50] More recent efforts reflect a more comprehensive "occupational health" or duty-of-care approach that recognizes an institutional responsibility to care for the whole person, through policies that begin with screening and recruitment efforts and cover the end of mission and beyond.[51] The latter approach reflects the professionalization and maturation of humanitarian action as a field of study and practice, embraces the effects of both the severe and nonlethal incidents and stresses of aid work, and is more consistent with a relational approach to aid. This approach represents a shift from mitigating the impact of the "disorder" of an individual traumatic event to supporting the inherent resilience of individuals working in and coping with difficult circumstances. The latter entails a more comprehensive approach that recognizes not only coping mechanisms (both constructive and destructive) but also the everyday and low-grade but cumulative stresses of aid work as a profession.

Although it is necessary to ensure the protection of civilians in wartime *and* peacetime, promoting compliance with civilian protection under IHL and renewing and redoubling efforts to prosecute those who harm aid workers both strengthen civilian protection and the rule of law. Likewise, caring for the emotional and mental health of aid workers, whether national or international staff, embodies a holistic commitment to the dignity of the person. These effects all help to equalize (as opposed to exceptionalize) aid workers and civilians and to uphold a relational approach to humanitarian and aid work. This perspective also suggests that humanitarian exceptionalism is earned and cannot be assumed from the virtue and altruism of aid work.

Operational Security Management: Field-Based Strategies of Ensuring Security and Access

Operational security management, which refers to the practical, field-based strategies of minimizing risk, is about protecting staff. Equally important from an organization's perspective, however, are maintaining access to vulnerable populations, ensuring the continuity of programming, and responding to and minimizing reputational risk. Short of a complete withdrawal, during an outbreak of intense violence agencies might temporarily evacuate and relocate staff members to a safer location or, if too dangerous, they might suspend movement and programs and "hibernate" in a predetermined location to wait out the violence. Security management, in short, is designed to ensure agencies can continue to operate in both violent and stable contexts. For most agencies, these security-management strategies encompass *deterrence, protection, acceptance,* and more recently *remote management* (Van Brabant 2000, 2001; Humanitarian Practice Network [HPN] 2010). Each strategy addresses different possible sources of insecurity, allowing an organization to develop a more comprehensive approach or to tailor its approach to a particular context.

Deterrence refers to amassing a counterthreat, such as withdrawal, armed protection of warehouses or compounds and armed escort for aid convoys, sufficient to deter or prevent an attack. Protection, known colloquially as "hardening the target", reduces vulnerability through technology, equipment, and mechanisms designed to prevent attack (HPN 2010, 55). Acceptance measures, in contrast, are designed to gain consent or tacit permission for agencies' presence and programs in a given area. Acceptance "is founded on effective relationships and cultivating and maintaining consent from beneficiaries, local authorities, belligerents and other stakeholders. This in turn is a means of reducing or removing potential threats in order to access vulnerable populations and undertake programme activities" (Fast and O'Neill 2010, 5–6). It requires the promotion of respectful relationships with and securing consent from those directly involved or peripherally affected by the programs and presence of an NGO.

The key to effective security management is to match an appropriate security approach to the security threats that exist in a particular context. While many agencies have increased their sophistication in the application of these strategies over time, the basic ingredients have remained essentially the same. The generally accepted wisdom is that an effective security-management strategy in a particular context will require a combination of two or more of the three strategies.

A fourth alternative, an evolution from the original three and generally used in situations with dramatic and serious deteriorations in the security conditions, is "remote management" or "remote control." In these situations, agencies partially or completely withdraw expatriate staff from high-risk areas, designate national staff to manage operations, or operate through local partners (HPN 2010, 94–99).[52] Frequently remote management includes operating without logos, conspicuous vehicles, or signage on their offices, thus choosing virtual anonymity (sometimes critically referred to as "stealth" programming) over visibility. In some places, agencies use magnetic logos that they can remove or attach, depending on the context and risks of clearly marking agency programs and assets. Many agencies that withdrew from Iraq after the 2003 Baghdad bombing used remote management to continue programs.[53] Those that did not completely close their programs adopted lower profiles, removing the insignia and flags on their vehicles, compounds, and projects (Vick 2003). A few eschewed armed protection, relying on an acceptance approach, working to establish good relationships with local leaders and communities (Murphy 2003; Callimachi 2003).

While these are the most commonly articulated strategies, others refer to community-based and systems-based (roughly equivalent to acceptance, and systematized protection and deterrence, respectively) approaches to security management (Bruderlein and Gassman 2006) or to the broader conceptualization of risk thresholds and risk management (Kingston and Behn 2010; Merkelbach and Daudin 2011). Deborah Avant and Virginia Haufler, in outlining various security strategies of nonstate actors including NGOs and private sector actors, propose five approaches: a fortress/protection strategy (roughly equivalent to the hardened approaches discussed below); avoidance (i.e., withdrawal); acceptance (closer to what I term "passive" acceptance); alliance, which refers to the development of partnerships with state or other actors to provide security; and engagement, which more closely approximates the consent-based approaches described below (Avant and Haufler 2012). The philosophy and use of the basic approaches and their variants have a variety of consequences, both positive and negative, when interpreted through the lens of a relational approach.

Hardened Security: Deterrence, Protection, and Remote Management

Deterrence, protection, and remote management most closely parallel the instinctual reactions of "flight" (withdrawal or evacuation) and "fight" (deterrence and to a lesser degree, protection). It is not that these reactive measures are misguided, because in the conflict zones in which aid workers deliver emergency assistance they are often necessary. Rather, from a relational perspective their consequences are implicit yet harmful. The deleterious consequences of deterrence are the best articulated, primarily because of the humanitarian community's reluctance to associate with the military or to use armed protection, at least in theory if not consistently in practice. Although some security directors assert that in some places such as Somalia, "it is impossible to function" without armed escort, its downsides are evident.[54] "Deterrence . . . is unidimensional. You can only deter part of the threat," observed one security director. Another advised that in situations of "open, armed conflict or violence . . . it is difficult to find someone without allegiances to one side." Moreover, he raised the intangible element of deterrence: "It is difficult to do this, to put security in the hands of others. It is completely out of our control."[55] Nevertheless, in some cases—more common in the most dangerous places—humanitarian agencies do use armed protection. Indeed, all the major relief and development agencies have used armed protection in at least one context. The use of international private security firms for armed protection, however, remains an exception (Stoddard, Harmer, and DiDomenico 2008).

The military's increasing involvement in humanitarian operations, such as the 2004 tsunami, the 2005 earthquake in Kashmir, and the 2010 earthquake in Haiti, and the war zones in which emergency operations often occur, make complete or even partial separation exceedingly difficult. Still, humanitarian actors argue for maintaining boundaries between military and civilian operations, especially in places such as Iraq and Afghanistan where military operations are large, politically charged, and fraught with controversy. Within the humanitarian community, the use of armed protection is contentious because of its effects on communities' perceptions of humanitarian actors, even in contexts where most deem it necessary. In particular, such tactics compromise their neutrality and independence. Less obvious are the implicit ethical messages that accompany the use of armed protection, such as the notion that violence works (and pays) and the question of who and what is protected with military force, with attendant implications about who and what matters (Anderson 1999; also Fassin 2012, chap. 9).

While deterrence is often equated with armed protection, it can also involve other measures, such as guard dogs,[56] or the threat of suspension of activities and aid agency withdrawal. The latter, however, is a tricky proposition. One aid expert observed, "In terms of a withdrawal, we have essentially given notice to others about how to get us to leave. We set it up to be kidnapped or killed if we say in advance 'if you attack us, we will leave.'"[57]

Protection, in contrast to deterrence, is pervasive as a security-management approach. It tends to be focused on education, policy, and equipment. Agencies send staff to personal security training courses or offer them online or by CD, and provide context-specific security briefings to new employees. Further training opportunities include a menu of specialty courses: first aid courses, land mine safety training, HEAT (Hostile Environment Awareness Training), or defensive driving courses that are designed to teach drivers to maneuver through war zones and evade land mines and improvised explosive devices. With "hostile observation" training, trainees learn to identify those who might be observing compounds, security measures, and the comings and goings of aid workers, with a view to planning an attack.

Recognizing the business opportunities and profit potential of working in dangerous places, private security providers now appear at relief and development conferences to sell their wares, actively soliciting business from humanitarian and aid actors and hyping their services at trade fairs and thereby encroaching on the terrain of the nonprofit organizations that have traditionally offered such services to the sector.[58] Disagreement exists, however, about whether this increased competition results in higher-quality services or simply drives up the cost of providing security. The increasing sophistication and range of service providers signals the significant human and financial resources devoted to security management.

In addition, aid agencies employ security managers and unarmed guards and have adopted policies and procedures related to perimeter and compound security (such as "welcome spaces" or separately secured entrances), office location, and vehicle safety—all protective measures. The more fortified aid agency compound entrances take the form of "air locks" where visitors, whether individuals or vehicles, enter a secure, enclosed area and are permitted further entry into the compound only after a search.[59] Others mark out perimeter or setback areas, with barricades preventing easy access to the main buildings. Aid workers live under curfew or other security restrictions, carry satellite phones, or travel in vehicle convoys, in recognition of the fact that the most dangerous locations are between places, whether home and office or office and program site. Where convoys are not sufficient to protect, armed escorts or aircraft allow aid workers to reach their destinations, all for a price. For many NGOs, traveling from a headquarters office in a capital city to a project site now involves multiple security checks at predetermined intervals, using short wave radio networks.[60] According to one aid worker, for some agencies security equates to the use of the "radio and an overreliance on guards." Furthermore, he charged that radio operators were underqualified or untrained and did not always speak a common language, increasing the possibility of miscommunication between operators and between organizations.[61]

Providing protection is often expensive and logistically complicated. One security director reported that his organization operates in a situation "if we have acceptance, safe transportation (this costs) and communication. Costs should be incorporated early in the budget process. It is not just about going in."[62] Budgeting and planning for security therefore requires not just responding to the current context, but also assessing the potential risk in the immediate and longer-term future. Thus, according to another aid worker "budgeting plays an important role in this process, as does logistics in terms of initially getting equipment to the field, and the speed with which extra equipment can be provided when an escalation in the security threat demands additional equipment."[63]

Ironically, the expensive equipment that characterizes protection, such as satellite antennas that adorn aid vehicles around the world, may increase risk. The equipment is often stolen, as satellite phones and armor-plated vehicles (to mitigate the potential impact of land mines or other explosive devices) are equally useful to rebel groups and criminal gangs. Protection, in general, is easier to reduce to a checklist of actions and carries with it an assumption that knowledge changes behavior or that hardening the target mitigates the risk. At its worst, a protection-focused security-management approach emphasizes security over programming and fosters a militarized security culture. As a result, protection and deterrence are better suited to address external threats. They therefore require agencies to react and mitigate the likelihood of incidents and their effect on the organization and its activities. Protection and deterrence privilege military and police approaches to security management that rely primarily on equipment, training, force, coercion, or hardened targets. They are akin to the "hard power" strategies of international relations, as opposed to the attraction-based "soft power" strategies (Nye 2004; Boulding 1989).

Despite the claims of security managers that security management is an "enabler" for programming, many staff disagree (Bruderlein and Gassman 2006; see also Autesserre 2014). Where agencies maintain operations in dangerous contexts, aid workers themselves frequently chafe at what they see as restrictive security measures that stifle flexible responses and impede their ability to reach and help the most vulnerable and therefore to fulfill their organization's purpose or mandate. This often becomes especially acute when the needs are overwhelming. One study of aid workers suggested frustrations with security restriction arose because security "prevents the efficient implementation of programs, but also because it prevents the experience of exotic locations and the interaction with locals." These two elements motivate people to get into the work in the first place and make it rewarding (Roth 2009, 17). Aid workers operate within particular security parameters for their safety, but these same restrictions elicit criticism from the local population and others who claim that aid workers are "jumping from one fortified compound to another."

Remote management, more commonly adopted in the recent past, offers a way to maintain programs in more dangerous contexts. As a strategy it is often hotly debated within organizations for its "unacceptable compromises" (see, e.g., Belliveau 2013). For organizations with a high percentage of national staff, it is often a viable option, even though in emergency contexts many organizations employ greater numbers of expatriate personnel. Operationally, program monitoring and evaluation are more challenging from afar. Remote management may potentially deprive remaining staff of accessible, outside expertise and technical support and could open the door to mismanagement or corruption, especially when organizations quickly ramp up new or existing programs. Operating by stealth, without branded vehicles, compounds, or projects, makes it more difficult for local populations to see tangible efforts of assistance, depriving them both of the solidarity of visible international support and of external witnesses to human rights violations or abuses that occur in armed conflict. In situations where kidnapping of foreigners is frequent or lucrative, remote management reduces risk by removing the target of attack. In some situations, however, it shifts the distribution of risk from expatriate staff to national staff or local partner organizations (many of which are less well equipped to manage security), or even to other organizations that choose to remain fully operational. In shifting the distribution of risk and eliminating the potential of presence and witnessing to curb the worst excesses of violence, remote management implicitly reinforces exceptionalism and the hierarchies that differently value categories of people.

The Normalization of Danger

The less recognized ramifications of the hardened security approaches are more insidious, but no less important. They highlight the tension between security-management approaches and the relational aspects of the work. These tensions concern the physical and emotional separation such measures engender, as well as the normalization of danger. Each of these relies on or reinforces humanitarian exceptionalism and undermines a relational approach.

Security concerns and management strategies can reshape both how agencies and aid workers operate and how they think about the environment in which they work and play and about the people with whom they interact. In the world of aid workers, walls and fences dominate, separating aid workers from those they help. The gated aid compounds represent an "oasis of private consumption" where "defensive living has been normalized. The walls and razor-wire fence off an external world that is otherwise threatening and unpredictable" (Duffield 2010, 468). Security guards, perimeter fencing, enclosed entrances, and sometimes X-ray machines greet visitors to aid agency compounds, serving to keep people out rather than opening up to engage them and their ideas and values. Separate compounds and curfews limit the possibilities for expatriate aid workers to interact with those around them. In many contexts, the separation is physical, via the operational security-management mechanisms agencies adopt and the architecture that simultaneously protects and separates them from those outside the walls. The result, one aid worker propounds, is a "fortress mentality."[64]

The ramifications of this separation are also psychological and emotional. The protective and deterrent strategies emphasize building more walls and barriers and at a certain point, the separation between humanitarians and the populations they seek to serve weakens the ability to see the humanity in others. Aside from the negative effects of such separation on programming effectiveness, it facilitates a frame that conceptualizes the people outside the walls as "other" at best and "enemy" at worst; they are people who are dangerous to those inside the walls, as opposed to people in need of help. In Iraq, for example, the mandatory UN Security Awareness Induction Training reinforced the "other" status, with "constant talk of 'the bad guys'" (Hansen 2008, 12). Months after the 2010 earthquake in Haiti, some observed that international aid workers arrived "indoctrinated that they're coming to this very dangerous place.... Then they get here and that only gets reinforced by their security regulations. If they do go into a neighborhood, go outside of Pétion-Ville even, they carry that fear with them. People sense that" (as quoted in Watkins 2012). An analysis of the Pakistan earthquake response quotes an INGO director as saying, "Many aid workers came to a country they perceived to have master-minded 9/11—a country full of terrorists. They thought everyone in Pakistan would have a turban and a Kalashnikov.... Some agencies were treating every road accident as a security incident. The paranoia was very irritating—it kept aid workers away from a large percentage of the population" (Wilder 2008, 76). The notion that "everyone in Pakistan would have a turban and a Kalashnikov" worryingly points to growing cynicism and fear, when aid workers look on those they are trying to help as simultaneously trying to hurt them.

Framing "beneficiaries" as subjects of fear as opposed to neighbors in need of help is detrimental to the principle of humanity that should motivate and inform humanitarian action and the way it is carried out. The humanitarian exceptionalism that codifies aid workers as a special category of civilians or assumes protection derives from humanitarian colors or principles that support rather than counter this psychological separation.

The separation also emerges from the professional expertise that characterizes the modern humanitarian endeavor and even the reforms designed to improve the efficiency and efficacy of the enterprise. As Michael Barnett observes in relation to the reforms that humanitarians instituted in the wake of the response to the Rwandan genocide, "In almost all respects, these reforms had a visible payoff. Yet their actions, designed to perfect the machinery, also seemed to be building a proverbial 'iron cage' that placed more physical, psychological, and moral distance between themselves and those they wanted to help" (Barnett 2011, 213). At another level, professionalized security management can make it easier to absolve individual aid workers of responsibility for their own security and to blame the "security experts" when something does go wrong (Fast et al. 2013). Taken together, these undermine the relational basis of humanitarianism.

Separation between aid workers and those they are helping is not necessarily new, even as its marriage to the normalization of danger and fortification of security are newer developments. As early as 1986, one commentator noted the separation between aid workers and refugees in camps, including eating facilities and housing, observing its role as a coping mechanism: "This physical, and perhaps more notably *emotional* separation is maintained as an institutional measure for dealing with the inequality that exists" (Fozzard 1986, as cited in Stearns 1993). In situations of extremity, emotional separation functions as a mechanism to cope with the fatigue induced by working in a fast-paced environment and the stress of witnessing firsthand the devastation and suffering of those around them. As Mark Duffield points out, "Care of oneself involves a psychological distancing that complements, and requires, the physical walls and razor-wire of the fortified aid compound" (Duffield 2010, 463). Self-care involves emotional distance that is at once necessary yet reinforcing of the separation inherent in a fortified compound.

The field security training that aid workers take helps to normalize risk. "Field security training," writes Mark Duffield about the mandatory UN training, "reinforces the idea that times have changed and, like it or not, *aid workers now face pervasive threats from a calculating and unpredictable enemy*. Since this enemy is faceless, follows no particular pattern and can strike anywhere, it requires constant vigilance and attention to one's surrounding environment" (Duffield 2010, 461, italics in original). This is particularly true precisely because the UN field security training is standardized, therefore generic, and is required regardless of the degree of risk in a particular country. In this way, risk becomes ubiquitous and normal rather than contextual and specific. Duffield continues, "Using generic messages and reinforcing techniques, the aim is to create a conformist and risk-averse aid worker subjectivity.

While in certain locations this might be necessary or even considered 'normal,' when institutionalized and universalized, even in areas where threats are more imagined than real, this subjectivity reshapes the perceptions, interactions and exchanges that link aid workers and host societies. Not least, it normalizes the segregation and bunkering of the aid industry within fortified aid compounds" (Duffield 2010, 461).

Moreover, protective and deterrent approaches assume that it is possible, with enough technology and money, to fix the "problem" of insecurity. They are, in a sense, the easier fixes. The approaches are clear and rational, if costly. They do not require an analysis of the aid system as a whole, with the discrepancies and inequalities it engenders, nor do they require attempts to ensure that programs and people are context-specific and culturally sensitive. They cannot address the internal vulnerabilities that may elicit or contribute to a "perfect storm" that results in a security incident. Highlighting this discrepancy, one aid worker stated, "In terms of operations, we invest in equipment, procedures, and advisors. We spend money. We don't invest in language, cultural sensitivity, and deep knowledge of a context."[65]

In addition, deterrence and protection are primarily reactive; these approaches presume that attacks will happen. And they likely will. Alarms, guards, and broken-glass-topped walls or concertina wire fences provide necessary barriers against attack, but incidents occur. Crime occurs at home, just as abroad, and in war zones and places wracked by violent conflict, the risks are higher. While these measures do offer protection, they cannot offer immunity from attack.

An approach to security management that relies primarily on isolating and insulating an agency from external threats produces and reinforces a sense of fear that can pervade and distort the humanitarian ethos. The social lives of humanitarians change as they leave refugee camps at night for security reasons to retreat to safer, fortified compounds farther away in which they interact primarily with other (expatriate) humanitarians. The fortified compounds also suggest that the beneficiaries of aid are passive (not able to help themselves) yet potentially dangerous individuals. The inequalities and social barriers that often exist between international and national staff fail to challenge these images and are even reinforced by security protocols. At worst, as Altheide suggests, fear "become[s] a perspective or orientation to the world, rather than a response to a particular situation or thing" (Altheide 2003, 22).

Aid agencies themselves are not often deliberately self-reflective about the ways in which they narrow humanitarian space. They need to be more so, however, regarding the ways in which their own security policies reinforce the blurring of lines between military and civilian actors. In particular, agencies either have neglected to examine the tangible and intangible walls and barriers that separate humanitarians from those they are there to help, or have calculated that such moves are a necessarily and affordable cost, with equally detrimental effect. Within this new frame of reference, the crisis or "emergency" moment is no longer extraordinary. Instead, a state of emergency is normal, and unseen yet imminent danger dominates.

The risk is that the focus has shifted from proactive policies designed to minimize risks and prevent incidents from occurring in the first place, to reactive tactics, which tend to neglect the everyday practices that render the organization vulnerable to certain kinds of security incidents: the internal vulnerabilities rooted in the behaviors of individuals and the actions and policies of organizations. This shift is reinforced by societal rhetoric emphasizing fear, danger, and uncertainty and replicated in discourses of security management and the changing context of providing aid. The emphasis on severe violence, including fatalities, kidnapping, and serious injury, punctuates this discourse. Thus, security management is situated within and mimics the broader discourses of fear and the trajectories of professionalization and fortification of aid.

While violence against aid workers is both criminal and intentional, in most places it is still not normal. Its dimensions are both commonplace, related to personal and organizational choices, and sensational, related to terrorism or politicized aid or some combination thereof. Recognizing the multiplicity of causes opens space to challenge the normalization of danger and to reassert the relational ethos of aid. In particular, the consent-based approaches of acceptance and negotiated access offer the possibility of security-management approaches more consistent with humanitarian principles.

Consent-Based Mechanisms: Acceptance and Negotiated Access

Of the three primary approaches to security management, acceptance is the most widely cited and the least understood. It dovetails most closely with the humanitarian ethos and principles and therefore corroborates a relational approach, since it seeks to gain consent and support for an organization's presence and programs. In contrast to protection and deterrence, acceptance is more flexible and is linked to internal vulnerabilities as well as external threats, even as its effectiveness as a security-management approach remains primarily anecdotal in many contexts and not empirically tested. It is an attraction-based, soft-power approach to security management. Consequently, its value in enhancing security is sometimes overlooked, especially in the most dangerous contexts. Security directors acknowledge that acceptance is "misapplied" or that organizations "tend to say they rely on acceptance but they don't really." Others go so far as to say that acceptance "is not relevant today" or that it "may not work now."[66]

The ways in which organizations choose to promote acceptance vary widely and are not well understood (O'Neill 2008; Fast et al. 2013). What is referred to as "passive acceptance" (see Egeland, Harmer, and Haver 2011, 18) corresponds with the assumptive mechanisms, by which agencies assume that principles protect or that the good works they do are enough to gain consent and ensure acceptance for their presence and programming. "We have relied on the principles to bring security," remarked one aid worker. "We talk about acceptance, and the principles are the primary piece of this."[67] Another suggested, "The acceptance model has come to mean 'no weapons' or unarmed security. If I use weapons, then how can I be neutral?"[68]

Acceptance, however, is not a passive approach. To conceive of it in this way is more likely indicative of the absence of an intentional and planned acceptance strategy or of its limited application in relation to communities and local populations. Instead, agencies must actively gain acceptance from *all* stakeholders, not only community members.[69] That the idea of passive acceptance is no longer reflective of the state of knowledge on acceptance is a reflection of the increasing sophistication of some agencies' approaches to security management.

Systematically and deliberately applying an acceptance approach is proactive; it ensures the benefits are actively sought, monitored, maintained, and earned, not assumed. Acceptance necessitates examining the agency's profile and its relationships with all stakeholders in a community or host population, especially those whose interests are threatened or enhanced by the activities or presence of the organization. It requires examining the organization's relevance and efficacy. Its full manifestation requires a more thorough examination of the ways in which the organization operates and interacts with all stakeholders in a context, not just its beneficiaries.

Conceptually, an acceptance strategy requires attention to an agency's principles and mission in a country, its relationships and networks, its programming, and its communications strategies. Organizations must cultivate relationships and networks, and recruit, hire, and train staff in ways that reflect the context. In addition, agencies need to pay attention to their image and how they are perceived in a community (Fast et al. 2013). Thus, relationships are central to such an approach, reflected in the metaphor that acceptance requires taking time to "drink tea"—an activity that involves conversation and time as opposed to measurable outcomes and that in many cultural contexts should not be hurried or ignored.

Research has demonstrated that gaining acceptance is clearly tied to meeting the needs of a population. As such, it is integral to an organization's programming approach and goals, even though aid agencies do not always deliberately or systematically link the two. Meeting needs, however, is not sufficient to gain acceptance; doing so should involve respectful interactions, transparency, accountability in how resources are managed, and participatory decision making, especially around an organization's entry into and exit from communities when implementing its programs (Fast, Freeman, et al. 2011).

Achieving the full potential of acceptance as a security-management approach implies respectful relationships *not only* with community members, but also with various stakeholders, including formal and informal local leaders and local militia or insurgent groups (Fast, Freeman, et al. 2011). Demonstrating the importance of respectful relationships, one aid worker in South Sudan told of the disrespect with which a colleague treated a local official, which caused a breakdown in the relationship between the official and the aid agency (Fast, Patterson, et al. 2011). In instances of kidnapping or other security incidents, these key stakeholders may become crucial negotiating partners, messengers, or sources of information. In Afghanistan, the ICRC has maintained contact with the Taliban, which has proved instrumental in negotiating humanitarian access and the release of kidnapped ICRC delegates, as well as in facilitating communication with other actors whose staff have been kidnapped.[70] In Gaza, NGO contacts with various groups have proved useful in times of insecurity (Fast 2006).

For some organizations, acceptance implies vigilance regarding hiring practices—making certain that national staff nominally represent, to the extent possible, the ethnic, religious, or political affiliations of the local population.[71] It may involve ensuring that drivers are respectful and courteous and that both drivers and guards, since they represent the most visible face of the organization, are fully aware and capable of explaining the organization's mission in a country. Local populations often resent what they see as dangerous and aggressive driving that foreigners exhibit on their roads, evidence of the importance of something as basic as driving habits to an acceptance approach. All of these factors, individually or in concert, influence the ways in which local communities perceive humanitarian actors, and thus influence their levels of security or insecurity. Without some degree of acceptance, it is difficult to operate safely.

Gaining acceptance takes time and resources, both in short supply in times of crisis when immediate needs are acute. Acceptance also faces additional obstacles of transferability, since acceptance for an individual, a program, or an agency does not necessarily scale up to multiple individuals, programs, or the NGO community as a whole. It is dynamic and can be fleeting (Fast, Freeman, et al. 2011; Fast et al. 2013). After the 2005 Pakistan earthquake, for example, agencies enjoyed the generalized consent of the community for relief operations. During this phase, few security incidents occurred and the security situation remained relatively safe. The situation deteriorated over time, however, as the relief phase gave way to reconstruction after the summer of 2007. Expressions of discontent and animosity toward UN and aid agencies involved in reconstruction efforts resulted in security incidents and the withdrawal of some agencies from the Mansehra and Battagram districts of the Northwest Frontier Province (Wilder 2008).

In the wake of a serious incident, such as one or more staff deaths or kidnapping, the challenge of security management only increases. Indeed, "Security keeps people awake at night—what are the consequences of pulling out, of not pulling out and then a staff member gets hurt/killed."[72] In the wake of an incident, should the agency evacuate staff or temporarily suspend programs and activities? How might this affect the population it serves? Should it hire or increase armed protection, or institute more restrictive security measures by constraining or limiting staff movement with geographical restrictions or a curfew? Or instead, should it revert to a more concerted effort to win acceptance? All of these constitute possible responses. Whereas ten years ago, a kidnapping might have prompted an agency to completely withdraw from a country, numerous agencies have decided to keep operating even after multiple kidnappings or staff deaths. After four staff members were killed and one wounded in ambush on the road between Kabul and Logar in 2008, for instance, the International Rescue Committee chose not to withdraw, but instead to reengage stakeholders in order to gain acceptance and remain operational in Afghanistan.[73] This is indicative both of the sophistication of security management and of a higher risk tolerance among aid actors generally.

A corollary to acceptance is the renewed emphasis on negotiating for access to populations in need. Humanitarian negotiation involves talking to belligerent parties in order to reach these populations, provide assistance, and ideally advocate for their protection, as spelled out in international law (Mancini-Griffoli and Picot 2004; McHugh and Bessler 2006). Recent research in Afghanistan indicates that structured negotiations, defined as "direct negotiations with Taliban at multiple levels, guided by internal policy or guidance" (Jackson and Guistozzi 2012, 6), can yield significant benefits, as high-quality and consistent programming helped to improve access and perceptions of aid agencies among the Taliban and community members. This type of dialogue, however, also may involve ethical and political compromises that call into question an agency's actions (or inactions) or force it to choose between other equally bad outcomes (Magone, Neuman, and Weissman 2011).

Negotiating for access to beneficiaries is integral to acceptance, but it refers specifically to dialogue with belligerents and not to the more holistic approach that acceptance implies. Because aid agencies may gain acceptance from some stakeholders and not others, whether belligerents or community members, acceptance is not an absolute; it is not black or white, either won or absent. Acceptance may be present in degrees, ranging from endorsement (where stakeholders actively intervene to protect an agency's staff, assets, or reputation) to targeting (where stakeholders actively and deliberately threaten or attack aid agencies). Between these extremes, from negative to positive, are rejection (where stakeholders undermine agency programs or activities), toleration (which is often related to the fact that agencies provide much-needed goods and services), and consent (where stakeholders provide safe and continued—as opposed to one-time—access to populations) (Fast, Freeman, et al. 2011). Likewise, the absence of an incident does not imply acceptance, nor does the occurrence of a security incident necessarily signal the loss of acceptance. Agencies might be caught up in the crossfire, or they might be mistaken for other actors. In Afghanistan, for example, ICRC and other aid workers have been kidnapped and subsequently released unharmed once the kidnappers learned of their actual affiliations. Indeed, one might argue that these cases of mistaken identity are actually examples of acceptance in action, rather than a failure of acceptance.

Acceptance therefore requires paying close attention to the perceptions of community members and other stakeholders. Indicators of the presence of acceptance include safe and continued access to populations in need, proactive sharing of security-related information by community members or other stakeholders with aid agencies, and interventions to protect aid agency staff members. In one East African community, community members formed units to protect aid workers living in their community in case of attack (Fast, Freeman, et al. 2011).

In spite of its security and programmatic benefits, however, acceptance is not a panacea. It is not always appropriate as a sole or primary strategy, nor is it feasible in every context. It is better suited to addressing political as opposed to criminal targeting, since good relationships with communities or armed actors may elicit a warning or, in the case of the former, preventive intervention. Targeting for economic or criminal reasons, in contrast, is less susceptible to such interventions. The challenges of gaining acceptance in urban contexts, which are becoming more important as areas in which aid agencies operate, are substantial since populations tend to be more transient and more isolated from neighbors or other social networks. Similarly, attempts to gain consent for an agency's programs and presence in complex emergency environments where dozens, if not hundreds, of aid agencies are operating alongside multiple and diffuse belligerents and other actors (e.g., governmental bodies, military forces, private security actors) are likely to be confusing for all involved and will require significant commitment to educate myriad parties about the agency's mission and goals. This, in turn, magnifies the effort required to gain acceptance, perhaps without immediate or tangible rewards.

Its benefits, however, are promising. Acceptance and negotiated access better account for the multiple ways in which humanitarians are embedded in complex systems and networks of relationships. Consent-based mechanisms, when deliberately and systematically employed, are more consistent with the principles of humanitarianism, particularly the principle of humanity. As an intrinsic element of a relational approach, these mechanisms could offer as-yet-undetermined program and security benefits and result in outcomes that are more consistent with the principles on which humanitarianism rests.

Conclusion

The highly visible attacks on aid workers have generated a continuum of responses, from laws delineating the special status of aid workers in order to protect them to the professionalization of security management. Particularly in the most dangerous countries, agencies operate by remote management, from behind bunkers, or in virtual anonymity. These strategies manifest most visibly in the most dangerous contexts, but also elsewhere. The security orientation and accompanying measures that prevail among many aid actors privilege a reactive security-management approach to specific, anticipated events. They also homogenize attacks, responding in a generic, one-size-fits-all manner. The bunker-type mentality functions as the humanitarian equivalent of force protection in military terms.[74] Remote management, however necessary, likewise harkens back to images of imperial rule from afar (Barnett 2011, 222). This is a reactive mode that creates protective walls and barriers in response to the threats the agency faces. Implicit in the logic of bunkerization is the message that humanitarians and other interveners are at risk from the host population, some of whom they are trying to help.

Reliance on reactive measures tends to obscure the internally generated image issues that also lead to security incidents. Blast plates, alarms, satellite phones, and security protocols are not likely to prevent the robbery of an aid worker at a nightclub in a dangerous part of the city. Nor will they address the grievances of a community that has been subject to numerous needs assessments without follow-up, grievances that could eventually cause a riot or other security incident. These types of issues relate more to the decision making of individuals and agencies, and represent self-generated risk or internal vulnerabilities.

Other negative consequences follow the shift in emphasis from proactively preventing incidents from happening in the first place to emphasizing external threats. The emphasis by key actors on fatalities, underscored by the fortification of security management, shapes security responses not only for one organization but for all. The increasing use of these strategies defines not only the dominant security-management responses, but also the realm of the possible. This occurs in multiple and mutually reinforcing ways.

Significantly, these measures dramatically increase the cost of humanitarianism, putting the emphasis on protecting the humanitarians at the potential expense of those whom they are there to assist. Walls, barriers, and communication equipment all cost money, a strain on the tight budgets of many agencies and enough justification for the skeptical that security is too costly. A worst-case scenario arises if those agencies without the resources to employ reactive strategies or that choose to adopt alternative strategies are found deficient in their security-management approaches, and therefore liable, if or when they are sued. This would only serve to further entrench a fortified response and undermine the relational ethos of aid.

Security measures, to be effective, must address the complete landscape of threat and not simply the external ones. Protection and deterrence and even remote management do not address the risk factors arising from individual behavior or organizational actions, risk factors that are better addressed by acceptance. External threats are more often beyond an organization's ability to influence, whereas the internal vulnerabilities represent a world over which aid workers and organizations exert a degree of control and where the ability to exercise agency is still intact. This helps to restore confidence in an ordered as opposed to uncontrollable world. Taking account of the internal vulnerabilities therefore reclaims the importance of the everyday practices of aid that give it meaning and that contribute both to security incidents and their mitigation.

Aid agencies must conceptualize security management as inherent in and reflective of the ways in which the organization defines itself and its mission. This is part and parcel of the call to better understand the choices organizations make in response to insecurity and how these, in turn, relate to broader questions of violence and governance (Avant and Haufler 2012). It is not that the reactive and fortified approaches are always misplaced, but agencies must employ them fully aware of the intrinsic cost to the humanitarian ethos and values. A fundamental assumption of humanitarianism and humanitarian response is a sense of connection to and compassion for others, even if people engage in the work for myriad reasons. It is precisely this connection and care for the stranger that acts as a motivating force for action and response. Agencies strive to create such a connection in their fundraising and advertising efforts, to bridge the distance between the individual donor in a Western country and the suffering of strangers who are geographically and often culturally distant. How this same connection can or should inform security management is part of conceptualizing aid work as a relational act. The way that agencies approach and provide security can help to distinguish them from others. In this, humanitarian exceptionalism must be rooted in principled actions and relationships and not assumed from the mythical images of humanitarianism.

A relational approach, therefore, offers a way forward. The assumptive mechanisms of relying on the protective coloring and emblems are not enough. Even in the most dangerous places for aid workers, such as Afghanistan and Somalia, aid agencies are proactively asserting their distinctiveness, in part by employing consent-based approaches. Anecdotal evidence suggests these approaches work, even if they cannot prevent all incidents. In Afghanistan, the ICRC and others are recommitting to acceptance, and in Somalia, negotiations with elders have led to the release of some kidnapped aid workers. At a minimum, they offer the possibility of retaining a consistency with humanitarian principles that the fortified measures do not.

A relational approach suggests that security management is subservient to the mission and principles of the organization and should be implemented across the organization, within programs and human resources and not only within a security unit. Such measures could also challenge the internal hierarchies within organizations. For example, while current legal regimes build on a perspective that exceptionalizes aid workers, a relational approach, by contrast, suggests strengthening the laws protecting all civilians, including aid workers, and implementing the duty of care for all staff members. With the latter, an individual agency would ideally commit to developing policies and practices that address the differential needs of all staff members, which begins to dismantle the internal hierarchies that ascribe differential value to categories of staff. A more radical approach could involve using the protection of civilians as the broader framework within which to advocate and manage security for an agency's staff and to advocate for strengthening and respecting existing international humanitarian law and human rights law as opposed to legal instruments that exceptionalize aid workers in context.

Conclusion: Reclaiming Humanity

On 28 October 2009, shortly before the Afghan presidential runoff in early November, Taliban militants attacked the UN guesthouse in Kabul. A lengthy gunfight occurred, and five expatriate UN staff died in the attack. Nine others were wounded. Three of the attackers were wearing suicide vests and were dressed in Afghan police uniforms. They arrived in police vehicles and carried IDs. After they were refused entry into the guesthouse compound, they killed four UN security guards and entered the compound. One victim, a UN security officer, engaged the attackers for close to an hour before he was killed. His actions allowed other staff members to escape.[1]

UN Secretary-General Ban Ki-moon and a Taliban spokesman attributed the tragedy to the UN's involvement in the disputed Afghan elections (Motevalli and Salahuddin 2009; Charbonneau 2009c). The assault itself created substantial fear on the ground. A BBC reporter wrote,

> These attacks on two high-profile targets [the UN guesthouse and the Serena Hotel in Kabul] have spread a lot of fear. Every building where UN staff work or live has to conform to minimum security rules and one question that will be asked is, how did these gunmen get into this building? President Hamid Karzai has said he wants more security for foreign workers but in all the years I have been coming here there is more security in place than ever before, more concrete blast barriers, more troops in the street, but that still cannot prevent determined militants getting through. (Andrew North, as cited in BBC News 2009)

The assumption here is that security is equal to deterrence (i.e., troops) and bunkers (i.e., concrete blast barriers). "Security," in this instance, refers to hardened measures to prevent the "determined militants" from attacking foreigners. The consequence of the attack, as the reporter indicates, is a generalized condition of fear. In response, UN Secretary-General Ban Ki-moon called for increased security to counter the "dramatically escalated threat to UN staff now widely considered to be a soft target" (as quoted in Charbonneau 2009c). It is unclear whether a "hardened target" with better perimeter security or more armed guards would have prevented the assault. The UN and other organizations restricted staff movement in Kabul after the attacks, even though other aid groups promised to remain in the country (Bhalla 2009).

The drama of repeated attacks on aid workers, when interpreted in light of the lenses of global dynamics and the perceived demise of the assumptive paradigm of protection, outlines a picture of aid workers under siege. The prominent security measures in situations of extreme danger and uncertainty advance humanitarian exceptionalism and emphasize the need to forcefully react. These measures reinforce the physical and psychological separation between aid workers and those they are trying to help, reflecting and reinforcing the broader discourses of fear and uncertainty that undermine the relational ethos of aid. The assumptions underlying the logic of the response to the attack on the UN Guest House illustrate the dangers inherent in being present in war zones as well as the exceptionalism narrative, begging a repeat of Kieran Prendergast's question after the 2003 Baghdad bombing: "If a fortress is required to ensure security, why be there?" (quoted in Power 2008, 503). The December 2007 Algiers bombing suggests that the extensive changes and programs the UN implemented after August 2003 did not work as intended. In his introduction to the report of the panel charged with investigating the Algiers bombing, Lakhdar Brahimi, the chairperson, acknowledges this failure: "Though the UN security management system, led by DSS, has been addressing very challenging global and local threats, the 11 December 2007 attack in Algiers put the new security arrangements to the test. Most unfortunately, the system as a whole and individuals who, both in the duty station itself and at Headquarters, held direct responsibility for the UN presence in Algiers and the security of its personnel and premises, have been found wanting" (Independent Panel 2008, 3).

Providing aid in danger is no easy task, particularly in an era when uncertainty and crisis dominate the headlines and when the range of mechanisms available sometimes leaves agencies between the proverbial rock and a hard place. While it is impossible to prevent all attacks, the failure of "security" should prompt questions about the causes of security incidents, about other approaches that exist, and about the implications of security-management approaches on the humanitarian principles and ethos.

The good news is that many in the aid community are asking these same questions. Some organizations are reexamining risk and security management and seeking options that better reflect their mission and principles. They are deliberately engaging with and listening to the perceptions of the recipients of aid, working to be more accountable and responsive. All of these incorporate elements of a relational approach to humanitarianism that conceives of humanitarianism as embedded within an interdependent system of actors and actions.

In this conclusion I reiterate the ways exceptionalism takes aid further from a relational approach and privileges certain tendencies with regard to security management. The previous chapters juxtaposed the practical and analytical challenges of providing aid in the contemporary context and exposed the dominant discourses that emphasize the fortification and professionalization of assistance and the narrative of humanitarian exceptionalism. In the second section, I summarize the ways a multidisciplinary and multidimensional analytical framework challenges exceptionalism and lays the foundation for a reorientation in analyzing security concerns and providing security. Finally, I discuss the implications of a relational approach for aid in danger and for the system as a whole. Whether agencies are guided by impartiality, neutrality, and independence and are engaged in humanitarian action in the narrow, principled sense, or in aid work in the broader sense, acts of mercy and justice are fundamentally relational. Conceptualizing aid in this way is radical, indeed, and requires a shift in the ways agencies interact with those they serve and how they protect those in their employ.

Revisiting Humanitarian Exceptionalism

The narrative of exceptionalism and the related issues of power and blame raise deep and fundamental questions about the relationship between humanitarianism and structures of inequality and the ways in which these issues might influence security. A closer look exposes provocative paradoxes and inherent contradictions related to power and humanitarian exceptionalism, which emphasize the political and global level of analysis and reinforce the reluctance to deal with self-generated risk as well as the tendency to attribute causation to external factors. In turn, it is possible to question the location of blame and responsibility and how, together, these issues influence conceptions of the causes of violence against aid workers and agencies. Of course, as previous chapters have demonstrated, humanitarian agencies are not monoliths or fully consistent in their policies and practices, nor are the government actors against whom they are often juxtaposed. Thus, the critiques I summarize here do not apply equally to all aid agencies.

Implicit in the politics-and-principles debate and the rescue and empire discourses is the issue of who gets to claim the symbolic power of the humanitarian label. Humanitarians and aid agencies have a complicated, paradoxical relationship with power. On the one hand, many deny or are at least uncomfortable with the ramifications of the power they do possess (Barnett and Weiss 2008b; see Barnett and Weiss 2008a, 38–43 for a more specific discussion of power; Donini 2010). Humanitarian agencies often characterize themselves as underdogs up against bigger and more powerful actors (i.e., governments and corporations), making a limited yet crucial contribution to relieving people's suffering, but not necessarily addressing root causes of injustice and violence.

Attacks against aid workers and operations in conflict zones are framed as unjustifiable because of what humanitarians do, who they are, and because of the principles they (ideally) espouse and personify. The navel-gazing and self-congratulation that too frequently characterize the humanitarian world feed this dynamic. The humanitarian principles themselves both set humanitarians apart and frame them in opposition to states and other conflict parties, thereby implicitly underlining their relative lack of power and their exceptional status relative to other actors and to conflict dynamics.

In claiming neutrality, humanitarians stand apart from the conflict and thus at a distance from the political forces that shape conflict and its dynamics. In claiming impartiality, humanitarians do not acknowledge the resource power they wield in providing assistance: the power to decide who and what get attention, the power to bring resources into a country in which scarcity predominates. The discourse of aid as rescue (and its individual partner, the mythical, superhero aid worker), in particular, is a morally laden story that is above reproach. The discourse's hero, who provides succor to the vulnerable, is an especially compelling figure. The rescue story perpetuates a vision of aid that does not recognize the power of discourse in constructing reality and therefore in defining how the public sees and responds to aid workers and agencies. It exclusively characterizes aid workers as exceptional individuals. Aid agencies are understandably reluctant to poke holes in this tale, since it serves their interests, even as they recognize the fundamental tension of profiting from the suffering of others.[2] Complicating the story risks feeding into the criticisms that others level against humanitarian actors for what they cannot accomplish and raises questions about liability and responsibility, both of which incur reputational risk, for incidents that do happen.

On the other hand, humanitarians and aid agencies generally do not hesitate to use the power they do possess. The growth of the sector in financial resources, size, and number as well as the politicization of mercy are all signs of the increasing influence of aid actors. To their credit, humanitarians are reluctant witnesses to atrocity in situations of extreme violence, serve as advocates on behalf of the voiceless, and are often the only foreigners present at the height of violence, all of which grants them moral authority and gravitas. Wearing the humanitarian label implies a degree of symbolic power related to the altruism and positive impressions that accompany helping another person (see also Fassin 2010b). The pictures that appear in the media of white Westerners offering solace and food have culturally defined relevance and influence, as does the political capital that aid agencies receive from operating in the world's hot spots despite obvious personal and institutional risk. Thus, the words and symbols of humanitarianism command different types and degrees of power and help to explain the widespread adoption of the humanitarian label (e.g., Kennedy 2005, Coyne 2013). Aid agencies wield these sources of power in fund-raising and advocacy campaigns, in urging a response or advocating for a particular policy option. Thus, aid agencies are instrumental in the ways that they claim and deny power, especially as it relates to violence against their staff and operations.[3]

These opposing tendencies—of using the power of humanitarianism to harness people's imaginations (and wallets) and of denying the influence that humanitarian actors do possess—contribute to an unwillingness to tarnish the convenient myths surrounding humanitarianism and to the tendency to conceptualize causes as externally initiated and motivated. The causes of violence against aid workers, therefore, are easily and convincingly attributed to the political machinations of governments that manipulate aid for their own purposes, to the blurred lines between civilian and military actors that confuse people and undermine humanitarian principles, or to the endemic violence that characterizes the context within which humanitarians operate.

These explanations remain external to the purview and realm of influence of aid agencies.[4] While relevant, humanitarians nonetheless exaggerate their situation by construing themselves as relatively powerless actors buffeted about by strong political winds. This world is one in which others attack them and their principles. In this rendering, humanitarians are then *acted on by others*, as opposed to claiming agency for themselves. This is fundamentally a passive stance, since it does not account for ways in which aid actors behave that might generate reasons—internal vulnerabilities—why others might wish to attack them. Nor does it account for the ways in which aid agencies do attempt to address the inequalities of the global system. While I do not doubt the altruism and good work of many aid workers and agencies nor refute the veracity of these externally generated causes of violence, my point here is to underscore that the axiomatic and externally focused cause explanations do not and cannot explain all violence.

The dichotomous portrayal of aid as either good or bad that characterizes the rescue and empire discourses helps to minimize internal vulnerabilities and magnifies external causes. Commentators and the public tend to either idolize individual aid workers or vilify the enterprise as a whole. Critics blame aid and aid agencies for failing to clean up the messes or fix the problems of complex emergencies and armed conflict, an impossible task for Band-Aid solutions for wounds in need of much more serious medical intervention. The purists who want to safeguard humanitarian action from other agendas contend its aims and possibilities are necessarily limited; humanitarian aid should not be and is not a substitute for political solutions, nor should it alleviate the responsibility of those who create the crisis in the first place. Others critique the humanitarian enterprise for displacing local, and arguably more effective, responses to aid (de Waal 2005; Dugger 2007) and the stereotypical "humanitarian international" for the privilege and arrogance he or she personifies.

On the other extreme, the public, and the media in particular, mythologizes aid agencies and aid workers in particular for self-sacrificial responses and their valiant efforts in the face of trying circumstances. Aid workers do perform very difficult work in the midst of horrendous and traumatic circumstances, either as observers or inadvertent participant observers. It is therefore difficult to critique humanitarians and humanitarian assistance in large part because of the job they do and the lifesaving assistance they provide, creating a "secular sanctity" (Benthall 1993, 123). One only has to watch news reports of aid-agency responses to famine and war to see this in action. This tendency to hold aid workers on a pedestal in the public Western imagination makes it difficult to critique, unpack, or challenge the role of aid and its characters in the public's imagination. Within those aid actors that have internalized this tendency, a perspective that rests on a "magical shield" results.

Emphasizing internal vulnerabilities appears to place blame on aid workers themselves, making them responsible for their own tragedies. Those reporting the stories are understandably hesitant to travel this path, nor is it necessarily accurate to do so. It is difficult to criticize or even to highlight ineffective or inadequate policies and procedures or specific individual behaviors because these shatter the myths and the pedestal on which aid workers stand in the general public's imagination.

In addition, blame functions in other ways, related to society's responses to violence and the suffering it causes, that impede understanding. It is far easier to blame "those people" and their "ancient hatreds" for their condition rather than to acknowledge the complex reasons why people kill each other, some of which may find some truth in stereotypes and pithy explanations but often relate to social, political, or economic inequality, shame, or other factors. Instead, these convenient explanations of "ancient hatreds" and the cultural or biological underpinnings of violence mask the moral judgments others hand down upon those caught up in war and conflict.

These moral judgments, in turn, shape the public's responses to violence, especially in relation to assistance. The public tends to open its pocketbooks more readily to natural disasters than to complex political emergencies, as the public outpouring of support in response to the 2004 Asian tsunami illustrated (see Brauman 2009). The enormity of the public response surprised many and dwarfed previous giving records.[5] In a natural disaster, the chances of getting caught in the disaster vortex are ostensibly equal, regardless of wealth, status, or guilt. It is an "act of God" or "the wrath of nature," about which we humans can do nothing. Thus, no one is to "blame" for the suffering that results. In comparison, the level of assistance for the human-driven, viciously violent wars in places such as the Democratic Republic of Congo or Syria rarely matches the enormous need that exists.

Humanitarian principles trade in a symbolic currency that agencies harness and use to practical and rhetorical effect. To reiterate, the humanitarian principles are seminal for their own sake and for their ability to facilitate access in contested and violent environments. Their value in relation to security lies in how they are demonstrated; they cannot be assumed. Many of those who target aid agencies are fully aware of the social power of the symbols and narratives of humanitarianism, which feature as reasons why they are targeted. Attacking humanitarians, particularly expatriates, is sure to generate attention-grabbing headlines for a group and its cause. As one aid worker remarked after the 1996 International Committee of the Red Cross (ICRC) murders in Chechnya, "They have realised that we make a good story" (Linda Doull, as quoted in Sweeney and O'Kelly 1996). Those who attack humanitarians are intelligent and often strategic about their choices; to ignore these calculations exhibits a damaging naïveté in analyzing the causes of violence. Indeed, humanitarians may be attacked precisely because of the shock factor, the ability to capture attention with a well-planned attack against those who, according to the predominant thinking in the public imagination, should be inviolable. "The theater value [of attacks against aid workers] is really underappreciated," remarked one aid expert, referring to the way in which this element is under-analyzed.[6] In this way, humanitarians may be attacked, and not protected, because of the principles and associated myths. Likewise, the portrayal of attackers as ruthless, irrational, and evil villains fits a narrative that casts the world into all-encompassing groups of "us" and "them" and serves to heighten the sense of fear so prevalent in a post-9/11 world.

Certainly global trends—tensions between the West and the rest, global inequalities, an increase in terrorism, the blurred lines between military and civilian actors—affect the operating environment and often the security of humanitarians. Whether or not aid is labeled as political is based on the ways in which communities, governments, rebels, and others perceive assistance and those who provide it. However, the way individual humanitarians behave, their decisions and actions (e.g., programs, staffing) and the inequalities they personify (i.e., haves and have-nots) also influence the ways in which humanitarians are perceived. Perceptions, in turn, feed into and exacerbate the global "culture wars." These perceptions, rooted in personal and structural dimensions of the aid workers' presence and amplified by global and cultural trends, elicit anger and make aid workers targets. At the same time, aid workers themselves bring their own cultural assumptions and attitudes to their work. So while aid workers perceived Sri Lankan authorities as obstacles and hindrances to access and assistance, Sri Lankan authorities saw aid workers as demanding luxurious vehicles that reflected the privilege of the affluent North, all of which further entrenched the cycle of misunderstanding (see Chapter 6).

Simple mono-causal explanations, while seductive, are not enough to capture the nuance and complexity driving violence against aid work. Without a multidimensional analysis, conceptualizing causes in exclusive and not interdependent ways privileges certain security-management tendencies (see Figure 2). A perspective that focuses primarily on individual actions can lead to a stance that "blames the victim" for security incidents. One response, therefore, is to emphasize personal security training. Overemphasis on organizational shortcomings or mistakes is more likely to promote responses that establish strict and inflexible security protocols and procedures (an "inflexible bureaucracy"). The discourses of external threat likewise correlate with an assumption of the protective effects of the principles, emblems, and symbols of humanitarianism (the "magic shield") or on a reactive, fortified response (the "gated community"). On its own, each tendency is problematic.

Internal vulnerabilities	External threats
"Blame the victim" *(blame individual actions; focus on personal security training)*	**"Magic shield"** *(external threats; reliance on principles, emblems, and symbols for protection)*
"Inflexible bureaucracy" *(focus on organizational shortcomings or mistakes; establish strict or inflexible security protocols and procedures)*	**"Gated community"** *(external threats; reliance on a reactive, fortified response)*
Hidden narratives	Dominant narratives

Figure 2. A Typology of Security Management Tendencies

Agencies need not be trapped into one or another of these tendencies, however. Missing from these options is an accounting of the interactions between dimensions and of reality and perception. The individual and collective actions of aid actors, set within the context of global dynamics, shape the way they are perceived, and vice versa. Thus, while external threats are important and even decisive in some contexts, humanitarian actors also need to take responsibility for the ways in which they contribute, either knowingly or inadvertently, to the perceptions others entertain about them. Such overlapping perceptions and misperceptions interact in potentially explosive ways. In short, these global and local perceptions and trends are mutually reinforcing. They deserve and require an analytical lens that can account for these complexities.

This sets the stage for a more complex discussion of the causes of violence, a complexity that the competing visions of aid and of the players in the aid drama tend to neglect. Without delving deeper into the reasons for why aid workers are attacked, with the messiness that emerges from challenging the blinders, it is impossible to proactively address the full range of risk, threat, and vulnerability.

Toward a Relational Approach to Analyzing the Causes of Violence

The arguments presented in the previous chapters, regarding the roots and implications of exceptionalism as they relate to the causes of and responses to violence and to the humanitarian system writ large, lay the foundation for the argument that security concerns have eroded the relational core of humanitarianism. Particularly in contexts of violence, providing assistance and protection and managing the security of aid providers are relational acts. That is, the process of giving and receiving humanitarian assistance unfolds within a relational web among aid workers as colleagues, friends, and partners; between aid workers and their host populations; among aid workers and local partners and officials; between governments and aid agencies. These relationships must be nurtured and maintained, all at the same time and with equal care and consideration. In this conception, they are both a manifestation of and response to the essential principle of humanity.

The increasing use of deterrent measures and fortified protective measures is at odds with a profession and field that sees as its first responsibility the need to respond to the exigencies and excesses of war. At some level, most aid workers are cognizant of the risks they are taking, even if they do not expect to pay the ultimate price. A model of security management that privileges protective and deterrent responses does not reflect what makes humanitarian work different—its emphasis on relieving suffering and its core principles—from other forms of political or military intervention. Moreover, it prevents humanitarians from providing assistance in a manner that maintains the relational character of the endeavor.

Essentially, an analysis of security concerns and an overly fortified and professionalized approach to security management threaten to overtake the relational ethos of humanitarianism, as embodied in the principle of humanity. The need to protect those providing assistance threatens to supersede both the moral imperative of responding to suffering and the imperative to provide assistance without discrimination and based on need. Providing security can and should be based on establishing and maintaining relationships with all sides, an idea central to the operational principle of neutrality. "No-go" zones imply working in only certain "safe" areas, without necessarily gathering a real sense of need, and often operating on one side of the conflict divide. In this way humanity, as the essential principle and a concept deeply rooted in the universal and inherent dignity and equality of all human beings, counters the negative aspects of humanitarian exceptionalism and the normalization of fear and danger, and offers a way forward that affirms a relational approach to aid.

Clearly, aid agencies need to think about the causes of violence against aid workers and aid agencies in a multifaceted and systemic way. Such a perspective supports a relational approach to aid work. Recognizing the complexity of causes implies surpassing the simplistic (and sensational) view of the dominant discourses of politics and principles, rescue and empire. Instead, a relational approach challenges exclusionary axioms and suggests that all of these causes and responses are mutually constituting and mutually reinforcing (see also Lynch 2011). An analytical framework that views causes in a reflexive way, as embedded in multiple dimensions and explanations, suggests a more proactive response to defining humanitarianism. It views aid workers as embedded within and not separate from the populations they assist, and follows a critical approach that emphasizes the importance of the everyday practices of aid (e.g., Fechter 2012; Autesserre 2014; also MacGinty and Richmond 2013). The framework emerges from a multidimensional and interdisciplinary approach that uncovers root causes and dynamics and aims to understand causation in the context of human frailty,

Internal vulnerabilities		External threats
Mythical figures and ordinary people (Personal/individual)	← → R E L A T I O N A L ← →	Empire and rescue (Cultural/metanarratives)
Informal past and bureaucratized present (Structural/organizational)		Politics and principles (Structural/humanitarian or aid system)
Hidden narratives		Dominant narratives

Figure 3. Analyzing Violence Against Aid Workers and Aid Agencies

organizational missteps and failures, as well as externally driven threats and dynamics (see Figure 3). Most important, however, it reclaims humanity as the guiding principle for action and reform.

The personal factors relate to those individual decisions and actions that increase individual vulnerability and may lead to a security incident. As described in Chapter 5, these include personal conduct and job stress, since stress deteriorates decision-making capabilities and may prompt people to behave in ways they might not otherwise act. Aid workers often find themselves in the midst of severe hardship, and the coping mechanisms they use often increase risk or are unhealthy. The motivations that draw people to aid work may also increase vulnerabilities, as individuals take exceptional risks to help others or lack the social support mechanisms that under normal conditions may lessen the negative effects of the context of hardship and suffering that surrounds them.

Acknowledging the role of individual behaviors in creating the conditions for violence functions as a counterweight to the vision of aid that sees aid workers as above reproach simply because of what they do. Aid workers are ordinary people, whose actions may be potentially generative of security incidents and who are vulnerable to different risks. Recognizing one's role and responsibility in creating risk emphasizes agency over passivity, restoring a sense of control rather than dwelling on vulnerability and fear. Therefore, it offers the possibility that individual agency may lessen the conditions of vulnerability and challenges the view that exceptionalizes aid workers as somehow more resilient or better able to cope. It encourages aid workers themselves to take ownership of their conduct and personal safety, keeping in mind the broader organizational and global context within which they work.

Organizational structural factors, also discussed in Chapter 5, include policies and procedures (or the lack thereof), such as hiring and firing practices and program activities that might result in or contribute to the conditions that lead to security incidents. This dimension covers incidents related to an agency's programming (who it serves, how, and where) and how this can lead to incidents. An agency that implements human rights programming might elicit the ire of those who benefit from the status quo or challenge local or cultural or religious customs and practices. Agencies that promise particular deliverables but do not explain or cannot deliver may generate resentment and cause retaliatory action. Most important, programming and security must be seen as interdependent and not isolated domains of activity.

In other cases, the internal, structural factors also refer to inappropriate or inadequate security procedures, such as the lack of blast film on the windows in the Canal Hotel despite security protocols necessitating such measures. In Sri Lanka, organizational decision making played into the ACF murders, primarily by not evacuating their national staff when the fighting began in Muttur. Although agencies cannot prevent all incidents, a risk-analysis perspective suggests the need to assess needs and protection for both staff members and those whom they help.

Conceptualizing internal vulnerabilities in this way provides a sense of normalcy of cause, in that many of these factors characterize many organizations and sectors and not just aid work. In that, they are quotidian as opposed to sensational and offset the dominance of the exceptionalism narrative. Self-generated risk and vulnerability capture the ways in which these factors become weaknesses in security-management terms. These dimensions increase in importance because of their interaction with the overall context of aid.

In the face of muddied or unclear motives or concrete explanations for why security incidents happen, the knowable and observable trends and patterns in the global system that can account for the increase in security incidents—targeted and random—against aid workers gain in importance. The competing discourses of aid and their associated explanations about the politicization, militarization, and securitization of aid and the cultural fault lines of humanitarianism as a tool and instrument of Western empire serve as convenient conceptual hooks to categorize the causes of violence against aid workers and aid delivery. In drawing on global trends and threats, analysts point toward the end of the Cold War and the changing nature of violence against civilians, the use of humanitarian action to mask weak political responses to violent conflict in strategically unimportant regions, the proliferation of actors in the humanitarian sector, the blurring of lines between civilian and military actors, crime or inequality, or the "war on terror" and ideological debates to explain the causes of security incidents. These conditions, in turn, undermine the neutral, impartial, and independent nature of traditional humanitarian action. Such explanations reflect the disciplinary dominance of political science and its analytical lenses, and reflect the narratives of the structural system and cultural levels.

These contextual narratives about cause emphasize factors external to humanitarian agencies' realm of influence. These causes are part of the context within which aid agencies and workers operate and represent external threats to agencies and their work and reputations. Aid agencies may not have direct influence over the foreign or military policies of states, nor do they control the actions of nonstate actors that result in violent conflict or war. Yet it is equally unrealistic to think that humanitarian agencies, individually or collectively, have no power to change the environment in which they operate. Although they might be able to only mitigate the impact of violence or contribute to volatility, they do wield symbolic and actual power and influence through their actions, programs, and the resources they control.

The instrumentalization and militarization of aid, with consequent negative ramifications for the security of aid workers, offer real and powerful, if convenient tools to critique the contraction of humanitarian space. Nevertheless, as exclusionary explanations they do not recognize how aid agencies themselves contribute to the contraction of that same space with the adoption of fortified security-management approaches and the ways in which their security profiles influence the perceptions of communities and other stakeholders.

At the same time, a relational focus illustrates several of the paradoxes and tensions inherent in aid work. For example, a focus on the behavioral responses to trauma and stress could help to reduce negative coping behaviors that may lead to incidents and could decrease personal vulnerability. Yet this also magnifies the inequalities—the access to resources that aid workers enjoy, when the people they are trying to help are so obviously lacking in such resources and care—that generate ethical and moral dilemmas in the first place. The professionalization of the field may make self-destructive actions less likely, even as it makes aid work more like a business, potentially detracting from the motivating power of acts of mercy.

The systems perspective inherent in the relational dimension also serves as an antidote to the narrative of humanitarian exceptionalism. Emphasizing only the external threats absolves individual aid workers and agencies of responsibility, while emphasizing only the internal vulnerabilities searches within the individual and organizational realms for scapegoats. The problem is that both explanations obscure the real issue. The ills and dynamics of causes exclusive to the cultural or structural realms deny agency to aid workers, whereas the rescue discourse and saintly images deny the role that aid workers themselves play in perceptions and cause. Seeing causes as interdependent and mutually constituting facilitates an understanding of aid workers and agencies as embedded within the systems in which they operate and as deserving of the protection due to all civilians.

The Implications for Aid Work in Danger

What are the implications of this analysis for aid work in danger? A humanity-based relational approach to humanitarianism is both pragmatic (setting out guidelines for interaction and analysis and requiring that agencies grapple with the inherent paradoxes of security management and aid as they are currently enacted) and aspirational (implying a long-term vision for reform of the aid system).

First, an analytical model of the causes of violence that accounts for a full landscape of causes shifts momentum in favor of proactive, flexible security-management approaches that reflect the guiding principles of aid work, whether these compose the animating principles of a purist humanitarian action or a broader set of principles. It embeds actors within the overall system and not outside of it. An incomplete or misguided analysis and understanding of causes can lead to inappropriate and ineffective security-management approaches. An analytical perspective that acknowledges internal vulnerabilities, external threats, and their interactive nature helps aid actors to recognize their own power and to claim agency, as opposed to promoting a reactive or passive approach to the violence that they experience or that hinders their work.

One way forward and beyond the competing visions is to focus on perceptions and the messy though imperative work of building relationships. Managing perceptions requires that agencies exert a concerted and continual effort to explain their actions and activities and that individuals consider their behaviors and the ways in which they affect the agency's image. This may include efforts to increase transparency and openness about programming successes and failures, thereby increasing the accountability of the sector.

Second, humanitarians and aid organizations need to reassert *and embody* their guiding principles, letting their organizational mission and principles shape not only their programs but also their security-management approaches. Principles matter, not as magical shields providing protection, but rather as guides for action. The dominance of protective and deterrent security-management strategies within the aid community suggests a perception of cause as due to external threat and neglects the internal vulnerabilities. At its most radical, a complete narrative that gives voice to and takes account of the unstated reasons goes to the very heart of the enterprise itself, calling for reform and a consistent application of values across an entire organization. This should manifest externally in an organization's programming, profile, and security-management approach, and internally, in its structures, policies, and procedures and its dealings with expatriate and national as well as headquarters and field-based staff members.

It is in the latter domain that agencies can address the internal hierarchies within their organizations, challenging the inequalities that characterize different categories of staff members and the push for continual growth and expansion. In doing so, agencies recognize the contributions of all causes, acknowledge differential risks, and take seriously the need for accountability, enmeshed as they are in the complex web of relationships that characterizes humanitarian work. Moreover, doing so involves reflexively examining and accepting their role as central actors within—and not outside—the system, scrutinizing their own power, mission, and orienting principles as well as their organizational footprint, physical architecture, and security approach.

Infusing an entire organization—programming and personnel—with its raison d'être and involving all segments in reflexive consideration of an organization's image and footprint are clearly long-term and complicated processes. They demand individual accountability, recognizing that all aid workers are to an extent "ambassadors" for the entire aid community, with concomitant responsibilities and privileges. Likewise, they insist on a cultural shift within the organizations themselves that reflects a relational approach to aid. This perspective implies the need to review discrepancies between categories of privilege inside and outside the organization and the dualities these discrepancies convey. Such a shift might emphasize mutual accountability, where staff are educated about and uphold the values of the organization and the organization adopts a clear and comprehensive duty-of-care approach to all those in their employ, and each is held accountable to the other. It could also involve significant financial costs, as agencies reassess and rectify the differential pay scales, benefits, and career opportunities for all staff members. A comprehensive approach balances the concurrent realities of the ethos of the informal past (an era less focused on standards and more oriented toward creative and flexible responses) and the realities and benefits of the professionalized present.

Taken seriously, a relational approach implies grappling with the paradoxes of compassion and repression inherent in the hierarchies of humanity (Fassin 2010a, 2012) that value, within organizations, expatriate over national staff and aid workers over civilians. Similarly, it challenges the Western bias of aid as well as the "othering" (Fechter 2012) that often characterizes the aid endeavor more generally. It calls for an internationalization of aid that engages nontraditional and non-Western actors in discussions about the various meanings and embodiment(s) of humanitarianism and for renewed emphasis on the protection of aid workers as inherently connected to the protection of all civilians.

In terms of security management, weaving together mission, programs, and security postures encourages security management to grow out of the raison d'être of the organization. Ideally, security management should inform programming (and vice versa) but not trump it. While many security officers espouse this idea, the reality is not always reflective of this approach. The ICRC's approach to security management, arguably one of the most advanced, is congruent with and embedded within its guiding principles and mandate.[7] The clarity of the ICRC's mandate in international law and practice facilitates this congruency. Other humanitarian and development actors would be well served to develop security-management approaches embedded in their distinctive history, missions, and values.

For many, this might entail a deliberate and systematic effort to adopt an acceptance approach to security that proactively demonstrates (and does not simply claim) a humanitarian exceptionalism based on principles and involves monitoring and adaptation to ensure that the perceptions of the organization match the image that the organization wants to project. Unless these security-management strategies are accompanied by a simultaneous strengthening of the aid system, primarily by making it more universal and less Western, aid actors risk further polarizing and weakening the norms of aid work. Such an approach would weaken the assumptive paradigm of humanitarian exceptionalism and contribute to making aid "exceptional" based on tangible efforts and actions. While it is possible to debate the extent to which agencies are responsible for unintended consequences, it is imperative that these become part of the ongoing conversation around security management and humanitarianism.

Third, the specter of Kouchner's "bureaucratized charity" has not abated. In the spirit of the trajectory of growth, standards, professionalization, and security, the aid community must remain attentive to its compassionate roots and avoid a primary focus on perpetuating its own survival. Professionalization privileges the technical and expert over the values of presence, witness, or solidarity that function on the basis of human connection. Thus, the push to professionalize must be tempered with the valuing and use of relational skills and not only technical expertise.

The danger of professionalization is that security becomes the domain of the professional and the expert, thereby devolving responsibility away from the individual aid worker. Especially when directly linked to programming, an acceptance strategy, for example, can generate the sense that security is the responsibility of all, whereas protection and deterrence strategies can function to make security the providence of things and specific individuals who are charged with security-management protocols and practices. Security management must not overshadow the humanitarian impulse or its relational foundations.

Fourth, a relational approach to aid can function as an antidote to the fortification of security management as well as enhance the operational principle of neutrality. Keeping humanity at the center forces a focus on relationships, which lie within the realm of individual and organizational agency. Relationally inspired security management requires strategic attention to the nature and quality of an organization's network of relationships and partnerships, and therefore to the ways in which the organization is perceived and to the image it projects. Clearly, neither relationships alone nor fortified security-management postures provide any assurance of not being attacked or targeted. Nevertheless, carefully cultivated relationships may provide insulation from attack and may function as safeguards when certain types of attacks do occur. A fortified security posture may mitigate impact, but its contribution to preventing attacks remains an empirical conundrum, for how does one prove a negative?

A community-policing model offers a middle ground that can include elements of a fortified stance but one modified with attention to relationships. Ideally, community policing is based on acceptance, with police looking to the community to alert them of problems. The police live in the neighborhoods they patrol, stop and converse with their neighbors, and patrol the streets on foot, bikes, or horseback rather than in armored cars. It is a relationally based model of providing protection, because the police live in and interact regularly with the community.

It is possible to change the ways in which agencies define the path forward in security management. If humanitarians do not take action, legal liability will do so for them. This has already begun. Legal proceedings resulting from insurance claims and alleged negligence are defining the parameters of legal responsibility and "due diligence" regarding agencies' duty of care to their staff, apart from any ethical or moral responsibilities that already exist. The strategies that agencies adopt and the specific decisions they make, however, have consequences far beyond the individual or agency processes that produce these strategies and decisions, ranging from immediate to long-term effectiveness for humanitarian action as a whole.

Finally, and most important, asserting that humanity is at the core of aid work, as well as risk and security management, embodies the universal and inherent dignity and equality of all human beings and recognizes humans as social beings. It models an alternative to the inhumanity of war and violence and, in so doing, suggests the possibility of countermanding the relentless dynamic of violence. At their core, humanitarian acts represent a relational and human response to suffering. Yet this is easily lost in the daily grind of aid work. The underlying morality of humanity is that humanitarian action is a response to people's suffering, an act in solidarity with that suffering and an attempt to provide lifesaving assistance and protection. Responding by putting up walls and other mechanisms designed to protect humanitarians runs counter to the animating principle of humanity. Instead, a relational perspective calls forth a response rooted in humility and the reality of connection, where aid workers are also civilians and the difference between those with and those without is only an accident of birth.

Clearly, some organizations and actors have successfully navigated the literal and metaphorical minefields of perception, image, and operational humanitarianism. It is crucial, however, that humanitarian professionals, policymakers, and power brokers in world capitals not lose sight of the fundamental compassionate response of the humanitarian ethos and the desire to assuage the suffering of those caught up violence and natural disaster. Fear has not yet captured the humanitarian imagination, but it stands poised to do so. Preserving the humanitarian image requires an unambiguous reclaiming of humanity and adoption of security-management policies and procedures with an eye to how they affect the guiding principles, the image of humanitarians, and the relationships that characterize the endeavor.

This is not an argument for naïve security-management policies and practices devoid of professional expertise or of tactics and strategies borrowed from the police and military professions. Rather, it is a call for an approach to humanitarianism and security management that is fully informed by humanity at the core and by the multitude of causes that lead to insecurity in the first place.

NOTES

Introduction

1. Even though I analyze situations of violence in this book, many of the same issues and lessons apply to those providing assistance in stable contexts as well.

2. I discuss the paradoxical and problematic aspects of humanity, including the tension between the universal and the particular, in the following chapter.

3. In particular, I am indebted to Maarten Merkelbach and the participants in the Security Management Institute (SMI) seminars from 2007 to 2010; to the coordinators of the European InterAgency Security Forum (EISF), especially Jean Renouf and Oliver Behn; and to the InterAction Security Advisory Group (SAG), especially John Schafer, for inviting me to numerous meetings over the past years. The feedback I received and conversations at those meetings were particularly helpful.

4. All project documents, including the concluding report, reports from Kenya and Uganda, interview protocols, and conceptual discussions, are available at http://www.acceptanceresearch.org.

Chapter 1. Three Stories of Aid in Danger

1. The confusion meant that one female staff member, originally reported among the dead, was alive in an Iraqi hospital but without contact with family and colleagues for several days after the attack (Independent Panel 2003). Samantha Power relates the story of Lyn Manuel, Sergio Vieira de Mello's secretary, in more detail. After the bombing, UN officials notified her family that she had died in the attack. In fact, Manuel, who was in the office directly beside de Mello's at the time of the bombing, was severely wounded in the attack and taken to a U.S. Army clinic outside Baghdad. On 21 April, several days after her family held a private memorial service, she was finally able to phone her family (Power 2008, 496–499).

2. Rescuers extracted Loescher from the rubble around 8:00 P.M. after amputating his legs to free him. This allowed them to reach de Mello, but according to survivor accounts, de Mello lost consciousness around 7:30 P.M. and died shortly after Loescher was airlifted to safety (Power 2008, 487–488, chap. 21).

3. At the time of the bombing, the UN security-management system designated four phases in addition to the full withdrawal of phase 5: phase 1 is precautionary, requiring staff to exercise caution; phase 2 specifies restrictions on the movement of staff and families and requires them to stay at home, with no additional movement authorized; phase 3 involves temporary relocation of staff and eligible dependents inside or outside the country; phase 4, Program Suspension, requires the evacuation of all international staff, except those involved in security, emergency, or humanitarian programming (Independent Panel 2003, 33–35).

4. Interview with aid expert, January 2007. Also reported in BBC News (2003).

5. The Security Management Team for Iraq established a ceiling for Baghdad of 200 international staff on 30 June 2003. Despite Iraq's phase 4 security designation (allowing only international staff involved in security, emergency, or humanitarian programming), at least 350 international staff and as many as 900 international staff were posted to Baghdad at the time of the bombing (UN Secretariat 2004, 9–10).

6. The Ahtisaari Report had previously found that the U.S. military deployed particular security measures, such as a roving guard, armed observation post, military patrols, and a truck that blocked the access road later used in the bombing, for the Canal Hotel premises. UN senior management, however, was "uneasy with this highly visible military presence" and requested these measures be dismantled (Independent Panel 2003, 11).

7. Although UNDSS is the central security department for the UN, the UN agencies (WFP, UNICEF, UNHCR, etc.) all employ their own security personnel. Sir David Veness resigned after the December 2007 Algiers bombing, although he stayed on in an interim capacity until his successor, Gregory Starr, a former director of the U.S. Diplomatic Security Service, began as the under-secretary-general for safety and security in May 2009.

8. Interview with UN official, May 2006.

9. The headline of one newspaper article on 20 August 2003 read, "U.N. Staff's Immunity from Terror Ends" (Lynch 2003). Catherine Bertini, a UN under-secretary-general, remarked in 2004, "If you were flying the blue flag you had this invisible aura of protection" (as quoted in Adler 2004). On the first anniversary, Annan observed, "But the attack on the Canal Hotel brought us face to face with danger in a new and more intimidating form—the danger that we, servants of the United Nations, may have become one of the main targets of political violence" (Annan 2004).

10. Interview with NGO aid worker, May 2006.

11. See Article 55, Fourth Geneva Convention, 12 August 1949. Article 55 states, "To the fullest extent of the means available to it, the Occupying Power has the duty of ensuring the food and medical supplies of the population; it should, in particular, bring in the necessary foodstuffs, medical stores and other articles if the resources of the occupied territory are inadequate."

12. The Ahtisaari Report mentions UN Security Council Resolutions 1483, 1502, and 1511 and the lack of an agreed-on formal arrangement for the security of the UN mission (Independent Panel 2003, 3, 5–6).

13. Multiple interviewees, both inside and outside the UN system, indicated the UN operates as a risk-averse actor, particularly after the 2003 Baghdad bombing. Interviews with aid expert, March 2006; aid expert, July 2006; and security director, January 2007.

14. Interview with UN official, May 2006; interview with UN official, May 2006.

15. Interview with NGO aid worker, May 2006.

16. Although more than seventeen people died in the UN Baghdad bombing, not all were UN employees. Twenty-three people died in the suicide attack on the UN compound in Abuja, Nigeria, on 26 August 2011, of whom eleven were UN employees (UN News Service 2011). Two additional UN staff members later died from the injuries they sustained in the Abuja attack, bringing the total deaths to twenty-five, of whom thirteen were UN employees (BNO News 2011).

17. In fact, the ICRC lost five delegates between December 2008 and the summer of 2009.

18. Personal correspondence with security official familiar with the incident, March 2009. The ACF report indicates the team was due to leave Muttur on 1 August due to intense fighting between the government and the LTTE, but was stranded in the city after an LTTE attack that caused the suspension of the ferry to Trincomalee. Several attempts to evacuate them after this time also failed. ACF did inform the Sri Lankan army, navy, and police of the team's presence in the city (ACF International 2008).

19. See AFP (2009). In August 2009, on the third anniversary of the deaths, Human Rights Watch called for an international investigation into the killings (HRW 2009). As of May 2013, no one has been prosecuted for the murders.

20. Jonathan Goodhand (2006) refers to peacebuilding work (i.e., working for positive impacts on the peace dynamics) as working "on" conflict, as opposed to working "around" conflict (i.e., conflict blind programming) or working "in" conflict (i.e., limiting the negative impacts of programming on conflict dynamics, akin to Mary Anderson's approach of "do no harm"; Anderson 1999).

21. The FIC report observes, "Scant attention was paid to the underlying pre-existing conflict situation and its likely effect on the modalities of providing tsunami-related assistance. Inadequate contextual analysis may have contributed to a culture of humanitarian operations in which many aid agencies failed to prioritize the need for conflict-sensitive programming, conflict awareness in human resource management and the development of security guidelines" (Harris 2007, 35). This, in turn, had significant ramifications for security.

22. Harris concludes that "humanitarian actors will need to better contend with the dynamics of nationalism [and sovereignty] in order to ensure that they can maintain a space in which to operate effectively" (Harris 2010, 10).

23. Interviews with aid expert (July 2006), security director (May 2006), and security director (January 2007), respectively.

24. RTE News broadcast a Prime Time documentary called *Kidnapped* about the experience of Sharon Commins and her Kenyan colleague, Hilda Kawuki, on 21

December 2010. See http://www.rte.ie/news/primetime/2010/1221/295791-21december2010_primetime/.

25. *Flavia Wagner v. Samaritan's Purse and Clayton Consultants Inc.*, Case 1:11-cv-03375-RJS/AJP, U.S. District Court for the Southern District of New York, filed 17 May 2011.

26. While all three stories are basically true, their details are not in the public domain. For this reason, I have chosen to maintain the anonymity of the individuals and organizations involved. The first is based on an incident that happened to a friend. The second derives from interviews I conducted in 2006 and 2007. The third is based on a conversation with the security director of the affected organization, March 2009.

27. The company Johnson & Johnson uses a red cross with a white background on some of its medical products, a design they have used since the late 1800s and for which the company registered a trademark in 1905. Because the emblem is not used on aircraft, vehicles, or structures, it is the subject of an exemption. For the exemption, see U.S. reservations regarding the 1949 Geneva Conventions (http://www.icrc.org/ihl.nsf/NORM/D6B53F5B5D14F35AC1256402003F9920?OpenDocument, accessed 30 August 2011). Their use of the emblem, however, has been the subject of repeated litigation. Ads for their products carry a disclaimer that "products bearing this trademark have no connection with the American National Red Cross." See http://www.jnjredcross.com/ (Accessed 30 August 2011; see also IRIN 2007a).

28. The other three core principles for the ICRC—voluntary service, unity, and universality—are not as widely shared within the humanitarian community as a whole (see http://www.icrc.org).

29. In a related analysis, Finnemore (2003) explores the changing meaning of the use of military force over time, documenting the increasing importance of international law and norms limiting the use of force.

Chapter 2. The Twin Challenges for Contemporary Humanitarianism

1. Several websites are devoted to tracking acts of terrorism. See the Global Terrorism Database at the University of Maryland (http://www.start.umd.edu/start/) or the Worldwide Incident Tracking System (http://www.trackingterrorism.org/resource/us-nctc-worldwide-incidents-tracking-system; both sites accessed 5 October 2013). Scott Atran (2004) has written on the increases and implications of suicide terrorism, while Talal Asad (2007) has written about the narrative construction of suicide terrorism.

2. I thank Abby Stoddard for compiling for me these figures from the Aid Worker Security Database (AWSD) in April 2008. In contrast, a dataset I compiled using a variety of humanitarian news media, including IRIN, ReliefWeb, Reuters AlertNet, local online news sources, and major online and print news sources, such as the *Christian Science Monitor*, the BBC, and the *New York Times*, contained reports of at least 116 aid workers killed in Afghanistan and thirty-seven kidnapped between October

2001 and July 2007. In Iraq, these same media sources reported at least seventy-two aid workers killed and forty-three kidnapped between January 2003 and July 2007. See Fast (2010) and Chapter 3 for a discussion of discrepancies and challenges of data collection on this topic.

3. Interview with UN aid worker, May 2006.

4. Interview with UN official, May 2006.

5. Interview with aid expert, May 2006.

6. Ruud Lubbers, then the UN high commissioner for refugees, used the phrase "Iraqisation of aid" in May 2004. An article quotes Lubbers as saying, "There is a tendency to think that the whole world is like Iraq, a tendency to think that the U.N. now has to bunker down everywhere and seal ourselves off in heavily fortified compounds no matter which country we are operating in" (Large 2004).

7. In 1988 Alex Schmid and Albert Jongman defined terrorism as "an *anxiety-inspiring* method of repeated violent action, employed by (semi-)clandestine individual, group or state actors, for idiosyncratic, criminal or political reasons, whereby—in contrast to assassination—the direct targets of violence are not the main targets" (Schmid and Jongman 1988, 28, italics added). More than twenty years later, scholars are still searching for a consensus definition.

8. Interview with UN official, May 2006.

9. Interview with security director, January 2007. He suggested internal staff management threats as vulnerabilities and threats as external. Furthermore, "Vulnerability is the most difficult to tackle, but it is also the thing that we have the most control over."

Chapter 3. The Dangers They Face

1. The 1936 issues of the *Revue Internationale de la Croix-Rouge* document multiple bombings of Red Cross ambulances during the Italian-Ethiopian conflict. For more on this particular incident, see Comité International (1936a) and Moorehead (1998, chap. 11).

2. A Dr. Melly died on 5 May 1936 (Comité International 1936b, 581). Moorehead (1998, 305–316) also lists the deaths of an American, Dr. Hockmann, and of Lundstrom, the ambulance driver, on 30 December 1935.

3. Information for earlier historical periods is unfortunately limited in that much of it remains anecdotal or incident-specific. I use examples of violence against the ICRC and its delegates because the ICRC maintains the most comprehensive and systematic records of its operations, and not to imply that it is the only or most affected humanitarian actor. While other humanitarian actors undoubtedly lost staff members in operations throughout the twentieth century, their archives, if they exist, are less accessible and/or complete as are stories about them and their work.

4. Interview with aid expert, July 2006.

5. Georges Olivet was killed in Zaire (Comité International 1969d).

6. The two were Malarchy Riddle and Jonathan Ampache (Comité International 1968d).

7. Alain Modoux died in a land mine explosion (Comité International 1966).

8. The two were Pierre Tacier and Pierre Gachoud (Comité International 1968c).

9. The ICRC has conducted additional visibility tests periodically since 1936, including for infrared electro-optical observation, thermal imaging, and visibility at sea, in recognition of technological advances in warfare that render ineffective a purely visual recognition of the emblem. The results are reported in Cauderay (1990).

10. Interview with security director, May 2006.

11. The two, a Yugoslav (Dragan Hercog) and a Swede (Robert Carlsson), were killed on 30 September 1968, together with two individuals from the World Council of Churches (Comité International 1968a). Moorehead (1998, 619) reports the Nigerian officer enticed them out of hiding, calling out, "Come out all members of the International Red Cross," and that they were shot while lying on the ground.

12. Dismayed at what they saw as a failure to confront the Nigerian government over its policies and the ICRC's public silence in the face of genocide, Bernard Kouchner (who worked as an ICRC doctor in Biafra) and other founders of MSF, split from the ICRC and established MSF. Kouchner publicly compared the ICRC stance of neutrality to its stance during the Holocaust (Walker and Maxwell 2009, 48). One of the key principles for MSF is *témoignage*, or witnessing, as a way of expressing solidarity with victims and drawing attention to their plight. MSF's website lists the following core principles: medical ethics, impartiality, independence, neutrality, and bearing witness and speaking out (http://www.doctorswithoutborders.org/).

13. While the JCA flights did sometimes contain weapons, the ICRC relief flights did not, in part because they originated in a different place and operated with the permission of the Nigerian federal government (de St. Jorre 1972, chap. 9).

14. See, for example, Comité International (1968e, 403) for more on bombings of the Uli airstrip and Comité International (1969e, 6 and 1969g) for descriptions of bombings of hospitals. In May 1969, a cargo plane crashed near Uli, killing the four team members on board (Comité International 1969a).

15. The journalist de St. Jorre (1972) provides a compelling firsthand account of the war. He includes an extensive account of the shooting down of the Swedish Red Cross DC-7 on pp. 242 and 331–333. The English pilot who shot down the plane experienced a reported breakdown after the incident and later died in the war. Goetz (2001) writes about the event, indicating three people died in the crash, but the Comité International (1969c; also 1969f, 416–418) reports four died on board: David Brown, Stig Caroson, Kiell Petterson, and Harry Axelsson.

16. See de St. Jorre (1972, chaps. 9 and 12). Von Rosen also flew planes for the Swedish Red Cross in Abyssinia in the 1930s (Moorehead 1998, 307).

17. The figures from the Aid Worker Security Database (AWSD) are compiled from media sources and aid agency statistics. As of the time of writing, these were the most

authoritative data about severe violence against aid workers. No systematic data exist for periods prior to 1997. See Stoddard, Harmer, and Haver (2006) for a discussion of the study methodology.

18. According to the AWSD, on which these studies are based, the seven most dangerous countries between 2006 and 2008, in decreasing order, were as follows: Sudan, Afghanistan, Somalia, Sri Lanka, Chad, Iraq, and Pakistan (Stoddard, Harmer, and DiDomenico 2009, 4; also http://www.aidworkersecurity.org/).

19. Conversations with other researchers in this area, among them Marianne Abbott, Adele Harmer, Elizabeth Rowley, and Abby Stoddard, have enhanced this discussion about the challenges of research on humanitarian security. Several other sources (Sheik et al. 2000; Barnett 2004; Stoddard, Harmer, and Haver 2006; Rowley 2007; Fast 2010) articulate similar challenges.

20. Existing NGO security coordinating bodies, such as those in Afghanistan (Afghan NGO Security Office), Iraq (NGO Coordination Committee in Iraq), Somalia (the NGO Safety Program), and Gaza (Gaza Strip NGO Safety Office), collate incidents and provide periodic incident summaries and security assessments. Other exceptions are the work of IMMAP-OASIS in select countries (see http://www.immap.org/) and the Centre for Safety and Development's initiative, SIMSON, in the Central African Republic (see http://www.centreforsafety.org/).

21. A number of earlier data-sharing efforts failed, including the Humanitarian and Security Protection Network initiative, funded by ECHO (Barnett 2004, 69–70). New efforts, however, are gaining traction. In the late 1990s, World Vision International contracted Virtual Research Associates to create a database, which other agencies (e.g., Save the Children) have since adopted and adapted for their own use. The UN has created an incident reporting system to compile UN-wide statistics, which feed into the annual report to the UN secretary-general on the safety and security of humanitarian personnel and the protection of UN personnel. Since 2010, OCHA has compiled statistics on impediments to aid access in select countries. AWSD, a project of Humanitarian Outcomes, contains the incidents compiled for the ODI/CIC research (Stoddard, Harmer, and Haver 2006, 2011; Stoddard, Harmer, and DiDomenico 2009). Numerous web sources have sprouted, compiling media reports of incidents (e.g., Patronus Analytical and other blogs), or reporting on violence against aid workers and offering resources (e.g., http://humanitarianprotection.org/AID_WORKER_SAFETY/aid_worker_safety.html). The Security in Numbers Database (SiND) compiles threats and incidents of violence against aid operations more generally. It uses both media reports as well as data reported directly from different humanitarian and aid agencies (http://www.insecurityinsight.org/). See Wille and Fast (2013b).

22. For example, the ODI/CIC study (Stoddard, Harmer, and Haver 2006, 5–9) contains a more extensive discussion of how they estimated the number of national and international staff in order to arrive at rates of violence against aid workers over time. The Johns Hopkins School of Public Health study (Rowley 2007; Rowley, Crape,

and Burnham 2008) calculates rates only for those participating organizations that were able to provide complete denominator data.

23. These are clearly not obstacles unique to the study of violence against aid workers. The older and vast literatures on political violence (including the causes of interstate and civil war) and contentious politics have dealt with similar data collection issues. Conflict scholars researching these topics publish in academic journals such as the *Journal of Peace Research* and the *Journal of Conflict Resolution*, and attend conferences such as the annual meetings of the Peace Science Society or the International Studies Association. While I do not engage this literature here, these scholars suggest methodological or other solutions to resolve many of these issues. For how scholars have dealt with these issues, see, for example, Sarkees and Schafer (2000), Sambanis (2004), Harbom and Wallensteen (2010), and Davenport and Ball (2002) for a comparison of three different data sources and its implications for research findings.

24. Security and risk management standards exist in other fields, and some argue for applying these standards, such as the ISO31000, to the aid industry (e.g., Merkelbach and Daudin 2011). See the International Organization for Standardization for more information, http://www.iso.org.

25. One of these volunteers, Tom Fox, was murdered, while the remaining three, Jim Loney, Norman Kember, and Harmeet Singh, were eventually released.

26. Early reports labeled the twenty-three as aid workers, while later ones referred to the group as missionaries. Two of these, both men, were killed, and two others, both women, were released early on. The Taliban released the remaining nineteen later in August 2007 after negotiations, facilitated by the ICRC and the Afghan Red Crescent Society. The eventual agreement included a promise from South Korea to pull out its troops and to not send missionaries to the country as well as rumors of a ransom paid for the hostages' release (Rohde and Sang-Hun 2007).

27. Peace Corps volunteers are typically not considered aid workers, in part because they work for a government agency. For this incident, see the Patronus Analytical Aid Workers Fatalities Database at http://www.patronusanalytical.com/. The incident was included as of June 2009. The database contains other discrepancies as well (e.g., the death of Rachel Corrie, an activist with the International Solidarity Movement, who was killed by an Israeli bulldozer in 2003) and includes safety incidents such as plane crashes.

28. Interview with aid worker, May 2006.

29. At least one internal memo from an aid agency (International Rescue Committee) gave credence to these assertions. Reuters obtained a July 2005 memo from an IRC employee who later headed IRC's Sudan program, indicating that cooperating with the ICC could help bring criminals to justice. The IRC denied this became organizational policy, but acknowledged it did consider such actions (Charbonneau 2009a).

30. Interviews with UN official, May 2006, and with aid expert, March 2006. One interviewee used the example of an organization in Afghanistan that, at the time, was contracted to provide mapping of tribal structures and actors to a Provincial Recon-

struction Team (PRT). This type of information contributed to a perception that aid agencies could be gathering "intelligence" information.

31. See Rieff (2002, 221–222) and O'Connell (2002); also personal conversation with aid worker, June 2009.

32. A classic account of anthropological fieldwork relates how the author confronted accusations of spying (Rabinow 1977). This is not a new phenomenon either, as social scientists faced similar accusations and dilemmas in their work in Central and South America during the Cold War (Glazer 1970). More recently, tensions have surfaced related to academics' affiliations with intelligence agencies and the military. Psychologists have debated the ethics of participating in interrogations, related to accusations of torture (e.g., debates within the American Psychological Association membership related to the presence of psychologists during interrogations at Guantanamo Bay). The APA passed a resolution in June 2009 that condemned torture as unethical and stated that the "APA Ethics Committee will not accept any defense to torture in its adjudication of ethics complaints" (APA Ethics Committee Statement, "No Defense to Torture Under APA Ethics Code," June 2009). The Human Terrain Project, which hires social scientists, such as cultural anthropologists and political scientists, to work alongside and within military and counterinsurgency operations, such as those in Iraq and Afghanistan, has elicited tremendous controversy within the academy and professional associations, in part because of the tension between academic knowledge and intelligence gathering. At least one social scientist, Michael Bhatia, working on a Human Terrain Team died in Afghanistan in May 2008. A study commissioned by the American Anthropological Association examined the various dangers anthropologists faced in the field, including spying and violence, among other dangers (Howell 1990). To my knowledge, this is the only survey in the academy chronicling the specific dangers of fieldwork, even though a growing body of literature exists about conducting research in dangerous contexts (see, e.g., Peritore 1990; Sluka 1990; Nordstrom and Robben 1995; Lee 1995; Lee-Treweek and Linkogle 2000; Sriram et al. 2009).

33. PBS's *Frontline* produced a documentary about Cuny and his life as an aid worker. The accompanying website indicates that the Chechens are likely responsible for his death, but the Russians contributed to his death with their accusations that he was a spy. See "Who Killed Fred Cuny?," http://www.pbs.org/wgbh/pages/frontline/shows/cuny/kill/. Accessed 13 November 2007. See also Anderson (1996).

34. Although the article appeared in the 6 April 1995 *New York Review of Books*, published around Cuny's disappearance, the date of the article is 9 March.

35. Based on the data, Rowley reports the Middle East and South/Central Asia regions have proportionally higher numbers of intentional violence cases relative to the overall number of cases for these regions.

36. In multiple interviews (with aid experts [three], July 2006, July 2006, and January 2007, and with security director, January 2007), aid and security experts highlighted the differential risks that staff members face. In research on acceptance as a security-management approach in East Africa (Fast, Freeman, et al. 2011), we identified

at least four categories of staff: local staff (hired to work in the village/town/area in which they live), national staff (from another part of the country in which they work), regional staff (from a neighboring country), and international staff (expatriates from a non-neighboring country).

37. While such measures may have prevented the former staff member from entering the compound, as in Joe's case, or may have safely ensconced Karen behind a heavily guarded compound, the bigger question is whether they would have been able to carry out their work, given such fortifications.

38. Interview with aid expert, January 2007.

39. According to the AWSD, between 10 March 2009 and 22 June 2010, twenty-six aid workers were killed, kidnapped, or severely wounded in Sudan. In the previous fourteen months (from 1 January 2008 to the end of February 2009), a total of forty-four aid workers were killed, kidnapped, or severely wounded in Sudan. It is unclear whether the rates of violence changed during these periods. See http://www.aidworkersecurity.org/. Accessed 4 November 2010.

40. Carle and Chkam (2006, 11–15) make a similar argument that organizations in Iraq failed to share data because they were averse to drawing publicity to themselves, especially in cases where the security incident occurred as a result of a mistake or failure of some kind. They also assert that media reports of the violence drove analyses of risk in Iraq, magnifying the risks and resulting in a disconnect between reports and reality.

41. Interview with security director, May 2006.

42. Like the ODI/CIC study but using a different method that makes the studies not directly comparable, they calculate a rate of six per ten thousand fatalities per year due to intentional violence only (Rowley, Crape, and Burnham 2008).

43. Interviews with security directors (two in May 2006 and three in January 2007). Bolletino (2006) suggests a similar discrepancy between scholars and policymakers, who emphasize the threat of targeted violence, and security managers, who point to criminal acts and safety incidents as most important. Also, the World Health Organization (WHO) regularly releases research on road safety, and the 2009 report found that low- and middle-income countries bear the burden of road accidents and carry the highest death rates (WHO 2009). Given that most humanitarian operations take place in these countries, it seems logical that accidents should represent a significant safety issue for humanitarian actors. Nevertheless, this is a controversial subject. Fleet Forum (http://www.fleetforum.org/) is dedicated to improving the safety records of relief and development organization vehicles.

44. For example, a 2004 media report cites the following: "By sending U.S. troops to conduct what would ordinarily be seen as development work, or by requiring aid workers to coordinate their activities with those of the Western coalition, it becomes easier to identify aid workers—however falsely—as pro-Western and therefore justifiable targets for violence" (Baldauf and Tohid 2004). Lischer (2007, 101) cites "terror

tactics" that fail to distinguish between soldiers and civilians as responsible for higher casualty rates for aid workers.

45. Interview with security expert, May 2006.

46. The ODI/CIC report indicates an unknown motive for 41 percent of the 408 incidents (Stoddard, Harmer, and Haver 2006, 19). In their 2009 update, 55 percent of incidents had "undetermined" motives, and the number of politically motivated incidents increased from 29 percent in 2003 to 49 percent in 2008. The latter refers only to incidents for which it was possible to discern a motive (Stoddard, Harmer, and DiDomenico 2009, 5).

Chapter 4. The Dominant Explanations

1. See Charbonneau (2009b). The Sudanese government declared these expulsions nonnegotiable (Bayoumy 2009). In June 2009, however, the Sudanese government agreed to let some of those expelled return with new logos and names (e.g., Mercy Corps returned under Mercy Corps Scotland, CARE under CARE Switzerland, and SCF US under Save the Children Sweden). PADCO was also allowed to return (Parsons 2009).

2. Quote attributed to Rajiva Wijesinha, Ministry of Disaster Relief and Human Rights, at a special session of the UN Human Rights Council on Sri Lanka (Deutsche Presse-Agentur 2009). Aid agencies countered, saying it was impossible to deliver food and medicine without vehicles. The critique highlights the differing perceptions that recipient countries and communities may hold of aid agencies (as driving "luxury vehicles"), as opposed to those of the aid agencies themselves (as needing the vehicles for operational reasons).

3. As highlighted in Chapter 1, the Ahtisaari Report concluded, "The level and military nature of the threats against the United Nations . . . demonstrate the urgent need for a more *forceful* approach to UN security." It recommended that UN activities, regardless of type, occur "only with security and *deterrence* capabilities appropriate to protect its staff and premises" (Independent Panel 2003, 22, italics added).

4. Walker has since expanded these to four types: containment (government and military), comfort (most NGOs), compassion (ICRC and MSF), and change (human rights groups and others) (personal correspondence with author, April 2009).

5. Source unknown. Several versions of this tale exist, and I thank Andre Gingerich Stoner for bringing this one to my attention.

6. The specific term "humanitarian action" tends to refer to the provision of lifesaving assistance in accordance with the principles of humanity, impartiality, neutrality, and independence. See Slim (1997b) and Terry (2002). I use "humanitarianism" (vs. "humanitarian action") in this book in a more generic sense that may or may not be wedded to these four principles.

7. In an article on moral dilemmas of humanitarian action, Hugo Slim discusses deontological ethics—focusing on aid or acts of mercy as good in and of themselves—and consequentialist ethics—focusing on the consequences, intended or not, of providing assistance—as necessary and useful tools for aid agencies' ethical analysis. He discusses the various ethical choices and moral dilemmas that agencies with increasingly broad mandates face in the course of providing humanitarian assistance (Slim 1997a). In this case, the first falls within a deontological ethical frame, and the second within a consequentialist ethical frame. See also the discussion in Keen (2007, 141–142).

8. This is analogous to the roots of the argument that humanitarians make against the term "humanitarian intervention." The intervention, humanitarians argue, is not humanitarian even if justified as such, because (a) it involves violence (and therefore loss of life vs. life-sustaining assistance), (b) it is not of an exclusively humanitarian character, and (c) it is not provided on a neutral, impartial, or independent basis. Military intervention, by definition, cannot be neutral.

9. O'Connell (2002) discusses the evolution of IHL with regard to humanitarian assistance, focusing particular attention on the rights and responsibilities that accompany the empowerment of NGOs in the 1990s (the "third" and "fourth" waves of development of international law).

10. A 15 July 1992 *New York Times* editorial on p. A20 referenced the "well-fed dead" in Bosnia, asserting, "The people of Bosnia remain unprotected. What good will it do for them to have food in their stomachs when their throats are slit?" (*New York Times* 1992). Minear (2002) traces the inclusion of a human rights/protection agenda within a humanitarian assistance framework to the critique implicit in this idea.

11. For more perspectives arguing for the space for purist humanitarian action, see Terry (2002) and Rieff (2002). For more discussion of the principles of humanitarian action, see, among others, Pictet (1979a, 1979b), Plattner (1996), Slim (1997b), and Weiss (1999).

12. Other characterizations of the "purist" perspective include "Dunantist" (Stoddard 2003) and "classicist" (Weiss 1999).

13. For more discussion of the Wilsonian or political humanitarian perspective, see Weiss (1999), Minear (2002), Stoddard (2003), and Hoffman and Weiss (2006). Minear and Weiss (1995) also include a "solidarist" perspective that sides with a particular group, and Stoddard separates out religiously inspired or faith-based agencies.

14. See especially critiques of the ICRC for its silence during World War II and charges that it knew what happened in the Nazi concentration camps and later, during the genocide in Rwanda. See Favez (1999) and Moorehead (1998) for more on the Holocaust as well as Bugnion (1997), Kellenberger (2004), and Sandoz (2007) for an ICRC perspective. On the other hand, aid agencies have several times publicly and repeatedly called for military intervention, only later to regret and critique this same intervention, notably in Somalia (Maren 1997) and Kosovo (Vaux 2004).

15. Barnett and Snyder (2008, 145–146) suggest an alternative typology, according to political and apolitical objectives and change goals (modest or ambitious). These two axes result in four different types of humanitarianism: bed for the night, do no harm, back a decent winner, and peacebuilding. In a later book, Barnett (2011) differentiates emergency from alchemical humanitarians.

16. European and North American NGOs tend to divide along these lines, with more European organizations closer to (or at least advocating) the purist end of the spectrum and North American ones more firmly ensconced in the political humanitarian camp. This may be due to the fact that many North American organizations are multimandate, engaging in both humanitarian and development programs. While many would place MSF in the "purist" camp, due to its stance of maintaining neutrality and independence from governments and offering impartial assistance, others, like Weiss (1999), place MSF in the solidarist camp because of its principle of witnessing/*témoignage*.

17. Interview with security director, May 2006.

18. OCHA in Afghanistan is a hard-fought exception to this general rule. See the report of the High-Level Panel on System-wide Coherence (Aziz, Diogo, and Soltenberg 2006).

19. A 2011 study suggests that despite attempts to minimize the negative effects of UN integration efforts on humanitarian space, UN integration "remains poorly understood amongst UN and non-UN staff and has been inconsistently applied in practice" (Metcalfe, Giffen, and Elhawary 2011, 1).

20. Anderson offers a similar critique directed at the UN and its claim of humanitarian inviolability in the wake of the 2003 Baghdad bombing. He evinces that the UN simultaneously claimed inviolability based on neutrality and impartiality, yet engaged in political activities that contradicted this claim. The result? "Iraqi terrorists," he writes, "with greater political clarity, attacked" (Anderson 2004, 43).

21. For media reports on this issue, see Cater (2002), Perlez (2003), and Rohde (2004). For further discussion, see Barry and Jefferys (2002), de Torrenté (2004a), and Lischer (2007).

22. Those falling in the latter category are mostly agencies that provide assistance based on a religiously inspired mission (e.g., Mennonite Central Committee, an agency founded and operated within the peace church tradition). For more about the internal debates within the Mennonite community on military force and armed escort in Somalia, see Burkholder and Koontz (1993), Friesen (1993), and Weaver (1993).

23. I thank Maarten Merkelbach for this formulation. Although the idea is common, I first heard him articulate it in this way.

24. Other commentators propose that outside military intervention in a complex emergency promotes insecurity for aid workers because of the media attention such events usually receive. A consequence of this media profile is increased targeting of aid workers (Adams and Bradbury 1995, 33–34).

25. Interview with aid worker, May 2006. Arguably, this quotation relates more to neutrality (defined as not taking sides) than to impartiality of assistance.

26. Max Glaser writes about the challenges of negotiating for access to civilian populations in this context. Access, he suggests, is dependent on two primary elements: the relationship of armed nonstate actors (ANSAs) to civilians (e.g., protective, competitive, antagonistic, or sectarian) and the structure of the ANSA (i.e., organization, command structure, discipline, and goals and objectives). Where the interests of the ANSA and the humanitarian actor coincide (e.g., a protective relationship with civilians) and the ANSA's structure is clear (e.g., clear goals, command structure and organization), a greater likelihood exists that the ANSA will enter into and respect access agreements. In these cases, it is also more likely that humanitarian actors will be more secure. Thus, he claims, "The key to understanding the dynamics of humanitarian engagement with ANSAs is understanding how civilians are configured in the latter's interests, or implicated with the ANSA or its opponents" (Glaser 2005, 23; see also Natsios 1997, 93 and Van Brabant 1998; see Wood 2011 for a broader perspective on ANSAs and violence against civilians).

27. The UN Panel of Governmental Experts on small arms defines small arms as "weapons designed for personal use" and light weapons as "those designed for use by several persons serving as a crew" (A/52/298, 27 August 1997, 11).

28. Interview with UN security official, May 2006.

29. Interview with security director, May 2006.

30. Interview with security director, May 2006.

31. Despite this claim, the Afghanistan NGO Safety Office (ANSO) believes it was "non-local fighters" who murdered the ten because they were foreigners (IRIN 2010a; see also Clark 2010a, 2010b, 2010c).

32. The MSF combined financial report lists a total income of €665,395,000, of which €572,449,000 originates from private sources (individuals and institutions). See 2009 MSF-International Movement Financial Report, 13, http://www.msf.org/msfinternational/. Accessed 18 October 2010.

33. See, for example, the lively debate about the ability of Save the Children–US and –UK to criticize their respective governments. A report in the *Guardian* newspaper claimed SCF-US exerted "enormous pressure" on SCF-UK in internal correspondence after the latter, in a public statement, accused Coalition forces of violating the Geneva Conventions (Maguire 2003). Mike Aaronson, director-general of SCF-UK at the time, rebutted the article several days later in an opinion piece, which the *Guardian* also published (Aaronson 2003). Others similarly questioned the independence of large NGOs, whose budgets are largely financed by government donors (Fielding-Smith 2004). In his op-ed, Ian Brown asserts a connection among the death of Margaret Hassan (country director for CARE in Iraq, who was killed in 2004), CARE's U.S. government funding, and its decision not to pull out of Iraq (Brown 2004).

34. Interview with aid expert, July 2006.

35. Its website states, "In carrying out humanitarian assistance, MSF seeks also to raise awareness of crisis situations; MSF acts as a witness and will speak out, either in

private or in public about the plight of populations in danger for whom MSF works." http://www.msf.org/msfinternational/ (accessed 18 October 2010).

36. In fact, MSF chose to discontinue its gender-based violence programming in order to stay and provide other essential services, but the Sudanese government expelled the organization several months later anyway (MSF 2009; also from conversation with MSF-Holland official, September 2010; and Kahn 2009). For a statement on Bashir's indictment, see ICC (2009).

37. The ICRC's claims of a separate status are rooted and codified in IHL. This legal status, however, does not extend to others that claim exceptionalism based on the same humanitarian principles.

38. Other scholars have made similar observations about humanitarianism, though not related to the violence perpetrated against them. Didier Fassin (2010b) interrogates the "sacredness" of humanitarians and their values that creates an "untouchability," while Barnett (2011) writes about the transcendental dimensions of the humanitarian endeavor.

39. Anderson develops this idea in relation to humanitarian operations in Iraq, post-9/11. This notion, though not named as such, existed well before 2004. Anderson defines humanitarian inviolability as "the ability of humanitarian relief agencies . . . to act in situations of extreme human need and suffering, particularly in circumstances of armed conflict, with the assurance that their personnel, their property, and their activities will not be made the object of attack." Writing post-9/11, he claims that the twin "pillars" of neutrality and impartiality underpin the concept of inviolability (Anderson 2004, 41), yet suggests that the UN and other international NGOs operating in Iraq did not uphold these values and thus undermined the concept.

40. Interview with security director, May 2006.

41. The two were meeting with UN Special Representative Sergio Vieira De Mello at the time of the 2003 Baghdad bombing. Arthur Helton died and Gil Loescher was severely injured in the attack.

42. Samuel Worthington, then the president of InterAction, an alliance of American relief and development organizations, asserted that such branding made "our jobs harder and more dangerous" (Worthington 2010). His op-ed appeared the day after a blog entry by Mark Ward (2010), the head of USAID's Office of Foreign Disaster Assistance. Ward's blog, published on the USAID Impact blog, called for more and better branding for USAID-supported projects in Pakistan.

43. As articulated in interviews with security directors (three—May 2006, July 2006, and January 2007), with an aid worker (May 2006), and with aid experts (three—March 2006, May 2006, and January 2007).

44. The Algeria bombing was the most devastating single incident for the UN in terms of the number of staff fatalities, surpassing the 2003 Baghdad bombing. After the release of the Independent Panel's report, Sir David Veness, head of the UN Department of Safety and Security (UNDSS) at the time, resigned. The report again

illuminated shortcomings in the UN's security procedures. The Senegalese UNDSS security officer, one of those killed in the attack, had called for more protection for the UN facilities in Algiers prior to the bombing. No one heeded his warnings.

45. Whether or not aid actually serves to win hearts and minds is a matter for debate. See Wilder and Gordon (2009) and Fishstein and Wilder (2011).

46. For a list of UN Goodwill Ambassadors, see http://www.un.org/sg/mop/gwa.shtml (accessed 30 November 2010). For an analysis of the phenomenon of celebrities and diplomacy, see Cooper (2007).

47. See also Kennedy (2009) on this issue. Barnett and Weiss (2008a) refer to "forces of salvation" in referring to the moral, ethical, and religious discourses that prompt generosity to strangers.

48. One possible response, she writes, is humanitarian, a practice rooted in compassion and neutrality. Edkins critiques famine and aid, offering a more complex and multifaceted argument than that which I include here. I use this particular example because of the direct relevance of the cartoon to the point above.

Chapter 5. Explanations in the Shadows

1. Email in possession of author. Email also available at http://groups.yahoo.com/neo/groups/CIMIC/conversations/topics/26.

2. In a similar reference, UN Secretary-General Ban Ki-Moon created a group of "superheroes" of development to advocate for the Millennium Development Goals (UN News Service 2010). These more recent superheroes are often celebrities or well-known public figures, recruited to raise the profile of particular issues in an attempt to gain public attention and support.

3. Interview with aid expert, July 2006.

4. Flashman or "Flashy" first appeared in the book *Tom Brown's Schooldays*, written by Thomas Hughes and published in 1857. He reappears as a fictional character in the Flashman books by George MacDonald Fraser, a twentieth-century author. Fraser's "Flashy" is an adventurer, heavy drinker, and womanizer. I thank Sarah Smiles Persinger for drawing my attention to the fictional Flashman. Poster on file with author.

5. Interview with security director, January 2007.

6. Similar critiques of the aid world, a growth industry in the late 1980s and 1990s, can be found in Hancock (1989) and Maren (1997) and others. These critical voices fall within the "mercenary" category, which typically characterizes this group of aid workers as cocooned in enclaves, out for profit, and often incompetent at their work (Stirrat 2008; Chambers 1997). See also Anderson (1999) and the "do no harm" efforts that aim to highlight the impact of the "implicit ethical messages" of aid and how aid can be used to support the "local capacities for peace" in a context of war or violence. Implicit ethical messages also shape the perceptions of the aid industry and can nega-

tively (or positively) influence the effectiveness of aid and, as a result, the security of aid workers and agencies.

7. Interview with aid worker, January 2007.

8. Interview with security director, May 2006.

9. For more on the scandal and implications, see UNHCR (2002) and Naik (2003). A December 2010 report by HAP International addressed this same issue (Davey, Nolan, and Ray 2010).

10. Save the Children–UK did a study of sexual abuse by aid workers, peacekeepers, and other foreigners constituting part of the "international community" in Cote d'Ivoire, Haiti, and southern Sudan. News outlets have also carried reports of sex scandals in DRC and Haiti (UN News Service 2004; Williams 2007). In discussing these abuses and their potential ramifications for security, the global reach of the humanitarian sector became apparent. One NGO that helped to bring the abuses of Haitians to light was attacked in another country—the country of origin of some of the accused peacekeepers—as a result of its actions (personal conversation with NGO official, December 2007).

11. Interview with security director, May 2006.

12. Interviews with security directors, May 2006 and January 2007.

13. A cursory search revealed a series of blogs written by aid workers, some of which are attributable to an individual and others of which are anonymous. One blog written by an aid worker in Sudan ("Sleepless in Sudan," active in 2005 and 2006) was deliberately anonymous because of the fear of repercussions for the blogger and her employer (see http://sleeplessinsudan.blogspot.com/). Other anonymous blogs include Pyjama Samsara (http://vasco-pyjama.livejournal.com/), Tales from the Hood (http://talesfromthehood.com/), and Stuff Expat Aid Workers Like (http://stuffexpataidworkerslike.com/). Other blogs are used to communicate particular messages or engage constituents and potential donors. These named bloggers include Joel Charney, then vice president of Refugees International, blogging for AlertNet (http://www.alertnet.org/db/bloggers/50892), Duncan Green of Oxfam (http://www.oxfamblogs.org/fp2p/), and Michael Kleinman's blog on Change.org. MSF posts a series of staff blogs written in multiple languages by national and international staff with archived postings (http://msf.ca/blogs/). This brief list is a sampling and by no means representative or comprehensive.

14. In fact, the actual number of aid workers and national and international staff working around the world is indeterminate. The best estimates come from a study on violence against aid workers (Stoddard, Harmer, and Haver 2006; Stoddard, Harmer, and DiDomenico 2009).

15. For example, in 1994, my aunt, who lived in Zaire/Democratic Republic of Congo for seven years in the 1960s and 1970s, volunteered for an international NGO that responded to the Rwandan refugee crisis in eastern Zaire. She served for six weeks as a medical laboratory technician, her profession at the time. She received no security training and only a minimal situation report at the time of her deployment. Her

fellow volunteers, most of whom had no prior experience in Congo, had a similar experience. While this is less common now, the immediacy of need often means that the training and screening for emergency deployments are expedited.

16. Interview with aid worker, May 2006.

17. Interview with security director, January 2007.

18. Interview with aid worker, May 2006.

19. Interview with aid expert, July 2006.

20. Mahoney and Eguren offer a similar basic typology of international accompaniment volunteers (those who accompany human rights activists to offer the activists a form of nonviolent deterrent protection): (a) volunteers with a prior personal connection to a region, (b) those with a religious, moral, or humanitarian motive, and (c) political activists. Volunteers in accompaniment work, they claim, frequently fall into the latter two categories. Many of the volunteers have careers in the "helping professions," but their primary motivation for volunteering is their political activism. Furthermore, they suggest that volunteers often come from Northern, wealthy countries and see their work as a way of "offsetting" their country's policies that contribute to economic disparity and human rights abuses (Mahoney and Eguren 1997, 51).

21. A related study found human rights workers in Kosovo were more at risk for mental health issues than were aid workers in Kosovo (Holtz et al. 2001).

22. Interview with aid expert, July 2007.

23. Few sources focus on national staff security. InterAction (2001), Ahmad (2002), Egeland, Harmer, and Stoddard (2011), and Stoddard, Harmer, and Haver (2011) describe the specific concerns and vulnerabilities of national staff.

24. Interviews with security director and aid expert, both January 2007; also with aid worker, May 2006.

25. In an intriguing parallel, one study of job insecurity and employee safety outcomes among food processing plant employees documents a relationship between higher job insecurity and decreased safety motivation and compliance. These, in turn, correspond with increased numbers of workplace accidents and injuries. The authors explain the finding as follows: "Employees who feel insecure perceive a greater emphasis on production, which then translates into lower job satisfaction and reduced motivation to attend to safety" (Probst and Brubaker 2001, 156). It is conceivable that the same might be true of aid workers: The contractual nature of much aid work leads to job insecurity, which, when combined with donor emphases on outcomes and results and high-stress jobs, translates into lower job satisfaction and less attention to security procedures.

26. For example, Saner (1990) documents the stresses of an ICRC delegate. See also McFarlane (2004), Jensen (n.d.), and Staff Welfare Unit (2001) for more about the psychological stressors and risk factors of aid work.

27. Interview with UN official, January 2007.

28. See Smith et al. (1996, 414–415). The Headington Institute has compiled a series of research reports about the psychological health of aid workers, including ones

on the links between stress and security, and created resources designed to promote healthy coping mechanisms (available from http://www.headington-institute.org).

29. Interview with security officer, January 2007.

30. Interview with UN official, January 2007.

31. The meteoric rise of Greg Mortensen, author of the bestselling *Three Cups of Tea*, and his dramatic and ugly fall after a *60 Minutes* exposé neatly illustrates this point. The *60 Minutes* story is available at http://www.cbsnews.com/video/watch/?id=7363068n, accessed 14 June 2011.

32. Interview with security expert, May 2006.

33. The ICRC was awarded the prize three times (1917, 1944, and 1963, shared with the League of Red Cross Societies). The Quakers and the AFSC shared the prize in 1947, and MSF won the prize in 1999. The UN family has won the prize five times: the UN and Kofi Annan in 2001, UN peacekeepers in 1988, UNICEF in 1965, and UNHCR in 1954 and 1981. UNHCR's precursor organization, the Nansen International Office for Refugees, won in 1938. A list of the winners of the Nobel Peace Prize is available from http://nobelprize.org/nobel_prizes/peace/laureates/. Accessed 15 September 2010.

34. Kennedy (2009) links the expansion of humanitarianism to the age of direct mailing and other media technologies designed to solicit and encourage support from individual donors.

35. This represents an increase of US$400 million from 2007, when WVI raised US$2.2 billion, to support programs in ninety-eight countries with approximately thirty-one thousand staff members (WVI 2007). The 2010 WVI revenues, from gifts in kind and cash, reached US$2.61 billion (WVI 2010, 4).

36. The IASC is a coordinating body for policy development and decision making composed of UN and non-UN humanitarian actors, with the UN emergency relief coordinator at its head. The Steering Committee for Humanitarian Response, founded in 1972, is composed of CARE International, Caritas Internationalis, the ICRC, the International Federation of Red Cross and Red Crescent Societies (IFRC), the International Save the Children Alliance, Lutheran World Federation, Oxfam, and the World Council of Churches. On both, see http://www.humanitarianinfo.org/iasc/ (accessed 5 August 2010).

37. The DAC is an international forum of governments and multilateral agencies to discuss issues of poverty, development, and the UN Millennium Development Goals. The DAC has twenty-four members, and an additional eight OECD members have full observer status. It regularly issues policy analysis and guidance. See http://www.oecd.org/dac (accessed 5 August 2010).

38. Humanitarian aid in 2009 decreased by US$1.8 billion (Development Initiatives 2010, 4). Encouragingly, for the first half of 2010 the UN OCHA received just under half the funds it solicited as part of the UN Consolidated Appeals Process (US$4.6 billion of the US$9.5 billion requested), according to IRIN (2010c).

39. Interview with aid expert, March 2006.

40. Interview with security director, May 2006.

41. Interview with aid worker, May 2006.

42. Interview with aid expert, March 2006.

43. See http://www.oxfam.org/ for more about Oxfam's history; http://www.savethechildren.org/ for more about SCF; and http://www.care.org/ about CARE (all accessed 6 August 2010).

44. Reportedly, Hollywood producer Tony Scott is planning a movie (starring Nicole Kidman) about McCune based on Scroggins's biography. The film, however, is generating controversy, as family members are upset with the book's portrayal of McCune and claim neither Scroggins nor the filmmakers have approached them for information or advice. See http://www.theage.com.au/news/World/Nicole-enters-movie-maelstrom/2005/04/15/1113509924831.html (accessed 12 August 2010).

45. Some aid agencies, such as the Mennonite Central Committee, and related quasi-government agencies doing development work, such as the U.S. Peace Corps or the Irish APSO (Agency for Personal Service Overseas, part of Irish Aid) or the British VSO International (Voluntary Service Overseas, http://www.vsointernational.org/) second people to small organizations based outside major population areas or send individuals or couples into rural areas to live and work among the people they are helping. The decision to operate in this way is often rooted in the organizational mission.

46. Benthall discusses this topic in relation to fund-raising and media, referring to the tension between raising funds domestically and the need to "maintain an institutional ethos appropriate to the organization's 'deprived' clientele and the professional practice of the field personnel directly concerned with them" (Benthall 1993, 56 and 26; see also chap. 2 and 4).

47. Interview with aid worker, July 2006.

48. Interview with security director, July 2006.

49. My conception of this idea of altruistic immunity is related to Anderson's (2004) notion of "humanitarian inviolability." Although I agree with much of his argument, I argue that inviolability as a function of neutrality and impartiality—more akin to principled inviolability—never really existed. Instead, principled inviolability existed (and indeed exists) as an assumption as opposed to a functioning reality. While a taboo against attacking foreigners, often aid workers, may have operated in many contexts, we have no definitive evidence, aside from that which is anecdotal, to prove that such a type of functioning inviolability ever truly existed.

50. Lindenberg and Bryant (2001, 9) actually propose six factors that created the rapid expansion of Northern NGOs in the 1980s and 1990s: the public fiscal crisis, the collapse of the Soviet Union, what they term "democratic openings, bilateral and multilateral incentives, and improvements in communication mechanisms."

51. Personal conversation with expatriate based in Kigali, fall 1999.

52. Some agencies (e.g., MSF-France and CARE) eventually did pull out of the camps, many citing security concerns (Borton, Brusset, and Hallam 1996, 52).

53. Barnett (2011) asserts that the move to professionalize humanitarianism began after World War II.

54. Interviews with aid experts, March 2006 and May 2006.

55. In a more recent and major move in this direction, the Conservative government elected in the United Kingdom in May 2010 promised to ensure better aid effectiveness, emphasizing positive and demonstrated results and outcomes (Mitchell 2010). A new "UKaid Transparency Guarantee" will publish information about the initiative (see IRIN 2010b for reactions).

56. For more about the Sphere Project and Charter, see http://www.sphereproject.org/. See http://www.hapinternational.org/ for more about HAP International and http://www.alnap.org/ for more about ALNAP (all accessed 6 August 2010). While many agencies have signed on to Sphere Project, some (e.g., MSF) critique it for focusing too heavily on standards as opposed to quality of assistance, arguing that the former does not necessarily result in the latter. On the Good Humanitarian Donorship initiative, see http://www.goodhumanitariandonorship.org/ (accessed 14 June 2011).

57. Interview with aid expert, March 2006.

58. Interview with aid worker, May 2006.

59. Respondents to a survey on the professionalization of the humanitarian sector raised these concerns, although the authors of the report suggest this represents a misunderstanding of the functions of professionalization. Instead, they argue, the move to professionalize in other fields reflected a desire to preserve cherished values (Walker and Russ 2010).

60. See Fast, Patterson, et al. (2011) and corresponding studies in Kenya (Freeman et al. 2011) and Uganda (Rowley et al. 2011), available from http://acceptanceresearch.org. This contrasts with interviews with an aid worker (May 2006) and security directors (May 2006 and January 2007) and other assertions, such as those cited above, that communities do not distinguish between NGOs and see them all as "the same." While both assertions are undoubtedly true in specific contexts or circumstances, blanket assertions about community members' ability to differentiate between NGOs questions their observational acumen and intelligence.

61. Interviews with security directors, May 2006 and January 2007.

62. Interview with security director, December 2000.

63. The organization is registered as a Christian organization with the Afghan government and has worked in the country since 1966 (IAM 2010a; see also Nordland 2010; Partlow 2010; Clark 2010b, 2010c).

64. Interview with aid expert, July 2006.

65. The organizational accident literature identifies the need to balance between too little regulation, which privileges funding over safety ("we must be spending enough, since we haven't had any accidents"), and too much regulation, which cuts into profits. After a catastrophic accident, organizations tend to move from too little to too much regulation (Reason 1997).

Chapter 6. Coping with Danger

1. Conversation with ICRC official, July 2008.

2. The UN employed security officers in Afghanistan as early as 1990 (personal correspondence with aid expert, September 2011).

3. Those killed were Fernanda Calado (Spain), Ingeborg Foss (Norway), Nancy Malloy (Canada), Gunnhild Myklebust (Norway), Sheryl Thayer (New Zealand), and Hans Elkerbout (Netherlands). Christophe Hensche (Switzerland) was severely wounded and evacuated to Geneva the next day. He and thirteen other delegates survived.

4. Interview with former ICRC delegate, November 2010.

5. One aid expert recalled hearing that the ICRC hospital had displaced an existing clinic and that the internal investigations revealed a stance that locals perceived as wealthy, pro-Western, and therefore insensitive to the local context (personal correspondence, September 2011).

6. Two staff persons for ACF were kidnapped in July and released to the ICRC on 22 August (*Glasgow Herald* 1996).

7. Attributed to Chris Giannon, medical coordinator for the ICRC in the North Caucasus at the time (as quoted in Beaumont 1996; see also Stanley 1996).

8. Boyes (2010) casts some doubt on the story, pointing out that the account of Major Aleksi Potyomkin, the defector, reveals an unplanned attack, when the details of the case clearly suggest a well-planned attack.

9. UNHCR did not have its own safety and security team until 1994, while UNICEF was the first UN agency to hire a security coordinator. Interviews with security directors, May 2006 and January 2007.

10. Interview with security expert, January 2007.

11. The ECHO Security Review was updated again in 2006, and translated into English, French, Spanish, and Arabic (http://ec.europa.eu/echo/evaluation/security_review_en.htm. Accessed June 2007).

12. Interview with security expert, July 2006.

13. The Interaction Security Advisory Group and the European Interagency Security Forum are two examples. The Security Management Institute (part of the Geneva Centre for Security Policy) meetings also served a similar function.

14. The International NGO Safety and Security Association has an advisory board comprising individuals working in the NGO security sector in the United States and Europe (https://ingossa.org/).

15. The lack of gender diversity among security managers and field officers may also affect the strategies an agency adopts, as could the gendered nature of security approaches. Acceptance, with its emphasis on relationships, is more "female," while the protective and deterrent strategies are more "male" in orientation, conforming to notions of what it means to be male in Western society. See Persaud (2012) for a discussion of the gender dimensions of security.

16. This is slowly changing, a function of the growing demand for security officers and a recognition of qualifications for these positions. One security director observed that military or police experience has moved from "required" to "desirable" in job postings in the sector (personal correspondence, April 2009).

17. Interview with security director, January 2007.

18. Interview with security director, January 2007; also interview with security director, May 2006.

19. A 2009 survey of humanitarian security professionals revealed the need for and appreciation of the SLT framework but noted that awareness and implementation of the framework and its ten principles in the field is generally poor (Micheni and Kuhanendran 2010).

20. See http://www.afgnso.org/ for more on the Afghanistan NGO Safety Office (ANSO) and http://www.gaza-nso.org/ for more on the Gaza NGO Safety Office (GANSO). Other similar organizations include the Pakistan Humanitarian Forum, which covers safety and security issues (http://pakhumanitarianforum.org/phf-safety and-security) and NSP (NSO Safety Programme, Somalia—http://www.nspsomalia.org/joomla/). A new organization, called the International NGO Safety Organisation (INSO), has been established to help NGOs set up security coordination bodies in other contexts, building on the experience of ANSO (see http://www.ngosafety.org/). All websites accessed 14 April 2012.

21. Interviews with aid expert, March 2006; aid expert, July 2006; and security director, January 2007.

22. This same argument has been used to refer to the presence of military forces in humanitarian emergencies, such as Iraq and Afghanistan.

23. OCHA has produced a series of maps showing areas of limited or no humanitarian access (e.g., OCHA access map, "Darfur, Sudan—Humanitarian Access Overview Map—Areas Consistently Limited Access and No Access (From Apr 2008 to Feb 2009)," http://reliefweb.int/node/12444 (accessed 19 September 2011). See also Young and Maxwell (2009).

24. Interview with aid expert, July 2006.

25. Interview with aid expert, July 2006.

26. The March 2011 earthquake and tsunami and the subsequent nuclear crisis in Japan raise the issue of the substantial risks that aid workers and other emergency personnel take to a new level. The head of the U.S. Nuclear Regulatory Commission, in testimony before the U.S. House of Representatives subcommittee, warned of the possible radiation risk that emergency personnel might face in traveling near the reactors (*Reuters* 2011).

27. Interview with aid expert, March 2006.

28. Interview with aid expert, March 2006.

29. UN Department of Safety and Security, "About Us—History," https://trip.dss.un.org/dssweb/aboutus/history.aspx. Accessed 9 October 2013.

30. Conversation with former aid worker, February 2009.
31. Interview with UN aid worker, May 2006.
32. Interview with aid worker, May 2006.
33. Interview with aid official, May 2006.
34. Conversation with ICRC official, August 2009. See also Terry (2010) and de Torrenté (2004a), and O'Brien (2004) for an opposing perspective.
35. Interview with aid expert, January 2007.
36. Personal correspondence with individual familiar with the case, April 2012.
37. Conversation with individual familiar with investigation, November 2010. At the time of Hassan's death, kidnapping was a prevalent criminal activity and those kidnapped or taken hostage were often "sold" to other criminal actors. It is possible that this was the case in Hassan's kidnapping and death, thus allowing for a morphing of motives that distinguishes between the motive for her kidnapping (criminal) and for her death (political).
38. The internal investigation was never made public and alternative explanations for her kidnapping and brutal murder still circulate. One aid expert told me of a rumor that she was killed because she got caught up in an intergroup conflict, rampant at the time of her death; in short, that she was murdered because of her knowledge of Iraq and ties to Iraqis and not protected because of them (conversation with aid expert, February 2009). This explanation could still be consistent with the criminal interpretation of her death. Carle and Chkam (2006, 9), in contrast, assert that the motive for her kidnapping and execution was political (versus criminal) and that it is "impossible that the perpetrators did not know of her humanitarian activities." These competing explanations underscore the difficulties of attributing motives—which are likely multiple and not singular—to attacks in the absence of information from the perpetrators themselves.
39. This is changing in dangerous contexts like Afghanistan, where agencies are pursuing acceptance as a security-management approach and reasserting humanitarian principles to distance themselves from the "war on terror." See Fast, Freeman, et al. (2011, 2013) for more on acceptance and Pont (2011), Macdonald (2011), and Terry (2010) on acceptance in Afghanistan, one of the most dangerous places for aid workers. This change supports my argument that aid agencies are at a crossroads in terms of approaches to security management in the future.
40. Interview with security director, January 2007. Séverine Autesserre (2014) points out, however, that the visible branding of aid projects also undermines local ownership and empowerment, since it implies that local populations cannot accomplish such projects on their own and without assistance.
41. Interview with security director, May 2006.
42. Interview with aid expert, March 2006.
43. UN Convention on the Privileges and Immunities of the United Nations (1946), Article 2, Section 3, states, "The premises of the United Nations shall be inviolable. The property and assets of the United Nations, wherever located and by whomsoever

held, shall be immune from search, requisition, confiscation, expropriation and any other form of interference, whether by executive, administrative, judicial or legislative action." Article 2, Section 2 refers to legal immunity.

44. The convention entered into force on 15 January 1999. As of 9 October 2013, it has ninety-one state parties and forty-three signatories (UN Treaty Collections, http://treaties.un.org/Pages/ViewDetails.aspx?src=TREATY&mtdsg_no=XVIII-8&chapter=18&lang=en , accessed 9 October 2013).

45. The United Kingdom ratified the Optional Protocol in July 2010, bringing the total to twenty-two ratifications, the number required for the protocol to enter into force (UN Secretary General 2010). As of 9 October 2013, it had twenty-eight state parties and thirty-four signatories (UN Treaty Collection, http://treaties.un.org/Pages/ViewDetails.aspx?src=TREATY&mtdsg_no=XVIII-8-a&chapter=18&lang=en, accessed 9 October 2013).

46. Chapter 1 includes some examples of misuse. A more recent example is the misuse of the emblem during a rescue operation to free hostages of Colombian rebel forces in July 2008. One of the rescuers, a Colombian soldier, wore a Red Cross insignia on an armband. The use of the emblem in this way placed Colombia, a state party, in contravention of the Geneva Convention, resulting in a protest from the ICRC.

47. Interview with aid expert, May 2006.

48. I thank Melker Mabeck, then working in the ICRC Security Unit, for planting this seed. I have heard him articulate numerous times that aid workers are civilians and thus deserving of the respect and protection afforded to all civilians under international humanitarian law.

49. For example, when I contacted one aid worker several months after our interview, he informed me that he no longer worked for the organization and had taken a leave due to the physical and emotional toll of his previous posting.

50. While employer practices can mitigate and address many of the mental health issues and stresses that arise, social support mechanisms are also crucial. Social support can come from the agency as well as family and friends and is critical to mitigating or decreasing the negative effects of traumatic events (Erikksson et al. 2001; Ozer et al. 2003). With good institutional and social support mechanisms and effective early intervention, it is possible to mitigate the consequences of experiencing trauma.

51. The Antares Foundation has developed a pamphlet titled "Managing Stress in Humanitarian Workers: Guidelines for Good Practice" (3rd ed., 2012) that builds on the principle that "managing staff stress is good management practice." Their approach moves from policy to screening and assessing, preparation and training, monitoring, ongoing support, crisis support, end of assignment support, and postassignment support (see http://www.antaresfoundation.org/download/managing_stress_in_humanitarian_aid_workers_guidelines_for_good_practice.pdf). People in Aid's "Code of Good Practice in the Management and Support of Aid Personnel" (revised 2003) offers a broader approach to human resource management in aid organizations that goes beyond managing the stresses of aid work. Nevertheless, the code underscores the

primacy of the seventh principle: "The security, good health and safety of our staff are a prime responsibility of our organization" (p. 20, available from http://www.peoplein aid.org/code/). The Headington Institute (http://www.headington-institute.org/) also offers resources on staff care (all sites accessed 9 October 2013).

52. This leaves many uncomfortable, as agencies ask national staff to assume risks that international staff are unable or unwilling to take. The reasoning behind such decisions is based on the fact that national staff are presumed to be less at risk and to know the context better, making them safer. A key question is whether national staff face increased risk due to the conflict or due to their employment or affiliation with the departing organization. This is one of several ethical debates within the field.

53. The ICRC, for example, withdrew its expatriates to Jordan but remained operational in Iraq with Iraqi staff (interview with ICRC official, May 2006).

54. Interview with security director, May 2006.

55. Interviews with security directors, January 2007 and May 2006.

56. Interview with aid worker, May 2006.

57. Interview with aid expert, March 2006.

58. Nonprofit security companies are also springing up to provide these services. For example, a former Canadian peacekeeper offers such a service on Aidworkers.net in a posting on 1 February 2009 ("Stormhaven a New Idea in Field Security"; see http://www.aidworkers.net/?q=node/2004).

59. Michael O'Neill, director of global safety and security for Save the Children International, remarked that these air locks can be innocuous if done well and do not need to reflect a sterile environment. "One can decorate the air lock with children's drawings, plants or comfortable chairs. It needn't look like/feel like a cell. At the same time anyone conducting cursory surveillance would immediately recognize it for what it is and understand the difficulty of bypassing this entry point" (personal correspondence, April 2012).

60. Interview with aid worker, May 2006.

61. Interview with aid worker, May 2006.

62. Interview with security director, May 2006.

63. Interview with aid worker, May 2006.

64. Interview with aid worker, May 2006. Autesserre (2014) documents similar processes with regard to peacebuilders.

65. Interview with aid worker, May 2006.

66. Interviews (three) with security directors, all January 2007. See also Jackson and Guistozzi (2012) about misunderstandings and misapplications of acceptance.

67. Interview with security expert, July 2006.

68. Interview with security director, January 2007.

69. As Michael O'Neill, a security director who is also an advocate of acceptance, writes, "Those who believe/assume they have gained acceptance 'passively' by virtue of espousing humanitarian principles, delivering good programming and creating a recognizable logo have (a) taken actions guided by humanitarian principles that dem-

onstrate to stakeholders organizational commitment, (b) designed and delivered good programs that meet beneficiary needs and contributed to some level of acceptance, and (c) at least imbued their logo with recognizable value. All of which reinforces the need for deliberate action. One may actually realize a modicum of 'acceptance' simply by virtue of local cultural beliefs treat strangers as honored (accepted) guests" (personal correspondence, April 2012).

70. In September 2007, the Taliban kidnapped four ICRC delegates and released them several days later. A Taliban spokesman claimed they did not realize who the ICRC delegates were. One news source (inaccurately) reported the four were involved in negotiations with the Taliban to secure the release of a German engineer, whom the Taliban kidnapped in July 2007 (Hemming 2007). Although the ICRC does not actually negotiate for the release of others, it will carry messages back and forth between the parties.

71. In one interview, an aid worker working in a violent conflict zone reported that his organization received threats because it was too closely affiliated with one particular ethnic group (interview with aid worker, May 2006).

72. Interview with aid expert, May 2006.

73. Conversation with security official, September 2010.

74. Larry Minear suggested "personnel protection" as a distinct but equivalent term (personal interview, March 2006).

Conclusion

1. Personal email correspondence with aid worker in Kabul at the time of the attack (October 2009). See also Zavis (2009).

2. While agencies recognize this tension, it is also clear that the rescue narrative serves them well in their fund-raising efforts. Benthall (1993, chap. 2) addresses this topic in more depth. The professional/volunteer debate discussed in Chapter 5 reflects this tension as well.

3. While agencies may not possess the threat or destructive power that characterizes the use of force (Boulding 1989), they do exercise power in the manner of the second dimension, including the ability to control or determine an agenda or what is defined as a "key issue" (Lukes 1986, 9), through their advocacy efforts on behalf of particular populations (i.e., helping to determine which countries and populations receive world attention) and even their decisions about who receives or does not receive aid.

4. David Keen makes a similar point about attributing the failures of the international aid system to external causes. "More generally," he states, "the tendency to explain unwelcome phenomena (disasters, relief inadequacy, terrorism) as the result of *extrinsic* factors ('drought,' 'evil,' 'chaos,' 'tribal violence,' 'problems of implementation') serves a function in removing responsibility from society as a whole (including key actors in the West)" (Keen 2007, 9).

5. It is conceivable that the overwhelming generosity in response to the tsunami was partly due to its timing—26 December—immediately after Christmas, a "season of giving" when many are home for holidays. The public responses to flooding from Cyclone Sidr in Bangladesh (2007), Cyclone Nargis in Myanmar (2008), and an earthquake in China (2008), all with high death tolls, did not approach the total donations for the tsunami.

6. Interview with aid expert, January 2007.

7. The ICRC's security approach draws on and reflects its mandate in IHL, its decentralized management approach, and humanitarian principles (Krähenbühl 2004; Dind 1999).

BIBLIOGRAPHY

Aaronson, Mike. 2003. Viewpoint: We will never be "silenced"—SC-UK. *Guardian*, 4 December. http://www.guardian.co.uk/politics/2003/dec/02/society.iraq.

Abbott, Marianne. 2006. Dangerous intervention: An analysis of humanitarian fatalities in assistance. Ph.D. dissertation, Ohio State University.

Abu-Sada, Caroline. 2011. MSF perception study results. Presented at Médecins Sans Frontières conference on "Perceptions of Humanitarian Action," 11 February, Montreal, Quebec.

———, ed. 2012a. *Dilemmas, Challenges and Ethics of Humanitarian Action: Contributions Around MSF's Perception Project*. Montreal: McGill-Queen's University Press.

———, ed. 2012b. *In the Eyes of Others: How People in Crises Perceive Humanitarian Aid*. New York: Médecins Sans Frontières, Humanitarian Outcomes, and NYU Center on International Cooperation.

ACF International. 2008. Sri Lanka, the Muttur massacre: A struggle for justice. Study report, June. Paris: Action Contre La Faim.

Adams, Mark, and Mark Bradbury. 1995. Conflict and development: Organisational adaptation in conflict situations. Oxfam discussion paper. Oxford: Oxfam UK and Ireland.

Adler, Leslie. 2004. Year after Baghdad attack, UN faces vulnerability. *AlertNet*, 18 August. http://www.alertnet.org.

AFP. 2009. Sri Lanka says aid worker massacre probe concluded. 18 June. http://www.google.com/hostednews/afp/article/ALeqM5hDR2u-f8tfFGBJVocULKGqY-ouc4A.

African Rights. 1994. Humanitarianism unbound? Current dilemmas facing multimandate relief operations in political emergencies. Discussion paper, November. London: African Rights.

Agency Coordinating Body for Afghan Relief. 2002. ACBAR policy brief: NGOs concerns and recommendations on civil-military relations. 7 December. http://www.careusa.org/newsroom/specialreports/afghanistan/12092002_ACBAR.pdf.

———. 2003a. ACBAR policy brief: NGO position paper concerning the Provisional Reconstruction Teams. 15 January. http://www.care.org/newsroom/specialreports/afghanistan/01152003_ngorec.pdf.

———. 2003b. Provincial Reconstruction Teams and the security situation in Afghanistan. ACBAR policy brief, 24 July. http://www.careusa.org/newsroom/specialreports/afghanistan/07242003_ACBAR.pdf.

Ahmad, Mokbul Morshed. 2002. Who cares? The personal and professional problems of NGO fieldworkers in Bangladesh. *Development in Practice* 12 (2): 177–191.

Alter, W. 1936. Les hôpitaux et les dangers de la guerre aérienne. *Revue Internationale de la Croix-Rouge* 18 (208, April): 257–265.

Altheide, David L. 2002. *Creating Fear: News and the Construction of Crisis*. New York: Aldine de Gruyter.

———. 2003. Mass media, crime, and the discourse of fear. *Hedgehog Review* 5 (3): 9–25.

Amis, Martin. 2008. *The Second Plane*. New York: Knopf.

Anderson, Kenneth. 2004. Humanitarian inviolability in crisis: The meaning of impartiality and neutrality for UN and NGO agencies following the 2003–2004 Afghanistan and Iraq conflicts. *Harvard Human Rights Journal* 17: 41–74.

Anderson, Mary B. 1999. *Do No Harm: How Aid Can Support Peace—Or War*. Boulder, CO: Lynne Rienner.

Anderson, Mary B., Dayna Brown, and Isabella Jean. 2012. *Time to Listen: Hearing People on the Receiving End of International Aid*. Cambridge, MA: CDA Collaborative Learning Projects.

Anderson, Scott. 1996. What happened to Fred Cuny? *New York Times Magazine*, 26 February. http://www.nytimes.com/1996/02/25/magazine/what-happened-to-fred-cuny.html.

Annan, Kofi. 2004. Secretary-General's message on the first anniversary of the attack of UN Headquarters in Baghdad. 19 August. https://www.un.org/sg/statements/?nid=1051.

Appleby, Timothy. 1996a. Relief missions more risky than ever: Non-combatants face new lawlessness, international paralysis that erodes their safety. *Globe and Mail* (Canada), 21 December, A13.

———. 1996b. Slain nurse no stranger to perils of war zone: Red Cross worker talked about fears. *Globe and Mail* (Canada), 18 December, A16.

Apps, Peter. 2007a. Rights group concerned about Sri Lanka massacre evidence. *AlertNet*, 26 June. http://www.alertnet.org/.

———. 2007b. Sri Lanka's escalating war of words over aid security. *AlertNet*, 16 August. http://www.alertnet.org/.

Arendt, Hannah. 1970. *On Violence*. San Diego: Harcourt Brace.

Arsanjani, Mahnoush. 1995. Defending the blue helmets: Protection of United Nations personnel. In *Les Nations Unies et le Droit International Humanitaire: Actes du Colloque International à l'Occasion du Cinquantième Anniversaire de l'ONU*, edited by L. Condorelli, A.-M. LaRosa, and S. Scherrer. Paris: Editions Pedone. Pp. 117–147.

Asad, Talal. 2007. *On Suicide Bombing*. New York: Columbia University Press.

Atran, Scott. 2004. Mishandling suicide terrorism. *Washington Quarterly* 27 (3): 67–90.
Autesserre, Séverine. 2014. *Peaceland: Conflict Resolution and the Everyday Politics of International Intervention*. Cambridge: Cambridge University Press.
Avant, Deborah D. 2005. *The Market for Force: The Consequences of Privatizing Security*. Cambridge: Cambridge University Press.
Avant, Deborah, and Virginia Haufler. 2012. Transnational organisations and security. *Global Crime* 13 (4): 254–275.
Aziz, Shaukat, Luísa Dias Diogo, and Jens Soltenberg. 2006. Delivering as one. Report of the High-Level Panel on System-wide Coherence. A/61/583, 9 November. http://daccess-dds-ny.un.org/doc/UNDOC/GEN/N06/621/41/PDF/N0662141.pdf?OpenElement.
Bader-Saye, Scott. 2007. *Following Jesus in a Culture of Fear*. Grand Rapids, MI: Brazos Press.
Baldauf, Scott, and Owais Tohid. 2004. Aid workers increasingly a target in conflict zones. *Christian Science Monitor*, 5 November. http://www.csmonitor.com/.
Barnett, Katy. 2004. Security report for humanitarian organizations. ECHO Security Review, October. Brussels: Directorate-General for Humanitarian Aid—ECHO, European Commission.
Barnett, Michael. 2011. *Empire of Humanity: A History of Humanitarianism*. Ithaca: Cornell University Press.
Barnett, Michael, and Jack Snyder. 2008. The grand strategies of humanitarianism. In Barnett and Weiss, *Humanitarianism in Question*. Pp. 143–171.
Barnett, Michael, and Thomas G. Weiss. 2008a. Humanitarianism: A brief history of the present. In Barnett and Weiss, *Humanitarianism in Question*. Pp. 1–48.
———, eds. 2008b. *Humanitarianism in Question: Politics, Power, Ethics*. Ithaca: Cornell University Press.
Barron, Ruth A. 1999. Psychological trauma and relief workers. In *Humanitarian Crises: The Medical and Public Health Response*, edited by J. Leaning, S. M. Briggs, and L. C. Chen. Cambridge, MA: Harvard University Press. Pp. 143–175.
Barry, Jane, and Anna Jefferys. 2002. A bridge too far: Aid agencies and the military in humanitarian response. HPN network paper 37, January. London: Overseas Development Institute, Humanitarian Policy Network.
Bauman, Zygmunt. 2006. *Liquid Fear*. Cambridge: Polity Press.
Bayoumy, Yara. 2009. Sudan says willing to admit new NGOs. *Reuters*, 6 May. http://www.reuters.com/.
BBC News. 2003. Baghdad terror blasts kill dozens. 27 October. http://news.bbc.co.uk/.
———. 2005. Timeline: Margaret Hassan. 1 May. http://news.bbc.co.uk/2/hi/uk_news/3946455.stm.
———. 2009. UN chief condemns Kabul killing. 28 October. http://news.bbc.co.uk/.
Beasley, Ryan, Cate Buchanan, and Robert Muggah. 2003. In the line of fire: Surveying the perceptions of humanitarian and development personnel of the impacts of

small arms and light weapons. Geneva: Centre for Humanitarian Dialogue and Small Arms Survey.
Beaumont, Peter. 1996. Do nothing, and other people die. Do something, and you might die. *Observer Review* (UK), 22 December, 3ff.
Beck, Ulrich. 1992. *Risk Society: Towards a New Modernity*. Thousand Oaks, CA: Sage.
Belliveau, Joe. 2013. "Remote management" in Somalia. *Humanitarian Exchange* 56 (January): 25–27.
Benhabib, Seyla. 2004. *The Rights of Others: Aliens, Residents and Citizens*. Cambridge: Cambridge University Press.
Benthall, Jonathan. 1993. *Disasters, Relief and the Media*. London: I.B. Tauris.
Benthall, Jonathan, and Jérôme Bellion-Jourdan. 2003. *The Charitable Crescent: Politics of Aid in the Muslim World*. London: I.B. Tauris.
Berdal, Mats, and David Keen. 1997. Violence and economic agendas in civil wars: Some policy implications. *Millennium* 26 (3): 795–818.
Berdal, Mats, and David M. Malone, eds. 2000. *Greed and Grievance: Economic Agendas in Civil Wars*. Boulder, CO: Lynne Rienner.
Bergman, Carol, ed. 2003. *Another Day in Paradise: International Humanitarian Workers Tell Their Stories*. Maryknoll, NY: Orbis Books.
Bhalla, Nita. 2009. Aid groups vow to stay in Afghanistan despite UN pulling out expat staff. *AlertNet*, 10 November. http://reliefweb.int/node/332741.
Bickley, Shaun. 2003. *Safety First: A Field Security Handbook for NGOs*. 2nd ed. London: Save the Children.
Biggs, Cassie. 2006. Aid workers targeted in Sri Lanka's resurgent conflict. *Associated Press*, 29 August.
Binder, Andrea, and Claudia Meier. 2011. Opportunity knocks: Why non-Western donors enter humanitarianism and how to make the best of it. *International Review of the Red Cross* 93 (884): 1135–1149.
Bjoreng, Eva. 2003. Taking a stand: Solidarity and neutrality in humanitarian action. *Humanitarian Exchange* 25 (December): 9–11.
Bloom, Evan T. 1995. Protecting peacekeepers: The Convention on the Safety of United Nations and Associated Personnel. *American Journal of International Law* 89 (3): 621–631.
BNO News. 2011. UN staff member dies of injuries sustained in August attack in Nigeria. 29 December. http://www.minews26.com/content/?p=12621.
Bolletino, Vincenzo. 2006. Designing security. HPCR policy brief, October. Cambridge, MA: Harvard University, Program on Humanitarian Policy and Conflict Research.
Bornstein, Erica, and Peter Redfield, eds. 2010. *Forces of Compassion: Humanitarianism Between Ethics and Politics*. Santa Fe, NM: School for Advanced Research Press.
Borton, John, Emery Brusset, and Alistair Hallam. 1996. Humanitarian aid and effects. Joint Evaluation of Emergency Assistance to Rwanda, Study 3. Copenhagen: Steering Committee of the Joint Evaluation of Emergency Assistance to Rwanda.

Bouchet-Saulnier, Françoise. 2001. The principles and practices of "rebellious humanitarianism". *Humanitarian Exchange* 19 (September): 15–17.
Boulding, Kenneth E. 1989. *Three Faces of Power*. Newbury Park, CA: Sage.
Bourloyannis-Vrailas, M.-Christiane. 1995. The Convention on the Safety of United Nations and Associated Personnel. *International and Comparative Law Quarterly* 44 (3): 560–590.
Bouvier, Antoine. 1995. "Convention on the Safety of United Nations and Associated Personnel": Presentation and analysis. *International Review of the Red Cross* (309, December): 113–130.
Boyes, Roger. 2010. Russian secret squad killed Red Cross staff in Chechnya, defecting spy reveals. *Times (London)*, 24 November, Features, 35–36.
Brauman, Rony. 2009. Global media and the myths of humanitarian relief: The case of the 2004 tsunami. In Wilson and Brown, *Humanitarianism and Suffering*. Pp. 108–117.
Brown, Ian. 2004. This fatal compromise. *Guardian*, 19 November. http://www.guardian.co.uk/.
Bruderlein, Claude. 2001. The end of innocence: Humanitarian protection in the twenty-first century. In *Civilians in War*, edited by S. Chesterman. Boulder, CO: Lynne Rienner. Pp. 221–235.
Bruderlein, Claude, and Pierre Gassman. 2006. Managing security risks in hazardous missions: The challenges of securing United Nations access to vulnerable groups. *Harvard Human Rights Journal* 19: 63–93.
Bryans, Michael, Bruce D. Jones, and Janice Gross Stein. 1999. Mean times: Humanitarian action in complex political emergencies—Stark choices, cruel dilemmas. NGOs in Complex Emergencies Project report, January. Toronto: Program on Conflict Management and Negotiation, University of Toronto and CARE Canada.
Buchanan, Cate, and Robert Muggah. 2005. No relief: Surveying the effects of gun violence on humanitarian and development personnel. Geneva: Centre for Humanitarian Dialogue and Small Arms Survey.
Bugnion, François. 1997. 17 December 1996: Six ICRC delegates assassinated in Chechnya. *International Review of the Red Cross* 317 (March–April): 140–142.
Burkholder, J. R., and Ted Koontz. 1993. A time for silence, a time for action. *The Mennonite*, 26 January, 10.
Burnett, John. 2005. *Where Soldiers Fear to Tread*. New York: Bantam Dell.
Burns, Robert. 2009. Envoy laments weak U.S. knowledge about Taliban. *Seattle Times*, 7 April. http://seattletimes.com/html/nationworld/2008961176_apusafghanistan.html.
Burton, John W. 1997. *Violence Explained: The Sources of Conflict, Violence and Crime and Their Provention*. Manchester: Manchester University Press.
Cain, Kenneth, Heidi Postlewait, and Andrew Thomson. 2004. *Emergency Sex and Other Desperate Measures: A True Story from Hell on Earth*. New York: Miramax Books.

Callimachi, Rukmini. 2003. Portland aid group accepts risks of Iraq duty: Aid workers become targets because their deaths spark outrage. *Statesman Journal* (Salem, OR), 10 December.

Cardozo, Barbara Lopes, and Peter Salama. 2002. Mental health of humanitarian aid workers in complex emergencies. In Danieli, *Sharing the Front Line and the Back Hills*. Pp. 242–255.

CARE International. 2003. A New Year's resolution to keep: Secure a lasting peace in Afghanistan. Policy brief, 13 January. London: CARE International. http://www.careusa.org/newsroom/specialreports/afghanistan/01132003_policybrief.pdf.

Carle, Alexandre, and Hakim Chkam. 2006. Humanitarian action in the new security environment: Policy and operational implications in Iraq. HPG background paper, September. London: Overseas Development Institute, Humanitarian Policy Group.

Cater, Nick. 2002. Soldiers in civvies alarm agencies in Afghanistan. *AlertNet*, 5 April. http://www.alertnet.org/.

Catholic Relief Services. 2000. Peacebuilding activities. Baltimore: Catholic Relief Services.

Cauderay, Gerald C. 1990. Visibility of the distinctive emblem on medical establishments, units, and transports. *International Review of the Red Cross* (277, August): 295–321.

CBC News. 2007. UN flag no longer protects workers, Arbour warns. 12 April. http://www.cbc.ca/world/story/2007/04/12/arbour-un-070412.html.

Chambers, Robert. 1997. *Whose Reality Counts? Putting the Last First*. Intermediate Technology Publications in Participation Series. Bourton-on-Dunsmore, UK: ITDG.

Charbonneau, Louis. 2009a. NGO expelled from Darfur considered ICC cooperation. *Reuters*, 16 March. http://www.reuters.com/.

———. 2009b. Sudan expulsions of NGOs leave aid gap: UN. *Reuters*, 9 March. http://www.reuters.com/.

———. 2009c. UN to boost Afghan security after Kabul attack. *Reuters*, 29 October. http://www.reuters.com/.

Chicago Tribune. 1998. The miracle merchants: Myths of child sponsorship. 15 March and 22 March.

Clark, Kate. 2010a. Ten dead in Badakhshan (Updated). 8 August. *Afghan Analysts Network*. http://www.afghanistan-analysts.org/.

Clark, Kate. 2010b. Ten dead in Badakhshan 5: Condemnation from a Taleb: Silence from the palace. 17 August. *Afghan Analysts Network*. http://www.afghanistan-analysts.org/.

Clark, Kate. 2010c. Ten dead in Badakhshan 6: Local Taleban say it was murder. 20 August. *Afghan Analysts Network*. http://www.afghanistan-analysts.org/.

CNN Wire Staff. 2010. Dead aid workers knew risks but loved Afghanistan. *CNN.com*, 7 August. http://www.cnn.com/.

Collier, Paul. 2000. Doing well out of war: An economic perspective. In Berdal and Malone, *Greed and Grievance*. Pp. 91–112.

Comité International. 1936a. Bombardement de Dessié. *Revue Internationale de la Croix-Rouge* 67 (401, January): 66–68, 70–73.

———. 1936b. Retour des ambulances étrangères. *Revue Internationale de la Croix-Rouge* 67 (407, July): 581.

———. 1936c. Visibilité du signe de la Croix-Rouge. *Revue Internationale de la Croix-Rouge* 67 (405, May): 408–412.

———. 1966. Retour d'un délégué blessé. *Revue Internationale de la Croix-Rouge* 48 (569, May): 241.

———. 1968a. Après la mort de deux délégués du Comité international de la Croix-Rouge. *Revue Internationale de la Croix-Rouge* 50 (599, November): 511–516.

———. 1968b. Au Yemen: Attaque contre un établissement sanitaire. *Revue Internationale de la Croix-Rouge* 50 (593, May): 236.

———. 1968c. Le CICR et l'incident du pont Allenby. *Revue Internationale de la Croix-Rouge* 50 (590, February): 70.

———. 1968d. Les délégations du CICR. *Revue Internationale de la Croix-Rouge* 50 (597, September): 399.

———. 1968e. Santa Isabel, CICR: Ouvrir des routes. *Revue Internationale de la Croix-Rouge* 50 (597, September): 401–404.

———. 1969a. 7 mai 1969. *Revue Internationale de la Croix-Rouge* 51 (606, June): 354–355.

———. 1969b. Activités extérieures: Au Nigéria. *Revue Internationale de la Croix-Rouge* 51 (608, August): 479–480.

———. 1969c. A Genève: Cérémonie d'hommage. *Revue Internationale de la Croix-Rouge* 51 (608, August): 492–493.

———. 1969d. Au Congo: A la mémoire de Georges Olivet. *Revue Internationale de la Croix-Rouge* 51 (608, August): 495–496.

———. 1969e. Au secours des victims du conflict du Nigéria. *Revue Internationale de la Croix-Rouge* 51 (601, January): 5–8.

———. 1969f. Au secours des victims du conflict du Nigéria. *Revue Internationale de la Croix-Rouge* 51 (607, July): 416–426.

———. 1969g. Au secours des victims du conflit du Nigéria: Bombardement d'un hôpital. *Revue Internationale de la Croix-Rouge* 51 (602, February): 95.

Cooley, Alexander, and James Ron. 2002. The NGO scramble: Organizational insecurity and the political economy of transnational action. *International Security* 27 (1): 5–39.

Cooper, Andrew F. 2007. *Celebrity Diplomacy*. Boulder, CO: Paradigm.

Cortright, David, George A. Lopez, Alistair Millar, and Linda Gerber-Stellingwerf. 2008. Friend, not foe: Civil society and the struggle against violent extremism. Notre Dame, IN: Kroc Institute for International Peace Studies and Fourth Freedom Forum.

Coupland, Robin. 2001. Humanity: What is it and how does it influence international law? *International Review of the Red Cross* 83 (844): 969–989.

———. 2003. The humanity of humans: Philosophy, science, health, or rights? *Health and Human Rights* 7 (1): 159–166.

Coyne, Christopher. 2013. *Doing Bad by Doing Good: Why Humanitarian Action Fails*. Stanford: Stanford University Press.

Crewe, Emma, and Elizabeth Harrison. 1998. *Whose Development? An Ethnography of Aid*. London: Zed Books.

Cuny, Frederick C. 1995. Killing Chechnya. *New York Review of Books* 42 (6, 6 April).

Cutts, Mark, and Alan Dingle. 1995. *Safety First: Protecting NGO Employees Who Work in Areas of Conflict*. London: Save the Children.

Danieli, Yael, ed. 2002. *Sharing the Front Line and the Back Hills: Peacekeepers, Humanitarian Aid Workers and the Media in the Midst of Crisis*. Amityville, NY: Baywood.

Darcy, James, and Charles-Antoine Hofman. 2003. According to need? Needs assessment and decision-making in the humanitarian sector. HPG report 15, September. London: Overseas Development Institute, Humanitarian Policy Group.

Davenport, Christian, and Patrick Ball. 2002. Views to a kill: Exploring the implications of source selection in the case of the Guatemalan state terror, 1977–1995. *Journal of Conflict Resolution* 46 (3): 427–450.

Davey, Corinne, Paul Nolan, and Patricia Ray. 2010. Change starts with us, talk to us! Beneficiary perceptions regarding the effectiveness of measures to prevent sexual exploitation and abuse by humanitarian aid workers. HAP commissioned study, December. Geneva: HAP International.

Deen, Thalif. 2008a. Politics: Kenya, Chad new danger zones for U.N. workers. *Inter Press Service*, 5 February. http://ipsnews.net/.

———. 2008b. Politics: Terror threats weigh on U.N. staff abroad. *Inter Press Service*, 24 January. http://ipsnews.net/.

DeMars, William E. 2001. Hazardous partnership: NGOs and American intelligence in small wars. *International Journal of Intelligence and Counterintelligence* 14 (2): 193–222.

Department of Foreign Affairs and International Trade. 2003. Defence: Canada's Commander in Afghanistan. *Canada World View* (20, Autumn): 8–9.

de St. Jorre, John. 1972. *The Brothers' War: Biafra and Nigeria*. Boston: Houghton Mifflin.

de Torrenté, Nicolas. 2004a. Humanitarian action under attack: Reflections on the Iraq war. *Harvard Human Rights Journal* 17: 1–30.

———. 2004b. Humanitarianism sacrificed: Integration's false promise. *Ethics and International Affairs* 18 (2): 3–12.

———. 2007. The professionalization and bureaucratization of humanitarian action: Some reflections from MSF's experience. Discussion draft, SSRC, 10 April. http://programs.ssrc.org/emergencies/publications/torrente.pdf.

Deutsche Presse-Agentur. 2009. Sri Lankan official: Aid workers must use bicycles. 26 May. http://www.reliefweb.int/.

Development Initiatives. 2010. Global humanitarian assistance report 2010, 6 July. Somerset, UK: Development Initiatives. http://www.globalhumanitarianassistance.org/reports.

de Waal, Alex. 1997. *Famine Crimes: Politics and the Disaster Relief Industry in Africa*. Oxford: James Currey.

———. 2005. *Famine that Kills: Darfur, Sudan*. Rev. ed. Oxford: Oxford University Press.

Dewan, Shaila, and Rod Nordland. 2010. Slain aid workers were bound by their sacrifice. *New York Times*, 9 August. http://www.nytimes.com/.

DiMaggio, Paul J., and Walter W. Powell. 1983. The iron cage revisited: Institutional isomorphism and collective rationality in organizational fields. *American Sociological Review* 48 (2): 147–160.

Dind, Philippe. 1999. Security in ICRC field operations. *Forced Migration Review*, April, 13–15.

Docherty, Jayne Seminare. 2001. *Learning Lessons from Waco: When the Parties Bring Their Gods to the Negotiation Table*. Syracuse, NY: Syracuse University Press.

Donini, Antonio. 2003. Issues note. Paper read at The Future of Humanitarian Action: Implications of Iraq and Other Recent Crises, Brainstorming workshop, 9 October, Boston.

———. 2010. The far side: The meta functions of humanitarianism in a globalised world. *Disasters* 34 (suppl. 2): S220–S237.

———, ed. 2012. *The Golden Fleece: Manipulation and Independence in Humanitarian Action*. Bloomfield, CT: Kumarian Press.

Donini, Antonio, Larry Minear, Ian Smillie, Ted van Baarda, and Anthony C. Welch. 2005. Mapping the security environment: Understanding the perceptions of local communities, peace support operations, and assistance agencies. June. Medford, MA: Tufts University, Feinstein International Center. http://sites.tufts.edu/feinstein/2005/mapping-the-security-environment.

Donini, Antonio, Larry Minear, and Peter Walker. 2004. The future of humanitarian action: Mapping the implications of Iraq and other recent crises. *Disasters* 28 (2): 190–204.

DuBois, Marc. 2011. AidWatch—UK undermines its own Somalia aid with a political agenda. *AlertNet*, 9 March. http://www.trust.org/alertnet/blogs/alertnet-aidwatch/uk-undermines-its-own-somalia-aid-with-a-political-agenda.

Duffield, Mark. 1997. NGO relief in war zones: Towards an analysis of the new aid paradigm. *Third World Quarterly* 18 (3): 527–542.

———. 2001. *Global Governance and the New Wars: The Merging of Development and Security*. London: Zed Books.

———. 2010. Risk management and the fortified aid compound: Everyday life in post-interventionary society. *Journal of Intervention and Statebuilding* 4 (4): 453–474.

Dugger, Celia W. 2007. Oversight report says U.S. food aid practices are wasteful. *New York Times*, 14 April. http://www.nytimes.com/.

Dunant, Henri. 1862/1986. *A Memory of Solferino*. Geneva: ICRC.

Easterly, William. 2006. *The White Man's Burden: Why the West's Efforts to Aid the Rest Have Done so Much Ill and so Little Good*. New York: Penguin.

Ebersole, Jon M. 1995. Mohonk criteria for humanitarian assistance in complex emergencies. *Disaster Prevention and Management* 4 (3): 14–24.

Edkins, Jenny. 2000. *Whose Hunger? Concepts of Famine, Practices of Aid*. Minneapolis: University of Minnesota Press.

Egeland, Jan, Adele Harmer, and Abby Stoddard. 2011. To stay and deliver: Good practice for humanitarians in complex security environments. Policy and studies series. New York: UN Office for the Coordination of Humanitarian Affairs, Policy Development and Studies Branch.

Ehrenreich, John H., and Teri L. Elliott. 2004. Managing stress in humanitarian aid workers: A survey of humanitarian aid agencies' psychosocial training and support of staff. *Peace and Conflict* 10 (1): 53–66.

Erikksson, Cynthia B., Hendrika Vande Kemp, Richard Gorusch, Stephen Hoke, and David W. Foy. 2001. Trauma exposure and PTSD symptoms in international relief and development personnel. *Journal of Traumatic Stress* 14 (1): 205–212.

EU Commission. 1998. Security of relief workers and humanitarian space. Working paper, 14 May. Brussels: European Commission—Humanitarian Aid and Civil Protection (ECHO).

Fassin, Didier. 2010a. Inequality of lives, hierarchies of humanity: Moral commitments and ethical dilemmas of humanitarianism. In Feldman and Ticktin, *In the Name of Humanity*. Pp. 239–255.

———. 2010b. *Noli me tangere*: The moral untouchability of humanitarianism. In Bornstein and Redfield, *Forces of Compassion*. Pp. 35–52.

———. 2012. *Humanitarian Reason: A Moral History of the Present*. Berkeley: University of California Press.

Fast, Larissa A. 2002. Context matters: Identifying micro- and macro-level factors contributing to NGO insecurity. Ph.D. dissertation, George Mason University.

———. 2006. "Aid in a pressure cooker": Humanitarian action in the Occupied Palestinian Territory. Humanitarian Agenda 2015 case study, November. Medford, MA: Tufts University, Feinstein International Center. http://hdl.handle.net/10427/37855.

———. 2007. Characteristics, context, and risk: NGO insecurity in conflict zones. *Disasters* 31 (2): 130–154.

———. 2010. Mind the gap: Documenting and explaining violence against aid workers. *European Journal of International Relations* 16 (3): 365–389.

Fast, Larissa, Faith Freeman, Michael O'Neill, and Elizabeth Rowley. 2011. The promise of acceptance: Insights into acceptance as a security management approach from field research in Kenya, South Sudan, and Uganda. Washington, DC: Save the Children. http://acceptanceresearch.org/reports/final-report/.

———. 2013. In acceptance we trust? Conceptualizing acceptance as a viable approach to NGO security management. *Disasters* 37 (2): 222–243.

Fast, Larissa, and Michael O'Neill. 2010. A closer look at acceptance. *Humanitarian Exchange* 47 (June): 3–6.

Fast, Larissa, Reginold Patterson, Alfred Amule, Simon Bonis, Lasu Joseph, Anthony Kollie, James Luer Gach Diew, Sirocco Mayom Biar Atek, Christopher Nyamandi, and Jimmy Okumu. 2011. South Sudan country report: Key findings from field research on acceptance in South Sudan. Washington, DC: Save the Children. http://acceptanceresearch.org/reports/south-sudan-country-report.

Fast, Larissa, and Dawn Wiest. 2007. Final survey report: Security perceptions survey. Unpublished paper, Notre Dame, IN.

Favez, Jean-Claude. 1999. *The Red Cross and the Holocaust*. Cambridge: Cambridge University Press.

Fearon, James D. 2008. The rise of emergency relief aid. In Barnett and Weiss, *Humanitarianism in Question*. Pp. 49–72.

Fechter, Anne-Meike. 2012. "Living well" while "doing good"? (Missing) debates on altruism and professionalism in aid work. *Third World Quarterly* 33 (8): 1475–1491.

Fechter, Anne-Meike, and Heather Hindman, eds. 2011. *Inside the Everyday Lives of Development Workers: The Challenges and Futures of Aidland*. Sterling, VA: Kumarian Press.

Feldman, Ilana, and Miriam Ticktin, eds. 2010a. *In the Name of Humanity: The Government of Threat and Care*. Durham, NC: Duke University Press.

———. 2010b. Introduction: Government and humanity. In Feldman and Ticktin, *In the Name of Humanity*. Pp. 1–26.

Fielding-Smith, Abigail. 2004. Muddying the world's conscience. *Guardian*, 9 January. http://www.guardian.co.uk/.

Finnemore, Martha. 2003. *The Purpose of Intervention: Changing Beliefs About the Use of Force*. Ithaca: Cornell University Press.

Fishstein, Paul, and Andrew Wilder. 2011. Winning hearts and minds? Examining the relationship between aid and security in Afghanistan. January. Medford, MA: Tufts University, Feinstein International Center. http://sites.tufts.edu/feinstein/2012/winning-hearts-and-minds.

Forbes, Cameron. 1996. Red Cross nurses serve under a frail emblem. *Australian*, 19 December, 3.

Forsythe, David P. 2005. *The Humanitarians: The International Committee of the Red Cross*. Cambridge: Cambridge University Press.

Freeman, Faith, Michael O'Neill, Peter Aura, Madeleine Kingston, Julius Mutuku, Clayton Omwanga, and Miriam Tharao. 2011. Kenya country report: Key findings

from field research on acceptance in Kenya. Washington, DC: Save the Children. http://acceptanceresearch.org/reports/kenya-report/.
Friesen, Duane K. 1993. Ethical dilemmas of Christian peacemaking in the post–Cold War context. Paper presented at the Mennonite Peacemaking after the Cold War conference, November, Akron, PA.
Galtung, Johan. 1969. Violence, peace and peace research. *Journal of Peace Research* 6: 167–191.
———. 1990. Cultural violence. *Journal of Peace Research* 27 (3): 291–306.
Ganguly, Dilip. 2006. 15 aid workers slain in Sri Lanka; 15 more Tamil civilians killed in shelling, rebels say. *Associated Press*, 7 August.
Gilligan, James. 2000. *Violence: Reflections on Our Deadliest Epidemic*. London: Jessica Kingsley.
Glaser, Max P. 2005. Humanitarian engagement with non-state armed actors: The parameters of negotiated access. HPN network paper 51, June. London: Overseas Development Institute, Humanitarian Practice Network.
Glasgow Herald. 1996. Family rejoice over freedom of aid worker; Briton held in Chechen maelstrom is released before bombardment. 22 August, 11.
Glazer, Myron. 1970. Field work in a hostile environment: A chapter in the sociology of social research in Chile. In *Student Politics in Chile*, edited by F. Bonilla and M. Glazer. New York: Basic Books. Pp. 313–333.
Glover, Jonathan. 2012. *Humanity: A Moral History of the Twentieth Century*. 2nd ed. New Haven, CT: Yale University Press.
Goetz, Nathaniel H. 2001. Humanitarian issues in the Biafra conflict. UNHCR New Issues in Refugee Research, working paper 36, April. http://www.unhcr.org/3af66b8b4.html. Accessed 4 June 2013.
Goodhand, Jonathan. 2006. Working "in" and "on" war. In *Civil War, Civil Peace*, edited by H. Yanacopulos and J. Hanlon. Athens: Ohio University Press. Pp. 280–313.
Goodhand, Jonathan, and Nick Lewer. 1999. Sri Lanka: NGOs and peace-building in complex political emergencies. *Third World Quarterly* 20(1): 69–87.
Gordenker, Leon, and Thomas G. Weiss. 1990. Humanitarian emergencies and military help: Some conceptual observations. In *Humanitarian Emergencies and Military Help in Africa*, edited by T. G. Weiss. New York: St. Martin's. Pp. 1–23.
Green, Linda. 1995. Living in a state of fear. In Nordstrom and Robben, *Fieldwork Under Fire*. Pp. 105–127.
Hackett, Ken. 2009. Humanitarian neutrality. *Washington Post*, 2 February, A12. http://www.washingtonpost.com/.
Hammond, Laura. 2008. The power of holding humanitarianism hostage and the myth of protective principles. In Barnett and Weiss, *Humanitarianism in Question*. Pp. 172–195.
Hancock, Graham. 1989. *Lords of Poverty: The Power, Prestige, and Corruption of the International Aid Business*. New York: Atlantic Monthly Press.

Hansen, Greg. 1997. Aid in war-ravaged Chechnya—A severe test for humanitarians. *Christian Science Monitor*, 31 December, 19.

———. 2007a. Coming to terms with the humanitarian imperative in Iraq. Humanitarian Agenda 2015 briefing paper, January. Medford, MA: Tufts University, Feinstein International Center. http://sites.tufts.edu/feinstein/2007/coming-to-terms-with-the-humanitarian-imperative-in-iraq.

———. 2007b. Taking sides or saving lives: Existential choices for the humanitarian enterprise in Iraq. Humanitarian Agenda 2015 case study, June. Medford, MA: Tufts University, Feinstein International Center. http://sites.tufts.edu/feinstein/2007/ha215-iraq.

———. 2008. Iraq: More challenges ahead for a fractured humanitarian enterprise. Humanitarian Agenda 2015 briefing paper, December. Medford, MA: Tufts University, Feinstein International Center. http://sites.tufts.edu/feinstein/2009/iraq-more-challenges-ahead-for-a-fractured-humanitarian-enterprise.

Harbom, Lotta, and Peter Wallensteen. 2010. Armed conflicts, 1946–2009. *Journal of Peace Research* 47 (4): 501–509.

Harmer, Adele, and Lin Cotterrell, eds. 2005. Diversity in donorship: The changing landscape of official humanitarian aid. HPG report 20, September. London: Overseas Development Institute, Humanitarian Practice Group.

Harr, Jonathan. 2009. Lives of the saints: International hardship duty in Chad. *New Yorker*, 5 January. http://www.newyorker.com/reporting/2009/01/05/090105fa_fact_harr.

Harrell-Bond, Barbara. 1986. *Imposing Aid: Emergency Assistance to Refugees*. Oxford: Oxford University Press.

Harris, Simon. 2007. Humanitarian Agenda 2015: Sri Lanka country study. October. Medford, MA: Tufts University, Feinstein International Center. http://sites.tufts.edu/feinstein/2007/ha2015–sri-lanka.

———. 2010. Humanitarianism in Sri Lanka: Lessons learned? Humanitarian Agenda 2015 briefing paper, June. Medford, MA: Tufts University, Feinstein International Center. http://sites.tufts.edu/feinstein/2010/humanitarianism-in-sri-lanka-lessons-learned.

Hassan, Abdiaziz. 2010. UN to return to Somalia within two months—envoy. *Reuters*, 8 August. http://www.reuters.com/.

Helton, Arthur C., and Gil Loescher. 2003. NGOs and governments in a new humanitarian landscape. *openDemocracy*, 24 June. http://www.opendemocracy.net/.

Hemming, Jon. 2007. Taliban free 4 ICRC staff kidnapped in Afghanistan. *Reuters*, 29 September. http://www.reuters.com/.

Hiebert, P. C., and Orie O. Miller. 1929. *Feeding the Hungry: Russia Famine 1919–1925*. Scottdale, PA: Mennonite Central Committee.

Higgins, Noelle. 2003. The protection of United Nations and associated personnel. *Journal of Humanitarian Assistance*, 14 April. http://www.jha.ac/articles/a116.htm.

Hilhorst, Dorothea, and Bram J. Jansen. 2010. Humanitarian space as arena: A perspective on the everyday politics of aid. *Development and Change* 41 (6): 1117–1139.

Hilhorst, Dorothea, and Nadja Schmiemann. 2002. Humanitarian principles and organisational culture: Everyday practice in Médecins Sans Frontières–Holland. *Development in Practice* 12 (3–4): 490–500.

Hockstader, Lee. 1997. The perils of doing good: The International Red Cross rethinks its role in a changing world. *Washington Post Magazine*, 17 August, 12–17, 28–30.

Hoffman, Peter, and Thomas G. Weiss. 2006. *Sword and Salve: Confronting New Wars and Humanitarian Crises*. Lanham, MD: Rowman & Littlefield.

Holtz, Timothy H., Peter Salama, Barbara Lopes Cardozo, and Carol A. Gotway. 2001. Mental health status of human rights workers, Kosovo, June 2000. *Journal of Traumatic Stress* 15 (5): 389–395.

Hopgood, Stephen. 2008. Saying "no" to Wal-Mart? Money and morality in professional humanitarianism. In Barnett and Weiss, *Humanitarianism in Question*. Pp. 98–123.

Hopkins, Mark, director. 2009. *Living in Emergency: Stories of Doctors Without Borders*. Documentary film. Red Floor Pictures.

Howell, Nancy. 1990. Surviving fieldwork: A report of the Advisory Panel on Health and Safety in Fieldwork. Washington, DC: American Anthropological Association.

Human Rights Watch. 2009. Sri Lanka: Adopt international inquiry for aid worker killings. 3 August. http://www.hrw.org.

Humanitarian Accountability Partnership. 2010. The 2010 HAP Standard in Accountability and Quality Management. Geneva: Humanitarian Accountability Partnership. http://www.hapinternational.org.

Humanitarian Policy Group. 2007. Humanitarian advocacy in Darfur: The challenge of neutrality. HPG policy brief, October. London: Overseas Development Institute, Humanitarian Policy Group.

Humanitarian Practice Network. 2010. Operational security management in violent environments. Good Practice Review 8 (rev.), December. London: Overseas Development Institute, Humanitarian Practice Network.

Hyndman, Jennifer. 2000. *Managing Displacement: Refugees and the Politics of Humanitarianism*. Minneapolis: University of Minnesota Press.

Independent Panel. 2003. Report of the Independent Panel on the Safety and Security of UN Personnel in Iraq. The Ahtisaari Report, 20 October. New York: United Nations.

———. 2008. "Towards a culture of security and accountability": The report of the Independent Panel on Safety and Security of UN Personnel and Premises Worldwide. The Brahimi Report, 9 June. New York: United Nations.

Integrated Regional Information Networks. 2007a. Global: U.S. company sues American Red Cross over use of Red Cross emblem. 24 August. http://www.irinnews.org/.

———. 2007b. Pakistan: Islamic extremists attack aid workers. 9 May. http://www.irinnews.org/.

———. 2007c. Sri Lanka: No tangible progress in investigations into murdered aid workers. 3 July. http://www.irinnews.org/.

———. 2008a. Kenya: Violence slowing down humanitarian effort. 5 February. http://www.irinnews.org/.

———. 2008b. Pakistan: Concerns about humanitarian access, safety of aid workers. 2 June. http://www.irinnews.org/.

———. 2009. Global: Less money for more work—the NGO double whammy. 21 April. http://www.irinnews.org/.

———. 2010a. Afghanistan: Criminal groups pose significant risk to NGOs. 4 October. http://www.irinnews.org/.

———. 2010b. Aid policy: Cautious welcome for new UK aid commitments. 4 June. http://www.irinnews.org/.

———. 2010c. Global: Donors deserve a pat on the back. 16 July. http://www.irinnews.org/.

InterAction. 2001. The security of national staff: Towards good practices. Report, 27 July. Washington, DC: InterAction.

Inter-Agency Standing Committee. 2002. *Growing the Sheltering Tree: Protecting Rights Through Humanitarian Action*. Geneva: UNICEF/Inter-Agency Standing Committee.

Inter-Agency Standing Committee Working Group. 2001. Use of military or armed escorts for humanitarian convoys. Discussion paper and non-binding guidelines, 14 September. Geneva: World Health Organization. http://www.who.int/hac/network/interagency/news/convoys_2001/en/index.html.

International Assistance Mission. 2010a. On the death of 10 of the 12 Nuristan Eye Camp team members. Press release 1, 9 August, Kabul, Afghanistan. http://www.iam-afghanistan.org/.

———. 2010b. On the death of 10 of the 12 Nuristan Eye Camp team members. Press release 3, 12 August, Kabul, Afghanistan. http://www.iam-afghanistan.org/.

International Committee of the Red Cross. 2003. Iraq: Two ICRC employees killed in Baghdad bomb attack. News release 03/71, 27 October. http://www.icrc.org/.

International Criminal Court. 2009. ICC issues a warrant of arrest for Omar al-Bashir, President of Sudan. Press release, Statement No. ICC-CPI-20090304-PR394. http://www.icc-cpi.int/.

International Federation of the Red Cross and Red Crescent Societies. 1997. Code of conduct for the International Red Cross and Red Crescent Movement and Non-Governmental Organizations (NGOs) in disaster relief. Geneva: International Federation of the Red Cross and Red Crescent Societies. http://www.ifrc.org/en/publications-and-reports/code-of-conduct/.

———. 2007. *Stay Safe: The International Federation's Guide to a Safer Mission*. Geneva: International Federation of Red Cross and Red Crescent Societies.

Jackson, Ashley, and Antonio Guistozzi. 2012. Talking to the other side: Humanitarian engagement with the Taliban in Afghanistan. Working paper, December. London: Overseas Development Institute, Humanitarian Policy Group.

Jensen, Soeren Buus. n.d. Taking care of the care-takers under war conditions—Who cares? Towards a comprehensive approach on mental health for humanitarian aid workers under war conditions. Unpublished report, Copenhagen.

Joint Evaluation of Emergency Assistance to Rwanda. 1996. The international response to conflict and genocide: Lessons from the Rwanda experience. Copenhagen: Steering Committee of the Joint Evaluation of Emergency Assistance to Rwanda.

Jones, Mervyn. 1965. *In Famine's Shadow: A Private War on Hunger.* Boston: Beacon.

Kahn, Clea. 2009. Case study of an integrated mental health program in Kalma camp: Challenges and pitfalls. Paper presented at the World Conference on Humanitarian Studies, 4–8 February, Groningen, Netherlands.

Kaldor, Mary. 2006. *New and Old Wars: Organized Violence in a Global Era.* 2nd ed. Cambridge: Polity Press.

Keen, David. 1998. *The Economic Functions of Violence in Civil Wars.* IISS Adelphi Paper 320. Oxford: Oxford University Press.

———. 2000. Incentives and disincentives for violence. In Berdal and Malone, *Greed and Grievance.* Pp. 19–42.

———. 2007. *Complex Emergencies.* Cambridge, UK: Polity Press.

Keizer, Michael. 2010. The professional volunteer: Impossible in aid? (And how about the salaried amateur?) *A Humourless Lot,* 27 June. http://michaelkeizer.com/humourless.

Kellenberger, Jakob. 2004. Speaking out or remaining silent in humanitarian work. *International Review of the Red Cross* 86 (855, September): 593–610.

Kemp, Edward, and Maarten Merkelbach. 2011. Can you get sued? Legal liability of international humanitarian aid organisations toward their staff. SMI policy paper. Geneva: Security Management Institute.

Kennedy, David. 2005. *The Dark Sides of Virtue: Reassessing International Humanitarianism.* Princeton, NJ: Princeton University Press.

Kennedy, Denis. 2009. Selling the distant other: Humanitarianism and imagery—Ethical dilemmas of humanitarian action. *Journal of Humanitarian Assistance,* 28 February. http://sites.tufts.edu/jha/archives/411.

Kent, Randolph. 2003. Humanitarian dilemmas in peace and war. *Conflict, Security and Development* 3 (3): 438–446.

King, Dennis. 2002a. Chronology of humanitarian aid workers killed in 1997–2001. UN Office for the Coordination of Humanitarian Affairs, 15 January. http://reliefweb.int/symposium/NewChron1997-2001.html.

———. 2002b. Paying the ultimate price: Analysis of the deaths of humanitarian aid workers (1997–2001). UN Office for the Coordination of Humanitarian Affairs, 15 January. http://reliefweb.int/symposium/PayingUltimatePrice97-01.html.

Kingston, Madeleine, and Oliver Behn. 2010. Risk thresholds in humanitarian assistance. EISF report. London: European Interagency Security Forum.

Klamp, Carolyn. 2007. Legal liability in the humanitarian sector. *RedR UK Safety and Security Review*, no. 7, 2–5.

Knox, Paul. 1996. Volunteers doing relief work face unpredictable risks: Red Cross workers struggle to absorb news of colleague's death. *Globe and Mail* (Canada), 18 December, A16.

Krähenbühl, Pierre. 2004. The ICRC's approach to contemporary security challenges: A future for independent and neutral humanitarian action. *International Review of the Red Cross* 86 (855, September): 505–514.

Lange, W. Robert, Diane L. Frankenfield, and John D. Frame. 1994. Morbidity among refugee relief workers. *Journal of Travel Medicine* 1 (2): 111–112.

Laqueur, Thomas W. 2009. Mourning, pity, and the work of narrative in the making of "humanity." In Wilson and Brown, *Humanitarianism and Suffering*. Pp. 31–57.

Large, Tim. 2004. U.N. refugee chief warns of "Iraqisation" of aid. *AlertNet*, 18 May. http://www.alertnet.org/.

LeBillon, Philippe. 2000. The political economy of war: What relief agencies need to know. HPN network paper 33, July. London: Overseas Development Institute, Humanitarian Practice Network.

———. 2005. *Fuelling War: Natural Resources and Armed Conflict*. IISS Adelphi Paper 373. Oxford: Oxford University Press.

Lederach, John Paul. 1995. *Preparing for Peace: Conflict Transformation Across Cultures*. Syracuse, NY: Syracuse University Press.

———. 1997. *Building Peace: Sustainable Reconciliation in Divided Societies*. Herndon, VA: U.S. Institute of Peace Press.

———. 2003. *The Little Book of Conflict Transformation*. Intercourse, PA: Good Books.

———. 2005. *The Moral Imagination: The Art and Soul of Building Peace*. New York: Oxford University Press.

Lee, Raymond M. 1995. *Dangerous Fieldwork*. Thousand Oaks, CA: Sage.

Lee-Treweek, Geraldine, and Stephanie Linkogle, eds. 2000. *Danger in the Field: Risk and Ethics in Social Research*. New York: Routledge.

Lindenberg, Marc, and Coralie Bryant. 2001. *Going Global: Transforming Relief and Development NGOs*. Bloomfield, CT: Kumarian Press.

Lischer, Sarah Kenyon. 2007. Military intervention and the humanitarian "force multiplier." *Global Governance* 13: 99–118.

Listening Project. 2008. Issue paper: International assistance as a delivery system. September. Cambridge, MA: CDA Collaborative Learning Projects.

Loquercio, David, Mark Hammersley, and Ben Emmens. 2006. Understanding and addressing staff turnover in humanitarian agencies. HPN network paper 55,

June. London: Overseas Development Institute, Humanitarian Practice Network.

Lukes, Steven. 1986. Introduction. In *Power*, edited by S. Lukes. New York: New York University Press. Pp. 1–18.

Lynch, Cecelia. 2011. Local and global influences on Islamic NGOs in Kenya. *Journal of Peacebuilding and Development* 6 (1): 21–34.

Lynch, Colum. 2003. U.N. staff's immunity from terror ends. *Washington Post*, 20 August, A11. http://www.washingtonpost.com.

———. 2007. The U.N. insignia emerges as a global target for Al-Qaeda attacks. *Washington Post*, 25 December, A14. http://www.washingtonpost.com.

———. 2010. UN embraces private military contractors. *Foreign Policy*, 17 January. http://www.globalpolicy.org/security-council/peacekeeping/analysis-and-articles-on-peacekeeping/48682.html.

Macdonald, Ingrid. 2011. Securing access through acceptance in Afghanistan and Pakistan. *Humanitarian Exchange* 49 (January): 9–11.

MacGinty, Roger, and Oliver P. Richmond. 2013. The local turn in peace building: A critical agenda for peace. *Third World Quarterly* 34 (5): 763–783.

Mackinlay, John. 1993. Armed relief. In Weiss and Minear, *Humanitarianism Across Borders*. Pp. 85–96.

Mackintosh, Kate. 2007. Beyond the Red Cross: The protection of independent humanitarian organizations and their staff in international humanitarian law. *International Review of the Red Cross* 89 (865, March): 113–130.

Macrae, Joanna. 1998. The death of humanitarianism? An anatomy of the attack. *Disasters* 22 (4): 309–317.

Macrae, Joanna, Mark Bradbury, Susanne Jaspars, Douglas Johnson, and Mark Duffield. 1997. Conflict, the continuum and chronic emergencies: A critical analysis of the scope for linking relief, rehabilitation and development planning in Sudan. *Disasters* 21(3): 223–243.

Macrae, Joanna, and Anthony Zwi. 1994. Famine, complex emergencies and international policy in Africa: An overview. In *War and Hunger: Rethinking International Responses to Complex Emergencies*, edited by J. Macrae and A. Zwi. London: Zed Books. Pp. 6–36.

Magone, Claire, Michael Neuman, and Fabrice Weissman, eds. 2011. *Humanitarian Negotiations Revealed: The MSF Experience*. New York: Columbia University Press and Médecins Sans Frontières.

Maguire, Kevin. 2003. How British charity was silenced on Iraq. *Guardian*, 28 November. http://www.theguardian.co.uk/.

Mahoney, Liam, and Luis Enrique Eguren. 1997. *Unarmed Bodyguards: International Accompaniment for the Protection of Human Rights*. West Hartford, CT: Kumarian Press.

Malkki, Liisa. 1996. Speechless emissaries: Refugees, humanitarianism, and dehistoricization. *Cultural Anthropology* 11 (3): 377–404.

Mancini-Griffoli, Deborah, and André Picot. 2004. Humanitarian negotiation: A handbook for securing access, assistance and protection for civilians in armed conflict. October. Geneva: Centre for Humanitarian Dialogue.

Maren, Michael. 1997. *The Road to Hell: The Ravaging Effects of Foreign and International Charity*. New York: Free Press.

Marriage, Zoë. 2006. *Challenging Aid in Africa: Principles, Implementation, and Impact*. Hampshire, UK: Palgrave Macmillan.

Martin, Randolph. 1999. NGO field security. *Forced Migration Review*, April, 4–7.

Matthews, David. 2009. A man with a mission. *Washington Post*, 25 January, W14. http://www.washingtonpost.com/.

Mauss, Marcel. 1954/2011. *The Gift: Forms and Functions of Exchange in Archaic Societies*. Translated by I. Cunnison. Mansfield Centre, CT: Martino.

Mayhew, Barney. 2004. Generic security guide for humanitarian organizations. ECHO Security Review, October. Brussels: Directorate-General for Humanitarian Aid—ECHO, European Commission.

McCall, Maureen, and Peter Salama. 1999. Selection, training and support of relief workers: An occupational health issue. *British Medical Journal* 318 (7176): 113–116.

McDonald, Henry. 2004. Hostage-taking "legitimate": Irish Muslims condemn radical who condones kidnapping of women aid workers in Iraq. *Observer* (UK), 7 November. http://www.guardian.co.uk/world/.

McFarlane, Colleen A. 2004. Risks associated with the psychological adjustment of humanitarian aid workers. *Australasian Journal of Disaster and Trauma Studies*. http://www.massey.ac.nz/~trauma/issues/2004-1/mcfarlane.htm.

McHugh, Gerard, and Manuel Bessler. 2006. Humanitarian negotiations with armed groups: A manual for practitioners. New York: UN Office for the Coordination of Humanitarian Affairs.

Médecins Sans Frontières. 2009. Dutch section of MSF expelled from Darfur, leaving hundreds of thousands without critical medical aid. 4 March. http://www.msf.org/msfinternational/.

Merkelbach, Maarten, and Pascal Daudin. 2011. From security management to risk management: Critical reflections on aid agency security management and the ISO Risk Management Guidelines. SMI discussion paper. Geneva: Security Management Institute.

Metcalfe, Victoria, Alison Giffen, and Samir Elhawary. 2011. UN integration and humanitarian space: An independent study commissioned by the UN Integration Steering Group. HPG report, December. London: Overseas Development Institute, Humanitarian Policy Group and the Stimson Center.

Micheni, Kiruja, and Janeki Kuhanendran. 2010. Saving Lives Together: A review of security collaboration between the United Nations and humanitarian actors on the ground. June. London: Christian Aid.

Miles, Tom, and Richard Lough. 2011. ICRC wants food for Somalia but can't take U.N. aid. *Reuters*, 4 August. http://www.publicbroadcasting.net/wprl/news.news-main/article/0/3/1836494/World/ICRC.wants.food.for.Somalia.but.can't.take.U.N.aid.

Minear, Larry. 2002. *The Humanitarian Enterprise: Dilemmas and Discoveries.* Bloomfield, CT: Kumarian Press.

———. 2003. NGOs and UN face pressure over Iraq. *AlertNet*, 7 July. http://www.alertnet.org/.

Minear, Larry, and Thomas G. Weiss. 1995. *Mercy Under Fire: War and the Global Humanitarian Community.* Boulder, CO: Westview Press.

Mitchell, Rt. Hon Andrew. 2010. Mitchell: Full transparency and new independent watchdog. 3 June. London: UK Department for International Development. https://www.gov.uk/government/news/mitchell-full-transparency-and-new-independent-watchdog.

Mohamed, Ibrahim. 2010. Somalia's al Shabaab rebels expel three aid groups. *Reuters*, 9 August. http://www.reuters.com/.

Moore, Jonathan, ed. 1999. *Hard Choices: Moral Dilemmas in Humanitarian Intervention.* Lanham, MD: Rowman & Littlefield.

Moorehead, Caroline. 1998. *Dunant's Dream: War, Switzerland and the History of the Red Cross.* London: HarperCollins.

Motevalli, Golnar, and Sayed Salahuddin. 2009. Five U.N. foreign staff killed in attack in Kabul. *Reuters*, 28 October. http://www.reuters.com/.

Mowjee, Tasneem. 2006. Humanitarian agenda 2015 Sudan country study. July. Medford, MA: Tufts University, Feinstein International Center. http://sites.tufts.edu/feinstein/2006/ha2015-sudan.

Moyo, Dambisa. 2009. *Dead Aid: Why Aid Is Not Working and How There Is Another Way for Africa.* New York: Farrar, Straus and Giroux.

Muggah, Robert. 2001. Perceptions of small arms availability and use among Oxfam-GB field personnel. Geneva: Small Arms Survey and Oxfam-GB.

Muggah, Robert, and Peter Batchelor. 2002. "Development held hostage": Assessing the effects of small arms on human development. April. New York: UN Development Program.

Muggah, Robert, and Eric Berman. 2001. Humanitarianism under threat: The humanitarian impacts of small arms and light weapons. April. New York: UN Inter-Agency Standing Committee.

Murphy, Dan. 2003. How an Iraq aid group stays safe. *Christian Science Monitor*, 18 December. http://www.csmonitor.com/.

Naik, Asmita. 2003. West Africa scandal points to need for humanitarian watchdog. *Humanitarian Exchange* 24 (July): 13–15.

Natsios, Andrew S. 1997. *U.S. Foreign Policy and the Four Horsemen of the Apocalypse: Humanitarian Relief in Complex Emergencies.* Westport, CT: Praeger.

New York Times. 1992. The well-fed dead in Bosnia. *New York Times*, 15 July, A20. http://www.nytimes.com/1992/07/15/opinion/the-well-fed-dead-in-bosnia.html.

Nordland, Rod. 2010. Gunmen kill medical aid workers in Afghanistan. *New York Times*, 7 August. http://www.nytimes.com/.

Nordstrom, Carolyn. 1997. *A Different Kind of War Story*. Philadelphia: University of Pennsylvania Press.

———. 2004. *Shadows of War: Violence, Power, and International Profiteering in the Twenty-First Century*. Berkeley: University of California Press.

Nordstrom, Carolyn, and Antonius C. G. M. Robben, eds. 1995. *Fieldwork Under Fire: Contemporary Studies of Violence and Survival*. Berkeley: University of California Press.

Nye, Joseph S. 2004. *Soft Power: The Means to Success in World Politics*. New York: Public Affairs.

O'Brien, Paul. 2004. Politicized humanitarianism: A response to Nicolas de Torrenté. *Harvard Human Rights Journal* 17: 31–39.

O'Callaghan, Sorcha, and Sara Pantuliano. 2007. Protective action: Incorporating civilian protection into humanitarian response. HPG report 26, December. London: Overseas Development Institute, Humanitarian Policy Group.

O'Connell, Mary Ellen. 2002. Humanitarian assistance in non-international armed conflict: The fourth wave of rights, duties and remedies. In *Israel Yearbook on Human Rights, 2001*, vol. 31, edited by Y. Dinstein and F. Domb. The Hague: Martinus Nijhoff. Pp. 183–217.

Office for the Coordination of Humanitarian Affairs. 2008. ReliefWeb/OCHA situation report: Somalia. Situation Report 4, 1 February. New York: UN Office for the Coordination of Humanitarian Affairs. http://www.reliefweb.int/.

O'Neill, Michael. 2008. Acceptance: An approach to security as if people mattered. *Monday Developments*, January/February, 22–24.

Ozer, Emily J., Suzanne R. Best, Tami L. Lipsey, and Daniel S. Weiss. 2003. Predictors of posttraumatic stress disorder and symptoms in adults: A meta-analysis. *Psychological Bulletin* 129 (1): 52–73.

Parsons, Claudia. 2009. Sudan letting back renamed aid groups: UN official. *AlertNet*, 11 June. http://www.alertnet.org/.

Partlow, Joshua. 2010. Taliban kills 10 medical aid workers in northern Afghanistan. *Washington Post*, 8 August, A1. http://www.washingtonpost.com/.

Paul, Diane. 1999. Protection in practice: Field-level strategies for protecting civilians from deliberate harm. RRN network paper 30, July. London: Overseas Development Institute, Relief and Rehabilitation Network.

Peritore, N. P. 1990. Reflections on dangerous fieldwork. *American Sociologist* 21: 359–372.

Perlez, Jane. 2003. Relief groups struggle to keep Pentagon at arm's length. *New York Times*, 16 April. http://www.nytimes.com/.

Persaud, Christine. 2012. Gender and security: Guidelines for mainstreaming gender in security risk management. EISF briefing paper. London: European Interagency Security Forum.

Peytremann, Isabelle, Michel Baduraux, Sinead O'Donovan, and Louis Loutan. 2001. Medical evacuations and fatalities of United Nations High Commissioner for Refugees field employees. *Journal of Travel Medicine* 8 (3): 117–121.

Pictet, Jean. 1979a. The fundamental principles of the Red Cross. *International Review of the Red Cross* 19 (210): 130–140.

———. 1979b. The Fundamental Principles of the Red Cross: Commentary. Geneva: Henry Dunant Institute.

Plattner, Denise. 1996. ICRC neutrality and neutrality in humanitarian assistance. *International Review of the Red Cross* 36 (311): 161–179.

Polman, Linda. 2010. *The Crisis Caravan: What's Wrong with Humanitarian Aid?* New York: Metropolitan Books.

Pont, Nigel. 2011. Southern Afghanistan: Acceptance still works. *Humanitarian Exchange* 49 (January): 6–9.

Porter, Benjamin, and Ben Emmens. 2009. Approaches to staff care in international NGOs. September. London: People in Aid and InterHealth.

Powell, Colin. 2001. Secretary of State Colin L. Powell Remarks to the National Foreign Policy Conference for Leaders of Non-Governmental Organizations. 26 October. http://avalon.law.yale.edu/sept11/powell_brief31.asp.

Power, Samantha. 2008. *Chasing the Flame: One Man's Fight to Save the World*. New York: Penguin.

Probst, Tahira M., and Ty L. Brubaker. 2001. The effects of job insecurity on employee safety outcomes: Cross-sectional and longitudinal explorations. *Journal of Occupational Health Psychology* 6 (2): 139–159.

Propp, Vladimir. 1968. *Morphology of the Folktale*. Translated by L. A. Wagner. 2nd ed. Austin: University of Texas Press.

Rabinow, Paul. 1977. *Reflections on Fieldwork in Morocco*. Berkeley: University of California Press.

Raftree, Linda. 2010. Amateurs, professionals, innovations and smart aid. *Wait . . . What? Bridging Community Development and Technology*, 26 June. http://lindaraftree.wordpress.com.

Rapoport, Anatol. 1995. *The Origins of Violence: Approaches to the Study of Violence*. New Brunswick, NJ: Transaction.

Reason, James. 1997. *Managing the Risks of Organizational Accidents*. Aldershot, UK: Ashgate.

Reeves, Phil, and Christopher Bellamy. 1996. Six aid staff killed in cold blood. *Independent* (London), 18 December, 1.

Reuters. 2011. Japan emergency workers may face lethal radiation—NRC. 16 March. http://www.trust.org/alertnet.

Rieff, David. 2002. *A Bed for the Night: Humanitarianism in Crisis*. New York: Simon & Schuster.

Roberts, Adam. 1996. *Humanitarian Action in War: Aid, Protection and Impartiality in a Policy Vacuum*. IISS Adelphi Paper 305. Oxford: Oxford University Press.

Roberts, David Lloyd. 1999. *Staying Alive: Safety and Security Guidelines for Humanitarian Volunteers in Conflict Areas*. Geneva: International Committee of the Red Cross.

Rogers, Charles, and Brian Sytsma. 1998. *A Shield About Me: Safety Awareness for World Vision Staff*. Monrovia, CA: World Vision.

Rohde, David. 2004. G.I.'s in Afghanistan on hunt, but now for hearts and minds. *New York Times*, 30 March. http://www.nytimes.com/.

Rohde, David, and Choe Sang-Hun. 2007. Taliban release 12 of 19 hostages from South Korea. *New York Times*, 30 August. http://www.nytimes.com/.

Ross, Steven S. 2004. Toward new understandings: Journalists and humanitarian relief coverage. San Francisco: Fritz Institute.

Roth, Silke. 2009. Becoming an aid worker: Biographies, careers, skills. Paper presented at the World Conference of Humanitarian Studies, 4–8 February, Groningen, Netherlands.

——. 2011. Dealing with danger: Risk and security in the everyday lives of aid workers. In Fechter and Hindman, *Inside the Everyday Lives of Development Workers*. Pp. 151–168.

Rowley, Elizabeth. 2005. Mortality and morbidity among humanitarian workers. Paper presented at the 46th Annual Convention of the International Studies Association, 2 March, Honolulu, HI.

——. 2007. Mortality and morbidity of humanitarian workers: Final narrative report. Baltimore: Johns Hopkins University, Bloomberg School of Public Health.

Rowley, Elizabeth, Jim Arbogast, James Byaruhanga, Daniel Etik, Robert Lochap, Gabriel Oling Olang, Stephen Okiror, Herbert Sabiiti, and Daniel Walusaga. 2011. Uganda country report: Key findings from field research on acceptance in Uganda. Washington, DC: Save the Children. http://acceptanceresearch.org/reports/uganda-country-report/.

Rowley, Elizabeth A., Lauren Burns, and Gilbert M. Burnham. 2010. Research review of nongovernmental organizations' security policies for humanitarian programs in war, conflict, and postconflict environments. *Disaster Medicine and Public Health Preparedness*, 26 July. doi: 10.1001/dmp.2010.0723.

Rowley, Elizabeth A., Byron L. Crape, and Gilbert M. Burnham. 2008. Violence-related mortality and morbidity of humanitarian workers. *American Journal of Disaster Medicine* 3 (1): 39–45.

Rubenstein, Jennifer. 2008. The distributive commitments of international NGOs. In Barnett and Weiss, *Humanitarianism in Question*. Pp. 215–234.

Ryan, M., and D. Heiden. 1990. Illness among expatriate relief workers during a refugee disaster. *International Ophthalmology Clinics* 30 (1): 66–67.

Saeed, Abdul Baseer. 2004. Minister scorns NGO's work. Institute for War and Peace Reporting. http://www.globalpolicy.org/. Accessed 3 November 2009.

Saffron, Inga. 1997. Relief workers losing their bystander status/They go to war zones to offer neutral help. More and more, they're becoming targets. *Philadelphia Inquirer*, 23 February, A1.

Sambanis, Nicholas. 2004. What is civil war? Conceptual and empirical complexities of an operational definition. *Journal of Conflict Resolution* 48 (6): 814–858.

Sandoz, Yves. 2007. Max Huber and the Red Cross. *European Journal of International Law* 18 (1): 171–197.

Saner, Raymond. 1990. Manifestation of stress and its impact on the humanitarian work of the ICRC delegate. *Political Psychology* 11 (4): 757–765.

Sarkees, Meredith Reid, and Phil Schafer. 2000. The Correlates of War data on war: An update to 1997. *Conflict Management and Peace Science* 18 (1): 123–144.

Save the Children. 2005. Code of conduct for Save the Children staff. Doc No. POL_34, February.

Schmid, Alex P., and Albert J. Jongman. 1988. *Political Terrorism: A New Guide to Actors, Authors, Concepts, Data Bases, Theories and Literature*. Rev. ed. Amsterdam: North-Holland.

Scroggins, Deborah. 2002. *Emma's War: Love, Betrayal and Death in the Sudan*. London: HarperCollins.

Senanayake, Shimali, and Somini Sengupta. 2006. Aid agencies stymied by war in Sri Lanka. *International Herald Tribune*, 18 August. http://www.iht.com/.

Shawcross, William. 1984. *The Quality of Mercy: Cambodia, Holocaust and Modern Conscience*. New York: Simon & Schuster.

———. 2000. *Deliver Us from Evil: Peacekeepers, Warlords and a World of Endless Conflict*. New York: Simon & Schuster.

Sheik, Mani, Maria Isabel Gutierrez, Paul Bolton, Paul Spiegel, Michel Thierren, and Gilbert Burnham. 2000. Deaths among humanitarian workers. *British Medical Journal* 321 (7254): 166–168.

Sida, Lewis. 2005. Challenges to humanitarian space: A review of the humanitarian issues related to the UN integrated mission in Liberia and to the relationship between humanitarian and military actors in Liberia. April. Monrovia, Liberia: Monitoring and Steering Group.

Siddique, Muhammad Haroon, and Mokbul Morshed Ahmad. 2012. Variables affecting fieldworkers of NGOs in Pakistan. *Development in Practice* 22 (2): 216–228.

Simmonds, Sandra, Pascale Gilbert-Miguet, Harald Siem, Manuel Carballo, and Damir Zeric. 1998. Occupational health of field personnel in complex emergencies: Report of a pilot study. July. Geneva: World Health Organization.

Slim, Hugo. 1995a. The continuing metamorphosis of the humanitarian practitioner: Some new colours for an endangered chameleon. *Disasters* 19 (2): 110–126.

———. 1995b. Military humanitarianism and the new peacekeeping: An agenda for peace? *Journal of Humanitarian Assistance*, 22 September. http://sites.tufts.edu/jha/archives/64.

———. 1997a. Doing the right thing: Relief agencies, moral dilemmas and moral responsibility in political emergencies and war. *Disasters* 21 (3): 244–257.

———. 1997b. Relief agencies and moral standing in war: Principles of humanity, neutrality, impartiality and solidarity. *Development in Practice* 7 (4, November): 342–352.

———. 1998. Sharing a universal ethic: The principle of humanity in war. *International Journal of Human Rights* 2 (4): 28–48.

———. 2001. Military intervention to protect human rights: The humanitarian agency perspective. ICHRP working paper, 14 March. Geneva: International Council on Human Rights Policy. http://www.ichrp.org/files/papers/50/115_-_Military_Intervention_to_Protect_Human_Rights_Slim_Hugo_2001_background_paper.pdf.

———. 2003. Marketing humanitarian space: Argument and method in humanitarian persuasion. Geneva: Centre for Humanitarian Dialogue.

———. 2007. *Killing Civilians: Method, Madness, and Morality in War.* London: Hurst.

Slim, Hugo, and Andrew Bonwick. 2005. Protection: An ALNAP guide for humanitarian agencies. London: Overseas Development Institute/ALNAP.

Slim, Hugo, and Luis Enrique Eguren. 2004. Humanitarian protection: A guidance booklet. London: Overseas Development Institute/ALNAP.

Sluka, Jeffrey A. 1990. Participant observation in violent social contexts. *Human Organization* 49: 114–126.

Smith, Barbara, Inger Agger, Yael Danieli, and Lars Weisaeth. 1996. Health activities across traumatised populations: Emotional responses of international humanitarian aid workers. In *International Responses to Traumatic Stress: Humanitarian, Human Rights, Justice, Peace and Developmental Contributions, Collaborative Actions, and Future Initiatives*, edited by Y. Danieli, N. S. Rodley, and L. Weisaeth. Amityville, NY: Baywood. Pp. 397–423.

Smith, Gayle E. 1993. Relief operations and military strategy. In Weiss and Minear, *Humanitarianism Across Borders*. Pp. 97–116.

Smock, David R. 1996. Humanitarian assistance and conflict in Africa. Peaceworks no. 6, February. Washington, DC: U.S. Institute of Peace.

Sphere Project. 2000. *Humanitarian Charter and Minimum Standards in Disaster Response.* Herndon, VA: The Sphere Project.

Sriram, Chandra Lekha, John C. King, Julie A. Mertus, Olga Martin-Ortega, and Johanna Herman, eds. 2009. *Surviving Field Research: Working in Violent and Difficult Situations.* London: Routledge.

Staff Welfare Unit. 2001. Managing the stress of humanitarian emergencies. July. Geneva: United Nations High Commissioner for Refugees, Career and Staff Support Service.

Stanley, Alessandra. 1996. Six Red Cross aides slain in Chechnya, imperiling the peace. *New York Times*, 18 December, A1.

Staub, Ervin. 1989. *The Roots of Evil: The Origins of Genocide and Other Group Violence.* Cambridge: Cambridge University Press.

Stearns, S. D. 1993. Psychological distress and relief work: Who helps the helpers? *Refugee Participation Network* 15 (September): 3–8.
Stein, Janice Gross. 1998. Loyalty, voice, and exit: Humanitarian NGOs, complex emergencies, and conflict resolution. Toronto.
———. 2000. New challenges: Humanitarian nongovernmental organizations. In *International Conflict Resolution After the Cold War*, edited by D. Druckman and P. Stern. Washington, DC: National Academy Press. Pp. 389–425.
Stirrat, Roderick L. 2008. Mercenaries, missionaries and misfits: Representations of development personnel. *Critique of Anthropology* 28 (4): 406–425.
Stoddard, Abby. 2003. Humanitarian NGOs: Challenges and trends. In Humanitarian Action and "the Global War on Terror": A Review of Trends and Issues, edited by J. Macrae and A. Harmer. HPG report 14, July. London: Overseas Development Institute, Humanitarian Policy Group. Pp. 1–4.
Stoddard, Abby, and Adele Harmer. 2006. Little room to maneuver: The challenges to humanitarian action in the new global security environment. *Journal of Human Development* 7 (1): 23–41.
Stoddard, Abby, Adele Harmer, and Victoria DiDomenico. 2008. The use of private security providers and services in humanitarian operations. HPG report 27, October. London: Overseas Development Institute, Humanitarian Policy Group.
———. 2009. Providing aid in insecure environments: 2009 update. HPG policy brief 34, April. London: Overseas Development Institute, Humanitarian Policy Group.
Stoddard, Abby, Adele Harmer, and Katherine Haver. 2006. Providing aid in insecure environments: Trends in policy and operations. HPG report 23, September. London: Overseas Development Institute, Humanitarian Policy Group.
———. 2011. Aid worker security report 2011. Spotlight on security for national aid workers: Issues and perspectives. New York: Humanitarian Outcomes.
Stoddard, Abby, Adele Harmer, and Morgan Hughes. 2012. Aid worker security report 2012. Host states and their impact on security for humanitarian operations. New York: Humanitarian Outcomes.
Suttenberg, Lindsay Jill. 2005. Curing the humanitarian crisis: Resolution 1502. *Washington University Global Studies Law Review* 4 (1): 187–204.
Sweeney, John, and Lisa O'Kelly. 1996. Who would be an aid worker? Four veterans give their answer. *Observer Review* (UK), 22 December, 3ff.
Tales from the Hood. 2010. Noble savages. *Tales from the Hood*, 28 June. http://talesfromethehood.com/.
Taylor, Mark. 2002. Economies of conflict: Private sector activity in armed conflict. Emerging conclusions. March. Oslo: Programme for International Co-operation and Conflict Resolution, FAFO.
Teitel, Ruti G. 2011. *Humanity's Law*. Oxford: Oxford University Press.
Terry, Fiona. 2002. *Condemned to Repeat: The Paradox of Humanitarian Action*. Ithaca: Cornell University Press.

---. 2010. The International Committee of the Red Cross in Afghanistan: Reasserting the neutrality of humanitarian action. *International Review of the Red Cross* 92 (880, December): 1–16.

Tilly, Charles. 2003. *The Politics of Collective Violence*. Cambridge: Cambridge University Press.

Topouria, Nikolai. 1996. Slaughtered as they slept/Six Red Cross staff shot in hospital. *Daily Telegraph* (Australia), 18 December, 32.

United Nations. 2000. Deputy Secretary-General tells "summit" on staff security that increasing threats "compel us to do more." UN Press Release DSG/SM/97 ORG/1306, 16 June. http://www.un.org/News/Press/docs/2000/20000209.dsgsm84.r1.doc.html.

---. 2003. Safety and security of humanitarian personnel and protection of United Nations personnel: Report of the Secretary-General. A/57/300, 15 August. New York: UN General Assembly.

United Nations High Commissioner for Refugees. 2002. Extensive abuse of West African refugee children reported. UNHCR press release, 26 February. http://www.unhcr.org/.

United Nations News Service. 2003. UN family honours terror victims one month after Baghdad bombing. 19 September. http://www.un.org/news.

---. 2004. Annan vows to end sex abuse committed by UN mission staff in DR of Congo. 19 November. http://www.un.org/news.

---. 2010. Ban unveils "collection of superheroes" to help eradicate poverty. 23 June. http://www.un.org/news.

---. 2011. UN re-assesses security threats in wake of deadly attack in Nigerian capital. 30 August. http://www.un.org/news.

United Nations Office of Internal Oversight Services. 2002. Investigation into sexual exploitation of refugees by aid workers in West Africa. A/57/465, 11 October. New York: UN Office of Internal Oversight Services.

United Nations Secretariat. 2004. Report of the Security in Iraq Accountability Panel (SIAP), UN Secretariat summary of main findings and conclusions. 3 March. New York: United Nations. http://www.un.org/News/dh/iraq/SIAP-report.pdf.

United Nations Secretary General. 2008. Decisions of the Secretary-General—25 June meeting of the Policy Committee. Decision No. 2008/24—Integration. New York: United Nations.

---. 2010. Secretary-General welcomes entry into force of optional protocol to Convention on Safety and Security of United Nations and Associated Personnel. Press release SG/SM/13059, L/T/4421, 13 August. http://www.un.org/News/Press/docs/2010/sgsm13059.doc.htm.

United Nations Security Council. 2003. Resolution 1502 (2003) Protection of United Nations personnel, associated personnel and humanitarian personnel in conflict zones. S/RES/1502 (2003), 26 August. New York: UN Security Council.

University Teachers for Human Rights. 2008. Unfinished business of the five students and ACF cases: A time to call the bluff. Special report 30, 1 April. Jaffna: University Teachers for Human Rights. http://www.uthr.org/SpecialReports/Spreport30.htm.

Uvin, Peter. 1998. *Aiding Violence: The Development Enterprise in Rwanda*. West Hartford, CT: Kumarian Press.

Van Brabant, Koenraad. 1998. Cool ground for aid providers: Towards better security management in aid agencies. *Disasters* 22 (2): 109–125.

———. 2000. Operational security management in violent environments. Good Practice Reviews 8, June. London: Overseas Development Institute, Humanitarian Practice Network.

———. 2001. Mainstreaming the organisational management of safety and security. HPG report 9, March. London: Overseas Development Institute, Humanitarian Policy Group.

vanOrden, Steven. 2008. *Africa: Stranger than Fiction. Memoirs of a Humanitarian Aid Worker*. Bloomington, IN: iUniverse.

Vaux, Tony. 2004. *The Selfish Altruist: Relief Work in Famine and War*. London: Earthscan.

Vayrynen, Raimo. 1999. More questions than answers: Dilemmas of humanitarian action. *Peace and Change* 24 (2, April): 172–196.

Vick, Karl. 2003. Facing "different kind of war," aid groups in Iraq adopt lower profile. *Washington Post*, 29 September, A15. http://www.washingtonpost.com.

Waddington, Richard. 2003. ICRC outraged by Baghdad attack, weighs withdrawal. *AlertNet*, 27 October. http://www.alertnet.org/.

Wagner, Johanna Grombach. 2005. An IHL/ICRC perspective on "humanitarian space." *Humanitarian Exchange* 32 (December): 24–25.

Walker, Peter. 2007. Future human resources challenges. Paper presented at The Heart of Humanitarian Relief: Managing and Supporting People Effectively in a Challenging Global Context, Baltimore, 14 November.

Walker, Peter, and Daniel Maxwell. 2009. *Shaping the Humanitarian World*. New York: Routledge.

Walker, Peter, and Catherine Russ. 2010. Professionalising the humanitarian sector: A scoping study. April. London: Enhancing Learning and Research for Humanitarian Assistance, SCF-UK.

Walsh, Nick Paton. 2005. Russian says "spies" work in foreign NGOs. *Guardian*, 13 May. http://www.guardian.co.uk/.

Walt, Vivienne. 2010. Terrorist hostage situations: Rescue or ransom? *Time*, 12 October. http://www.time.com/time/world/article/0,8599,2024420,00.html.

Ward, Mark. 2010. USAID assistance in Pakistan. *USAID Impact Blog*, 9 October. http://blog.usaid.gov/2010/10/usaid-assistance-in-pakistan/.

Watkins, Tate. 2012. Rebuilding Haiti: Why is it taking so long? *American Interest*, 10 May. http://www.the-american-interest.com/article.cfm?piece=1255.

Wax, Emily. 2009. Red Cross barred from Sri Lankan refugee camp. *Washington Post*, 21 May. http://www.washingtonpost.com/.

Weaver, J. Denny. 1993. Violence does not bring peace. *The Mennonite*, 13 April, 12.

Weiss, Thomas G. 1999. Principles, politics, and humanitarian action. *Ethics and International Affairs* 13: 1–22.

———. 2004. *Military-Civilian Interaction: Intervening in Humanitarian Crises.* 2nd ed. Lanham, MD: Rowman & Littlefield.

Weiss, Thomas G., and Larry Minear, eds. *Humanitarianism Across Borders: Sustaining Civilians in Times of War.* Boulder, CO: Lynne Rienner.

Whitman, Jim, and David Pocock, eds. 1996. *After Rwanda: The Coordination of United Nations Humanitarian Assistance.* New York: St. Martin's.

Wilder, Andrew. 2008. Perceptions of the Pakistan earthquake response. Humanitarian Agenda 2015 case study, February. Medford, MA: Tufts University, Feinstein International Center. https: //sites.tufts.edu/feinstein/2008/humanitarian-agenda-2015-perceptions-of-the-pakistan-earthquake-response.

Wilder, Andrew, and Stuart Gordon. 2009. Money can't buy America love. *Foreign Policy*, 1 December. http://www.foreignpolicy.com/articles/2009/12/01/money_cant_buy_america_love?page=0,0.

Wille, Christina and Larissa Fast. 2013a. Humanitarian staff security in armed conflict: Policy implications for the international community from changes in the operating environment for humanitarian agencies. Insecurity Insight policy brief. Vevey, Switzerland: Insecurity Insight. http://www.insecurityinsight.org/.

———. 2013b. Operating in insecurity: Shifting patterns of violence against humanitarian providers and their staff (1996–2010). Report 13-1. Vevey, Switzerland: Insecurity Insight. http://www.insecurityinsight.org.

Williams, Carol J. 2007. Sex scandal in Haiti hits U.N. mission. *Baltimore Sun*, 16 December. http://www.baltimoresun.com/. Reprinted from the *Los Angeles Times*.

Wilson, Richard Ashby, and Richard D. Brown, eds. 2009. *Humanitarianism and Suffering: The Mobilization of Empathy.* Cambridge: Cambridge University Press.

Wood, Elisabeth Jean. 2011. Rape is not inevitable during war. In *Women and War: Power and Protection in the 21st Century*, edited by K. Kuehnast, C. d. J. Oudraat, and H. Hernes. Washington, DC: U.S. Institute of Peace Press. Pp. 37–63.

Working Group on NGO Security. 1997. NGO security training. Washington, DC: InterAction.

World Health Organization. 2009. Global status report on road safety: Time for action. Geneva: World Health Organization.

World Vision International. 2007. World Vision International 2007 annual review. Hope for the most vulnerable. Monrovia, CA: World Vision International. http://www.wvi.org/annualreviews. Accessed 5 August 2010.

———. 2008. World Vision International 2008 annual review. Hope for the most vulnerable. Monrovia, CA: World Vision International. http://www.wvi.org/annualreviews.

———. 2009. World Vision International 2009 review. Working together with joy. Monrovia, CA: World Vision International. http://www.wvi.org/annualreviews.

———. 2010. World Vision International 2010 annual review (summary). Monrovia, CA: World Vision International. http://www.wvi.org/annualreviews.

Worthington, Samuel. 2010. Why American aid workers in Pakistan need to keep a low profile. *Washington Post*, 10 October, B04.

Yamashita, Hikaru. 2004. *Humanitarian Space and International Politics: The Creation of Safe Areas*. Aldershot, UK: Ashgate.

Yancho, Paul J. 2005. Catholic humanitarian aid and the Nigeria-Biafra civil war. In *Religion, History, and Politics in Nigeria: Essays in Honor of Ogbu U. Kalu*, edited by C. J. Korieh and G. U. Nwokeji. Lanham, MD: University Press of America. Pp. 158–171.

Young, Helen, and Daniel Maxwell. 2009. Targeting in complex emergencies—Darfur case study. April. Medford, MA: Tufts University, Feinstein International Center.

Zaks, Dmitry. 1996. Chechen accuse Russia in murders. *Moscow Times*, 20 December, sec. 1111.

Zavis, Alexandra. 2009. Afghan attack puts aid programs at risk. *Los Angeles Times*, 29 October. http://www.latimes.com/.

INDEX

Abu-Hafs al-Masri Brigades, 18. *See also* Baghdad; Iraq (2003)
Abyssinian War (Ethiopia and Italy, 1936), 66, 153–54
Acceptance. *See* Security management, specific strategies
Access. *See* Humanitarian access
Accountability. *See* Donors and donor communities; Humanitarianism, principles
Action Contre la Faim (ACF; Action against Hunger), 26–30, 238. *See also* Muttur, Sri Lanka (2006)
Active Learning Network for Accountability and Performance (ALNAP), 159–60
Actors, humanitarian. *See* Aid workers; Humanitarians; Threats, external; Violence and violent contexts; Vulnerabilities, internal
Actors, integrationist. *See* Humanitarians, Wilsonian
Addis Ababa (Ethiopia), 66
Additional Protocol III (2005; to Geneva Conventions, 1949), 202
Adventist Development and Relief Agency, 168
Afghanistan: acceptance in, 270n39; armed escorts in, 202; culture clashes in, 134, 135; deaths of IAM workers in, 192; deaths of UN workers in, 226; funding from U.S. and UK governments in, 108; humanitarian negotiations in, 221; ICRC in, 48, 219, 222, 225, 273n70; increase in incidents in, 75; kidnappings, murders, and attacks in, 78, 221, 222, 250n2, 254n26, 260n31; media coverage of, 49; military and humanitarian linkages in, 117–19; NGOs and aid agencies in, 133, 260n31; ransoms paid in, 107; reconstruction in, 116; security for humanitarians in, 47; security management and, 49, 225; Taliban in, 168, 192, 219, 221, 226, 273n70; U.S. bombing in, 116; violence against aid agencies and workers, 48, 50, 51, 103, 116, 117, 122, 166, 168, 250n2
Afghanistan NGO Safety Organization (ANSO), 183, 260n31, 269n20
Africa, 81. *See also individual countries*
Ahmad, Mokbul Morshed, 166
Ahtisaari, Martti, 19
Ahtisaari Report (2003), 19–20, 22, 24, 91
Aid agencies: acceptance of, 207, 208, 218–23; aid compounds, 213–14; armed protection for, 103–4; codes of conduct of, 147–49; competing visions and images of, 7, 45, 152, 164–65; criticisms and critiques of, 113–16, 134, 159, 161–62, 229–35; decision making of, 32–33; emphasis on external threats by, 56, 239; ethical messages of, 160; exceptionalizing of, 91, 187, 195; faith-based agencies, 168; hiring policies of, 142, 165–66; as humanitarian and multimandate agencies, 81; interference by, 106; internal hierarchies and inequalities in, 241; localized grievances, 34–35; military and, 103, 117–19, 217, 258n14; neutrality and impartiality of, 96–97, 103; organizational issues, 33, 56; payment of ransoms, 106–7; perceptions of, 166–67, 230, 241, 257n2; professionalization of, 163; power and, 229, 230, 239; programming of, 29–30, 102, 109, 118, 152, 165, 168–69; recognition of external threats and internal vulnerabilities, 56; resources of, 155, 164; risks of, 41–42, 83, 96–97, 103,

Aid agencies (*continued*)
195, 213–17; role of, 155; security incidents and, 53, 238; security management and, 13–14, 168–69, 170–72, 183, 194–95, 207, 217, 224, 238; security officers and directors, 181–82; staffing of, 33–34, 194–95; stress and, 271n51; suits against, 143–44; time-bound images of, 128; withdrawal and evacuation from dangerous places, 75, 207. *See also* Aid organizations; *individual countries; headings under* Security *and* Staff

Aid and aid work: branding of assistance, 117, 119; business model of, 152, 162, 164, 240; as a career path, 137, 162–63; criticisms and critiques of, 113–16, 134, 159, 161–62, 229–40, 262n6; decreases in, 265n38; definitions and concepts of, 2, 4, 8, 227; dilemmas of, 7, 11, 42, 103, 108, 139, 140, 161, 240; early aid and humanitarian work, 37, 153; effects of, 206; exceptionalizing of, 4–8, 187, 225, 229; expansion and institutionalization of, 160–61; foreign policy and, 116–17; funding for, 160–61; implicit ethical messages in, 160, 262n6; internal vulnerabilities and, 31; Iraqisation of, 50, 251n6; micro-management of, 151; militarization of, 50, 102–3, 120–21, 259n24; normalization of danger and risk, 213–17; paradoxes of, 43, 83, 115–16, 193–94, 196, 202, 205, 229, 239–40, 242; paths to aid work, 138; perceptions and interpretations of, 2, 4, 229, 231, 232; politicization of, 29–31, 232; questionable and unethical side of, 134–35; relational nature of, 8, 42, 44–45, 53, 93, 157, 194, 195, 207, 215, 224–25, 243; rescue story of, 229–30; securitization of, 102; self-interests of, 115, 160–61; separation of aid workers and others, 9, 24–26, 45, 53, 161–62, 193–94, 213–17, 227; stresses of, 5, 86, 138–45, 206–7, 240; violence and, 2–3, 5, 30–31, 53, 83, 120, 125; Western agendas of, 116, 117, 119–20. *See also* Humanitarian assistance; Humanitarianism

Aid in danger: ambushes, 81; attacks on hospitals, 69–70; Biafran crisis as an illustration of, 70–74; concept of humanitarian exceptionalism and, 68, 186–87, 228–35; degree of danger, 74–77; history and trends of, 67–70, 74–75, 81, 82, 83; implications of analysis of a humanity-based relational approach, 240–45; military involvement and, 256n44; motives for, 257n46; normalization of danger, 213–17; pillaging and, 106; recommendations for a way forward, 58–65, 82, 147, 240–45; risks of, 84; sensationalism of, 67; targeted and intentional violence, 50–51, 53, 66–67, 69–72, 73, 74, 81, 84, 99, 105, 222. *See also* Baghdad, Iraq (2003); Muttur, Sri Lanka (2006); Research and analysis; Solferino, Italy (1859); Violence and violent contexts

Aid organizations. *See* Aid agencies; Organizations

Aid workers: actions and lifestyles of, 6, 57, 134–35; blogs by, 263n13; characteristics of, 136–37; codes of conduct, 147–49; communications and, 120, 154, 155, 219; contractors as, 77; criticisms and critiques of 113–16, 134, 159, 161–62, 229–35; cultural contexts of aid work, 57, 134, 135; decrease in violence and, 83, 157–58; definition of, 77; early work of, 153–56; either/or images of, 86; emergencies and, 263n15; emotional rewards of, 131; as fairy-tale heroes, 122–25, 156, 169–70, 174–75, 193, 229–32, 237–38; general picture of, 227; as humanitarians, 4–5, 53, 80–81, 115–16; humanity as a guiding principle of, 5; legal issues of, 6, 197–207; localized grievances, 34–35; loss of life of, 26–27, 30, 32, 83, 48, 75, 81, 102, 249n16, 250n2; media and, 78; military and, 117–19, 259n24; as misfits, 129, 130, 137; as misfits and "third-country nationals," 163; as mythical figures or ordinary people, 129–38; normalization of danger and risk and, 213–17; numbers and proliferation of, 149, 151, 158; organizational management and personnel conflicts, 33; paths to aid work, 138; perceptions of, 2, 6, 171, 236, 241; pillaging and, 106; politicization

Index

discourse and, 32; power of, 229–30; professionalism and effectiveness of, 162–63; reckless and sexual behavior of, 33–34, 134, 144; relational issues of, 195; risks and security of, 2, 41–42, 137–39, 142, 144–47, 153, 156–57; security restrictions for, 211; separation of aid workers and others, 9, 24–26, 45, 53, 161–62, 193–94, 213–17, 227; sexual abuse by, 263n10; skill set of, 130–31; stress and security of, 138–45, 215, 237, 240, 271n51; violence against, 50–51, 53, 66–67, 69–74, 75t, 81, 84, 99–100, 105, 171, 176–79, 188, 193, 205, 222, 223, 250n2, 259n24; volunteers, 264n20. *See also* Aid agencies; Civilians; Cuny, Fred; Humanitarian exceptionalism; Threats, external; Violence and violent contexts; Vulnerabilities, internal; *headings under* Staff *and* Humanitarian

Aid workers, attacks: in Afghanistan, 48; in Baghdad, Iraq, 32, 48; in Burundi, 177; in Cambodia, 177; in Chechnya, 83, 121–22, 176–79; in Muttur, Sri Lanka, 27–28, 32; of 2011, 1–2, 75t

Aid workers, competing visions of: assumptions about security and, 145; attributes-based image, 131; colonial legacy of, 132; critical images of, 147; culture clashes and, 134, 135; empire and profit and, 113–21, 125–26; identities of aid agencies and, 128; labeling and self-images of aid workers, 128–29; as mythical figures, 128, 130–36, 146–47; NGO workers, 132–33; as ordinary people, 128, 136–38, 147; perks and privilege of, 132–33; portraits emphasizing greed and incompetence, 131–32; as rescuers, 113–14, 121–26; responses to violence and, 128–29, 147

al-Bashir, Omar, 89, 109
Algiers, Algeria bombing (2007), 26, 117, 184, 227, 261n44
al-Kurdi. *See* Awraz Abd Al Aziz Mahmoud Sa'eed
al-Qaeda, 107, 117
al-Massri, Abu Farid 19
ALNAP. *See* Active Learning Network for Accountability and Performance

Al-Shabaab (Somalia), 107–8, 168
al-Zarqawi, Abu Mussab, 18, 19
American Friends Service Committee, 149
American Red Cross. *See* Barton, Clara
Anderson, Mary B., 106, 160, 249n20. *See also* CDA Collaborative Learning Projects; Do-no-harm approach; Local Capacities for Peace project
Angola, 196
Annan, Kofi, 17, 19, 22, 49, 117. *See also* Baghdad, Iraq (2003); United Nations
Antares Foundation, 271n51
Appia, Louis, 39
Arbour, Louise, 187
Assumptive mechanisms. *See* Protection and protective measures; Security management, paradigms
Awraz Abd Al Aziz Mahmoud Sa'eed (al-Kurdi), 18–19, 55
AWSD (Aid Worker Security Database). *See* Databases

Baghdad, Iraq (2003), 15; bombing, blame, and bunkers, 16–19, 26, 47–48, 53–56, 84; causes of bombing in, 55–56; command structures and planning in relation to bombing, 18–21; effects of bombing on survivors, 54; escalation of violence in, 49; fatalities and injuries in, 77; humanitarian crisis in, 49; investigations of and reports on bombing in, 19–20, 24, 25, 76; lessons of bombing in, 21–22, 45; security management before and after bombing, 19–25, 49, 54, 56, 93, 170, 208, 248n3; staffing in, 248n5; targeted violence against aid workers, 50; UN in, 16–24, 26, 49, 54–56, 93, 184; U.S. in, 22–24, 54–55. *See also* Iraq
Balkans, 177
Balkan wars (1875), 40
Ban Ki-moon, 226, 227. *See also* United Nations
Bangladesh, 141, 166
Barton, Clara, 16, 38, 39
Berlin Airlift (1948), 70
Betancourt, Ingrid, 96
Biafra, 69, 71, 108
Biafran War (Nigeria-Biafra; 1966–1970), 67–74, 102, 121, 153

Blame: "blaming the victim," 56–57, 62, 65, 147, 232; complexities of, 56–57, 62, 232; exceptionalism and, 126; in morality-play narratives of violence, 124–25; "moral untouchability," 56; "public secrets" and, 57; recommendations for a way forward, 58–65; relational aspects of, 64–65; understanding and, 61. *See also* Baghdad, Iraq (2003); Muttur, Sri Lanka (2006)
Bono. *See* Hewson, Paul David
Bosnia, 95, 150, 158
Brahimi, Lakhdar, 117, 227
Brescia, Italy. *See* Solferino, Italy (1859)
Brown, Sidney, 66
Brussels Document (1874), 40
Bush (George W.) era, 46–47, 116–17
Buxton, Dorothy, 152

Canal Hotel (Baghdad, Iraq), 16, 17, 20, 22, 49, 55, 238. *See also* Baghdad, Iraq (2003); Iraq
CARE Canada, 79
CARE International, 27, 118, 150, 189, 190
CARE USA, 150, 153
Caritas (relief and development agency of the Catholic Church), 27
Caseres, Carlos, 127
Castiglione. *See* Solferino, Italy (1859)
Catholic Relief Services (CRS), 78, 79, 108, 150
Causes of violence, 58–65
CDA Collaborative Learning Projects, 160
Central America, 108
Change, 59–60
Charity: aid agencies and, 163; bureaucratized charity, 152, 243; Christian charities, 35; humanitarian assistance as, 4; humanity enacted as charity, 43–44; militarized charity, 103; NGOs' use of, 133; perpetuation of violence and, 159; "technocrats of charity," 152. *See also* Aid and aid work; Humanitarian assistance
Cheadle, Don, 123
Chechnya: Fred Cuny in, 79, 80; kidnapping in, 178, 179; security issues in, 2, 176, 179; violence and withdrawal of aid agencies from (1996), 83, 121–22, 176–79, 187
Chicago Tribune, 121, 159
Christian Peacemaker Teams (CPT), 78
Churches, 71–73. *See also* Joint Church Aid

CISD. *See* Critical Incident Stress Debriefing
Civilians: aid workers as, 128, 148, 170, 175, 188, 192, 194, 205–7, 225, 240, 242, 244–45, 271n48; aid workers as special category of, 3, 6, 65, 128, 174–75, 205, 214, 242; blurred lines between military actors and, 2–3, 50, 68, 73, 102–3, 118, 120, 188, 210, 217, 230–31, 233, 239, 256n44; definition of, 103; legal codification of exceptionalism, 197–204, 225; negotiating for access to, 260n26; protection of, 23, 41–45, 95, 96, 103, 105, 109, 128, 175, 197–207, 225, 235, 242, 271n48; security concerns and access to, 83, 104, 106; security of aid workers and, 41–42, 104, 117, 194; as targets of violence, 103–5, 188, 192, 239. *See also* Humanitarian access
Civil War (American; 1861–1865). *See* Barton, Clara
Clooney, George, 123
Codes of conduct, 96, 147–48, 159
Coelho, Paulo, 123
Cold War (1985–1991), 153, 157–58
Commins, Sharon, 31, 84, 143
Common Article 3 (Geneva Conventions, 1949), 202
Compassion, 94. *See also* Humanitarianism
Comprehensive Peace Agreement (South Sudan; 2005), 155
Concern/Concern Worldwide, 70, 153
Conflicts. *See* Violence and violent contexts; Warfare and armed conflict
Conrad, Joseph, 155
Consortium for Humanitarian Agencies, 27
Containment, 94–95
"Control Arms" campaign, 109
Convention on the Privileges and Immunities of the Specialized Agencies (1947), 23
Convention on the Privileges and Immunities of the United Nations (1946), 23, 198, 270n43
Convention on the Rights of the Child (1989), 153
Convention on the Safety of UN and Associated Personnel (1994), 13, 23, 197–98, 199, 200, 203, 204
Cooperative for American Remittances to Europe, 153. *See also* CARE USA
CPT. *See* Christian Peacemaker Teams

Crime and criminals: attacks on humanitarians, 13, 22, 26–30, 73, 105, 191–92, 198–204, 217; availability of conventional weapons and, 106; kidnapping and murder of Hassan, Margaret, 191–92, 270n37; media coverage and fear of, 51–52; misuse of flags and emblems, 198; politically motivated crimes, 85–86; war crimes, 13, 22, 105, 191–92. *See also* Legal issues

Crimea. *See* Nightingale, Florence

Critical Incident Stress Debriefing (CISD), 206

CRS. *See* Catholic Relief Services

Culture and cultural mores, 57

Cuny, Fred, 79–80, 176, 179

Darfur, Sudan: accusations of spying by aid agencies in, 79; aid work in the 1980s in, 151; expulsions of aid agencies in, 83, 109, 257n1; indictment of President Bashir for war crimes in, 89, 109; kidnapping in, 31–32, 84; security and security management in, 181; study on neutrality in, 109; trust of staff in, 167. *See also* Republic of the Sudan

Databases and data: Aid Worker Security Database (AWSD), 75t, 252n17, 253n18, 253n21; data-sharing efforts, 253n21; Patronus Analytical Aid Workers Fatalities Database, 254n27; Security in Numbers Database (SiND), 253n21

Declaration of the Rights of the Child (Jebb; 1924, 1959), 153

de Mello, Sergio Vieira, 16, 17, 24, 53–54, 93, 144. *See also* Baghdad, Iraq (2003)

Democratic Republic of Congo, 2, 134, 151, 158

Derviş, Kemal, 117

de Silva, Ramiro Lopes, 16–17, 21. *See also* Baghdad, Iraq (2003)

Dessié/Dessye, Ethiopia (1936), 66

Deterrence. *See* Security management, specific strategies

Development, 115, 119–20

Development Assistance Committee (DAC; Organisation for Economic Co-operation and Development), 150, 265n37

Diakonia (Swedish NGO), 168

Do-no-harm approach, 98, 160, 262n6

Donors and donor community: amounts donated, 158; demands for accountability and oversight, 152, 159, 164; expansion of, 150–51. *See also* Funding and fund raising; Resources

Dost, Bashar, 133

Dufour, Guillaume Hénri, 39

Dunant, Henri, 16, 37–38, 40–42. *See also* Solferino, Italy (1859)

Dunantist actors. *See* Humanitarians, Dunantist (purist)

Duty of care, 143–44, 149, 164, 175, 206–7, 225, 244. *See also* Mental health issues

East Africa, 166–67, 222

Economic issues, 151, 157

Emergencies and emergency operations: agency logos and emblems during, 196; criticism of, 158; funding for, 149, 150; military involvement in, 210; training for, 263n15; UN and, 184; U.S. and European humanitarian assistance and, 158

Emergency Relief Coordinator (ERC). *See* United Nations

Escorts (armed), 3, 103–4, 110, 170, 174, 176, 202, 207, 208, 211. *See also* Security management, specific strategies

Ethiopia. *See* Dessié/Dessye, Ethiopia (1936)

Ethiopian-Italian War (1936), 69–70

Ethiopian Medical Service, 66

Europe, 158

European Commission, 180

Exceptionalism and exceptionalizing: acceptance approach to security and, 243; aid worker as distinct and apart, 139; approaches to aid and, 90–92; assumption of altruistic immunity, 156, 170, 186–87, 190, 193; causal mechanisms and, 229; changing circumstances of aid workers and, 177; definition and implications of, 6; exclusionary analysis and, 2–3; Geneva Conventions and legal issues of, 199–207; legal codification of exceptionalism, 197–207; normalization of danger and, 213–17; politicization discourse and, 32; remote management and, 213; security management and, 169–70, 175. *See also* Aid agencies; Aid and aid work; Aid in danger; Aid workers; Humanitarian exceptionalism; Humanitarians, exceptionalist

Fear: discourse of, 51–52; of humanitarians, 47; in modern life, 46; principle of humanity and, 236; protective and deterrent security management and, 216–17, 226–27; severe violence and, 51; terror and, 46–47, 55; "us" versus "them" perspective and, 232

First Geneva Convention. *See* Geneva Convention for the Amelioration of the Condition of the Wounded and Sick in Armed Forces in the Field

Fourth Geneva Convention. *See* Geneva Convention relative to the Protection of Civilian Persons in Time of War

Franco-Prussian war (1870–1871), 40

Fréchette, Louise, 204

Funding and fund raising, 123, 151. *See also* Donors and donor community; Resources

Gaza, 219

Gaza Strip NGO Safety Office (GANSO), 183–84, 253n20, 269n20

Geneva Convention for the Amelioration of the Condition of the Wounded in Armies in the Field (First Geneva Convention; 1864), 39–40

Geneva Convention relative to the Protection of Civilian Persons in Time of War (Fourth Geneva Convention; 1949), 23, 39, 92, 248n11

Geneva Conventions and Additional Protocols (1949, 1977, 2005), 92, 96, 197–200, 202, 205, 250n27, 260n33

Genocide, 158–59. *See also* Rwanda

GHD. *See* Good Humanitarian Donorship

Gilligan, James, 59–62, 124

GOAL (Irish NGO), 31

Goodall, Jane, 123

Good Humanitarian Donorship (GHD), 159, 160

Good Practice Review 8 (GPR8; Overseas Development Institute), 180

Governments and states: aid in agendas of, 116, 120; as donors to NGOs, 108; duty to protect all civilians, 205–6; investigation of attacks by, 204; humanitarianism of, 4, 98; humanitarians as underdogs, 229; legal codification of humanitarian exceptionalism, 197–207; mechanisms of protection of, 204; purpose of, 94, 96; regulation of use of emblems, 202; states as partners in aid, 157

Greece, 153

Green Zone. *See* Baghdad, Iraq (2003); Iraq

Grozny. *See* Chechnya

Hackett, Ken, 78

Hague Conventions (1899, 1907), 23, 40

Haiti earthquake (2010), 134, 140, 210, 214

HAP International. *See* Humanitarian Accountability Partnership International

Hassan, Margaret, 189–93, 270n37, 270n38

Health issues, 206. *See also* Mental health issues

"Healthcare in Danger" campaign (ICRC), 109

Heart of Darkness (Conrad), 155

HEAT. *See* Hostile Environment Awareness Training

Helton, Arthur, 116

Hewson, Paul David (Bono), 123

Hiring practices. *See* Aid agencies; Security management; Staff

Holbrooke, Richard, 117

Holmes, John, 28

Hostile Environment Awareness Training (HEAT), 210

Humanitarian access, 3, 38, 47, 89, 104–7, 109, 112, 151, 171, 174, 176, 184–85, 193–94, 205–8, 219, 233, 260n26; and security, 48, 83, 104, 109, 221–22. *See also* Humanitarian negotiation

Humanitarian Accountability Partnership International (HAP International), 159

Humanitarian action, 1, 4, 8, 10, 25–26, 41, 91–100, 111, 112, 116, 125, 157, 206, 228, 231, 240–41, 258n7; challenges to, 48, 50–51, 239; definition of, 5, 257n6

Humanitarian agencies, 81. *See also* Aid agencies

Humanitarian assistance: advocacy and information campaigns, 107, 108–9; armed security forces and, 103; branches of humanitarian tradition, 92; business model of, 152, 162, 164, 240; criticisms and critiques of, 113–16, 134, 159, 161–62, 229–35; definitions of, 90, 93–94; expansion and institutionalization of, 160–61, 163–69; funding for, 160–61;

history of, 92; instrumentalization of humanitarian aid, 100–110, 239; integration and coherence agendas for, 102; justice, politics, and principles of, 90, 92–93, 160–61; militarization of, 102–4, 116–21, 239; military escorts and, 104; neutrality and, 101; politicization of, 99–102; professionalization and standardization of, 162–69, 243; securitization of, 102–4, 117–21; violence against aid workers and, 99–101; who and what of, 93–100. *See also* Aid and aid work; Aid workers

Humanitarian exceptionalism: aid workers as mythical figures or ordinary people, 129–38, 170; challenges and paradoxes, 128–29, 228–35; concepts and definition of, 6–9, 47–48, 65, 87, 90–91, 224–25; legal codification of, 197–207; logic of, 110–13; relational dimensions and, 240; security management and, 174–75, 213, 227, 243; separation of aid workers and aid recipients and, 9, 45, 53, 161–63, 193–94, 213–17, 227; winning of, 196. *See also* Aid and aid work; Aid workers; Exceptionalism and exceptionalizing; Humanitarian assistance

Humanitarian intervention, 258n8

Humanitarian inviolability, 261n39, 266n49

Humanitarianism: agendas of, 97, 120; blame and, 125; as a career, 137, 162–63; compassion tradition of, 94, 110–11, 157; contemporary post-9/11 humanitarianism, 1–4, 48, 50, 53, 68–69; crisis of, 1, 51, 188–89; deconstruction of, 44; definitions of, 94–95; essence of, 41; exploitation of, 112; founding story of Solferino, 37–41; goals of, 94, 97; integration/coherence agenda of, 91, 102, 112, 201, 259n11; justice, 112, 195; legal codification of humanitarian exceptionalism, 197–207; mercy and, 110–12, 193–95; "moral untouchability" of, 6, 56, 87; motives and agendas of, 92, 97, 224; perceptions of, 42; politics of, 92–100; privilege and paternalism of, 195; recommendations, 58–65; relational nature of, 8, 42, 44–45, 53, 93, 157, 194, 195, 207, 215, 224–25, 235–40; security management and, 25–26, 50–51, 119–20, 224; themes of, 90; typologies of, 259n15; whole of government approach of, 98, 102. *See also* Aid in danger

Humanitarianism – principles, 8–9; acceptance and, 222–23; accountability, 159, 164, 241, 242; accompaniment, 194; demonstration of, 194, 232; dilemmas of, 161, 194, 210, 229; function of, 193–94, 232; hiring and staffing and, 194; of the ICRC, 41, 96, 101, 112; importance of, 241; justice, politics, and principles of, 90, 92–93; primary principles of humanitarian action, 95–96, 245; principled inviolability, 266n49; protective measures, 112, 171, 177, 218; security management and, 93, 185, 218, 235–36, 242; solidarity, 98, 194, 243; violence and, 100; visual and fundraising representations of disaster-affected populations, 159

Humanitarianism, principles

—humanity: aid agencies and workers and, 80, 149, 160; definitions and concepts of, 5, 8, 41–45, 80, 95–100, 131, 195, 205, 244; equality and, 195; erosion and reclaiming of, 50, 53, 88, 145, 226–35, 237; hierarchies of, 43–45, 195, 199, 204–6, 213, 225, 241–42; instrumentalization of humanitarian aid and, 100–110; protection of civilians and, 205; a recommended way forward and, 58–59; relational approach and, 8–9; security management and, 8, 175, 222–23, 236, 243–45; separation of aid workers and recipients and, 9, 45, 53, 161–63, 193–94, 213–17, 227

—impartiality: aid agencies and workers and, 149, 194, 228; aid delivery and, 78, 80; Biafran operation and, 72; blame and, 57; Code of Conduct and, 96, 159; definitions and concepts of, 5, 8, 41–43, 95–100, 171, 177, 186–87, 193; Dunant and, 38; erosion and reclaiming of, 50, 158; hiring policies and, 194; humanitarian exceptionalism and, 6; humanitarian inviolability and, 111–12, 186–87, 193, 261n39; humanitarians and, 229; instrumentalization of humanitarian aid and, 100–110; security management and, 25; Sri Lankan killings and, 29; UN and, 24, 93

Humanitarianism, principles (*continued*)
—independence: aid agencies and workers and, 34, 80, 149, 194, 228; armed escort and, 202; definitions and concepts of, 8, 41–43, 95–100, 187, 193; Code of Conduct and, 96; erosion and reclaiming of, 50, 158; humanitarian inviolability and, 193; instrumentalization of humanitarian aid and, 100–110; legal protection and, 201; security management and, 25; Sri Lankan killings and, 29; UN and, 24
—neutrality: aid agencies and workers and, 34, 57, 80, 149, 194, 201, 228; aid delivery and, 78, 80; armed escort and, 202; Biafran operation and, 72; blame and, 57; Code of Conduct and, 96; definitions and concepts of, 5, 41, 42, 95–102, 171, 177, 186–87, 193; Dunant and, 38; erosion and reclaiming of, 50, 131, 158, 177; Geneva Conventions and, 40; genocide and, 97; hiring policies and, 194; humanitarian exceptionalism and, 6; humanitarian inviolability and, 111–12, 186–87, 193, 261n39; humanitarians and, 95, 229; instrumentalization of humanitarian aid and, 100–110; legal protection and, 201; Red Cross and, 178; security management and, 236, 243; staff in Darfur and, 167; UN and, 91, 93
Humanitarian negotiation, 38, 105–6, 175, 221–22. *See also* Security management, specific strategies
Humanitarians: civilian character of, 202, 204; legal codification of humanitarian exceptionalism, 197–207; power and, 229–31; risks of, 41, 42; targeted attacks against, 201–2, 222, 232; UN and, 201; view of humanitarianism, 42; view of military involvement, 210; views of, 163; as visibly branded outsiders, 193. *See also* Aid workers; Civilians; Humanitarianism
Humanitarians, Dunantist (purist): arguments of, 112–13; ICRC as, 96; political dimensions of aid and, 102; primary principles of humanitarian action and, 95–96; as purist humanitarian actors, 96, 97
Humanitarians, exceptionalist: arguments of, 91–92, 110–13; exceptionalizing aid and aid workers, 4–8, 65, 68; implications of, 6; preserving the logic of, 110–13; recommendations for a way forward, 58–65; relational approach to, 8–9; roots of, 6–7, 90–91; violence and, 47, 110, 112
Humanitarians, Wilsonian (integrationist or political): arguments of, 91, 97, 112–13; minimalist and maximalist, 98; neutrality and, 97–98
Humanity. *See* Humanitarianism, principles: humanity
Humanity law, 43
Human resource management, 143
Human Rights Commission (Sri Lanka), 29
Hutus. *See* Rwanda

IAM. *See* International Assistance Mission
IASC. *See* Inter-Agency Standing Committee
ICC. *See* International Criminal Court
ICRC. *See* International Committee of the Red Cross
IDPs. *See* Internally displaced persons
IFRC. *See* International Federation of the Red Cross and Red Crescent Societies
IHL. *See* International Humanitarian Law
IIL. *See* Institute of International Law
Immigration, 203
Impartiality. *See* Humanitarianism, principles: impartiality
Independence. *See* Humanitarianism, principles: independence
Indonesia. *See* West Timor, Indonesia (2000)
Institute of International Law (IIL), 93–95
Insurance issues. *See* Security
Integrated Regional Information Networks (IRIN), 167
InterAction, 170, 179–80, 184
Inter-Agency Standing Committee (IASC), 150, 265n36
Internally displaced persons (IDPs), 150, 167, 169. *See also* Refugees
Internal vulnerabilities. *See* Vulnerabilities, internal
International Assistance Mission (IAM; Afghanistan), 107, 122, 168, 192, 267n63
International Committee for Relief to the Wounded, 39

International Committee of the Red Cross (ICRC): attacks against, 18, 27, 66, 69–70, 72, 77, 83, 121, 176–79, 189, 222, 251n3, 273n70; Code of Conduct, 148; criticisms and critiques of, 258n14; exploration of security measures by, 69–70; founders, founding, and history of, 39, 40, 153–55; funding of, 107; Geneva Conventions and role of, 40–41; humanitarian security and, 176; immunity from attack of, 112; Nobel Peace Prize winner, 149, 265n33; principles of, 41, 96, 101, 112; protective value of the Red Cross emblem, 202; security cell of, 176; security management and, 242; Taliban and, 219; use of military escorts by, 104; withdrawal of delegates, 189

International Committee of the Red Cross (ICRC), specific countries: Afghanistan, 219, 273n70; Baghdad, Iraq, 18, 189; Biafra, 108; Chechnya, 83, 121–22, 176–79; Dessié, Ethiopia, 66; Nigeria/Biafra, 70–73; Somalia, 107–8, 176; Sri Lanka, 27, 189

International Criminal Court (ICC), 89, 198, 254n29

International Federation of the Red Cross and Red Crescent Societies (IFRC), 159, 202

International Humanitarian Law (IHL), 95, 96, 207

International organizations. *See* Organizations, international; *individual organizations*

International Organization for Migration, 184

International Rescue Committee, 150, 221

International Review of the Red Cross. *See Revue Internationale de la Croix-Rouge* (RICR)

International Save the Children Alliance, 150

International Security Assistance Force, 103

Intertect, 79

Iraq: aid agencies in, 161, 173, 201; armed escorts in, 202; CARE International in, 190; deaths of aid workers in, 48; funding from U.S. and UK governments in, 108, 161; Green Zone, 22–24, 42, 54, 173; Hassan, Margaret and, 189–93; humanitarianism in, 25, 111, 119; insecurity in, 51; military involvement in, 117–18, 210; reconstruction in, 116; security and security management in, 181; UN in, 54–55, 111, 259n20; U.S. and U.S. Coalition in, 23, 54–55, 117, 161; violence and kidnappings in, 18, 48, 51, 103, 117, 189, 191–92, 250n2. *See also* Baghdad, Iraq (2003); Operation Provide Comfort

Iraqi Red Crescent, 189

IRIN. *See* Integrated Regional Information Networks

Israel, 203

Italian Red Cross, 66

Italy, 66

Japanese Red Cross, 69

JCA. *See* Joint Church Aid

Jebb, Eglantyne, 152–53

Joint Church Aid (JCA), 71, 74

Jolie, Angelina, 123

Juba, South Sudan, 119–20

Kabul. *See* Afghanistan

Karzai, Hamid, 226. *See also* Afghanistan

Kashmir, Pakistan earthquake (2005), 210, 214, 220

Katanga, Zaire, 69

Kawuki, Hilda, 31, 84

Kellenburger, Jakob, 108

Kenya, 167

Khartoum. *See* Republic of the Sudan

Kidnappings. *See* Afghanistan; Chechnya; Darfur; Iraq; Violence and violent contexts

"Killing Chechnya" (article; Cuny), 80

Kosovo, 79

Kouchner, Bernard, 152, 164, 243

Kratz, Clayton, 69

League of Nations, 153

Lederach, John Paul, 59–60, 63

Legal issues: aid workers and, 6, 13, 22, 195, 205; contrasting approaches to, 204–7; duty to protect and of care, 205–7, 225, 244; humanity law, 43; ICRC mandate, 242, 261n37; inhumanity, 43; insurance and liability, 143–44, 185, 224, 230, 244; investigations, arrests, and punishments, 204, 207; laws regulating armed conflict

Legal issues (*continued*)
and war, 197, 199–200, 202; legal codification of exceptionalism, 197–207; misuse of Red Cross emblem, 40, 202–3, 271n46; relational approaches to the law, 225; respect for the law, 204. *See also* Crime and criminals; United Nations Resolutions; *individual laws and conventions*
Leslie, Andrew, 118
Liberation Tigers of Tamil Eelam (LTTE; Sri Lanka), 26–30, 89
Liberia, 40, 176
Lifestyle choices. *See* Aid workers; Vulnerabilities, internal
Lindt, August, 72
Local Capacities for Peace project, 160. *See also* CDA Collaborative Learning Project
Loescher, Gilburt, 17, 116. *See also* Baghdad, Iraq (2003)
Loss of life. *See* Aid workers; Violence and violent contexts
LTTE. *See* Liberation Tigers of Tamil Eelam

Ma, Yo-Yo, 123
Maathai, Wangari, 123
Machar, Riek, 155
Malloy, Nancy, 178
Matthews, David, 78
Maunoir, Théodore, 39
McCune, Emma, 154–55
MDGs. *See* Millennium Development Goals
Médecins Sans Frontières (MSF): advocacy activities of, 108; after-work activities of, 134; in Angola, 196; Biafran aid operation and, 70; in Chechnya, 177–78; in the Democratic Republic of Congo, 151; founding of, 252n12; income of, 260n32; in Iraq, 189; Nobel Peace Prize of, 149; programming of, 261n36; revenues of, 107; in Rwanda, 161; witnessing by, 252n12, 259n16, 260n35
Médecins Sans Frontières International (MSF International), 150
Media: coverage of aid and aid workers, 78, 121; coverage of aid-worker attacks, deaths, and kidnappings, 51, 76, 191, 232; coverage of Baghdad, Iraq bombing, 49; coverage of Biafran War, 70; coverage of crime and violence, 51–52, 84–85; coverage of death of Hassan, Margaret, 191; coverage of deaths of ICRC expatriate staff members in Chechnya, 177–78; coverage of deaths of national staff members, 32; images of aid as rescue and, 123; fairy-tale narratives of, 122–25; military and, 259n24; relationships between aid workers and the media, 121
Memory of Solferino, A (Dunant), 37, 39. *See also* Solferino, Italy (1859)
Mennonite Central Committee/Mennonite Relief Unit, 69
Mental health issues, 138–45, 206, 215, 237, 271n51
Menu of Options (United Nations), 184
Mercy Corps, 150, 257n1
Merlin (British aid agency), 79
Military issues: child soldiers, 105; irregular forces, 105–6; blurred lines between military actors and civilians, 2–3, 50, 68, 73, 102–3, 118–21, 188, 210, 217, 230–31, 233, 239, 256n44; militarized charity, 103; neutrality and negotiating with, 104; pillaging, 106; purpose of, 94, 95, 96; targeting of aid workers, 105, 119, 259n24
Millennium Development Goals (MDGs), 262n2
Minimum operating standards for security (MOSS; United Nations, InterAction), 21, 25, 183, 184
Mohonk Criteria for Humanitarian Assistance (1994), 159
Mortensen, Greg, 265n31
MOSS. *See* Minimum operating standards for security
Moynier, Gustave, 39, 41
Mozambique, 102
MSF. *See* Médecins Sans Frontières
MSF International. *See* Médecins Sans Frontières International
Multimandate agencies, 5, 81, 259n16
Multi-National Force, 119
Muslim Home Guard (Sri Lanka), 28
Muttur, Sri Lanka (2006), 15; accusations, investigations, and explanations, 28–30; lessons of, 30–32, 45, 53; politicized nature of aid in, 27–32; secessionist war in (1983–2009), 27, 29–30; security management in, 56; violence and loss of life in, 26–28, 30, 32, 249n18. *See also* Action Contre La Faim; Sri Lanka

Nairobi, 89
Napoleon III, 37
Natsios, Andrew, 116
Neutrality. *See* Humanitarianism, principles: neutrality
New York Review of Books, 80
NGOs. *See* Organizations, nongovernmental
Nigeria, 69, 70–73. *See also* Biafran War
Nigerian Red Cross, 72
Nightingale, Florence, 16, 38–39
Nobel Peace Prize, 149, 265n33
No-go zones, 184–85, 236
Nongovernmental organizations. *See* Organizations, nongovernmental
Norwegian People's Aid, 98

Obama (Barack) administration, 46–47, 117
OCHA. *See* Office for the Coordination of Humanitarian Assistance
ODI. *See* Overseas Development Institute
OECD. *See* Organisation for Economic Co-operation and Development
Office for the Coordination of Humanitarian Assistance (UN; OCHA), 102, 166, 259n18
Office of the UN Security Coordinator (UN; UNSECOORD), 21, 179, 248n7
"One" campaign, 109
Operation Provide Comfort (Iraq; 1991), 80
Optional Protocol to the Convention on the Safety of United Nations and Associated Personnel (2005), 198, 199, 200
Organisation for Economic Co-operation and Development (OECD), 150
Organizations: acceptance approaches and, 218–23, 243; attacks on, 190; demands for accountability and oversight for, 152; effects of incidents on, 206; founding stories of, 153; informal and idealized past, 149–57, 163–69, 171; institutional and professional present, 149–52, 157–63, 171; level of security of, 165; management issues of, 174; numbers of, 149; perceptions of, 165; recession of 2008 and, 151; security incidents and, 238; security management of, 184; shift from charity to business model of, 152, 162, 164, 240; types of, 149; winners of Nobel Peace Prizes, 149. *See also* Aid agencies; Security; Security management; Staff; *individual organizations*
Organizations – nongovernmental (NGOs): in Afghanistan, 133, 260n31; "big seven" American organizations, 150; business model of, 152, 162, 164, 240; codes of conduct of, 96, 159; demands of, 166; fortification and militarization of security by, 119; founding and history of, 155–58, 164; funding and revenues of, 108, 149–50; hiring policies of, 165; humanitarianism of, 259n16; insecurity and, 185; in Iraq, 18, 201; legal protections of, 201; mission requirements of, 151–52; NGO voluntarism, 155; numbers and proliferation of, 149, 161–62; perceptions of, 29, 155–56, 166–67; perks and privilege of, 132–33; professionalization of, 53, 157–58, 161–65, 175, 181, 185, 206, 217, 240, 243; safety offices, 183–84, 260n31, 269n20; scandals of, 159; security and security management of, 52, 179–80, 184, 211; security coordinating bodies for, 253n20; in Sri Lanka, 26, 29; task expansion of, 150, 158; visibility of, 196; in war zones, 201. *See also individual organizations*
Overseas Development Institute (ODI), 109, 180
Oxfam, 150, 153
Oxfam International, 150
Oxford Committee for Famine Relief (1942), 153
Oxford Manual on War (1880), 40

Pakistan: earthquake response of 2005, 165, 167–68, 170, 210, 214, 220; risks in, 2; security and security management in, 47, 181; Taliban in, 116; USAID logos in, 117, 261n42; violence in, 117, 167–68
Peace Corps, 78
Pictet, Jean, 42–43, 70, 96, 101
Political issues: change and, 94; development and peacebuilding, 94; need for political awareness, 113; politically motivated crimes, 85; politicization of humanitarianism, 44, 87, 92–100, 187; politicization and violence, 99; politicization of violence, 47; U.S. and European use of humanitarian assistance, 158

Political issues, politicization of aid: causes of violence and, 47, 114, 126, 239; criticism of, 87; foreign policies and, 116–17; government agendas and, 93, 101–2, 239; increase in incidents and, 82; influence of aid workers and, 230; in Sri Lanka, 28–32; threat and risk and, 2–3; violence against aid workers and, 99

Posttraumatic stress disorder (PTSD), 139

Poverty and violence, 120

Powell, Colin, 116–17

Prendergast, Kieran, 22, 227

Principles of humanitarian action. *See* Humanitarianism, principles

Private security actors, 103, 117–18, 120–21, 135, 170, 182–84, 209–11, 222

Professionalization. *See* Aid agencies; Humanitarian assistance; Organizations, nongovernmental; Security management; Staff

Protection and protective measures: for aid workers and civilians, 205; assuming protection in an age of fear and terror, 188–97; effects of, 3; end of symbolic protection, 26, 105, 186–90, 225; Geneva Conventions and, 96; hierarchies of differential protection, 195, 199, 204–6, 225, 241–42; humanitarian principles, 112; law as protection, 197–207; "magic shields," 112, 174, 186–87; mental and emotional effects of aid work and, 206; minimum set of protections in armed conflict, 202; legal use of, 40; misuse of, 40, 96; remote management and, 208; targeting of, 66. *See also* Exceptionalism and exceptionalizing; Humanitarian exceptionalism; Security; Security management

Protection and protective measures, emblems and logos: of agencies, 187, 193, 195–97, 202–3; exemptions, 250n27; protective coloring, 186–88, 190, 194–96; Red Cross/Red Crescent, 39, 40, 66, 69–70, 96, 178, 186, 187, 202–3, 250n27, 271n46; Red Crystal, 202; UN flag and laurel, 22, 26, 32, 186, 187, 202–3. *See also* Exceptionalism and exceptionalizing; Humanitarian exceptionalism; Security management, specific strategies

Protection of civilians. *See* Civilians, protection of

Providence Principles (1993), 159

Provincial Reconstruction Teams (PRTs; Afghanistan; Iraq), 118, 254n30

PTSD. *See* Mental health issues; Posttraumatic stress disorder

Ransom. *See* Violence and violent contexts

Red Cross/Red Crescent, 39, 40, 69, 72, 79, 186, 189. *See also* International Committee of the Red Cross; *individual countries*

Red Cross emblem, 40, 66, 69–70, 96, 186–88, 198, 202–3, 250n27

Red Cross Movement, 41

Red Cross NGO Code of Conduct in Disaster Response, 96, 159

Refugees, 150, 158, 161, 169

Registry for Engineers in Disaster Relief (RedR), 180

Relationships. *See* Aid and aid work; Aid workers; Humanitarianism; Security management

Relief actors. *See* Aid workers; Humanitarians; Staff

Relief work. *See* Aid and aid work; Humanitarianism

Remote management. *See* Security management, specific strategies

Republic of South Sudan, 78, 119–20, 135, 154, 219

Republic of the Sudan: activities of Stephen Templeton in, 78; aid agency accusations, 79; dangers in, 156; expulsion of aid agencies from, 83, 257n1, 261n36; fortified aid compounds in, 119–20; humanitarian access and assistance in, 101, 102, 184–85; increase in incidents in, 75; Khartoum, 119–20; trust of aid workers in, 167; violence, kidnappings, and deaths in, 256n39; withdrawal of UN from, 89, 186

Research and analysis: aggregated and global numbers, rates, and trends in, 82–84; analytical challenges of, 47–48, 53–58, 76–77, 82; definitional challenges of, 77–81; differential risk, 85; emphasis on violence and fatalities, 83–84; fieldwork challenges and controversies of, 255n32, 255n36; global trend analysis, 82;

interdisciplinary and multidimensional approach to, 91; methodological challenges of, 68; necessity of analyzing differential risks, 145; necessity of disaggregation, 145; practical challenges of, 47–53; recommendations for a way forward, 58–65; research findings, 81–86; "why" question, 85. *See also* Aid in danger; Violence and violent contexts

Resources, 160, 161. *See also* Donors and donor community; Funding and fund raising

Revue Internationale de la Croix-Rouge (RICR; *International Review of the Red Cross*), 69

Risk management, 2, 86–87, 145, 148, 208–9, 254n24

Risk threshold. *See* Security management

Risk transfer. *See* Security management

Risks. *See* Aid agencies; Aid workers; Security management; Threats, external; Vulnerabilities, internal

Rome Statute (1998), 198

Russia, 80, 179

Russian Federal Security Service, 79

Russian Red Cross, 79

Russo-Japanese War (1904–1905), 69

Rwanda (1994): conflict resolution in, 157; development aid in, 115; humanitarian assistance in, 101; military protection in, 103; "One UN" pilots in, 102; reforms in, 215; refugees in, 158–59; security challenges in, 176

Rwandan Patriotic Front, 158

Safety, 77

Samaritan's Purse, 31–32

Sana'a, Yemen, 69

Sarajevo, Bosnia-Herzegovina, 80. *See also* Yugoslavia

Save the Children, 69, 148, 150, 152–53, 260n33, 265n36

Saving Lives Together (SLT; United Nations), 183, 184, 260n19

Security: aid as rescue and, 123–24; for aid operations, 2; evolution of humanitarian assistance and, 163–69; humanitarian security, 176; individual responsibility for, 148–49; insurance and liability issues, 185, 224, 230; merging of development and security, 119–20; militarization of, 119–20; relational ethos of humanitarianism, 193; staffing issues and, 137–38, 165, 166; stress of aid work and, 138–45. *See also* Violence and violent contexts

Security incidents and lapses: of aid agencies, 5, 31–32, 142, 147; aid-agency programming and, 168–69; cultural clashes and, 134–35; definition of, 77; driving habits and incidents, 132, 135, 210, 220; historical views of, 156; increase in, 75t, 238–39; recommendations for, 58–65; risks of, 173; staffing issues and, 137–38, 165, 166, 238; stress and, 142, 237–38. *See also* Baghdad, Iraq (2003); Biafran War (Nigeria-Biafra; 1966–1970); Chechnya; (Muttur, Sri Lanka (2006); Solferino, Italy (1859); Threats, external; Violence and violent contexts; Vulnerabilities, internal

Security management: aid agencies and, 13–14, 168–73, 211, 224, 242; analytical approach to violence and, 240; approaches to and delegation of, 173–74, 182–83, 205–7; armed escort/protection, 3, 103–4, 110, 170, 174, 176, 202, 207–9, 211; community-policing model of, 244; core principles of aid and, 9; countermeasures of, 52; costs of, 211, 224; dilemmas of, 210; effectiveness of, 82, 208; effects of, 9, 13–14, 25, 26, 52, 53; evolution of, 156, 175–80; exceptionalism and, 156–57; general picture of, 227, 234; humanitarianism and, 25–26, 53; of the ICRC, 242; inadequate or inappropriate procedures and measures, 170–71, 227, 237; individual responsibility and, 152; military and private security and, 182, 209–12; need for additional information regarding, 82–83; operational measures of, 13; perceptions of organizations and, 165, 243–44; principles or politics and, 93; procedures related to perimeter and compound security, 20, 176, 211, 213, 227; professionalization and standardization of, 24–26, 175, 180–85, 215, 243; programming and, 208, 212, 219, 238, 242, 243; relational character of aid and, 8, 175, 209, 225, 235–40, 243–45; risks of, 211–12; risk thresholds, 77, 173, 184; risk

Security management (*continued*)
  transfer, 36, 138, 184; security officers and directors, 181–83, 190, 218, 268n15; security restrictions for aid workers, 211, 212; "soft" targets, 22–23, 25, 54, 55, 103–4, 119, 184, 227; staff and staff hiring and turnover, 168, 183; training for, 179–80, 203, 210, 214, 215, 234, 263n15; typology of security management tendencies, 234–35; of the UN, 22–25, 184, 203; withdrawal and evacuation, 192, 195, 207, 210. *See also* Baghdad, Iraq (2003); Chechnya; Protection and protective measures
Security management, paradigms: assumptive paradigm, 174, 186–97, 218, 225, 227, 243; basic paradigms of, 13, 174–75; legal mechanisms, 174–75; operational security management, 175
Security management, specific systems: contrasting approaches, 193–97; field-based strategies, 207–9; fortified/fortress, 12, 25, 26, 49, 53, 104, 119, 175, 190, 239, 244; hardened approaches, 182, 184, 192–93, 207, 209–13; militarized, 22, 119–20, 170, 176, 239; operational, 207–9; professionalized, 53, 175, 236; relationally-based approaches, 192–93. *See also* Baghdad, Iraq (2003)
Security management, specific strategies: acceptance and negotiated access, 167, 190, 207–9, 211, 217–23, 243, 244, 267n60, 268n15, 270n39, 272n69; alliance, 209; avoidance, 209; community-based approaches, 208; consent-based approaches, 209, 225; deterrence, 207–14, 216, 218, 224, 227, 235–36, 243, 268n15; effective strategies, 208; engagement, 209; fortress/protection strategies (hardened security), 207–8, 209–14, 216–18, 223–24, 226–27, 235–36, 243, 244, 250n6, 268n15; hard and soft power strategies, 212, 218; normalization of danger and, 213–17, 236; remote management or control, 49, 119, 189, 207–13, 223, 224; risk management, 208–9; stealth programming, 208; systems-based approaches, 208
Self-generated vulnerabilities. *See* Vulnerabilities, internal
September 11, 2001, 46, 49

Sierra Leone, 108
SiND (Security in Numbers Database). *See* Databases
SLT. *See* Saving Lives Together
Small arms and light weapons, 31, 106
Solferino, Italy (1859), 15, 37–42
Solidarity, 98, 194, 243
Somalia: armed escorts in, 202, 209; expulsion of faith-based aid agencies from, 168; humanitarian access and assistance in, 102, 184–85; ICRC in, 107; increase in incidents and violence in, 75, 158, 176; negotiations in, 225; risks in, 2; security and security management in, 181; "technicals" in, 173; UN withdrawal from, 89; World Food Programme in, 107–8
Somaliland, 166
Soros Foundation, 80
South Sudan. *See* Republic of South Sudan
Sphere Project (2000), 98, 159, 162
Sri Lanka, 27, 29, 32, 89, 234, 238. *See also* Muttur, Sri Lanka (2006)
Sri Lanka Monitoring Mission, 28
Sri Lankan Naval Special Authorities, 28
Staff: differential risks of, 195; duty-of-care standards and, 143–44, 225; hierarchies of, 195; hiring policies, 165–66, 168, 194, 219–20, 238; lines between private and public, 146; professionalization of, 162–64; qualifications of, 162, 165; as representatives of organizations, 146, 148; security issues and, 90, 137–38, 164, 168, 185, 207, 225; sought-after skill sets of, 163; stresses and vulnerabilities of, 138–45. *See also* Aid agencies; Aid workers; Humanitarianism, principles: humanity; Humanitarians
Staff, expatriate and international: acceptance of, 167; activities and behaviors of, 146; blogging by, 136; characteristics of, 137, 138; in Chechnya, 176–77; cultural contexts of aid work of, 57, 146; driving and driving habits of, 132, 135, 210, 220; early research and, 77; in emergency situations, 212; evacuation of, 160, 220; inequalities of, 216; lines between private and public, 146; loss of life of, 81; ordinariness of, 136; remote management and, 208, 213; as organization representatives, 146; risks of, 272n52;

Index 319

as security professionals, 181; in Sri Lanka, 28; stresses, vulnerabilities, and security of, 140–43; in violent contexts, 5; value of lives of, 44; withdrawal of, 49, 195
Staff, local, 28, 49, 213
Staff, national: acceptance of, 167; characteristics of, 137; early research and, 77; in emergency situations, 212; employment and placement of, 151; evacuation of, 160, 195; hiring policies and, 219–20; increases in, 194; inequalities of, 216; loss of life of, 81; protective coloring and, 194; remote management and, 208, 213; as reputational interlocutors for aid agencies, 135; risks of, 272n52; as security officers, 181; stresses and vulnerabilities of, 140–41; value of lives of, 44; violence against in Sri Lanka, 27–28, 32; in violent contexts, 49; work in active war zones, 201
Starr, Gregory, 248n7
States. *See* Governments and states
Steering Committee for Humanitarian Response, 150, 265n36
Sudan. *See* Republic of the Sudan
Swedish Red Cross, 72
Swiss Confederation, 40

Tafari Makonnen American hospital (Dessié, Ethiopia, 1936), 66
Taliban, 107, 116, 192. *See also* Afghanistan; Pakistan
Targeted violence. *See* Aid in danger; Humanitarians
Templeton, Stephen, 78
Terror/terrorism and counterterrorism, 55–56, 117, 120, 191, 232, 251n7. *See also* War on terror
Threats – external: acceptance and, 208; aid agencies and, 56, 239; analysis of, 58–65, 68, 86, 100; causes of, 230–31; embedded framework of violence and, 63–64; deterrence and, 209; dominance of external threats, 32, 47, 56, 91; after Pakistan earthquake of 2005, 165–66; reactions to, 3; responsibility for violence of, 3, 36–37; security management and, 212, 216. *See also* Security management; Violence and violent contexts; Vulnerabilities, internal

Training. *See* Security management
Tsunami (Indian Ocean, 2004), 29, 98–99, 150, 210, 232, 269n26, 274n5
Tutsis. *See* Rwanda

Uganda, 109, 169, 202
UN. *See* United Nations
UNDSS. *See* United Nations Department of Safety and Security
UNICEF. *See* United Nations Children's Fund; United Nations International Children's Emergency Fund
United Nations (UN): al-Qaeda threats against, 117; contracting with, 204; deaths and murders of staff members, 204; Declaration of the Rights of the Child and, 153; emergency relief coordinator (ERC) in, 102; field security training, 52; humanitarianism of, 98; integration agenda of, 102, 201; in Iraq and, 54–55, 111–12; legal protections for, 200–201; linkage with independent humanitarians, 201; mission requirements of, 151; neutrality and impartiality of, 111–12; NGOs and, 184; Nobel Peace Prize and, 265n33; One UN pilots, 102; peacekeepers, 198, 199, 201; perceptions of, 24; sanctions, 55; security management of, 22–25, 49, 56, 179, 184, 215, 248n3, 261n44; security standards for, 21; situations of exceptional risk and, 199; targeting of, 21, 132, 203; treaties and conventions of, 197–98, 199; U.S. and, 23–24, 55; violence against, 105, 198, 203. *See also* Algiers, Algeria bombing (2007); Annan, Kofi; Baghdad, Iraq (2003); Iraq; Office for the Coordination of Humanitarian Assistance; Protection and protective measures; *individual countries*
United Nations, programs, 21, 55, 77
United Nations Charter, 23
United Nations Children's Fund (UNICEF), 154
United Nations Department of Safety and Security (UNDSS), 21, 179, 184, 185, 227, 248n7, 261n44
United Nations International Children's Emergency Fund (UNICEF). *See* United Nations Children's Fund

United Nations Office for the Coordination of Humanitarian Affairs Consolidated Appeals Process, 179. *See also* Office for the Coordination of Humanitarian Assistance

United Nations Security Council, 22, 23, 105, 198, 199

United Nations Security Council Resolutions: 1483 (role of the UN in Iraq, 2003), 23, 248n12; 1502 (protection of UN personnel, 2003), 13, 22, 198–99, 205, 248n12; 1546 (humanitarian and security functions in Iraq, 2004), 23

United States (U.S.), 158. *See also* Afghanistan; Baghdad, Iraq (2003)

United States Agency for International Development (USAID), 116, 117, 149–50, 261n42

Universal Declaration of Human Rights (UN, 1948), 44

University Teachers for Human Rights (UTHR), 28

UNSECOORD. *See* Office of the UN Security Coordinator

UN Security Awareness Induction Training, 214

UN Staff Association, 25

U.S. *See* United States

USAID. *See* United States Agency for International Development

UTHR. *See* University Teachers for Human Rights

Veness, David, 21
Vietnam, 108
Vietnam, South, 79
Violence and violent contexts: accidents, 256n43; aid agencies and workers and, 41–42, 48, 191, 230, 249n20; analysis of, 236–37, 240; assistance and, 5, 160; decrease in violence, 83; deterrence and, 209; dynamics of, 45; effects of, 89; embedded framework of, 63–64; external threats and, 47, 48; historical view of, 156–57; humanitarianism and, 43; humanitarian principles and, 100, 235–40; internal vulnerability and, 47, 48, 57–58; kidnappings and ransom, 1, 18, 31–32, 48, 51, 67, 74, 75t, 78, 83–84, 106–7, 178, 179, 189–92, 213, 217, 219–22, 225, 250n2, 270n37; loss of life in, 26–27, 30, 32, 48, 220–21; military and, 95, 188; need for multidimensional analysis of, 12; normalization of danger, 213–17; as performance or theater, 191; pillaging and, 106; political motivations of, 85, 100; poverty and, 120; provision of aid in, 5, 232; recommendations for, 58–65; relational approaches and, 62, 64, 235–40; search for blame for, 56–57; soft and hard targets, 119, 227; as tragedy, 60–62, 64; understanding and prevention of, 60–62; withdrawal and evacuation during, 207. *See also* Aid in danger; Aid workers; Baghdad, Iraq (2003); Chechnya; Muttur, Sri Lanka (2006); Security incidents and lapses; Solferino, Italy (1859); Threats, external; Vulnerabilities, internal; Warfare and armed conflict

Violence and violent contexts, causal mechanisms: exclusionary analysis and, 2–3; external threats and internal vulnerabilities and, 47–48, 90–91, 230–40; framework of violence, 63; humanitarian exceptionalism and, 6; humanitarian principles and, 100–110; kidnapping and murder of Hassan, Margaret, 191–93; motives for, 85–88, 100; in Muttur, Sri Lanka, 28–32; politicization of aid, 47, 100, 114, 126, 239; public secrets and, 58; social and relational processes, 60–62; vignettes of, 32–37. *See also* Political issues; Threats, external; Vulnerabilities, internal

von Rosen, Carl Gustaf, 72–74

Vulnerabilities, internal: accounting for, 145–49; aid agency programming, 168–69; aid agency reluctance to recognize, 56–58; boundaries between civilians and the military and, 119–20; in Chechnya, 178; codes of conduct and, 147–49; culture clashes, 134; in Darfur, Sudan, 167; embedded framework of violence and, 63–64; implicit messages, 160; invisibility of, 90–91; after Pakistan earthquake of 2005, 165–66; perceptions of humanitarians and, 233–34, 240–41; public silencing and public secrets of, 12, 30, 57–58, 125; security management and, 217, 224; staff actions and staffing and, 146, 166–67,

194–95, 238. *See also* Baghdad, Iraq (2003); Muttur, Sri Lanka (2006)
Vulnerabilities, internal: responsibility for violence: analysis and framework of, 236–38; concepts and explanations of, 6, 31–37, 62–65, 91–92, 223, 231–32; differential risk and, 86; humanitarian exceptionalism and, 3; Pakistan earthquake response and, 165–66; silencing and invisibility of, 125, 171–72

Wagner, Flavia, 31–32, 84, 143
Walker, Peter, 94–95
Walzer, Gerald, 20
Walzer Panel, 20–21, 24
War crimes. *See* Crime and criminals
Warfare and armed conflict: civilians and humanitarians, 205; efforts to limit, 40; humanitarianism and, 43; international and internal conflicts, 201–2; protections in, 201–2, 205. *See also* Violence and violent contexts

"War on terror," 1, 23, 46, 48, 50, 116, 117, 161. *See also* Terrorism
Washington Post, 78
Weapons and weaponry, 106
Well-fed dead, 95
West Africa, 134
West Timor, Indonesia (2000), 127, 169
WFP. *See* World Food Programme (UN)
Wilsonian actors. *See* Humanitarians, Wilsonian
Witnesses: humanitarians as, 41, 108, 131, 213, 230; ICRC delegates as, 154; MSF as, 252n12, 259n16, 260n35
World Food Programme (UN; WFP), 21, 77
World Vision International (WVI), 150, 168, 265n35

Yemen, 69, 154
Yugoslavia, 40, 176. *See also* Sarajevo

Zaire, 158, 166. *See also* Democratic Republic of Congo

ACKNOWLEDGMENTS

This book represents more than a decade of research and practice. Although my name appears on the front cover, I owe a debt of gratitude to many individuals who have encouraged me and contributed to my thinking about the dilemmas of providing aid in danger, especially those named and unnamed individuals who trusted me with their stories. I thank all of those who gave of their time and shared their insights with me as I conducted research for this book. In accordance with their wishes, I have not listed those individuals who agreed to speak with me but asked to remain anonymous. The people who participated in formal interviews and who agreed to share their names and affiliations include the following: Mary Anderson (executive director, Collaborative for Development Action, Inc. [CDA]); Shawn Bardwell (safety and security coordinator, Office of Foreign Disaster Assistance, U.S. Agency for International Development [USAID]); John Berry (consultant); Susan Brock (consultant); Patrick Brugger (delegate in charge of the Security Unit, International Committee of the Red Cross [ICRC]); Warren Buttery (global security advisor, Mercy Corps); Penelope Curling (stress counselor, United Nations Children's Fund [UNICEF]); Mark Cutts (chief, Field Response Section, Internal Displacement Division, Office for the Coordination of Humanitarian Assistance [OCHA]); James Darcy (director of humanitarian programmes, Overseas Development Institute [ODI]); Pascal Daudin (director of global safety and security, CARE International); Paul Davies (independent aid and security consultant); Antonio Donini (senior researcher, Feinstein International Center, Tufts University); Daniel Endres (acting deputy director, Division of Operational Services, Emergency Technical Support Service, UN High Commissioner for Refugees [UNHCR]); Paul Farrell (deputy security coordinator and Operations Centre manager, Office of Emergency Programs, UNICEF); Bill Gent (security coordinator, UNICEF); Paul Harvey (research fellow, ODI); Lucy Hodgson (security training coordinator, Registry for Engineers in Disaster Relief–IHE); Sulayman Khuri (senior field safety advisor, Field Safety Section, Emergency and Security Service, UNHCR); Dennis King (analyst, Humanitarian Information Unit, U.S. Department of State); Eric LeGuen (global safety and security advisor, International Rescue Committee); Gil Loescher (senior research fellow, Centre for International Studies, Oxford University); Randy Martin (director of global emergency operations, Mercy Corps); Larry Minear (director, Humanitarianism and War Project, Feinstein International Center, Tufts University); Sorcha O'Callaghan (research officer, ODI); Michael O'Neill (director, Global Safety and Security, Save the Children–US); Robert Painter (humanitarian security advisor, UN Department of Safety and Security [UNDSS]); Laky Pissalidis (senior security advisor, International Services, American Red Cross); Karina Purushotma (Feinstein International Center, Tufts University); Elisabeth Rasmusson (resident representative, Geneva, Norwegian Refugee Council [NRC]); Jean Renouf (coordinator, European InterAgency Security Forum [EISF]); John Schafer (security coordinator, InterAction); Hugo Slim (chief scholar, Centre for Humanitarian Dialogue); David Snider (liaison officer, Emergency and Security Service, UNHCR); Ravi Solanki (senior field safety advisor, Field Safety Section, Emergency and Security Service, UNHCR); Nick Stockton (director, Humanitarian Accountability Partnership International); Lars Tangen (manager, Security Unit, International Federation of Red Cross and Red Crescent Societies [IFRC]); Peter Walker (director, Feinstein International Center, Tufts University); Thomas Weiss (presidential professor of political science and director, Ralph Bunche Institute for International Studies, Graduate Center, City University of New York); Victoria Wheeler (research fellow, ODI); and Aimee Wielechowski (field response officer, Internal Displacement Division, OCHA). Individuals' affiliations are listed as of the time of the interview.

The names of interviewees and details on the focus group participants in the field research in the occupied Palestinian territory appear in Fast (2006) and in Fast, Patterson, et al. (2011) for the research in South Sudan. The Institutional Review Board at the University of Notre Dame approved all research conducted for this book.

In addition, I offer thanks to the following people: Oliver Behn, Amaury Cooper, the late John Darby (and Marie Darby), Jan Davis, John Dyer, Chris Finucane, Heather Hughes, Trevor Hughes, Madeleine Kingston, Melissa Labonte, Melker Mabeck, Julie MacFarlane, Maarten Merkelbach, Marc Michaelson, Will Moore, Norah Niland, Michelle Parlevliet, Reg Patterson,

Christine Persaud, Elizabeth Rowley, Norm Sheehan, Sam Sherman, Jackie Smith, and Christina Wille.

In particular, I have been privileged to learn from multiple and extended conversations over the past decade with a series of colleagues turned friends. The insights of Shawn Bardwell, Pascal Daudin, John Schafer, and especially Michael O'Neill have significantly influenced the ideas I present here, and their generosity of time and ideas has proven invaluable. Likewise, Mary Anderson and Antonio Donini have profoundly shaped my thinking about the dilemmas of aid and humanitarianism and as a result about violence against aid workers. Hugo Slim's innocuous questions at the end of our interview—"Why focus on violence against aid workers? Why not violence against civilians?"—planted a seed that eventually culminated in this book. While not all of these individuals or my other interlocutors would fully agree with the argument I make here, I have benefitted greatly from their contributions and stories. Nonetheless, any mistakes herein are mine alone.

The International Committee of the Red Cross permitted me access to its archives. Maria-Helena Ariza, Faith Freeman, Vonda Polega, Solomiya Pyatkovska, and Alicia Simoni diligently and ably assisted me with research tasks. Various friends and my current and former colleagues at the Kroc Institute, too numerous to name, provided valuable encouragement along the way. In addition, research funding from the U.S. Institute of Peace permitted me to conduct interviews and field research in 2006 and 2007. Support from the Institute for Scholarship in the Liberal Arts, College of Arts and Letters, at the University of Notre Dame enabled the book to come to fruition.

I presented earlier versions of various chapters at the International Studies Association (2006, 2008, 2010), the World Conference on Humanitarian Studies (2009), and a conference on humanitarianism at the University of Manchester (2012). Portions of earlier versions of Chapters 2–5 previously appeared in my 2010 article "Mind the Gap: Documenting and Explaining Violence Against Aid Workers," *European Journal of International Relations* 16(3, September): 365–389, and my 2013 article "A Reflexive Approach to Risk and Intervention for Third Party Intervenors," *Conflict Resolution Quarterly* 30(4, July): 467–489. I thank these journals and their publishers for permission to adapt these materials here.

I appreciate the careful and insightful feedback from the following individuals who read all or parts of the manuscript in its various stages of development and offered their encouragement and constructive critiques: Christian Davenport, John Paul Lederach, Atalia Omer, Ernesto Verdeja, and especially Scott Appleby, whose uncompromising editing, particularly of the early versions of the manuscript, pushed me toward parsimony of words and a sharper argument. I benefitted greatly from the critiques and comments of Jennifer Hyndman, Thea Hilhorst, and the anonymous reviewers whose insight and careful engagement with my words and ideas saved me from several errors and whose feedback greatly improved the cogency and clarity of the manuscript. Julia Petrakis ably copyedited the manuscript, responded amiably to tight deadlines, and provided valuable advice. The interest and support of Peter Agree, my editor at Penn Press, and the meticulous editing of the editorial team at Penn, especially Noreen O'Connor-Abel, proved crucial in the process.

Finally, I would be remiss if I did not express my profound gratitude to Dick Sutphen and the voices of the monks who facilitated a clear head for writing, to Donna, Danielle, Emma, and MJ for their friendship and accompaniment, and to my immediate and extended family for their love and encouragement throughout this process. Thank you.